The Many and the One

THE ETHIKON SERIES IN COMPARATIVE ETHICS

Editorial Board

The Ethikon Series publishes studies on ethical issues of current importance. By bringing scholars representing a diversity of moral viewpoints into structured dialogue, the series aims to broaden the scope of ethical discourse and to identify commonalities and differences between alternative views.

TITLES IN THE SERIES

Brian Barry and Robert E. Goodin, eds.
Free Movement: Ethical Issues in the Transnational Migration of People and Money

Chris Brown, ed.
Political Restructuring in Europe: Ethical Perspectives

Terry Nardin, ed.
The Ethics of War and Peace: Religious and Secular Perspectives

David R. Mapel and Terry Nardin, eds.
International Society: Diverse Ethical Perspectives

David Miller and Sohail H. Hashmi, eds.
Boundaries and Justice: Diverse Ethical Perspectives

Simone Chambers and Will Kymlicka, eds.
Alternative Conceptions of Civil Society

Nancy L. Rosenblum and Robert Post, eds.
Civil Society and Government

Sohail H. Hashmi, ed.
Foreword by Jack Miles
Islamic Political Ethics: Civil Society, Pluralism, and Conflict

Richard Madsen and Tracy B. Strong, eds.
The Many and the One: Religious and Secular Perspectives on Ethical Pluralism in the Modern World

Margaret Moore and Allen Buchanan, eds.
States, Nations, and Borders: The Ethics of Making Boundaries

The Many and the One

RELIGIOUS AND SECULAR PERSPECTIVES
ON ETHICAL PLURALISM IN THE
MODERN WORLD

❖

Edited by
Richard Madsen
Tracy B. Strong

PRINCETON UNIVERSITY PRESS
PRINCETON AND OXFORD

Copyright © 2003 by Princeton University Press
Published by Princeton University Press, 41 William Street,
Princeton, New Jersey 08540
In the United Kingdom: Princeton University Press,
3 Market Place, Woodstock, Oxfordshire OX20 1SY

All Rights Reserved.

Library of Congress Cataloging-in-Publication Data

The many and the one: religious and secular perspectives on ethical pluralism in
the modern world / edited by Richard Madsen, Tracy B. Strong.
p. cm—(Ethikon series in comparative ethics)
Includes bibliographical references and index.
ISBN 0-691-09992-8 (alk. paper)—ISBN 0-691-09993-6 (pbk.: alk. paper)
1. Ethics, Comparative. 2. Pluralism (Social sciences) I. Madsen, Richard, 1941–
II. Strong, Tracy B. III. Series.
BJ69 .M26 2003
170—dc21   2002024306

This book has been composed in Sabon

Printed on acid-free paper. ∞

www.pup.princeton.edu

Printed in the United States of America

10 9 8 7 6 5 4 3 2 1

Contents

Acknowledgments

The editors join with Philip Valera, president of the Ethikon Institute, and Carole Pateman, series editor, in thanking all who contributed to the dialogue project that resulted in this book. We are especially indebted to the Ahmanson Foundation and its trustees, Robert F. Erburu and Lee Walcott, who provided major support for the project, and to other important donors, including the Carrie Estelle Doheny Foundation, Joan Palevsky, and the Sidney Stern Memorial Trust.

In addition to the authors' contributions, the project and its results were greatly enhanced by the active participation of other dialogue partners: Gerald Doppelt, Harold Guetzkow, Eugene Mornell, and Peter Nosco, many of whose ideas have also found their way into this book.

Finally, we also thank Ian Malcolm, our editor at Princeton University Press, for his valuable guidance and continuing support.

The Many and the One

Introduction:
Three Forms of Ethical Pluralism

Richard Madsen

Tracy B. Strong

> We are placed into various life-spheres, each of which is governed by
> different laws.
> —Max Weber, *Politics as a Vocation*

The war on terrorism, say America's leaders, is a war of good versus evil.
But in the minds of the perpetrators, the 11 September attacks on the
World Trade Center and the Pentagon appear to have been justified as
ethically good acts required by Islam against American evil. How can different ethical systems become so polarized that, to paraphrase the great
German sociologist Max Weber, one person's God is another person's
devil? In the world today, is such polarization leading inevitably to a violent "clash of civilizations"? Or can differences between ethical systems be
reconciled through rational dialogue rather than political struggle? When
this book was begun, the issues posed by ethical pluralism in the modern
world were of considerable academic interest. Since the 11 September attacks, they have become matters of the most urgent public interest.

Taken as a whole, this book provides resources for thinking more
clearly about the range of different ways in which humans understand the
difference between good and bad, right and wrong, the universal and the
parochial, as well as the tension between ecumenical and flexible versus
fundamentalist and rigid responses to such difference. It contains nine
major essays about how the problem of ethical pluralism can be understood by different philosophical and religious traditions: classical liberalism, liberal egalitarianism, critical theory, feminism, natural law, Confucianism, Islam, Judaism, and Christianity. Each of the principal essays is
paired with a shorter "response essay" that helps to highlight the range
of understandings possible within each tradition. Unlike most works in
ethical theory, this book juxtaposes modern secular philosophical traditions with older religious traditions. A concluding chapter summarizes
the themes that emerge from these juxtapositions. In this introduction,
we explore some of the philosophical considerations that can bring these
juxtaposed traditions into genuine dialogue with one another.

The problems of ethical pluralism present themselves in the modern world on three different levels—what we might call the existential level, the cultural level, and the civilizational level.

THE EXISTENTIAL LEVEL

The epigraph from Max Weber reflects a common modern understanding. Human beings find themselves, whether they will it or not, in a world of incommensurable values. In our individual lives, we are pulled in incompatible directions. It is the lot of the modern person, in this understanding, to have to make choices between values—to choose *this*, such that this choice excludes *that* one. As Isaiah Berlin wrote in "Two Concepts of Liberty": "The world we encounter in ordinary experience is one in which we are faced with choices between ends equally ultimate and claims equally absolute, the realization of some of which must inevitably involve the sacrifice of the other."[1]

Although, as Donald Moon notes in his conclusion, some of the chapters in this book use the term "ethical pluralism" to refer to such a situation, we in this introduction call it "existential pluralism," to highlight the ways in which it confronts us with incommensurable choices, with our identities as particular persons. By "incommensurable" we mean here that there is no common standard by which the choices may be evaluated. The classical paradigm for this is Antigone who chooses to bury her brother in full consciousness that in doing so she is rejecting the authority of the laws of the city of which she is a member. In the modern world, however, the conflict between different values has become even more intense than in the age of Sophocles, because, as Max Weber observed, the various spheres of life—that is, religion, kinship, economics, politics, the realms of the aesthetic, the erotic, and the intellectual—have become increasingly differentiated. Thus, the values required to succeed in business are sharply separate from those required to be a loyal family member or a dedicated artist or devout believer.

The religious traditions (Judaism, Christianity, Islam) and classical philosophical traditions (natural law and Confucianism) represented in this book are all, as Joseph Chan puts it in his essay on Confucianism, "perfectionist," that is, they assume that it is good to live a coherent ethical life, they have a substantive vision of such a life, and they hold that both state and society should help people to achieve this. One way to achieve such coherence would be to limit the development of diverse value spheres. The Taliban, for instance, banned television, restricted the content of education, and strictly confined women to the domestic sphere. Within most perfectionist ethical traditions one can find "fundamentalist" arguments for limiting value spheres and thus saving society from the burdens of existential pluralism.

But each of the perfectionist traditions represented in this book also contains resources for accepting a wide range of values. They can be quite generous in their recognition that different persons can and should be able to pursue the good in different ways, and deserve the benefit of the doubt when their ways differ from conventional ways. All of the authors of the chapters on perfectionist traditions in this book emphasize the adaptability of their traditions to existential pluralism. (Fundamentalists would probably not have wanted to contribute to such a book.) Still, they all hold that a plurality of ethical practices is legitimate only insofar as it contributes to a transcendent substantive good. By comparing the main chapters and the response essays, the reader can get a sense of the arguments between more liberal and conservative positions within each tradition.

On the other hand, the modern secular philosophies represented here (classical liberalism, egalitarian liberalism, critical theory, and feminist theory) are resigned to the impossibility of integrating the diverse value spheres into a commonly accepted, ethically coherent order. They are procedural rather than perfectionist. Eschewing any final substantive understanding of the good, they focus on procedures that would allow individuals freely to pursue their versions of the good without interfering with the liberty of others. In theory at least, the painful, existential struggles that individuals must undergo when confronting incommensurable values are relegated to the private realm, where they cannot undermine the universally accepted public procedures that ensure an overall social order. Especially for liberalism, even though the boundaries between the two realms may not be always in the same place, this entails making a sharp separation between the public realm (the realm of universal legal procedures) and the private realm (the realm of particular versions of the substantive good).

It is important to recognize that such secular, procedural moral philosophical traditions have their own forms of fundamentalism that restrict the existential pluralism of a morally complex society. For instance, the supposedly neutral legal procedures prescribed by classical liberalism can be so constructed as to support the hegemony of a market economy that turns all values into mere commodities; and the distinction between public and private may be so defined as to shield the values of the market economy or the bureaucratic state from challenge by other values.[2] The debates among the secular philosophies represented here are partly debates about how to accommodate the full polyvalence of human ethical existence.

THE CULTURAL LEVEL

Different religious and philosophical traditions have different ways of accommodating the existential pluralism that is endemic to human social experience. Those intellectual traditions are rooted in the assemblages of lived practices that we call "cultures." Global migration, communication, and commerce, of course, bring about an intermingling of cultures that can confuse and torment as well as immeasurably enrich. If the circumstances under which an individual makes choices between opposing and incommensurable values can resound of the "tragic," as Berlin puts it in his essay, the situation seems even more intractable when it comes to the conflict between different cultural traditions. Antigone chooses between two alternatives that are both recognizably *hers*. I may have to choose, as a citizen of a Western country, between the demands of self-interest and the requirements of charity, but both of those choices are recognizable parts of a world that I recognize as *my own*. It is quite a different matter when the choice appears to be between two systems of value, one of which is acknowledged as mine, whereas the other is—*other*. In this introduction, we focus most of our attention on this level and we call this form of pluralism, manifested at the level of tension *between* rather than *within* cultures, "ethical pluralism."[3]

Ethical pluralism, in this sense, is the recognition that there are in the world different ethical traditions, that these distinguish themselves at least in name one from the other, and differ not only in matters of practical judgment on moral issues (for instance, citizenship, euthanasia, relationships between the sexes) but in modes of reasoning used to reach such judgments. How can such traditions be brought into a mutually fruitful dialogue?

The Problem of Objectivity

First of all, we must confront the basic epistemological issues. Is it possible to attain any objective knowledge that transcends the broad historical, cultural, and political contexts within which one is embedded? Even philosophers of natural science are no longer certain that this is possible. Consider the discontinuity between Newtonian mechanics and quantum mechanics. From the framework of Newtonian mechanics, motion can be understood in deterministic terms. The relation from cause to effect is singular and in principle predictable. When, however, one looks at very small scale phenomena (the movement of electrons or protons), neither Newtonian mechanics nor, for that matter, Einsteinian relativity any longer "works." Instead, depending on the measurement, protons sometimes behave like particles and sometimes like waves and the relation of "cause" to "effect" is one of probability rather than determination. Is the universe a discontinuous "quantized" reality or a smoothly curved space-time continuum? Is it lawlike or not? What you see, it might appear, depends on where you sit.

The apparent irresolvability of such issues has raised questions in other branches of science. Might not all claims about physical reality be in some sense relative to the particular frameworks within which the scientist works, a framework so general and all-encompassing that to step outside of it would be in a real sense "revolutionary"? Thomas Kuhn gave the name "paradigm" to such frameworks and claimed, or at least appeared to claim, that basic terms (such as "length," "time," "velocity") had different meanings in each paradigm.[4]

In philosophy, this situation came to be known as the "theory-ladenness of observations,"[5] and it has been a topic of violent debate in the philosophy of science. At stake was, or seemed to be, the very possibility of objective knowledge. Was it really true that scientific judgments were relative to the theoretical framework of the scientist? If so, it would seem that the framework itself was subject to social and historical factors. There was, to recall Hegel, to be no jumping over Rhodes, no escape from the circumstances of one's knowledge.[6]

Similar developments can be found in the human sciences.[7] And here the matter is much more intense than in the physical sciences, for in the humanities "paradigms" claim more than simple epistemological actuality—they have histories, of greater or lesser length, and have, demonstrably, "worked" for those who have grown up "in" each system. Hence one may understand the world as a Christian, as a proponent of natural law, as a Muslim, as a Confucian, and so forth: what is important is that when one does so, one actually *is* a Christian, a Muslim, and so forth. In the ethical realm one does not so much *adopt* a particular perspective as *manifest* it. Whereas in the natural sciences quantum mechanics might have a pragmatic justification (i.e., it explains a lot even if not gravitation), in the ethical and moral realms, all systems not only seem to work but they rarely if ever offer themselves as choices. Generally one is born and brought up as a Muslim or a Christian or a Buddhist, or without religious belief. Even if one changes one's beliefs, to the degree that one chooses an ethical framework that choice is less likely to be the results of pragmatic considerations than of some kind of conversion experience. Furthermore, by and large people do not live and die over the question of quantum versus relativistic physics, but various peoples have slaughtered others over differences in religious and ethical beliefs. In human relations, what appears to be at stake when one set of ethics confronts another is often personal identity.

Faced with such fundamental epistemological problems, is there any way we can transcend the differences between ethical traditions? It is important to note that in practice the encounter of different traditions has often provided the basis for a genuine mutual enrichment. There is, for instance, a line of social criticism that goes from Diderot to Margaret Mead that looked—with greater or lesser accuracy—to the South Seas as paradigms of enlightened sexual morality when compared with straiter-laced Anglo-European practices.[8] Here the encounter with others can serve as the foundation for a critique of practices in one's own society. But the encounter can also be violent, as we have recently seen in the confrontation between Western cultural traditions and militantly fundamentalist understandings of Islam.

Moral Relativism?

What are the philosophical bases for harmonious rather than conflictual encounters? One basis might be a principled acceptance of moral relativism—but this is undermined by the fear that power will then determine what counts as morally and ethically true.

Generally speaking, moral relativism is the doctrine that in matters of morality there are no universals. By universals one means here the actuality of standards by which to judge moral action, standards that are themselves independent of historical and individual contingencies.

Historically, the experience of moral relativism did initially provoke a move toward toleration. Precisely because there were no universal standards divorced from particular practices, one could not claim a privileged status for any practice, including one's own. The foundations for contemporary moral relativism were laid in Europe in the reactions to the wars of religion in the sixteenth and seventeenth centuries. David Hume can perhaps stand in for the others. When Hume argued that "it was not irrational for me to prefer the destruction of the entire world to the merest scratching of my little finger,"[9] he was specifically denying that rationality could settle moral quandaries. Thus, the purpose of Hume's social thought was to replace contingency with practice.[10] An accumulated set of practices defined a people (call it a moral tradition) and thus an identity. Hume was struck by this power of historical identity and did all he could to foster that power. "Nothing," he proclaimed, "is more surprising to those who consider human affairs with a philosophical eye than the easiness with which the many are governed by the few." The surprise, however, was due to the "philosophical eye," that is, to the desire to want from moral practices something that one could not have, namely a universal standard. He continues: "It is . . . on opinion only that government is founded, and this maxim extends to the most despotic and most military governments as well as to the most free and most popular."[11] He concludes this essay with a ringing endorsement to "cherish and encourage our ancient government as much as possible." The opinions that the English have are to be encouraged and each of the six volumes that Hume wrote on the *History of England* was designed to further that aim.[12] A modern version of this is the "value pluralism" that Donald Moon associates in this in this volume with the thought of Isaiah Berlin: once societies meet a certain minimal standard for decency (itself perhaps harder to define than Berlin thought), ranking different forms of life is in principle impossible.

The message here is that if a people have a set of practices that work, it will by definition have accepted them, have found them viable, and should in general continue to pursue them. Other peoples will have different practices. As long as they "work," there is nothing definitive that one people can say about the other. Moral relativism is premised on the notion not only that philosophy has in the end little to say to resolve tensions between different moral and ethical practices, but also that it should not attempt to resolve them.

Such a relaxed acceptance of moral relativism has proved hard to maintain, especially in the past century, as it succumbed to a second fear, the fear that power will determine what counts as "truth." This fear can be summarized as "What if Hitler had won?" Here the anxiety derives from the recognition that prevailing power and historical success may become the determinant of what might count as morally (or indeed factually) true. As such the fear is most characteristic of modern Western times. In her essay "Truth and Politics," Hannah Arendt recalls and updates a story from the second decade of the past century: "Clemenceau, shortly before his death, found himself engaged in a friendly talk with a representative of the Weimar Republic on the question of guilt for the outbreak of World War I. 'What in your opinion,' Clemenceau was asked, 'will future historians think of this troublesome and controversial issue?' He replied, 'this I don't know. But I know for certain that this will not say that Belgium invaded Germany.'" Arendt continues: "[T]o eliminate from the record the fact that on the night of August 4, 1914, German troops crossed the frontier of Belgium . . . would require no less than a power monopoly over the entire civilized world. But such a power monopoly is far from being inconceivable."[13] World War II and the increasing power of technology and the media dramatically exacerbate Arendt's worry.

Given that toleration of Nazism as "just another system" appeared to be an impossibility, the need for something other than a pragmatic justification of moral and ethical practices became pressing. It is noteworthy that Anglo-European liberal democracies and in general those cultures that draw their moral inspiration from monotheistic religion have often been more concerned about moral relativism than have countries in other regions of the world.[14] The People's Republic of China and Singapore, among others, regularly insist that certain Western views about, for instance, the universality of human rights, are out of place in those countries.[15] To insist on them would constitute a kind of category mistake, an epistemological error, as it were. Against this view, the justification of the destruction of the World Trade Center as an attack on the "enemies of Islam" appears simply unacceptable to most all who share the ethical point(s) of view broadly characteristic of the North Atlantic countries. Acknowledgment of the legitimacy of difference goes only so far before it becomes hostility.

The reasons that these issues seem to give rise to the greater anxiety in the "West" have several possible origins. In part they may be consequent to the fact that the past 200 years of human history have seen the balance of world power move to the North Atlantic nations. In part, they also arise because after the horrors of the first part of the twentieth century, the Western tradition—or at least important parts of it—now seemed to require a foundation for itself that transcended questioning. Betraying a note of anxiety, the American Founding Fathers had already written that they held certain "truths to be self-evident," by which it was meant that anyone denying them questioned the evidence of his or her senses. But suppose someone, or some set of events, did? Put bluntly, the inherited practices of supposedly civilized Western nations no longer seem adequate against their rivals.

Beyond Relativism

What might be the philosophical basis for transcending moral relativism while respecting the integrity of different moral traditions? What kinds of valid judgments can someone from one tradition make on those from another? Three issues appear.

First, is the system flexible on its own terms? If so, one would be able to say that in certain areas of moral life, those who identify themselves with a given system might have, in the terms of that system, made a mistake. Thus someone who considers him or herself a Muslim might think that the practice of *requiring* that women wear a burqa is mistaken, without this negating his or her self-identification as a Muslim.[16] It is important to understand all systems are to some degree flexible and thus permit criticism, *on their own terms*, both by those inside the system and by those outside it. As Donald Moon notes in his essay, one might think this a form of "perspectival pluralism," itself consequent to a "structural pluralism" characteristic of (at least) "modern" societies.

The question is how far that flexibility can extend without calling self-identification into question. The pronouncements of Osama bin Laden to the effect that Islam requires the destruction of the forces of the Christian West and of Israel reflect the deep sense that Islam is corrupted, potentially beyond repair, by the connivance of those presently governing many Muslim countries with the forces of the "West." All moral systems contain a range of interpretations of what it means to be a member of that system: this is consequent to the fact that moral systems are historical accumulations of practices and interpretations and by nature not completely consistent. The claim, however, that a moral system *requires* one particular practice and excludes all those in contradiction with it (wearing a burqa or not) cannot be refuted in terms of the system.

Thus we have a second issue: can particular judgments of the system be brought under the criteria of a moral code that is broader than that of the system itself? It is one thing to argue that in terms of Islam the practice of veiling women is not *necessary*, but quite another to say that it is wrong because of some standard that transcends Islam and is derived from a general understanding of morality—for instance, that men and women ought to as a general principle enjoy similar autonomy. Here it is a matter of whether the demand that a particular practice in a given system be abolished or changed threatens the self-identification of individuals as members of that system. (As a parallel, one might argue that one could play something that was recognizably the game of chess without using the *en passant* capture rule, where one could not play it if all the pieces moved in the same manner.) To the degree that it does, such a change will tend to be rejected by those who identify themselves as members of a given system.

If, however, one cannot determine a universal moral system in terms of which one might make a judgment about practices characteristic of individual moral systems, a third issue arises. Now the question is, can one declare certain systems as a whole to be so deeply flawed as to require rejection by some general moral standards? One might argue that the economic and social system in the antebellum American South not only practiced but required slavery to survive, in that the mode of life practiced and admired there depended on the free-slave distinction.[17] In such a case, nothing more than the elimination of such a system would be necessary. Elimination, however, on what grounds? Such a question reflects an anxiety about how one *knows* that something like slavery, or Nazism, or religiously intolerant cultures are morally wrong.

This returns us to and forces us to consider the question of what kind of knowledge would permit us to reject enough of the practices of another moral system such that those who adhered to it no longer recognized themselves in its terms. There are, roughly speaking, three ways in which one might approach this problem.

The most dominant Western approach to this problem presented by ethical pluralism has been to identify a core of values on which all reasonable people might agree and then to try to extend that core rationally to different practices and cultures. The work of John Rawls can stand in for the others.[18] Rawls has powerfully argued that rational individuals choosing from behind a "veil of ignorance" (such that they do not know what their position will be in a society they might choose to establish) will choose institutions that do not severely advantage or disadvantage anyone who might have a given quality (handsome, rich, white, smart, and so forth). Such choices will then not be made in terms of an individual's self-interest, but in terms of what common arrangements one would be willing to take one's chances at living under. They would so choose, Rawls argues, because they would not rationally want to undergo the possibility of winding up in a seriously disadvantaged position. Thus, Rawls tries to identify a core to moral and ethical judgments to which any person, no matter of what culture or social circumstances, would rationally assent.

Rawls's argument powerfully establishes a core of judgments that humans might rationally agree upon; but it is less successful when attempting to extend those judgments to particular policy controversies. While religious toleration, opposition to slavery, and perhaps some degree of civil disobedience seem rationally entailed policies, matters are much less clear on other pressing issues (abortion or euthanasia, for instance).[19] Indeed, if we were to agree with Sir Isaiah Berlin that some systems of value are truly incommensurable, we could not hope to find such a common rational core. A second approach to resolving the problem of ethical pluralism is exemplified by John Gray.[20] Instead of trying to resolve the conflicts between different systems of value by subordinating them to a common standard of rationality, he assumes that they all are, or can be, right. He insists only that they limit their claims on human beings for the sake of what he calls a "modus vivendi"—a kind of live and let live that permits others to coexist without forcing their standards of moral right and wrong on one another. Universals are thus for Gray a kind of negative: all have a right not to be tortured, not to be separated from their friends and family involuntarily, not to be humiliated, not to be subject to avoidable disease, and so forth.

Gray's position would accept a contradictory system of value as long as its advocates accepted it voluntarily and did not try to force it on others. But suppose an ethical system is so rooted in a culture's language and basic socialization processes that people voluntarily accept practices that other ethical systems regard as dehumanizing. Some young girls in some cultures accept clitoridectomy as a "natural" part of maturing and the need to regulate sexual desire. Is there any basis for criticizing this?[21] If the young women are socially conditioned to accept such a practice, why is this a problem—we are socially conditioned to accept many things. Why should we think that the standards by which a person lives his or her life be in some strong sense of the word his or her *own* standards, in the sense of having been chosen consciously? There is a line of thought in the Western tradition that dates back to Socrates that holds that they should. There is, however, a line of thought in, say, the Confucian framework that holds precisely that they should not.

A problem with both the position of Rawls and that of Gray is that they are derived from fundamental assumptions of the Western Enlightenment about the possibility and indeed necessity for human individuals to achieve moral autonomy through the use of reason. It is difficult to use them as a basis for genuine dialogue with non-Western traditions, especially religiously based ones, that do not fully accept such fundamental assumptions. It is also difficult to reconcile them with recent perspectives in Western thought that emphasize the extent to which our notions of freedom and rationality are constructed by language and culture. Thus, there is a third approach to transcending the differences among ethical systems. Exemplified in North America by the work of Charles Taylor, with roots in the philosophical hermeneutics of Hans-Georg Gadamer and the sociology of Emile Durkheim, this approach would not merely tolerate ethical difference but would engage it as a path toward deeper forms of human community. As Charles Taylor puts it, "The crucial idea is that people can bond not in spite of but because of difference. They can sense, that is, that their lives are narrower and less full alone than in association with each other. In this sense, the difference defines a complementarity."[22]

According to this approach one needs to strive for a full understanding of the other, because without such an understanding, one cannot truly know oneself. Full self-understanding is initially restricted by our horizon of unexamined assumptions. The attempt to understand other cultures and systems of morality leads to a "fusion of horizons" in which we gain a broader set of terms to reflect critically on our identity.[23] This approach by no means precludes criticisms of other moral systems. But it insists that for such criticism of particular moral practices to be valid, the criticism must be predicated on a broad understanding of what the practices mean in their overall contexts—and criticism of the other should be accompanied by self-criticism.

In each case, what needs to be criticized is the tendency to deny our relationship with that which is inextricably connected to us. Jean-Luc

Nancy, a French philosopher, concludes an essay entitled "La comparution/compearance" as follows:

> But to exclude, exclusion must designate: it names, identifies, gives form. "The other" is for us a figure imposed on the unpresentable [*le infigurable*]. Thus we have for us—to go to a heart of the matter—the "Jew" or the "Arab," figures whose closeness, that is their in-common with "us," is no accident.[24]

"Us" here reflects that Nancy speaks as a Frenchman and a member of the French moral "community." The problem of the "other," as he goes on clearly to recognize, will be specifically different for other communities, although not structurally different. The double question is thus always: "How to exclude without fixing [*figurer*]? And to fix without excluding?"[25]

The answer to Nancy's question is at the heart of the questions raised by ethical pluralism, and it is difficult. We think it might go something like this. Let us consider the problem of the outsider or the other—for Nancy here the "Arab," but in the context of this book it could be the Muslim, the Confucian, the Christian, the woman, and so on. One has to admit that in some sense this other—who or whatever it may be—is different from us. Indeed, not to admit this would be to deny the actuality of the other's presence to me (and of mine to it).

Western liberalism has tended to sidestep this encounter with difference, by relegating incommensurable values to the "private" realm. It is only in the public realm that considerations of justice and enforcement of moral standards are relevant: thus one can believe what one wants, do in one's bedroom what one wants (with "consenting adults," tellingly), and so forth. Issues such as race therefore and sexual orientation must generally be deemed private matters. Such considerations, however, seem to us to raise a serious question. How can it be that what may be centrally important to me (my sexual orientation, my race) be irrelevant to how I appear to others in the public realm, and likewise that the race and sexual preference of others should be publicly insignificant to me?[26] Part of what justice requires may include not denying the other's presence to me.

To overcome such denial we may need to criticize the Rawlsian assumption that the other and I could or do have common understandings of primary goods. If we assume all reasonable people ought to share such common understandings, then we easily dehumanize those who in fact do not. ("Can you believe how they treat women?" "They are animals and killers: they think abortion is all right." And so forth.)

But how can we criticize without dehumanizing? How, for instance, could we criticize a culture that justified slavery? We could do so on the basis of its inability to account for the full humanity of others. When we claim that so and so is a "slave" or attribute an other such definition to what an individual is, what is it that we are missing about them, or what is it that we want to miss? Stanley Cavell's *The Claim of Reason* helps us here: "[W]hat [a man who sees certain others as slaves] is missing is not something about slaves exactly and not exactly about human beings. He is missing something about himself, or rather something about his connection with these people, his internal relation with them, so to speak."[27] Cavell goes on to point out that my actions show that I cannot mean in fact that the other is not human, or is less then human.

> When he wants to be served at the table by a black hand, he would not be satisfied to be served by a black paw. When he rapes a slave, or takes her as a concubine, he does not feel that he has by that fact itself, embraced sodomy. When he tips a black taxi driver . . . it does not occur to him that he might more appropriately have patted the creature fondly on the side of the neck.[28]

No matter what the slave owner, the Frenchman, and the Christian can claim (and assert that they truly believe), their actions show that they hold to something quite different. They can allow that the others have qualities (their cuisine, their music, for instance), but what they cannot allow is for them to see themselves as the other sees them. For then, they would see themselves as they are seen. (Montesquieu saw this refusal and in the *Persian Letters* named it the central quality of tyranny.)

From this it would seem that the question that the actuality of ethical pluralism raises is not so much the status of the practices of other ethical systems, but *what it would mean actually to acknowledge the status of one's own*. Such an approach—and perhaps one of the achievements of this book—is not (only) to gain recognition of the other but of oneself.

THE CIVILIZATIONAL LEVEL

By giving us resources for understanding the world's major ethical traditions and for reflecting philosophically on how to reconcile them, this book may help us confront the political and social challenges of our time. It is said that we live in a global village, but the more apt metaphor is that of a global city. Villages were traditionally tied together by a common culture and by thick bonds of interlocking social relations. The modern city brings into abrasive contact people from many different cultures, encourages them to compete with one another in a common marketplace, and yet hopes that they will perceive enough mutual interdependence and achieve enough mutual understanding to live together in peace. Often this works, but sometimes cities break down into ugly strife. In an increasingly globalized world, the opportunities for constructive interconnection are tremendous, but so are the dangers of deadly conflict.

A key factor in maintaining peace in the global city is the capacity of people to cooperate constructively with those who share different beliefs and ethical commitments. This involves establishing institutions that both protect and limit ethical pluralism—that protect the right of different people to carry out practices that others find incomprehensible and disagreeable and yet establish enough of a limit on diversity to prevent anarchy. But different types of societies have different ways of doing this, differences based not simply on moral principles but on configurations of political arrangements bolstered by economic interests. The United States contains the potentially divisive forces of ethical pluralism through a kind of liberal hegemony. Although many Americans are morally multilingual, drawing on a variety of ethical traditions to make major life decisions, their public lingua franca, as it were, is mainly based on some combination of classical and egalitarian liberalism. The major institutions of the United States are based on this liberal understanding and continuously reinforce it. Central to this institutional order are laws that separate church and state and that relegate many contentious ethical disagreements to the private realm, a secular public education system, and an occupational system that primarily rewards technical competence. Though constantly challenged, these arrangements have proven quite robust. The United Kingdom and Anglophone Canada have very similar institutional arrangements and those of most continental European countries are broadly similar. In the Middle East, however, there have been attempts to govern diverse societies through institutions based on Islamic law; and in Singapore there is an attempt to organize a society on the basis of a modernized state Confucianism. Is it possible for societies whose public life is based on the hegemony of moral principles other than Western liberalism—for example, societies whose major institutions are based on Islamic Sharia or Confucian ideology—to accommodate the relatively high degrees of ethical pluralism that come with modernization?

There are some in the West—could we call them "liberal fundamentalists"?—who say that it is not possible, that "they" have to become like "us" if they are to be fully modern, stable, and peaceful.[29] Such liberal fundamentalists would tolerate only those forms of Islam, Judaism, or Christianity that were content to relegate themselves to a private sphere, as they are in the United States, and they would find a state based on Sharia—even if it was a fairly flexible form of Sharia—to be in principle intolerable. Are we then really destined for a "clash of civilizations"[30] that cannot be resolved until the whole world adopts the liberal institutions of the West? Or are there multiple models for a humane, flexible modernity? Can the modern globally interdependent world accommodate "civilizational pluralism" as well as ethical pluralism? The essays presented here may help us ask such questions, but answers would entail sociological and political discussions that are beyond the scope of this book.

The practices that led to the creation of this book, however, may at least give us hopeful examples of how the challenges posed by existential, ethical, and civilizational pluralism can be resolved in a constructive, peaceful way. This volume is the third in a series from an Ethikon Institute project on "Ethical Pluralism, Civil Society, and Political Culture." A nonprofit and nonsectarian organization concerned with the social implications of ethical pluralism, the Ethikon Institute sponsors programs to explore a diversity of moral outlooks, secular and religious, and to identify commonalities among them. As with the other volumes in the series, this book began in a dialogue conference engaging spokespersons for nine different ethical perspectives. In this case, the conference was held 25–27 June, 1999 in La Jolla, California. Participants were requested to address a common set of questions:

GENERAL CONSIDERATIONS: Is the ideal society one that embodies or aims for ethical uniformity, or one that emphasizes instead the accommodation of ethical pluralism?

SOCIAL REGULATION: Should the power of the state ever be invoked to protect, ban, or otherwise regulate ethically based differences? If so, where and how should the state be involved?

CITIZENSHIP: How should ethically based disagreements on the rights and duties of citizenship be dealt with? For example, how should dissenting positions on the civil status of women be handled in civil society?

LIFE-AND-DEATH DECISIONS: To what extent, if any, should the power of the state be utilized to regulate decision making on life and death issues? For example, how should ethically based conflict on physician-assisted suicide be handled?

HUMAN SEXUALITY: To what extent, if any, should conflicting ethical positions on sexual relationships be accommodated? For example, should society agree or decline to recognize same-sex unions as a form of marriage?

These questions forced participants to confront some of the most contentious areas of disagreement among the various traditions. Yet the discussions were carried out with a great deal of openness and civility, a testament not only to the personal qualities of the participants but to the richness of the various traditions.

Every major ethical tradition is the product of a long historical conversation among many different, often contradictory voices. Within any tradition, including the liberal tradition, one can find currents of thought that would sharpen the differences between its basic ideas and those of other traditions and would draw out the implications of those differences with rigid logic. For all traditions, judgments about concrete moral and political issues require something akin to what Thomas Aquinas, following Aristotle, called "practical reason." As quoted in John Haldane's essay on natural law in this volume, Aquinas wrote:

> Speculative reason . . . is different . . . from practical reason. For, since speculative reason is concerned chiefly with necessary things, which cannot be otherwise than they are, its proper conclusions, like universal principles are necessarily true. Practical reason, on the other hand, is concerned with contingent matters, about which human actions are concerned, and consequently, although there is necessity in the general principles, the more we descend to matters of detail, the more frequently we encounter deviations. . . . Accordingly, in matters of action, truth or practical rectitude is not the same for all in respect of detail but only as to the general principles, and where there is the same rectitude in matters of detail, it is not equally known to all.

Even where ethical traditions differ as to general principles, therefore, people working within different traditions can find many areas of overlapping consensus when it comes to evaluating practical policies for living and working together. Our Ethikon dialogue demonstrated that it is indeed possible to find common ground, even on some of the most contentious issues, among people deeply committed to and highly articulate about widely different ethical traditions. And even where common ground is not possible, it is possible to find robust justifications within each tradition for resolving disagreements peacefully.

Through dialogue it is even possible to soften the differences between "general principles" because the meaning of these principles can change when they are understood within different social and cultural contexts. Giving a serious account of major ethical traditions never takes place in a historical vacuum. It is always a response to the moral predicaments arising in certain political and social contexts. Thus the style and content of the essays in this book bear the marks of the state of the world at the beginning of the twenty-first century. The specific questions that frame each essay would not have been addressed several generations ago. For instance, physician-assisted suicide has only recently become an issue for contentious public debate, made so at least partially because of recent advances in life-prolonging medical technology. Likewise, same-sex marriage has only become debatable in recent decades (in the United States and Europe at least) because of changing social mores. Meanwhile, increasing flows of international migration have shattered the cultural homogeneity of many societies, leading to new debates about how to respect the citizen rights of minority communities.

Besides generating the questions that structure this book, the contemporary social context has an important influence on the style of answering the questions. Especially since the end of the Cold War, the eruption of religious and ethnic warfare has raised the stakes in discussions about ethical pluralism. Ecumenically oriented scholars feel increasing urgency to build bridges to other traditions. This may lead them to develop the implications of their tradition with a greater degree of circumspection than during times when they did not have to fear that wars of words might lead to wars with weapons.

Above and beyond these more immediate political considerations, however, are ways in which the general conditions of late (or post?) modernity shape the understanding of ethical traditions. Even when representing traditions that are thousands of years old, the chapters in this book interpret them in a distinctly modern light. David Little's chapter on Christianity, for instance, quotes less from the New Testament than from Roger Williams, the seventeenth-century dissenting Calvinist who did much to shape American thinking about freedom of conscience. Menachem Fisch writes from the point of view of Orthodox Judaism, which accepts the halakha—the code of Jewish law developed in late antiquity—as "the first place of reference and sole arbiter of authority." But he interprets this ancient law through the rulings of nineteenth- and twentieth-century rabbis, and he applies these rulings to contemporary dilemmas faced by Jews in the modern state of Israel.

The conditions of modernity include a pervasive, now globalized, market economy, which both enables and propels people to take individual initiative in seeking their comparative advantage. This leads to a heightened stress on individual autonomy, at odds with the emphasis in most classical religious traditions on the individual's embeddedness in society. Even though classic texts (though not the historical practice) of all of the religious traditions presented here emphasize the need for morality to be based on voluntary commitment rather than force, the expectations of modernity increase this emphasis and demand a focus on it. Most classical religious traditions assumed that the different spheres of life could be integrated into a harmonious whole, and the authors of this book's chapters on the religiously based ethical traditions advocate somewhat different forms of modernity—different patterns of relationship between economy, polity, society, and culture—than that of Anglo-American liberalism. But they each assume that the tensions between the various value spheres are here to stay, and that their traditions must be interpreted in such a way as to meet the complex ethical demands of such a world.

On the other hand, the authors of the chapters on the modern, secular traditions of liberalism, critical theory, and feminism are not without challenges in trying to formulate their traditions in ways that take account of early twenty-first-century modernity. In general, they stress the need for individual autonomy more than the religious traditions, but at the dawn of the new millennium they have to contend with a world dominated by huge multinational organizations. The apparent pluralism promised in such a world often seems superficial—a "Benneton pluralism," as one of our authors puts it.[31] As is apparent in the essays in this book, modern, secular ethical theories, which stress the autonomy of the empowered individual, have to struggle with basic definitions of fundamental concepts like "individual autonomy" and "empowerment," and they have to be critically sensitive to the possibility of ethnocentrism within their traditions. All of our authors therefore struggle to maintain a balance between what Lee Yearley, in his commentary on Joseph Chan's essay on Confucianism, calls "elaboration" and "emendation." The former tries to use the best historical and textual scholarship to understand the foundational documents of a tradition, the latter tries to reformulate the ideas to answer new questions. Part of the debate during the Ethikon conference concerned the extent to which the authors could remain faithful to their traditions while emending them sufficiently to respond to the pressing public questions of today.

There was no easy resolution to such debates, because the current condition of the world is full of paradoxes that no major ethical tradition can easily comprehend. Modernity inspires and indeed demands a quest for personal autonomy, to be achieved through constant criticism of all traditions and by the unmasking of the relations of power beneath all high-sounding principles. Yet it also delivers what Max Weber called an iron cage (or, in the more sunny formulation of the journalist Thomas Friedman, a "golden straitjacket").[32] People are encouraged to express their freedom by creating their own unique forms of life, but they find themselves under increased pressures to conform to the demands of the state and the needs of the market. When the perfectionist ethical traditions of the major world religions are institutionalized within the structures of the modern state, the result is all too often the forced imposition of officially approved ethical standards upon a population—a result that core texts of all these traditions say is unacceptable. Yet, when secular, procedural ethics are institutionalized within modern political economies, the result is often a combination of bureaucratic regulations and market pressures that stifles authentic pluralism—a result that contradicts the fundamental aspirations of such modern theories.

The scholars who represent each of the major ethical traditions included in this book all realize that, in their present form, none of their traditions can easily resolve such paradoxes. Therefore they genuinely need to listen to one another and learn from another. The dialogue around the table at the Ethikon conference was marked by this spirit of earnest listening and critical but sympathetic argument. Unfortunately, the fluidity and effervescence of that spoken, face-to-face dialogue cannot be reproduced on the printed page. Still, we hope that enough of its aura emanates from these essays that readers will begin stimulating dialogues of their own about how to utilize the richness of insight made possible by the world's ethical pluralism to meet the social and political challenges of a diverse, yet interdependent world.

NOTES

1. Isaiah Berlin, *Four Essays on Liberty* (Oxford: Oxford University Press, 1970).

2. For a lively critique of what one might call "neoliberal fundamentalism," see Harvey Cox, "Mammon and the Culture of the Market: A Socio-Theological Critique" in Richard Madsen, William M. Sullivan, Ann Swidler, and Steven M. Tipton, eds., *Meaning and Modernity: Religion, Polity, and Self* (Berkeley: University of California Press, 2002), pp. 124–35.

3. For the sake of making our argument in this introduction as clear as possible, we reserve the term "ethical pluralism" for pluralism at this cultural level. As Donald Moon points out in his conclusion, however, the essays in this book use the term "ethical pluralism" in a number of senses. Sometimes they refer to what we are here calling "existential pluralism." Other times they use it in the way we are using it in this introduction. Other times they use it to refer to the theory of value we have associated with Isaiah Berlin, that it is impossible in principle to adjudicate differences among values.

4. Thomas A. Kuhn, *The Structure of Scientific Revolutions* (Chicago: University of Chicago Press, 1970). See also Stephen Toulmin, "Conceptual Revolution in Science," *Boston Studies in the Philosophy of Science*, vol. 3, ed. R.S. Cohen (Dordrecht: Riedel, 1966).

5. See, for instance, C. R. Kordig, "The Theory-Ladenness of Obervations," *Review of Metaphysics* 24, 3 (March 1971): 448–84. For a discussion, see Tracy B. Strong, *The Idea of Political Theory* (Notre Dame, Ind.: University of Notre Dame Press, 1990), chap. 3.

6. The phrase comes from the end of the introduction to Hegel's *Philosophy of Right*.

7. This has been a subject of repeated concern to Alasdair MacIntyre, among others. See his *Whose Judgement? Which Rationality?* (Notre Dame, Ind.: University of Notre Dame Press, 1988). For specific studies, albeit from a point of view different than that of MacIntyre, see, inter alia, Steven Shapin and Simon Schaffer, *Leviathan and the Air-pump: Hobbes, Boyle, and the Experimental Life* (Princeton: Princeton University Press, 1985); Bruno Latour, *We Have Never Been Modern* (Cambridge, Mass.: Harvard University Press, 1993). See also Peter Winch,

The Idea of a Social Science and Its Relation to Philosophy (Atlantic Highlands, N.J.: Humanities Press, 1990), as well as his "Understanding a Primitive Society," *American Philosophical Quarterly* 1, 4 (1964): 307–24. For critique of Winch that would be relevant to the others, see Martin Hollis and Steven Lukes, *Rationality and Relativism* (Oxford: Blackwell, 1982).

8. See Denis Diderot, *Supplement au Voyage de Bougainville*, ed. G. Chanard (Paris: Draz, 1935); Margaret Mead, *Coming of Age in Samoa* (New York: New American Library, 1949).

9. David Hume, *A Treatise on Human Nature*, II, ii, 3 (London: Penguin, 1983) p. 463. Toward the beginning of the *Critique of Pure Reason* (p. 55 (B 20); see also pp. 44 and 127–28), Kant famously remarked that it was "destructive of philosophy" that no one had been able successfully to resolve the argument in Hume as to the apparently purely contingent character of the relation between facts and understanding. One may read Kant's project in the *Critique of Pure Reason* and the *Critique of Practical Reason* as an attempt at resolving Hume's argument first on the epistemological level and secondly on the ethical one.

10. See Kant, *Critique of Pure Reason*, p. 127 (B 127).

11. Hume, *Political Essays* (Indiannapolis, Ind.: Bobbs Merrill, 1974), p. 24.

12. The most brilliant dissection of this kind of history is by J.G.A. Pocock, *The English Constitution and the Feudal Law* (New York: W. W. Norton, 1967).

13. Hannah Arendt, *Between Past and Future* (Viking: New York, 1968), p. 239.

14. See Barrington Moore Jr., *Moral Purity and Persecution in History* (Princeton: Princeton Universtiy Press, 2000).

15. For a discussion of this question, see Daniel Bell, *East Meets West: Human Rights and Democracy in East Asia* (Princeton: Princeton University Press, 2001).

16. For the importance of veiling, see Lila Abu-Lughod, *Veiled Sentiments* (Berkeley: University of California Press, 1986).

17. See here Eugene Genovese, *The Political Economy of Slavery* (New York: Pantheon, 1965); in the nineteenth century, the writings of Calhoun and Fitzhugh argued something like the same position but from the other political standpoint.

18. John Rawls, *A Theory of Justice* (Cambridge, Mass.: Harvard University Press, 1970).

19. This may in fact be due to the "core-periphery" model on which Rawls works.

20. See John Gray, *Two Faces of Liberalism* (New York: New Press, 2000); see also the work of Charles Taylor, Michael Sandel, and William Kymlicka among others.

21. For a discussion of the inadequacies of some standard Western understandings, see Anne Norton's "review" of three books on women and multicultural questions in *Political Theory* 29, 5 (October 2001): 721–26.

22. Charles Taylor, "Democracy, Inclusive and Exclusive," in Richard Madsen, William M. Sullivan, Ann Swidler, and Steven M. Tipton, eds., *Meaning and Modernity: Religion, Polity, and Self* (Berkeley: University of California Press, 2002), p. 191.

23. Ibid. p. 191. See also, H. G. Gadamer, *Truth and Method*, ed. Garret Barden and John Cumming (New York: Seabury Press, 1975).

24. Jean-Luc Nancy, "La Comparution/Compearance," *Political Theory* 20, 3 (August 1992): 392 (translation by Strong).

25. Ibid., p. 393.

26. For a discussion of this on race, see Utz Lars McKnight, *The Political Theory of Liberalism and Race* (Lund: University of Lund Press, 1998).

27. Stanley Cavell, *The Claim of Reason* (Oxford: Clarendon Press; New York: Oxford University Press, 1979), p. 377.

28. Ibid., p. 428.

29. One might adduce here Susan Moller Okin, ed., *Is Multiculturalism Bad for Women?* (Princeton: Princeton University Press, 2000). See some of the responses to her chapter collected in that book as well as the review by Anne Norton in *Political Theory*.

30. Samuel P. Huntington, *The Clash of Civilizations and the Remaking of World Order* (New York: Simon and Schuster, 1996).

31. See, for example, Benjamin R. Barber, *Jihad or McWorld* (New York: *Times Books*, 1995).

32. Thomas L. Friedman, *The Lexus and the Olive Tree* (New York: Farrar, Straus and Giroux, 1999).

PART I

Liberal Egalitarian Attitudes toward Ethical Pluralism

William A. Galston

Definitions

"Liberal egalitarianism" names a family of views rather than a single canonical standpoint. This immediately suggests the question of what one must believe to be a member in good standing of the family. From a Wittgensteinian perspective of course, that question would evoke the response, "Nothing, if you mean a characteristic such that not possessing it strictly entails nonmembership." This perspective makes a certain amount of sense for political theory, a discipline in which traditions tend to be defined in the manner of chain letters rather than in reference to defined sets of formal bright-line characteristics. Still, the effort to push matters farther in the direction of formal definitions is worthwhile, with the caveat that even those who believe in the broad project of defining liberal egalitarianism may well disagree about the specific conception.

Here is my list:

1. Liberal egalitarianism brings together two principles—liberty and equality—that possess independent standing and cannot be reduced to a master concept or a common measure of value. For that reason, among others, liberty and equality are reciprocally limiting, in that some collective acts to promote equality are restrained by the principle of liberty rightly understood; and vice versa.[1] Among its other connotations, the "liberal" component of liberal egalitarianism names a sphere of privacy (the contours of which are contested) protected from both coercive state intrusion and the requirements of public justification.

2. Equality constrains liberty in one decisive respect: in liberal egalitarianism, liberty is understood as *equal* liberty, at least for all normal adults. For liberal egalitarians, the claim that some *citizens* or persons may rightly be deprived of liberties that all others standardly enjoy must discharge a heavy burden of proof. The operating presumption, though rebuttal, points strongly in the opposite direction.

3. There is a distinction, and also a connection, between moral and distributional equality, as follows. Moral equality is, roughly speaking, the idea that many of the empirical differences we observe among human beings

are irrelevant to how they ought to be regarded and treated. Historically, moral equality has been supported by three quite different (and not wholly consistent) considerations: theological—as God's children, all human beings are alike in God's sight; metaphysical—as possessors of moral capacities (practical reason, say), all human beings are alike in dignity; and empirical—on inspection, the observable differences commonly adduced to justify differences of treatment are based on individual vanity, arbitrary social convention, or (as Rawls insists) background conditions for which we are not responsible, and we are alike in the crucial respects (say, fear of violent death and desire for commodious life).

Distributional equality is (again roughly speaking) the idea that, in at least some respects, fairness requires the equal or at least equalizing assignment of goods to persons. This formulation is strong enough to rule out the libertarian claim that it is morally wrong for societies to concern themselves with or intervene in overall patterns of distribution. (In the face of Nozick-like declarations that liberty upsets patterns, liberal egalitarians will retort that some patterns are morally powerful enough to limit liberty—at least as libertarians understand liberty.) At the same time, this formulation is vague enough to suggest what is in fact the case, that liberal egalitarians disagree among themselves concerning the extent to which equality of distribution is required, and on what basis.

I said earlier that moral and distributional equality are linked as well as distinct. The undisputed connection is this: for liberal egalitarians, no pattern of distributional equality is acceptable if its justification ineliminably employs a premise that denies moral equality. The nineteenth-century Brahmin's claim that he was entitled to twenty times as much happiness as anyone else because his worth qua Brahmin was twenty times that of a member of lower orders is an example of what all liberal egalitarians agree on ruling out.[2]

Another link (only slightly more contested) between moral and distributional equality is this: liberal egalitarians believe that while individuals must be free to shape their own lives, even unwisely, their ability to develop and exercise their gifts should not be restricted by vastly unequal distributions of resources. The familiar phrase "equality of opportunity," though open to competing interpretations, expresses this intuitive connection.

Another link embraced by many though not all liberal egalitarians might be termed the "equality presumption." The idea here is that substantial deviations from equal distribution of resources require an affirmative justification, that the burden of proof is on those who would defend unequal outcomes. (Rawls's "Difference Principle" represents one way in which that burden might be discharged.)

A final possible link between moral and distributional equality has been much discussed of late. Among other implications, moral equality may be thought to entail that each individual should have an equal say in determining the distributional principles for his or her society. (One interpretation of "equal say" is that under suitably defined circumstances of choice, no individual can be bound legitimately by distributional principles to which he or she has not consented.)

Given this account, it is not hard to see how the liberty component of liberal egalitarianism can come into conflict with its equality component. A society in which individuals enjoy freedom of association will tend to proliferate groups with varying impacts on equality. Some patterns of exclusion may significantly impair equality of opportunity for those excluded. The internal norms of specific groups may make some of their members less likely to regard themselves as equal to the others and to make claims on that basis. A crucial question for liberal egalitarians is when the state is justified in coercively restricting choice-based social pluralism in the name of equality, moral or distributional. The more weight liberal egalitarians give to ethical pluralism, the more difficult this question becomes.

General Considerations

It has long been believed that ethical pluralism is the likely if not inevitable consequence of social liberty. In *Federalist* 10, James Madison argues that:

> As long as the reason of man continues fallible, and he is at liberty to exercise it, different opinions will be formed. As long as the connection subsists between his reason and his self-love, his opinions and his passions will have a reciprocal influence on each other, and the former will be objects to which the latter will attach themselves. . . . The latent causes of faction are thus sown in the nature of Man; and we see them everywhere brought into different degrees of activity, according to the different circumstances of civil society. A zeal for different opinions concerning religion, concerning government, and many other points, as well of speculation as of practice; an attachment to different leaders ambitiously contending for pre-eminence and power; or to persons of other descriptions whose fortunes have been interesting to the human passions, have, in turn, divided mankind into parties, inflamed them with mutual animosity, and rendered them much more disposed to vex and oppress each other than to co-operate for their common good.

Madison's view of the pluralistic consequences of liberty is far from unrelievedly affirmative. In the background is the Enlightenment idea of a unified and knowable truth. From this standpoint, diversity of opinion is evidence of reason's retail fallibility, not its wholesale infirmity. A society of philosophers should be able to reach agreement (at least on secular matters), provided of course that its members can set aside their vanity. Nor are the political effects of diversity wholly benign: Madison sees the subcommunities that form around diverse opinions as "factions" likely to be opposed to the rights of other members of the polity or to its "permanent and aggregate interests," that is, to the common good.

These animadversions against the consequences of liberty are staples of antiliberal thought, secular as well as theological. But Madison does not drive them to antiliberal conclusions; restricting liberty in the name of ethical uniformity is a cure worse than the disease: "Liberty is to faction what air is to fire—an aliment without which it instantly expires. But it could not be less folly to abolish liberty, which is essential to political life, because it nourishes faction than it would be to wish the annihilation of air, which is essential to animal life, because it imparts to fire its destructive agency."

Many contemporary thinkers offer a more favorable assessment of the consequences of liberty, in part because they back away from Madison's belief that nonfallible reasoners will reach convergent conclusions. For example, John Rawls asserts that "a plurality of reasonable yet incompatible comprehensive doctrine is the normal result of the exercise of human reason within the framework of the free institutions of a constitutional democratic regime."[3] Like Madison, Rawls asks why this is so: "Why should free institutions lead to reasonable pluralism, and why should state power be required to suppress it? Why does not our conscientious attempt to reason with one another lead to reasonable agreement?"[4] But unlike Madison, Rawls traces this pluralism, not to the fallibility of individual reasoners, but rather to the "burdens of judgment" under which we all labor. These burdens include at least the following:

- The evidence bearing on specific issues is complex, often conflicting, and hard to assess.
- Even when we agree about the considerations that are relevant, we may disagree about their weight.
- The concepts we use in political discourse tend to be vague, somewhat indeterminate and vulnerable to the pressure of hard cases.
- The way we assess evidence and weigh moral and political values is shaped to some extent by our life experiences, which in complex modern societies are bound to differ from individual to individual.
- Often there are important normative considerations on both sides of an issue.
- Any society is limited, in the sense that it cannot accommodate the full range of choices and ways of life that individuals may in the abstract find worthy of respect.[5]

Another key difference is that Rawls is less inclined than is Madison to regard diversity as a threat to basic liberal egalitarian regime principles. Rawls distinguishes between reasonable and unreasonable comprehensive views. The latter represent "factions" in the Madisonian sense—that is, bodies of belief and practice hostile to the polity's constitutive principles. But the range of reasonable views—and thus of reasonable subcommunities organized around those views—is encouragingly wide. In the face of ethical pluralism, Rawls suggests, liberal egalitarians should be alert but not anxious.

Within the liberal egalitarian camp, there are stances toward ethical pluralism even more positive than Rawls's. For example, Isaiah Berlin argues that pluralism reflects not the burdens of judgment but rather the nature of things. It is simply the case that the moral universe we happen to inhabit contains a multiplicity of valid principles and valuable goods that cannot be definitively ranked-ordered, cannot be reduced to a common measure of value, and cannot be combined into a single internally harmonious and comprehensively worthy way of life. Reason and experience allow us to distinguish between decency and barbarism. But beyond that, decency is inherently plural rather than singular. So ethical pluralism reflects our inherent moral liberty, the zone in which choice must come to the aid of reason in the construction of our moral lives. That is not to say the moral life is necessarily or always an individualist construction. We may equally *manifest* our moral liberty by identifying ourselves with a long-established community, religious as well as secular, and by pursuing the distinctive goods that give that community its particular shape and purpose.

To these views we may add the most affirmative of all: John Stuart Mill's belief that ethical and social plurality should be actively encouraged, in part because encouragement represents the social principle most likely to lead to the fullest development of individual human powers, and also because social plurality makes it more likely that ideas will be tested against continuing opposition, promoting the acquisition of new truths and preventing established truths from stultifying into mere dogma.

Having said all this, there are clear limits to ethical pluralism within the liberal egalitarian tradition. After all, this tradition is a political as well as moral theory. Its point is to constitute regimes organized in morally appropriate ways. Whether or not this organization takes the form of a written constitution, there is a presumption (rebuttable, but not easily) that the general principles guiding the organization of the polity take priority over beliefs and practices of individuals and subcommunities in cases of conflict. While a regime that is liberal as well as egalitarian will endeavor to limit the sway of general public principles to the essentials, the scope for pluralism, although wide, is necessarily limited. For example, core liberal egalitarian moral commitments such as commitment to equal liberty and the dignity of every human being are typically translated into individual rights protected by the institutions of the liberal democratic polity. Clearly, pluralism ends when the violation of rights begins. Indeed, the protection of individual rights is one of the highest duties of the national community.

Another example: in circumstances in which the general commitment to liberty and equality has been translated into reasonably just institutions and policies, most liberal egalitarians will argue that individual citizens have an obligation to do their part to uphold them. Citizenship is an office with duties as well as rights, and ethical pluralism is not ordinarily a defense against the enforceability of those duties. I say "not ordinarily" because there are exceptional circumstances in which features of ethical particularity may shield individuals against otherwise valid general policies—for example, when religious beliefs ground conscientious objection to military service.

A third kind of limit: because a liberal egalitarian polity requires a citizenry with a core of regime-specific beliefs and virtues, it is justified in establishing a standard of civic education that seeks to create such citizens. This standard will specify what all members in good standing of the polity ought to have in common, regardless of their ethical differences. Here again, there may be exceptions and accommodations in the face of strong competing claims. For example, an otherwise binding requirement to recite a pledge of political allegiance may be set aside if it violates the dictates of a particular religious conscience.

I conclude this section by noting that, for most liberal egalitarians, the scope of what might be thought of as "constitutional requirements" is limited and the potential sphere of pluralist variation is accordingly quite wide. For example, Brian Barry grounds liberal political theory in the motivation of fairness or impartiality: "The essential idea is that fair terms of agreement are those that can reasonably be accepted by people who are free and equal."[6] He goes on to observe that justice understood as impartiality "does not have a substantive answer to every question. Rather, in very many cases it can set limits to what is just but has to leave the choice of an outcome within that range to a fair procedure."[7] To which it must be added: a fair procedure will not always involve the collective determination of a single choice binding on all. Often the zone of moral indeterminacy can be filled by varied individual and group decisions.

SOCIAL REGULATION

The liberal egalitarian stance toward state regulation of ethically based differences flows directly from the liberal egalitarian understanding of constitutional requirements and individual liberties. On this understanding, there is a substantial zone of protected liberty within which individual and group differences, ethical as well as interest-based, may be freely expressed. But this zone is limited by (among other considerations) enforceable individual rights, basic state-protected interests, and the requirements of social coordination, order, and peace.

Consider, for example, a religious or ethnic group that seeks to restrain adult members from leaving. While it may use various strategies of persuasion, including intense emotional and moral pressure, it may not use physical force or threats. If it does, the state is required to intervene to protect individuals' ability to exit. This is so because liberal egalitarians believe in the right of individuals freely to alter what might be termed their "ethical identity" through identification with new ways of life and new groups, and in the state's obligation to protect this right. (This is not to say that liberal egalitarians must systematically prefer lives characterized by shifting ethical identities.)

Basic interests can also place limits on ethically based differences. If a religious ritual requires virgin sacrifice, the state must intervene to prevent it—even if the virgins have consented. (If you want a slogan: No free exercise for Aztecs.) Human life is a basic interest that the state is required to protect in a wide range of circumstances. Similar considerations suggest that parents may not cite ethical or religious considerations to justify withholding blood transfusions or other medical treatments needed to save children from life-threatening illness or injury. Reflecting this principle, U.S. laws against child abuse and neglect trump claims based on the First Amendment.

Of course, the definition of "basic interests" is sometimes the occasion of deep controversy. The best example of this is abortion, where much of the debate revolves around competing metaphysical and theological understandings of human life. While considerations other than the status of the fetus are significant, those who favor a relatively permissive state stance toward abortion typically embrace the view that the fetus is something less than a "Person" entitled to equal protection of the laws. Those who equate abortion with murder are committed to the opposite view, that the fetus is an instance of human life, full stop.

There is nothing in the core of liberal egalitarianism as I have defined it that commits liberal egalitarians to one side or the other of this controversy. A liberal egalitarian could without inconsistency believe that the fetus is within the circle of moral equality—for example, that the empirical differences between a fetus and a newborn infant are not such as to warrant differences of concern or respect. Nor is it possible to say without further ado that abortion is within the sphere of liberal "privacy," because that proposition is parasitic on the resolution of the underlying controversy: depending on your beliefs about the status of the fetus, you may believe that abortion represents the taking of (another's) life, which no one would place outside the purview of the state. The closest liberal egalitarianism can come to a case against abortion restrictions is the claim that such restrictions inevitably place women in a position of disadvantage, even "involuntary servitude." But without further controversial theses about the status of the fetus, it is hard to see why these considerations would trump claims based on the life and future liberty of the fetus.

Finally, reasons of social order may warrant state restriction on some expressions of ethical pluralism. Imagine, for example, ethnic groups whose core cultural practices require loud ceremonies in the late night or early morning hours. Or consider religious groups whose internal norms require vigorous efforts to convert the adherents of other faiths—efforts that others may regard as aggressively intrusive. Liberal egalitarianism is fully compatible with what U.S. law calls "time, place, and manner" restraints on manifestations of ethical particularity that affect the well being of others in ways that threaten the peace of society. (This is not to say that individuals and groups are entitled to a hermetic seal from practices they may find offensive, or that the state could create one.)

CITIZENSHIP

Central to liberal egalitarianism is the commitment to equal citizenship. The arbitrary exclusion of any individual or group from the rights and duties of citizenship is taken as an affront against basic public morality that cries out for correction, through the coercive use of public power if necessary. And the presumption is that exclusion is arbitrary unless compelling reasons can be adduced to justify it.

It is not often noted that the liberal egalitarian commitment to equal citizenship presupposes certain background conditions. Inherent in the distinction between adults and nonadults for purposes of voting, jury duty, and the like is the proposition that a minimum level of intellectual and emotional maturity and independence is needed to discharge the offices of citizenship. In the past, versions of this principle were invoked to justify the systematic exclusion of women and others from the franchise, but these arguments (and the restrictions relying on them) eventually collapsed under the weight of their empirical implausibility. Indeed, the thrust of liberal egalitarianism over time has been to tear down barriers to full and equal citizenship. For example, the Vietnam War created a powerful rationale for lowering the voting age from twenty-one to eighteen: the argument that "If he's old enough to die for his country, he's old enough to help select the leaders who send him to die" proved irresistible.

Liberal egalitarians are open in principle to the possibility that empirical differences among individuals or groups may sometimes justify unequal assignments of rights and duties. For example, the question whether women should be eligible to participate in the full range of military combat roles revolves around the physical and psychological requirement of those roles. Typically, liberal egalitarians favor distinctions among individuals rather than groups whenever possible. Rather than excluding women as a class from certain combat roles on the grounds that the average woman could not satisfy the eligibility standards, most liberal egalitarians would prefer an open competition in which (by hypothesis) a smaller percentage of women than men would succeed. But sometimes it is impractical to forgo group judgments: in the case of voting, an effort to substitute individualized standards of adult maturity for a single chronological criterion would be wholly unworkable.

Liberal egalitarians are also open to the possibility of minimum moral qualifications for full citizenship. For example, individuals convicted of serious crimes may forfeit basic rights such as voting. The argument is that participating in the process of legislation presupposes the willingness to be bound by the legitimate outcome of that process, and the commission of a serious crime is sufficient evidence of the rejection of that obligation.

The management of ethically based disagreements concerning the rights and duties of citizenship is structured by two decisions, one located in the state, the other in civil society. From the state perspective, it matters greatly whether a particular dimension of citizenship is defined as a right or a duty. Liberal egalitarian principles will not always require one or another decision. For example, some modem democracies establish voting as a right, whereas others define it as a duty such that the failure to perform it subjects the individual to state-imposed fines or other penalties. Clearly, the more the state defines citizenship as an ensemble of duties binding on all individuals, the greater the possibility of abrasion with ethical diversity in society. Conversely, the more citizenship is defined in terms of rights, the greater the room left for accommodating individual and group differences.

Some liberal egalitarians argue that specific circumstances may transform citizen rights into duties. For example, Will Kymlicka contends that when serious injustices exist that can only be rectified through political participation, citizens have an obligation to become actively engaged; doing one's fair share to create and uphold just institutions requires no less.[8] This attractive argument may do less work in practice than it does in theory, however. There may be legitimate disagreement as to what justice requires, or a reasonable case may be made (indeed, several political scientists have made it) that nonvoters as a class do not differ significantly from voters and that decisions made by half the citizenry will not diverge materially from those that would result if all participated.

However this may be, there is another crucial distinction, this one at the level of civil society. It makes a difference whether a civil association prevents (some of) its members from exercising a right of citizenship, or rather persuades them on ethical or religious grounds not to do so. The first case is straightforward, at least conceptually: civil associations may not transgress what the state legitimately defines as citizenship rights, and the state is obliged to step in if they try. So civil associations may embody a range of views about the role of women in politics. But if a group locked up all its female members on election day to prevent them from voting, surely the state would have to intervene.

Matters become more complicated if, as part of its core doctrine, a civil association simply instructs its members in what it takes to be deep differences between the appropriate political roles of men and women. Rawls's response is, I believe, roughly what liberal egalitarianism requires: the state must ensure that all citizens are aware of their rights and are at least minimally prepared to exercise them if they choose.[9] The state cannot allow a civil association to deprive its members of the knowledge that they possess basic public rights, or of the basic competencies they would need to exercise them.

Within limits, the liberal egalitarian state may also respond to a civil association's view of how a particular right of citizenship should be exercised. For example, it is inconsistent with liberal egalitarian principles for the government to forbid marriage across racial lines, as the laws of many U.S. states did until quite recently. But what if a civil association teaches its members that interracial marriage is morally repugnant (or contrary to nature, or forbidden by God)? A liberal egalitarian government surely cannot require members of civil associations to give equal opportunity and fair opportunity to all potential mates without regard to race, and it cannot prevent associations from teaching that race matters. What it can rightly do is withhold recognition and legitimization from associations that speak and act along racialist lines. For example, the U.S. government grants tax-favored status to a wide range of charitable institutions. In the early 1980s, the Supreme Court was presented with the issue of whether Bob Jones University, which preached and practiced racially based policies, could have its tax-exempt status withdrawn. The Court answered that question in the affirmative: while government could not prevent a private university from discriminating, it could certainly deny that university political legitimation and practical support.[10] And to the extent that law has an expressive as well as instrumental function, the state could also send the message that it considered the policy of Bob Jones University to be morally illegitimate as well.

LIFE-AND-DEATH DECISIONS

At the outset of this essay, I suggested that "liberal egalitarianism" names a family of approaches rather than a single canonical theory. Nowhere is this clearer than in the contemporary debate over life-and-death issues, especially physician-assisted suicide. Members in good standing of the liberal egalitarian family are found arrayed at different points along the continuum of possible responses to this challenge, in part because of disagreements as to the meaning and extent of individual liberty, and in part because of the tension between liberty and equality.

A well-entrenched principle of law runs as follows: if it is a crime for A to do X, then it is also a crime (though not necessarily the same crime) for B knowingly to assist A in the commission of X. This may readily be transposed into the ethical realm: if it is morally wrong for C to do Y, then it is morally wrong (though not necessarily in the same way) for D to help C to do Y. This suggests that, in considering the liberal egalitarian approach to physician-assisted suicide, we must begin with the morality of suicide itself.

Liberal egalitarians do not speak with one voice on this question. Most begin with a robust conception of individual liberty, understood as self-ownership, self-determination, or autonomy. Faced with the question, "Whose life is it, anyway?" most liberal egalitarians would respond, "Mine" (as distinguished, say, from God's or society's). On this basis, many liberal egalitarians are inclined to place the issue of suicide in the private sphere, outside the purview of legitimate state action.

At the same time, most liberal egalitarians believe that there are some limits to self-determination or self-ownership, that these limits may reflect (paternalistic) concern for individual agents as well as others, and that the state may step in to enforce them. Most would agree that the prohibitions found in the U.S. Constitution against slavery and indentured servitude are valid and enforceable even if the individual consents to this status. Most would agree that prior consent of the deceased does not constitute a valid defense against an indictment for murder. Most would agree (although this is a closer call for some) that the state may prohibit prostitution even when it qualifies as one of Robert Nozick's capitalist acts between consenting adults. None of these cases rests on the appeal to diminished agency; each of the acts may be prohibited even when the individuals involved are fully competent to make the decision to perform them.

The appeal to pain (more broadly, to a stable, intense, subjective sense of the disutility of one's continued existence) is frequently taken to be a powerful justification for suicide. The difficulty is that from a utilitarian standpoint, one's life is not (only) one's own. In considering suicide, the cessation of pain from terminating one's cancer-riddled existence must somehow be compared with the pain inflicted on friends and family as well as the broader consequences for society. That is an important reason why most contemporary liberal egalitarians are not utilitarians and are drawn instead to some form of Kantianism.

But there is an immediate difficulty: taking as his point of departure the concept of autonomy, the best-known Kantian (Kant himself) reaches the conclusion that suicide is always wrong. Autonomy is the basis of equal respect for persons. To respect persons is to treat humanity as an end in itself, never as means alone. But suicide treats humanity as a means to something else, such as the cessation of pain, and it is therefore wrong. Most Kant-inspired contemporary liberal egalitarians are uncomfortable with this rigorous position and try to relax it in some way. For example, Thomas Hill distinguishes among possible motives for suicide. Impulse, apathy, self-abasement, and utilitarian calculation are impermissible motives; however, suicide may be acceptable when human agency is vanishing, when pain is irremediable and so intense as to disfigure life, or when it may promote important and defensible moral beliefs and goods. The core intuition at work here is that at least some instances of suicide are consistent with respect for humanity in one's own person.[11]

It is also possible to argue against the morality of suicide based on the harm that it may inflict on others or on the obligations that one may have toward them. Typically, a parent's suicide leaves a child or spouse with profound feelings of abandonment, rejection, and guilt ("If he had really loved me, he would never have deprived me of his presence this way" or "If only I had been more caring, he would never have been driven to this act of ultimate desperation"). The force of such arguments will vary depending on the circumstances of the agent: the case of the married parent of a minor child is very different from that of an elderly nursing home resident who has outlived spouse, children, and friends.

I think it is fair to say that, although there will be disagreements in defining the zone of acceptability, for most liberal egalitarians suicide is not always wrong. In these cases, practices such as physician-assisted suicide cannot be ruled out on the grounds that they aid and abet wrongful acts. This conclusion is especially plausible once one grants, as nearly all liberal egalitarians do, that patients have the right to refuse life-sustaining treatment even when the clearly foreseeable consequence of that refusal will be one's death. The philosopher Dan Brock speaks for many when he says that "The central ethical argument for euthanasia . . . [i]s that the very same . . . fundamental ethical arguments (individual self-determination and well-being] supporting the consensus on patients' rights to decide about life-sustaining treatment also support the ethical permissibility of euthanasia."[12]

Even if this point is granted, which some do not,[13] there may nonetheless be other grounds for liberal egalitarian caution. If physician-assisted suicide is regularized, families may put pressure on gravely ill relatives to terminate their existence before their inheritance disappears. The patient-physician relationship, always vulnerable to abuse, may be disrupted, especially when patients are poor, old, or uneducated. Doctors may lose their moral moorings if the orientation of their craft is broadened beyond health and life. The availability of this option might weaken the general societal presumption against homicide or create a classic slippery slope in which the zone of societal permissibility is progressively broadened beyond the initial core of moral justification. The weight attached to these considerations varies from one liberal egalitarian to the next, but few dismiss them outright.

Everything considered, it is fair to say that there is a significant range of disagreement concerning physician-assisted suicide, both among liberal egalitarian philosophers and (at least in the United States) within the general populace. In practice, U.S. political and social institutions have adopted two complementary strategies for managing this ethically based conflict. First, the Supreme Court has resolutely resisted calls, from liberal egalitarian philosophers among others,[14] to craft a one-size-fits-all standard binding on the nation as a whole. There is neither a constitutional right to assisted suicide nor a constitutional prohibition against it. This zone of constitutional permission allows for geographically based diversity of laws in accordance with the principles and institutions of federalism. To date, one state has availed itself of the opportunity to legalize physician-assisted suicide; others may follow.

Second (as most families in the United States have learned), hospitals and other medical institutions have allowed an informal shadowy gray zone to develop. Appearing before the Supreme Court to present the government's case against a constitutional right to assisted suicide, acting solicitor general Walter Dellinger declared, "We agree that state law may . . . not only allow withdrawal of medical treatment but also allow physicians to prescribe medication in sufficient doses to relieve pain even when the necessary dose will hasten death . . . so long as the physician's intent is to relieve pain and not cause death."[15] It does not take a lot of imagination to see what kind of regime this declaratory position creates in practice. At some point the patient, family, and doctor will quietly agree that the time has come to administer a dose of pain-reliever large enough to cause death. Unless the surviving parties to the transaction are so indiscreet as to discuss their real motives with others, who will read their hearts?

The management of this issue may usefully be contrasted with that of abortion. As is well known, faced with local controversies and a diversity of state laws, the U.S. Supreme Court decided in 1973 to establish a national constitutional right to abortion in a wide though not unlimited range of circumstances. Many people sympathetic in principle to the claim that abortion should be more widely available have concluded that, in practice, a strategy of compelled constitutional uniformity was not well suited to the ethical conflicts that divided U.S. society on this issue and may even have exacerbated those conflicts while slowing the formation of a coalition of the center that over time might have rendered this debate less socially divisive and politically disfiguring. This is, obviously, an empirical claim about which reasonable people can differ, and they may also disagree about the relative weight of social division as opposed to the unequal burdens imposed by the prior status quo.

This case suggests the general proposition that the powers of the state should be deployed cautiously on behalf of any public philosophy, liberal egalitarianism included, in circumstances of diversity. This is not to say that it is always wrong to do so; the standard example is the judicially led use of state power to overcome widespread resistance to constitutionally guaranteed racial equality. But uniform public law that violates the deep convictions of individuals or groups is bound to generate resistance that diminishes both the perceived legitimacy and practical efficacy of the system of law as a whole. It may be frustratingly slow to allow public dialogue to find its point of equipoise, there is no guarantee that the political process will lead to a broadly acceptable settlement, and there may be substantial hardship and injustice in the interim. Still, informal social deliberation can often reduce deep conflict and point toward ethical compromise that can be sustained over time.

HUMAN SEXUALITY

At least three kinds of considerations lead liberal egalitarians to question "traditional morality," and public policies that reflect this morality, in sexual matters. First, liberal egalitarians tend to place most sexual conduct in the zone of liberty or privacy that should be insulated (so far as possible) from state interference.

Second, liberal egalitarians believe that arguments based on traditional practices and public consensus are inherently unsound. They note that entrenched traditional practices and understanding have often yielded to rational criticism over time. (For example, the arguments formerly deployed to justify antimiscegenation statutes now seem grotesque.) For similar reasons, policies based on considerations such as "innate repugnance" are suspect because such moral sentiments, even when widely shared, often reflect ungrounded prejudice. When challenged, even near universal norms such as incest prohibitions stand in need of justification.

Third, liberal egalitarians believe that public policies that claim to be binding on all must be based on reasons that are in principle accessible to all. There is a range of disagreement among liberal egalitarians as to the nature and scope of "public reasons." But there is broad agreement that (for example) it is not appropriate to justify a generally applicable restriction on sexual conduct by referring to God's law or plan unless this divine intention can be discerned through the use of faculties that are shared by all normal adults, regardless of denominational affiliation and the content of individual faith. From this perspective, public laws against polygamy cannot be based on the principles of Christianity but must plausibly link monogamy to important features of liberal egalitarian governance such as respect for persons, democracy, nonexploitation, or the equal protection of the laws. (It is a further question to determine whether or to what extent these public reasons trump individual or communal liberties such as religious free exercise.)

There are circumstances in which public policy cannot be silent or neutral on sexual relationships. For example, the institution of marriage is defined by law. When the law restricts marriage to a single man and single women, it must be prepared to offer a public justification. For the reasons just stated, liberal egalitarians cannot accept justifications of the form "this is the way we've always done things around here" or "same-sex sex is disgusting, so how could we allow them to get married?" or "God says it's an abomination."

Discussion of same-sex marriage, which began in the United States more than twenty-five years ago, escalated in the mid and late 1990s as first Hawaii and then Vermont moved toward the conclusion that the prohibition against same-sex marriage violated its state constitution. It has proved remarkably difficult to frame arguments in favor of this prohibition without falling back on tradition, revelation, or natural law claims that turn out to rely on premises not available to unaided reason. A standard modern natural law thesis is that heterosexual marriage is a purposive institution, oriented toward procreation, in a way that same-sex unions cannot be. But what about aged or sterile heterosexual couples, incapable of procreation? Are they are to be prevented from marrying as well? That was the position of Philo, a Judeo-Platonist philosopher of the early Christian period: "Those who woo women who have been shown to be barren . . . are simply mounting them in the manner of pigs or goats."[16] But few would take this line today. On the contrary: from a liberal egalitarian perspective, it is not hard to define general public purposes that would be well served by expanding the boundaries of marriage. Married couples tend to be the sources of social stability and to discharge mutual responsibilities within the family that would otherwise be performed less effectively by public authorities at public expense. Nor does there seem to be any empirical basis for believing that same-sex couples are less able than others to raise children successfully.[17] In short, the liberal egalitarian presumption is that same sex partners should be treated equally with others for purposes of marriage unless a compelling reason not to do so can be adduced, and the liberal egalitarian conclusion is that no such reason has yet made its appearance.

Conclusions

I suggested at the outset that "liberal egalitarianism" names a family of views rather than a single conception of political philosophy. Nonetheless, the exposition should have made it clear that the members of the family do have some important common features, that liberal egalitarianism at least rules out some approaches to politics and creates strong though rebuttable presumptions in favor of others. The moral equality of citizens tends to favor more tangible forms of equality, including equal liberty and at least a tendency toward the reduction of distributional inequalities. The moral liberty of persons undergirds both a protected zone of privacy and a presumption against state paternalism. Liberal egalitarians will therefore accept, even welcome, a wide though not unlimited ethical and social pluralism.

The tension between liberty and equality manifests itself in several ways, including issues of the state's proper stance toward voluntary civil associations whose internal principles and policies may not mirror those of the liberal egalitarian polity. The state can probably enhance certain kinds of equality by intervening in the affairs of these associations, but delimiting the point at which such interventions exact an excessive price in diminished liberty will continue to be a matter of contestation within the liberal egalitarian camp.

Notes

1. This point of departure implicitly rejects efforts to derive liberal egalitarianism from a single value, such as equality. For a well-known example of such an approach, see Ronald Dworkin, "Liberalism," in *A Matter of Principle* (Cambridge, Mass.: Harvard University Press, 1985).

2. For the full and much more charming account, see Brian Barry, *Political Argument: A Reissue with a New Introduction* (Berkeley: University of California, 1990), p. 15.

3. John Rawls, *Political Liberalism with a New Introduction and the "Reply to Habermas"* (New York: Columbia, 1996), p. xviii.

4. Ibid., p. 55.

5. Ibid., pp. 56–57.

6. Brian Barry, *A Treatise on Social Justice*, vol. 2: Justice as Impartiality (Oxford: Clarendon, 1995), p. 112.

7. Ibid., p. 113.

8. Will Kymlicka, "Civil Society and Government: A Liberal Egalitarian Perspective," paper prepared for Ethikon conferences, Santa Fe, January 1999, p. 6.

9. Rawls, *Political Liberalism*, p. 199.

10. *Bob Jones University v. United States*, 461 U.S. 574 (1983).

11. Thomas Hill. "Self-Regarding Suicide: A Modified Kantian View," in Howard J. Curzer, ed., *Ethical Theory and Moral Problems* (Belmont, Calif.: Wadsworth, 1999), pp. 732–43.

12. Dan Brock, "Voluntary Active Euthanasia," *Hastings Center Report* 22, 2 (1992): 10–12.

13. See, for example, Daniel Callahan, "When Self-Determination Runs Amok," *Hastings Center Report* 22, 2 (1992): 52–55; and Paul J. Weithman, "Of Assisted Suicide and The Philosophers' Brief," *Ethics*, 109, 3 (April 1999): 548–78. This issue of *Ethics* features a state-of-the-art philosophical symposium on the mind-numbing theoretical complexities of physician-assisted suicide. By comparison, this section of my essay barely scratches the surface.

14. See the famous (notorious?) "Assisted Suicide: The Philosophers' Brief," drafted by Ronald Dworkin, Thomas Nagel, Robert Nozick, John Rawls, Thomas Scanlon, and Judith Jarvis Thomson, *New York Review of Books*, 27 March 1997.

15. Quoted in Judith Jarvis Thomson, "Physician-Assisted Suicide: Two Moral Arguments," *Ethics* 109, 3 (April 1999): 508. 1 have added the italics for emphasis.

16. Quoted in Andrew Koppelman, "Is Marriage Inherently Heterosexual?" *American Journal of Jurisprudence* 42 (1997):, 64.

17. For all this and more, see ibid. and Stephen Macedo, "Homosexuality and the Conservative Mind," *Georgetown Law Journal* 84 (1995).

Liberal Egalitarian Platitudes?

Brian Barry

Anyone who is asked to give a liberal egalitarian account of an issue is faced by the problem that, within the Ethikon framework, liberalism comes in only two flavors: classical and egalitarian. Moreover, "classical liberalism" turns out in practice not to be as catholic as it sounds. It would exclude a presumptively classical liberal such as John Stuart Mill on account of (among other things) his support for the redistribution of market-derived incomes. What goes under the name of classical liberalism is in fact libertarianism, a doctrine with almost no resonance outside the United States—where it may even make a limited amount of sense in sparsely populated parts of the Southwest. What is left over is thus the entirety of liberalism. One option, which is the one I myself followed when placed in Galston's position in a previous Ethikon symposium, is to define liberal egalitarianism narrowly, tacitly accepting that most of historic and current liberalism will fall between the two variants discussed. Another possibility would be to stipulate that egalitarian liberalism is to be conceived of as everything that is left over when libertarianism is subtracted. The obvious problem with this inclusive conception is that it makes egalitarian liberalism a very amorphous doctrine in which equality will of necessity play no very distinctive part.

Galston seems to me to straddle both of these approaches—and more. What I mean by this last is that some of the ideas that he attributes to liberal egalitarianism are actually foundational to liberalism of any kind, including libertarianism. Thus, although libertarianism rejects criteria of justice that concern themselves with inequality of outcomes, what admits it into the family of liberal doctrines is its demand that whatever rights people have must be equal. I would therefore suggest that, of Galston's three points, the second is definitional of liberalism in any form. Similarly, the moral equality that forms the first half of his third point is an essential feature of liberalism, if only because it is necessary to underwrite the equality of rights.

A couple of Galston's specific discussions of public policy issues illustrate the way in which he sometimes appeals to pan-liberal principles. Thus, even libertarians (and this is what distinguishes them from their anarchist cousins) accept that acts of certain kinds must be prohibited by law. Killing another human being is the most basic example of such an act. As Galston says, it is possible to take the view "that the fetus is an instance of human life, full stop." Those who subscribe to this belief can derive from the general prohibition on murder that it should include abortion. Galston observes that liberal egalitarians can take either side on the question of the status of the fetus. But there is no reason for limiting the application of this point to liberal egalitarians: it is equally valid in relation to anybody who accepts that murder should be prohibited.

Galston's discussion of abortion, then, turns on a thesis—that murder should be prohibited by law—that is common ground to liberals of all kinds, and, indeed, is also shared by just about everybody else except anarchists. In his discussion of human sexuality, Galston calls on a principle that is not so widely accepted outside the ranks of liberals but is equally congenial to libertarian and nonlibertarian liberals. This is the principle, given its classic expression in John Stuart Mill's *On Liberty*, that practices engaged in by consenting adults that do not harm third parties in some tangible way (which rules out counting as harm having one's moral convictions affronted) should not be subject to legal sanctions. Libertarians are, if anything, even more enthusiastic than other liberals about this principle, because they wish to use it to defend from state intervention market transactions that other liberals (including Mill) have wished to regard as adversely affecting the interests of those not party to the transaction. Galston writes that "liberal egalitarians tend to place most sexual conduct in the zone of liberty or privacy that should be insulated (as far as possible) from state interference." This takes us back to his first point where he wrote that "the 'liberal' component of liberal egalitarianism names a sphere of privacy . . . protected from both coercive state intrusion and the requirements of public justification." The context there was assumed to be one in which the value competing with liberty was (substantive) equality: "[S]ome collective acts to promote equality are limited by the principle of liberty rightly understood." In the case of sexual relationships, however, there is no egalitarian purpose that can be advanced by intervention. Rather, intervention will be driven by convictions of a traditional or religious form about what is sinful or "unnatural." Liberals, as Galston correctly says, reject these as reasons that should shape the criminal law. But egalitarians have no special stake in this standard liberal move.

As far as same-sex marriage is concerned, the case for recognition turns, according to Galston, on a notion of equal treatment. But this is the notion of equal treatment by the state incorporated in Galston's second point, which I have suggested should be thought of as a defining feature of liberalism itself. Whether the case for recognizing same-sex marriages as a requirement of justice is sound depends on the degree to which the situation of same-sex couples is in the relevant regards sufficiently similar to that of different-sex couples to engage the principle of equal treatment.

I am inclined to agree with Galston that it does, but again this is a question in which egalitarians have no special stake. It may be that this whole discussion will be of little concern to libertarians, because their glorification of contracts is liable to make them uncomfortable with one whose terms are set by the state. Nevertheless, if libertarians are prepared to discuss the form to be taken by marriage law, they too will have to argue about the requirements of equal treatment and will have no distinctive take on this question qua libertarians.

We can find clearer instances in which Galston's premises would be rejected by a libertarian but are not distinctively egalitarian. If these premises are to be subsumed within egalitarian liberalism, it can be only by stipulating that egalitarian liberalism is to be taken to be any sort of liberalism except libertarianism—the second of the alternatives that I canvassed earlier. A more perspicuous description of the doctrine invoked would perhaps be "nonlibertarian liberalism" or (giving it a positive twist) "interventionist liberalism." Again, I offer two examples.

Galston writes that "because a liberal egalitarian polity requires a citizenry with a core of regime-specific beliefs and virtues, it is justified in establishing a standard of civic education that seeks to create such citizens." This is a principle that, ever since the era of mass education began in the nineteenth century, has been embraced with especial fervor by nonliberal regimes. Libertarians will presumably reject it because they will either say that the state should have nothing to do with education or will specify some minimal level of literacy and numeracy that children should be equipped with in order to avoid their threatening the interests of others. Either way, libertarians may be expected to balk at the idea that the state should lay down a set of beliefs and values to be inculcated in children. But the enthusiasm of nonliberal regimes for Galston's principle should, I suggest, give nonlibertarian liberals pause as well.

As a consequence of their justifying grounds, nonliberal regimes need have no qualms about turning the school system into an engine of political indoctrination. Bolsheviks, who split from other socialists on the question of "vanguardism," are committed to the idea that only a small elite can discern the imperatives of History. (Lenin and Trotsky disagreed about what these were, but neither would at any time have dreamed of turning the question over to the population at large of the Soviet Union.) Fascists and Nazis hold that the Leader knows what is best and that the only obligation of the citizens is obedience. In a theocracy, the legitimacy of the regime flows from its conformity to the Will of God, and in a regime founded on nationalism the interests of the nation cannot be left to the vagaries of popular opinion. Hence, for example, in Turkey the military, in the guise of guardians of the nation, intervene periodically to eject popularly elected governments, and it is no accident that the mandatory history textbooks provide an exceedingly unreliable record, which refuses to accept the existence of national minorities.[1]

Liberal regimes, in contrast, rest their legitimacy on the consent of the population governed. As Harry Brighouse has persuasively argued, the quality of this consent is compromised if it can be seen to arise from indoctrination undertaken at the behest of the government itself: the process of justification becomes uncomfortably circular.[2] Galston's discussion of the issue in his essay is too brief to enable the reader to get much idea of what he is driving at. Elsewhere, however, he has laid out his agenda for political education in a way that seems to me to bring out the dubious nature of its affiliation to liberalism, as against some sort of Burkean conservatism. Thus, he has written that

> [F]ew individuals will come to embrace the core commitments of liberal society through a process of rational inquiry. If children are to be brought to accept these commitments as valid and binding, the method must be a pedagogy that is far more rhetorical than rational. For example, rigorous historical research will almost certainly vindicate complex 'revisionist' accounts of key figures in American history. Civic education, however, requires a nobler moralizing history: a pantheon of heroes who confer legitimacy on central institutions and are worthy of emulation.[3]

If Galston were right that the great majority of citizens in a liberal democracy are incapable of giving rational assent to its political institutions, liberalism (whether egalitarian or any other kind) would be an untenable doctrine. Fortunately, there is no reason for thinking that the advantages of living in a liberal democracy cannot be easily understood. That hundreds of millions of people in the rest of the world would like to migrate to one of the liberal democracies reinforces the supposition that those advantages are not so arcane as Galston supposes and that deceitful propaganda is not therefore needed to evoke an attachment to liberal democratic institutions. Moreover, most liberal democracies manage perfectly well without requiring children to engage in grotesque displays of patriotism such as saluting the flag or reciting a pledge of allegiance. Galston is prepared to concede in his essay that "an otherwise binding requirement to recite a pledge of allegiance may be set aside if it violates the dictates of a particular religious conscience." This is too little, too late. It is the whole business that is pernicious, from a liberal point of view.

My second example is also one in which, while Galston's treatment of the issue is incompatible with libertarianism, I have similar doubts about its compatability with liberalism of any kind. Where doctor-assisted suicide is concerned, I take it that libertarians would appeal to Mill's principle, already invoked in relation to issues of sexuality. Thus, while there are a variety of views (some based on religious beliefs) about the morality of suicide, we can scarcely deny that taking one's life is a decision that primarily affects the person whose life it is unless we are prepared to eviscerate the principle by conceding that extraordinarily few kinds of act are going to be covered by it. Mill's principle then entails that, if a legally permissible act arises from the cooperation of consenting adults, that activity is also legally immune.

The problem is: can any liberal fail to draw the same conclusion? Galston's own discussion of the question gets off to a disastrous start. He proposes that "we must begin with the morality of suicide itself." But why must we? This, it should be recalled, was not at all the way in which Galston approached questions of public policy involving sexuality. There, he held that even deeply held moral and religious convictions, often with many thousands of years of history behind them, could be disregarded because individual liberty trumped attempts to implement moral and religious beliefs that are, inevitably, not acknowledged by all as valid. I can see no possible justification for departing from this approach when the issue is suicide.

Whatever the morality of suicide, and whatever its relevance to public policy, attempted suicide is not a criminal offence in liberal countries today, nor are the goods of successful suicides confiscated by the state, as a form of public vengeance in lieu of prosecution. We are therefore left with this simple question: if the law accepts suicide, how can it coherently prohibit assisted suicide—whether the assistance is given by a doctor or a friend or relative? As I grow older I become increasingly aware of how rare it is for public policy issues to be simple and straightforward. I also become increasingly clear that this is one of the few exceptions. The only arguments adduced by Galston to suggest that this is an open question are paternalistic. I do not think that liberals (and this distinguishes them from libertarians) have to be fanatically antipaternalistic. Normal people quite reasonably give a low value to the liberty offered by the ability to buy dangerous appliances and poisonous food, and are prepared to trade it in for other benefits. They would sooner have the state regulate the sale of goods than have to subscribe to some private information service to find out about risks of electrocution or salmonella poisoning. But to extend paternalism to a point that prevents an adult of sound mind from terminating his or her life with dignity rather than face a future of pain and degradation seems to me to carry it to a point that makes nonsense of any commitment to individual liberty.

No doubt the principle that assisted suicide should be legal needs to be qualified by safeguards, so as to ensure that death really has come about at the will of the deceased. But there is no reason for regarding the problem of erecting such safeguards as unsuperable. The alternative favored by Galston, which relies on nods and winks exchanged between the attending physician and the patient and/or the patient's family, seems to be fundamentally objectionable on liberal grounds, because it takes away the autonomy of the person primarily concerned and vests ultimate power in doctors. But it is, I suggest, especially obnoxious to liberals who are also egalitarians, because it violates equality of treatment. If we ask what are the conditions under which nod-and-wink euthanasia is going to be most readily available, two spring to mind. One is that it is better to have some illness resulting in progressive deterioration over some time during which the sufferer is still *compos mentis*, so as to allow time to develop a personal relationship with the physician primarily responsible for treatment. (Victims of a severe stroke, for example, will be disadvantaged by this condition.) The second condition is implied already in the assumption underlying the statement of the first, that the patient *has* a single physician primarily responsible for his or her care, as against whoever happens to be on duty in the ward from day to day. In the United States and, increasingly, in Britain, this condition is met only for those fortunate enough to be in a position to afford private medical care. Thus, equal access to physician-assisted suicide demands that it be put on a formal basis.

I have to say that I am rather baffled by the purport of the two paragraphs following Galston's discussion of physician-assisted suicide. He begins by saying that "the management of this issue may usefully be contrasted with that of abortion." But what exactly is the contrast that he has in mind? The set-up that he appears to find acceptable in the former case is, as we have seen, one in which euthanasia falls within "an informal shadowy gray zone." Does he believe that abortion fell into a similar "gray zone" before it was legalized? It did, of course, do so (in the United States and elsewhere) in the sense that quite a few abortions were actually performed and the proportion that resulted in prosecution was relatively small. But the procedure was hardly a standard one among the medical profession generally, as is the practice of deliberately shortening the lives of terminally ill people. In any case, we may ask if Galston is advocating that abortion should be treated as euthanasia is now handled: illegal but widely connived at. Some of the time he sounds as if he may. Thus, he tells us that "uniform public law that violates the deep convictions of individuals or groups is bound to generate resistance that diminishes both the perceived legitimacy and practical efficacy of the system of law as a whole." Is the alternative to "uniform public law" the kind of "gray area" that (according to him) euthanasia now falls within? It is hard to see what else could constitute an alternative to "uniform public law," since it is in the nature of law to be uniform in application, except where (as in the "gray area" cases) it is actually applied only haphazardly. However, the rest of what Galston says suggests that the contrast he intends is not really between "uniform public law" and some other sort of law but rather between legislated law and "judicially led use of state power."

This directs our attention to the other difference between Galston's two cases: the American Supreme Court's refusal to rule in favor of a constitutional right to be helped to die and its decision about abortion in *Roe v. Wade*. This is clear enough, and so is Galston's preference for the Supreme Court to leave both issues to legislation rather than preempting them. But I am puzzled by the conclusion he draws to the effect that it "suggests the general proposition that the powers of the state should be deployed cautiously on behalf of any public philosophy, liberal egalitarianism included, in circumstances of diversity." He appears to assume here that a liberal egalitarian public philosophy must unequivocally lead to the substantive conclusions (or something like them) reached by the Supreme Court. Yet this conflicts with his prior assertion that liberal egalitarians can come down on either side of the question of legalizing abortion, depending on their views about the status of the entity to be aborted. We might restate Galston's objection to *Roe v. Wade* by couching it as advice to those who are in favor of making abortion on demand legal. But what exactly is his advice? He appears to me to run together two distinct ideas, one procedural and the other substantive.

The procedural point is that "compelled constitutional uniformity" is not a good way to resolve the issue. This taps into a familiar argument to the effect that most of those who thought abortion should be illegal would have been reconciled to losing in a political battle and were only galvanized into an antiabortion crusade by the Supreme Court's line that there was some kind of constitutional principle underwriting the pro-abortion side. Two kinds of evidence have been advanced in defense of this thesis. The first is that liberal abortion legislation had already passed in some states (such as California) before the Supreme Court decision and had not produced the sort of backlash *Roe v. Wade* did. The other kind of evidence draws on a comparison between the experience of the United States and that of Western Europe. It is pointed out that opinion about abortion is as much divided in Western Europe as it is in the United States, but that controversy has been held at a much lower level of intensity there. This is then attributed to the way in which (with the exception of a regrettable intervention on the antiabortion side by the German Supreme Court) the abortion issue has been handled by legislatures.

It would be beyond my purpose to evaluate this argument here. I simply observe that Galston appears to rely on it to some degree. But what I wish to make more of is that he seems to me to run together this procedural argument with a substantive one that is highly dubious. Thus, he envisages that the outcome of "allow[ing] public dialogue to find its point of equipoise" must be "ethical compromise that can be sustained over time."

But there is no a priori reason for expecting the operation of the political process to lead to a compromise. American anti-abortionists propose a variety of restrictions that would make obtaining an abortion slower, more vexatious, more difficult, or more legally risky merely as a device to reduce the total number of abortions, their objective remaining a complete ban. This being so, those in favor of the availability of abortion have no reason for making any concessions, because these would not appease the anti-abortionists anyway. This a priori analysis is supported by experience. In the United Kingdom, for example, a settlement providing for abortion de facto on demand (and free on the National Health Service) has been sustained over more than thirty years, and periodic challenges having been beaten off by comfortable majorities in the House of Commons. I believe that the same story can be told of a number of other Western European countries.

So far I have not come up with any evidence for Galston's adopting the strategy of distinguishing liberal egalitarianism from liberalism generally, or at least nonlibertarian liberalism. Indeed, if Galston's views on political education and physician-assisted suicide are liberal at all, they exemplify a liberalism that is not libertarian but justifies intervention without invoking equality as a value. However, the second half of his third point, at the beginning of his essay, might scare off some nonlibertarians in as far as it allows that "at least in some respects, fairness requires the equal or at least equalizing assignment of goods to persons." In his discussion of public policy issues, however, Galston offers us very little in the way of state interventions to bring about "equal or at least equalizing assignments of goods to persons."

In the context of the institutions of civil society, a crucial question is how far the value of freedom of association should be permitted to license discrimination based on such characteristics as "race," ethnicity, religion, gender, sexual orientation, or age. All such discrimination is a denial of equal opportunity and therefore prima facie suspect, but nobody would wish to deny that (say) those who take part in a weekly poker game in the house of one of them should not be free to choose whom to invite, even if they self-consciously exclude anybody except old straight male WASPs. The question is how far this kind of immunity should extend. Fairly clearly, a church should be able to use the profession of a certain set of religious beliefs as a condition of membership. But the equivalent in the case of a golf club would be to exclude nongolfers or perhaps even those whose handicap exceeded some large number: it would not be to exclude Jews or blacks.

Liberal egalitarians will tend to be more impressed by the value of non-discrimination and less impressed by that of freedom of association than will nonegalitarian liberals. In particular, they will wish to see rigorous enforcement of antidiscrimination measures in relation to those associations that have the most impact on overall life chances, such as educational institutions and employers. Nonegalitarian liberals, in contrast, tend to hold that firms should be free to make whatever choices of employees are, in their judgment, best calculated to maximize their profits. This claim is commonly supported by the claim that, because discrimination does not pay, it cannot possibly occur. This view is held with remarkable tenacity in the teeth of evidence to the contrary that is depressingly easy to obtain: it is only necessary to send two people with the same qualifications but different characteristics such as sex or race to discover pretty soon a case in which one is told the job has been filled and the other is subsequently offered it. We are, after all, talking here about a school of economists whose members (according to the apocryphal story) refuse to accept ocular evidence for the existence of a twenty dollar bill lying on the sidewalk on the strength of the belief that, if there had been such a bill, somebody would already have picked it up.

Only in the final paragraph of his discussion of legitimate reasons for intervention does Galston cite a case in which egalitarian liberals might reach a different answer from nonegalitarian liberals. This is the case in which Bob Jones University was denied tax-exempt status because it "preached and practiced racially based policies." A recent Supreme Court decision that came down on the other side was that which permitted the Boy Scouts of America to exclude homosexuals from the organization. On one side, it was argued that the Scouts should have the power to determine their own criteria for membership. On the other, it was said that none of their published criteria mentioned sexual orientation and that to add it at this point was to practise arbitrary discrimination.[4] Working out the principles that should apply in such cases is difficult, but it is, I believe, a large part of what needs to be done to relate the demands of liberal egalitarianism to the claims of civil society.

NOTES

1. I am indebted to Murad Akan for a detailed analysis of the content of the textbooks sponsored by the Ministry of Education in Turkey and the role this material plays in the legitimation of the military's interventions in politics to protect "the nation."

2. Harry Brighouse, "Civic Education and Liberal Legitimacy," *Ethics* 108 (1998): 719–45.

3. William Galston, *Liberal Purposes* (Cambridge: Cambridge University Press, 1992), pp. 243–44.

4. At this moment, the King, who had been for some time busily writing in his note-book, called out "Silence!" and read out from his book "Rule Forty-two. *All persons more than a mile high are to leave the court.*"

Everybody looked at Alice.

"*I'm* not a mile high," said Alice.

"*You are*," said the King.

"Nearly two miles high," added the Queen.

"Well, I shan't go, at any rate," said Alice; "besides, that's not a regular rule: you invented it just now."

"It's the oldest rule in the book," said the King.

"Then it ought to be Number One," said Alice.

Alice's Adventures in Wonderland in *The Complete Works of Lewis Carroll* (New York: Vintage Books, 1976), pp. 124–25.

PART II

Ethical Pluralism from a Classical Liberal Perspective

Chandran Kukathas

> In fact, the real disturbers of the peace are those who, in a free state, seek to curtail the liberty of judgement which they are unable to tyrannize over.
> —Spinoza, *Theologico-Political Treatise*

GENERAL CONSIDERATIONS

Is the ideal society one that embodies or aims for ethical uniformity, or one that emphasizes instead the accommodation of ethical pluralism? From a classical liberal perspective the answer can only be that ethical pluralism should be accommodated.

But here some caveats are in order. First, such a society would be "ideal" only in a limited sense: in the sense that it is the best kind of society to try to sustain given ethical disagreement—even though it would be a better society if it were governed by the right ethical values. The classical liberal perspective assumes that a society that *embodies* ethical uniformity can only be a society in which uniformity is coerced; and that a society that *aims* for ethical uniformity must either resort to coercion or fail to attain uniformity (or, more likely still, both). Humans tend to disagree, and the larger the society the greater the likelihood of substantial disagreement. As Hume observed, "such is the nature of the human mind that it always lays hold on every mind that approaches it; and as it is wonderfully fortified by an unanimity of sentiments, so is it shocked and disturbed by any contrariety. Hence [our] impatience of opposition, even in the most speculative and indifferent opinions."[1] Ethical pluralism is ideal because of these constrained circumstances and because coercion is undesirable.

Second, even though it is necessary to offer a straightforward answer to the question of the classical liberal response to ethical pluralism, and to the subsidiary question of the extent to which ethical pluralism is acceptable, within the classical liberal tradition there is a measure of diversity—indeed, of ethical pluralism—regarding this very issue. There is a considerable disagreement within that tradition over the extent to which

diversity should be accommodated; over the principles by which such issues should be decided; and, indeed, over the question of what is classical
liberalism[2] and who are its exponents.[3]

Third, in view of the fact that the classical liberalism in question is a
tradition, it is worth noting that the classical liberal pantheon of heroes is
equally contested. For some it is very much a modern European tradition,
whereas others see traces of classical liberal thought not only in ancient
and medieval ideas but also in the writings of Confucius and Laozi.[4] And
many of the heroes of classical liberalism are also claimed by other political traditions: by republicans, conservatives, socialists, democrats, and
egalitarian liberals.[5] Equally, classical liberals disagree among themselves
over rights of membership in the club: some consider Burke a conservative, others find Hume too skeptical, and to a few Mill is an apostate who
must be forever barred.

The point of these caveats is to make clear that any account of classical
liberalism and its injunctions is bound to be contestable to a considerable
degree. It is not possible to offer an account of the classical liberal tradition without offering, in effect, a particular theory within it—one that, in
the end, takes sides on issues that are, to varying degrees, in dispute. Indeed, there are some issues on which there is no settled position not because there are competing views but because the tradition is itself evolving. On such matters as the status of women, and human sexuality, and
over issues arising out of medical treatment, health, and mortality, classical liberal thinking is evolving in response to developments in technology
as well as to changes in society more generally.

The account offered here, then, is as much a particular theory as it is a
summary of "the classical liberal position." While it might be expected
to be viewed critically (or with disdain) by other ethical traditions, it will
surely also be questioned within classical liberalism. It will certainly be
questioned by egalitarian liberals, many of whom view themselves as heirs
of the classical liberal tradition. Nonetheless, this essay offers one view
of what classical liberalism amounts to, leaving the demarcation disputes
and issues of inheritance to be settled by the reader.

Putting these qualifications to one side, then, what is classical liberalism, and by what principles does it determine the limits of ethical pluralism? Clearly, classical liberalism will have to be distinguished from other
forms of liberalism—notably egalitarian liberalism. But the first point that
has to be made about classical liberalism is that it is a *political* philosophy
rather than an ethical doctrine. In this respect it differs from religious
traditions such as Christianity and Confucianism, and from the natural
law tradition. Classical liberalism does not purport to answer a range
of important questions about the nature of the human good, or about
humanity's place in creation, or about the forms that are most appropriate

in relations among people. Neither does it offer any vision or promise of human liberation, as do various kinds of feminism and critical theory; or, for that matter, any theory of social justice, as does liberal egalitarianism. Although its proponents find its moral commitments compelling, it is, for all that, an austere and somewhat prosaic dogma.

As a tradition of political philosophy, then, classical liberalism has two strands or dimensions: social theory and moral theory. Social theory here refers to that dimension of classical liberal thinking which concerns itself with accounting for the nature of human society. Many of the most important figures in classical liberal thought devoted considerable effort to the understanding of society because they were as much interested in the question of what kinds of human arrangements were *feasible* as they were in the question of what arrangements might be desirable. Indeed, some, like Montesquieu, argued that a wise legislator looking to govern well would look carefully at the society his laws would shape, for its nature would bear decisively on his prospects of success. Society had a life of its own and could not be designed and shaped at will. It was already governed by economic, historical, and moral forces that demanded investigation (and which were capable of being understood). From the beginning classical liberals were thus not only philosophers but also economists, historians, and sociologists, as well as moralists.[6]

Although it would be foolish to try to reduce the social theories of these various figures to a single, unambiguous, doctrine, they share a number of important convictions. First, and most generally, they agree that order is possible without design. Society is a self-ordering or self-regulating structure that is not the product of deliberate construction. Order is certainly not the product of government; rather, order, in Tom Paine's words, "has its origin in the principles of society and the natural constitution of man. It existed prior to government, and would exist if the formality of government was abolished. The mutual dependence and reciprocal interest which man has upon man, and all the parts of a civilized community upon each other, create that great chain of connection which holds it together."[7]

In this view, government is necessary to deal with problems or tasks that cannot so readily be addressed through spontaneous cooperation. The precise tasks that are appropriate for government have always been a matter on which classical liberals have held a range of views. While writers like Paine saw little that society could not accomplish itself, others, like Adam Smith and F. A. Hayek, thought there was an important case for government activity to provide not only national defense but also programs for the general welfare. What was not disputed, however, was that society was a self-regulating structure whose tendency was to order, and which could not be shaped or directed by the impatient legislator or what Smith called "the man of system."

This last point is important not so much because this thinking marked a sharp departure from earlier social theory as because it stood in sharp contrast to the coming challenge of modern socialism. Particularly in its Marxian variant, socialist thought focused on the wasteful competitiveness of modern market or commercial societies and looked to centralized, collective planning to overcome the evils such societies were thought to produce: notably, poverty and alienation. Classical liberalism was, and remains, resistant to the idea that such a means can ever be available to redesign or reshape society that it might accord with this, or any, preconceived ideal.

This leads to the second important feature of classical liberal social theory: it includes within it a wariness of and skepticism about governmental power, and political power more generally. While individuals in society act from a variety of motives and with a variety of purposes, in politics, as David Hume observed, they must be presumed to act like knaves. Indeed, they must be understood as agents with ambitions that often lead them to act in concert with others—in factions—to serve their particular (rather than general) interests. For this reason, sound political institutions were ones that divided and separated power. Concentrations of power were dangerous to liberty and also dangerous for the stability of regimes.

Third, and most generally, classical liberalism stands in contrast to those social doctrines which have looked at the diversity of human religious and moral commitments and wondered how they might be brought into closer harmony, into a closer social unity. For some, an organic—almost spiritual—unity, in which the interests of society would be brought into harmony with the interests of the individual, was the highest ideal for which to strive. For classical liberalism, on the other hand, the assumption has always been that such a unity is impossible, if not altogether undesirable, because society is by its nature pluralistic, and individuals are prone to disagreement and conflict. The social problem was not how to bring about unity and cultural, or religious, or moral harmony, but how to preserve an order within which conflict was kept in check, and the plurality of ways allowed to coexist, if not flourish.

It is worth noting here that some classical liberals, such as Lord Acton, argued explicitly and vigorously that diversity was not simply desirable in itself but also essential if liberty was to be preserved. In his treatment of the issue of nationalities, he argued against John Stuart Mill who, in *Considerations of Representative Government*, presented a defense of nationalism as a new phase in the progress of freedom and had also averred that freedom required that the boundaries of the state should coincide with those of nationalities. For Acton, however, this was a profound error. Far from being likely to preserve free institutions, such a condition would jeopardize liberty. A state marked by homogeneity would also turn out to be one whose power was most difficult to limit. A state of a diversity of peoples, however, contained an important check on that power in the form of associations independent of central power. "Liberty provokes diversity, and diversity preserves liberty by supplying the means of organisation."[8]

For Acton, the theory of nationality represented not progress but a retrograde step in the history of liberty. "If we take the establishment of liberty for the realisation of moral duties to be the end of civil society, we must conclude that those states are substantially the most perfect which, like the British and Austrian Empires, include various distinct nationalities, without oppressing them." Indeed, he argued that those states with no mixture of races were imperfect, whereas those in which the effects of that mixture had disappeared were decrepit. And the state that "is incompetent to satisfy different races condemns itself," and one that "labours to neutralise, to absorb, or to expel them, destroys its own vitality."[9]

Saying this put Acton squarely within the classical liberal tradition. His contention here is a variant of James Madison's claim that the liberty of the extended republic rested, in good measure, on the plurality of interests that lay within it. Diversity might bring with it problems of destabilizing social conflict; but it also offered the very resource most needed to address social instability: the pluralism that made difficult the rise of irresistible power. This is why federalism has also been an important strand of classical liberal argument. If it is important that power be dispersed rather than concentrated, a federal structure offers one way of weakening the hold of central authority on society—by devolving power to provincial authorities. The basis of this is not an attachment to states' rights, or to any form of group rights, but simply the recognition of the importance of having in place institutions that will resist or impede the concentration of power.[10] Indeed, federalism is an important way of resisting the power of the majority, which is all too likely to tyrannize over the minority if unchecked. In any decision-making process, the majority will have its way at any particular step. Checking majority power can only be accomplished by institutions that do not enable the same majority to be decisive on all occasions. Federalism accomplishes this, at least to some degree, by creating multiple majorities. Power is concentrated when majorities collude, and dispersed when they collide.

In this social theory can already be detected the commitments that make up the second strand or dimension of classical liberalism: its moral theory. Here, however, it must be borne in mind that this liberalism is a political rather than an ethical doctrine. It rests on a moral theory but with respect to one dimension of moral life: the political. It does not offer an account of what kinds of life are valuable or what morality should govern all our relations. Indeed, it takes as its starting point the fact of ethical pluralism. In classical liberal moral theory two commitments are preeminent and also importantly related—the first to liberty and the second to the conviction that the liberty in question is the liberty of individuals. Classical liberalism is, broadly speaking, libertarian and individualist.

Within this tradition, it must be acknowledged, the proper understanding of liberty is a matter of some dispute. Conceptions of liberty vary, with some falling into Berlin's category of negative liberty, and others into the category of positive liberty.[11] And the justification of liberty has also varied, with some appealing to natural right, others to utility, and some to perfectionist[12] doctrines of the good life. For some, freedom is secured if individuals are merely unimpeded; for others, freedom means autonomy or self-direction. But however differently freedom has been construed philosophically, the concerns of classical liberals have been more plain: to argue that individuals ought to enjoy some liberty so that they might live by their own religious beliefs, and not be subject to arbitrary power. States should not deprive people of freedom—or of their property without their consent (or without just compensation). Liberty of conscience ought to be respected, along with freedom of association. In general there should be a presumption in favor of toleration of differences.

Within classical liberalism, toleration holds an especially important place, although there are surprisingly few substantial treatments of the idea by the great figures in the tradition. It is defended implicitly by J. S. Mill (in his defense of freedom of thought and discussion), explicitly but briefly by Spinoza in his *Theologico-Political Treatise*, and vigorously by Locke in a series of letters concerning toleration; however, the most powerful and comprehensive defence remains that offered by Pierre Bayle in his *Philosophical Commentary* (1686).[13] The roots of the liberal theory of toleration lie in arguments offered by these thinkers (and by others such as Bodin, Althusius, and Milton) for religious tolerance. But it ought to be noted that the status of toleration within liberalism is philosophically problematic. If liberalism is indeed a political doctrine that maintains that ethical disagreements must be put aside, along with questions about the nature of the human good, then toleration has a fundamental place in liberalism. Liberalism becomes, in effect, a doctrine of toleration. If, however, liberalism were to be regarded as a doctrine with particular substantive commitments—say, to the promotion or upholding of individual autonomy—then toleration would become much less important.[14]

Tempting though it is to say that a commitment to toleration is central to classical liberalism, whereas in other versions of liberalism (notably egalitarian liberalism) toleration is subordinated to other, substantive, commitments, such a view would be difficult to sustain historically. Too many classical liberal thinkers have revealed to us important, substantive, convictions guiding their thought. Nonetheless, if there is a philosophical distinction to be drawn between classical and egalitarian liberalism, it is surely here. Classical liberalism is committed to a toleration of difference or diversity, which makes substantive equality an implausible goal. Equality can only be pursued if diversity is brought under control so that there is at least one common dimension to social life, and so one common subject of value—which might then be equalized. But in a regime of diversity there will not be sufficient agreement to make this possible. Toleration would make for a regime in which different traditions coexisted, including different traditions of social justice. What makes a regime a liberal one is not its commitment to equality but its toleration of dissent. The greater its capacity to tolerate dissenting views or traditions or ways of life, including nonliberal ones, the more liberal the regime.

This does, however, raise the important question of the place of "equality" in classical liberal thinking. After all, classical liberal thinkers such as F. A. Hayek have maintained that equality is a notion that is central to the liberal standpoint: "The great aim of the struggle for liberty has been equality before the law."[15] Yet the equality to which classical liberalism is committed is only equality before the law. No individual or category of persons is to be regarded as above the law; nor is anyone without the right to the protection that the law affords. The basis for this attitude is the commitment to liberty: taking liberty seriously means not denying it to anyone. It does not, however, mean a commitment to making people more equal in any respect; nor does it mean assuming that they are equal. On the contrary, the classical liberal view rests on the assumption that individuals are different (and, so, unequal in all sorts of ways), but maintains that these differences provide no grounds for treating them differently.[16] Much of this, of course, classical liberalism shares with egalitarian liberalism; but the two traditions differ inasmuch as the latter evinces a positive concern to secure a substantive equality of persons—whether that be an equality of income, or wealth, or welfare, or resources, or capabilities, to name just a few of the important egalitarian ideals. Classical liberalism is not interested in substantive equality.

Equality figures in classical liberal thinking, then, only insofar as formal equality is implicit in the liberal commitment to liberty. But one other implication also needs to be recognized. Classical liberalism upholds the liberty of people as *individuals*. What this means, however, needs fuller explication. It would not be true to suggest that individuals are all that exist in society, for society is made up not only of individuals but also of other sorts of entities, from collectivities such as crowds to agents or institutions such as corporations. All of these have not only their own places in society and social life but also, to varying degrees, *interests* of their own. Liberalism is not committed in any way to denying the existence of such entities, nor to asserting that individuals are all that are to be found in society. Liberalism is committed, however, to the view that it is the interests only of individuals that matter. Even though groups or institutions may have interests, they do not matter—except insofar as the fates of such entities may bear on the interests of individuals (both those within and those beyond those groups or institutions).

In summary, then, the principles of classical liberalism suggest that the good society is one in which individuals are free to pursue their own ends—and ends, here, are no more than desires—in concert with others or alone. In such a society, the purpose of law, and authority, is to make possible a peaceful coexistence among human beings who will, inevitably, exercise their freedom to live differently and find themselves in conflict with others who might covet the same goods, or seek to take an interest in the beliefs and activities of their fellows. The function of law and government is to adjudicate—to act as umpire in—any disputes that might arise; but not to direct any to better or more popular ends.[17] In this society, the capacity of any authority to amass the power to push society in a particular direction would be constrained by a division and separation of powers. To put it in another way, the model of sovereignty that describes such a society would a Humean rather than a Hobbesian one: sovereign power would not rest in the hands of a single person or body but be dispersed into the hands of different authorities. In such a society there is no ultimate authority but numerous authorities, each superior to some and subordinate to others.

The centrality of the metaphor of the umpire to the classical liberal outlook is worth noting. An umpire is someone to whom players turn when there is a dispute. That dispute may be over the application of a rule, or the interpretation of a rule, or the question of whether a rule exists at all. But it is not the existence of the rules or the fact that there is a game that is critical for understanding this metaphor. What is important about the umpire is that he is a third party to whom the disputants turn for a *ruling*—and a ruling that is *authoritative*. The umpire's ruling is decisive not because the umpire is smarter, or better informed, or more just but because he is *authorized* (either tacitly or explicitly) to make it. He is taken to be, in principle, both an *un*interested party and a *dis*interested one. (If he is taken to have an interest in the outcome of his decision, or to be partial to one of the disputants, his authority is likely to wither, as one or more of the disputants cease to regard his rulings as authoritative.) In the context of society, the umpire or ruler adjudicates disputes over justice. Because people hold to different views about justice, and endorse different standards of social justice, ruling authorities settle matters by determining what standard(s) should prevail.

On this understanding there is nothing about the nature of the *state* as umpire that makes it uniquely capable of discovering or determining what is indeed just. But the point of the state is not to create a just social order— its purpose is not the establishment of social justice. The purpose of the state is to preserve order by averting conflict so that people might live freely; and it does this by exercising its authority to resolve conflict among beings who cannot help but disagree with one another. This understanding of the state stands in contrast to that of egalitarian liberalism, which views the state as having a larger purpose: to create and uphold a socially just political order.

SOCIAL REGULATION

The question now is, should the power of the state ever be invoked to protect, ban, or otherwise regulate ethically based differences—and, if so, where and how? Most societies exhibit such differences to some degree or another, to the extent that they contain individuals who belong to different religious or cultural traditions, or hold to different moral and political principles. In modern societies such differences are given expression in disagreements over many things, from the defensibility of particular customs, to the duties of parents to their children, to the permissibility of pornography, to the right of some political parties to participate in the political process. Does the state have some role to play here in addressing these differences of opinion or outlook?

In the simplest terms, the answer is: yes, the state cannot help but have a role to play. But to understand why this is so, and to go on to see the proper nature and extent of this role, it is necessary to gain a better appreciation of the nature of the state in classical liberalism. The best classical liberal statement of the purpose or point of the state is offered by Spinoza, who writes in his *Theologico-Political Treatise*: "the ultimate aim of government is not to rule, or restrain, by fear, nor to exact obedience, but contrariwise, to free every man from fear, that he may live in all possible security; in other words, to strengthen his natural right to exist and work without injury to himself or others . . . the object of government is not to change men from rational beings into beasts or puppets. . . . In fact, the true aim of government is liberty."[18] In other words, the purpose of the state is to provide that security which would not be available to people in the absence of the order made real by the exercise of the authority of the state. That security is the security that enables people to pursue their goals or ends in safety—without fear. And that security is the security that is consonant with liberty.

If this is the point of the state, the basis of or justification for any action it takes to regulate differences in society rests on the necessity for it to act to preserve the ongoing order of such a society. The state may—for it must—act to preserve the safety and security of its citizens; and to prevent the disintegration of the state into lawlessness or civil war. And if the state is understood as an umpire, it is also responsible for determining when the society is in danger, and what action ought to be taken. It has to decide when and what action has to be taken to protect a person or group, or ban a practice, or regulate a form of behavior.

But because the purpose of the state is liberty, it is also the case that it has no cause to protect or ban or regulate for any other purpose. It is not for the state to regulate to improve society: to make it healthier, or more noble, or more equal, or simply right-thinking. It is not for the state to ensure that some ways of life survive or that others die out; that some are saved or others damned; that one tradition prevail or another sink into oblivion. Indeed, the state has to recognize that human desires or purposes are innumerable, and that even traditions of thought about what are the proper ends humans ought to pursue are numerous and varied. The point of the state is not to settle what disagreements there might be among these different ways of thinking but to preserve an order in which such disagreement does not lead into disorder. To put it another way, the point of the state is to preserve an order in which the exercise of liberty does not lead to disorder—which is to say that the point is to preserve liberty.

By this understanding of the nature and function of the state, the state should regulate, when necessary, so as to preserve an order in which different traditions or practices can continue to operate. It should regulate to preserve an order of toleration rather than to reshape society according to the lights of any one particular tradition—including the majority tradition. This means that, to the extent that it should regulate, it should regulate to make possible, rather than to stifle, *dissent* from the majority view.

In practical terms, this means regulating, when necessary, to ensure that those who adhere to different ethical beliefs are free to try to live by those beliefs, even if they run counter to the attitudes of other groups or traditions. For a free society will be one in which those who dissent are not forced to assimilate into the tradition of the dominant majority but are able to find niches for themselves—spaces within which they might live differently.

To the extent that dissenting practices differ only trivially from the ways of the mainstream of society, of course, the problem dissent poses is also trivial (though, like the Lilliputians, humans are more than capable of turning trivial differences into occasions for violent conflict). But according to the classical liberal view, the freedom to practice dissent should also be upheld even when differences are substantial. It should even be upheld for those who dissent from the principles of classical liberalism—and, so, from the principle of toleration of dissent.

Given that the state cannot but be involved in social regulation—since even to do nothing is to sanction some kinds of activity that may be controversial—the question is, How should the principle of toleration be given practical expression? This question is better addressed through some concrete issues rather than in the abstract, so it may be worth considering social regulation of some particular ethically based disagreements. Two topics might usefully be addressed: sexuality and life-and-death decisions.

Human Sexuality

Human sexual practices, and attitudes toward them, have been as changeable as they are diverse. And from the earliest times to the modern day societies have sought to regulate, as well as to regularize, sexual conduct. The description and evaluation of sexual behavior has undoubtedly been the subject of contention; but it has also been the object of legal sanction. The legal regulation of sexuality addresses a range of issues, from the permissibility of marriage (e.g., in same-sex unions); to the acceptable age of consent to sexual activity; to the allowability of some forms of sexual relationships (such as homosexuality) or sexual conduct (such as sodomy). Yet while the legal regulation of sexuality may appear, on the face of it, to be essentially a formalizing of sanctions reflecting established public attitudes, it needs to be recognized that the law is also implicated in a larger story about the cultural construction of identity, and sexual identity in particular.[19]

Given the history of disputation about sexual conduct and sexual identity, what is the attitude of classical liberalism to the handling of ethically based disagreements in this area? The first point that has to be made is that, because classical liberalism suggests that individuals should be left free to pursue their own purposes, and that differences should be tolerated, it also advocates a principled tolerance of different attitudes toward sexuality and different traditions of marriage. In its terms, a society is a liberal social order if it is one which will tolerate differences of attitude and practice within that order. Indeed, the state has no principled interest in matters of marriage or sexuality. It is not part of its purpose to sanction one form of marriage or another, or to promote any form or understanding of sexuality as more appropriate (or, for that matter, to define any forms as deviant).

Two problems that flow from this stance, however, need to be addressed. The first is that it is not possible to ignore the fact that the modern state is already implicated in the regulation of these matters, and in ways that make it almost impossible for it to withdraw. The existence of welfare benefits, or tax concessions, which vary according to marital status, for example, means that the definition of marriage is already a state interest. Short of reforming—or reconstructing—the entire edifice of political society, what should be done? Classical liberalism's answer to the question of social regulation needs to be offered in this context. The second problem is that, even while the state is to be discouraged from pronouncing on marriage and sexuality, the reality is that not only the state as central authority is responsible for regulation on such matters. Within many, if not most, states a number of different jurisdictions may have chosen to regulate differently. Thus, for example, laws about sexual conduct, marriage, and divorce vary from state to state in the United States, as they do in different states in Australia. How these differences should be addressed is also an issue for classical liberalism.

A part of what must be said in response to the first problem is that the state has to regulate, when it must, in ways that avoid presuming the correctness of one ethical stance as against another on matters of marriage and sexuality. But the reality is that this is possible only to a limited extent when the state acts as more than merely an umpire but becomes involved in substantive enterprises: assisting families (and upholding or promoting "the family"); improving community (or "national") health standards; or providing a system of education. To the extent that the state is implicated or involved in such enterprises, it will not be able to avoid adopting substantive ethical positions. It will have to say what does *not* count as a family; what kinds of conduct are not consistent with safe sexual lifestyles; and what it is appropriate for children to be taught about sexuality and sexual conduct. In liberal societies this creates a problem because the stance of ethical neutrality cannot plausibly be regarded as anything but a substantive position by those whose ethical perspectives differ. Taxpayers whose idea of the family envisages only husband and wife, and their children, may not condone public definitions that include same-sex, polygamous, or incestuous relationships.

To the extent that it is possible, however, the classical liberal reaction to ethical differences here would be to say that a good society would be one that left people with different ethical views the opportunity to distance themselves from the ethical position of the state—to disengage from "mainstream" society. Thus, in such a society, even if the state exercises its interest in defining marriage to advance its own purposes, there will be the freedom for those who dissent from this ethical view to live by their own, alternative standards or definitions. There will be an opportunity for dissenters to exit, and to reconstruct communities of their own. For those, for example, who wish to live in same-sex unions, there would be the opportunity not so much to have such unions recognized as a form of marriage as to reject the salience or necessity of such recognition altogether. In the free society according to classical liberalism, the dissenters are free to leave, even if acceptance or recognition of their dissenting stance(s) is not possible.

There is, however, a troubling aspect to this position, which egalitarian liberals in particular will notice. Dissenters are given no substantial rights or entitlements to pursue or defend their beliefs or practices. Classical liberalism argues that they should be offered the freedom to establish or live within alternative jurisdictions; but not that they should have a fixed set of entitlements regardless of the jurisdiction. The reason for this here has much to do with the classical liberal conviction that in the good society power or authority is not concentrated but dispersed. For this reason, alternative regimes or communities would be accepted as capable of exercising authority over their members—even if those communities are themselves not liberal in their attitudes.

A useful example is supplied here by the case of *Rodney Croome & Another v. The State of Tasmania*, brought before the High Court of Australia in November 1995. The aim of the plaintiffs in this case was to reform the Tasmanian Criminal Code, which provided (in sections 122[a] and [c] and 123) that any person who has sexual intercourse with any person "against the order of nature" or engages in acts of "gross indecency" be deemed guilty either of unnatural sexual intercourse or indecent practice between male persons. In their Statement of Claim the plaintiffs asked the High Court to find these sections inconsistent with the Human Rights (Sexual Conduct) Act 1994, by virtue of being an arbitrary interference with the right to privacy, and that the Tasmanian laws were therefore invalid (by virtue of their inconsistency with federal law, which takes precedence over state law under section 109 of the Australian Constitution). The solicitor general for Tasmania submitted that, because no proceedings had been brought or threatened against the plaintiffs in respect of the conduct pleaded in their statement of claim, there was no "matter" within the meaning of that term in section 76 of the Constitution (and section 30 of the Judiciary Act 1903 [Cth]) that can be judicially determined in proceedings between plaintiffs and defendant and, consequently, that there can be *no federal jurisdiction* to entertain the action commenced.

The decision of the High Court on 26 February 1997 to hear the case, recognizing that the plaintiffs had a legitimate interest in the matter even though they had not been prosecuted under the laws in question, placed the Tasmanian government at risk of losing a case fought on the defensibility of the state's laws on sexual conduct. Yet the importance of the case was sufficiently well recognized that the government of Western Australia announced that it would intervene with a submission in support of the Tasmanian government's position. (Its concern was that a successful outcome for the plaintiffs would provide a precedent for the invalidation of Western Australia's own age of consent laws, which discriminated against homosexuals.) In these circumstances, the Tasmanian government decided to repeal the laws in question, and this was effected on 1 May 1998. This also effectively brought the High Court case to a close.

From a classical liberal point of view, this particular outcome appears as a mixed blessing. On the one hand, the repeal of laws criminalizing sexual activity between consenting males can only be welcomed, because the freedom to dissent, not only in word but in deed, is properly upheld. And the propriety of a state's sanctioning or promoting particular views about sexuality is rightly repudiated. On the other hand, the independence of a separate jurisdiction—the state of Tasmania—was weakened insofar as it decided to change its laws in order to avoid having them declared invalid by a central authority. If classical liberalism is a doctrine that looks to deal with ethically based disagreement by ensuring that authority on ethical matters is not centralized and concentrated, it must also view the success of the Tasmanian Gay and Lesbian Rights Group as a victory that has come at a troubling price.[20] Indeed, it ought to be noted plainly that there is a certain tension in place here. A classical liberal in Tasmania would be bound to argue for law reform. But a classical liberal looking to answer a question about the best institutional arrangements would want to protect the autonomy or independence of states and preserve a federal structure as one best suited to allowing ethical differences to coexist.

The significance of this tension ought not to be underestimated, for it reveals that classical liberals can be forced to defend outcomes they dislike or even find repellent on some of their own principles (though it also displays a distinctive characteristic that marks all liberalisms: a willingness to defend the rights or freedoms of those for whom liberals have no sympathy). What it does not suggest, however, is any concession to majoritarianism because the majority view in the state appears to be allowed to trump the right answer. On the contrary, what must be resisted here, from the classical liberal point of view, is the temptation to use the greater (majority) power of the federal government to crush the weaker authority. Tasmania would be wrong to exert its power to uphold majority values and deny homosexuals the right to dissent from majority thinking and practice. Australia would equally be wrong to assert its power over the dissenting authority of Tasmania. In the end it is not majoritarianism that must be allowed to trump the right answer; rather, it is certain principles that must prevail: those political principles which govern human relations when "the right answer" is in dispute.

Life-and-Death Decisions

Just as there are differences among ethical traditions over sexuality, so are there equally profound disagreements among them over matters of life and death. The importance of these disagreements stems from the fact that they reflect fundamental differences in belief about the nature of persons, and about what is the nature and source of value. Attitudes to abortion and infanticide, or to various forms of euthanasia, or to a range of medical procedures from blood transfusions to organ transplant, or indeed to the very definition of death (which can affect the timing of decisions to remove organs from "deceased" donors) reflect the diversity of religious and cultural traditions extant in society. And this diversity of traditions makes some of these issues peculiarly difficult—if not altogether intractable.

Once again, there are two dimensions to the classical liberal response to dealing with ethically based conflict over such matters. In the first instance, in view of its commitment to the coexistence of different ethical perspectives, classical liberalism sees it as no part of the state's purpose to promote or uphold particular ethical views about abortion or euthanasia or blood transfusions.[21] Within society there are different traditions with different attitudes to life and death; the purpose of the state is to make it possible for these to coexist rather than to ensure that one or the other dominates. The problem (once again), however, is that the modern state is already implicated in the assessment of some of these questions inasmuch as it has been a party to the development of laws and institutions that cannot but take positions on these questions. To the extent that the state is not only a provider of health insurance but a supplier of medical care, it has to make some decisions about what kinds of treatment it may—or is morally bound to—offer. Thus, in many societies, the site of ethical disagreement is government health policy. In this situation, however, because some particular ethical perspective has to be adopted, those from dissenting ethical perspectives will have to condone—and maybe subsidize—ethical practices with which they disagree, or, on occasion, which they find unconscionable.

One part of the classical liberal response to this situation is to recommend that the state not concern itself with matters like health care. It is not possible to be concerned with such things and not take some stance on a range of questions that it is no part of the state's purpose to settle: questions about what constitutes a good life, or what is required for a good death. This would not, however, resolve the problem entirely, because ethical disagreement results not only in resentment on the part of some that they are forced to be accessories to practices they find ethically dubious, but also in outrage on the part of others that such things are condoned anywhere at all. Private abortion clinics are as much targets as public hospitals.

Given this problem, another part of the classical liberal response to disagreement is to say that, in the absence of any basis on which ethical disputes on fundamentals can be settled, ethical priority must be given to the freedom to dissent from the dominant view. (To put it differently, no special weight should be given to any ethical stance simply because it is a majority stance or a position taken by the stronger.) The reality, however, is that this approach favors those who take particular sides on certain life-and-death issues. For example, it favors those who wish to see abortion accepted as a legitimate medical procedure, because the principle of freedom to dissent offers no additional support to those who view abortion as immoral; after all, the pro-abortion (or pro-choice) lobby was never likely to challenge the freedom of antiabortionists to exercise their own dissenting choices.

Nonetheless, given that the problem is how to find a settlement to ethically based disagreement, some form of compromise is necessary. Is there within classical liberalism anything to suggest how compromise ought to be reached? In political life, compromises will be made along all sorts of dimensions when disputes can only be settled, not resolved. In the abortion case, compromises are made by restricting the opportunities for termination without disallowing it altogether—say, by specifying procedures that have to be followed, disallowing intervention after the second trimester, and making counseling mandatory. Such compromises do not so much reflect any classical liberal commitment as reveal the variety of forms compromise might take.

What is, perhaps, more distinctive to classical liberalism, however, is the suggestion that compromise might be effected by accepting that different rules can apply in different places—in different jurisdictions. The purpose of the state is not to establish the truth, or to enforce its implications, when disputes arise because ethical standpoints differ. Its purpose is simply to preserve the order in which people can be secure in their freedom. In such an order, there is no necessity that all people fall under the one jurisdiction in all matters. States can be—and typically are—made up of many, often but not always, overlapping jurisdictions; and laws generally differ from one to another. In a federal republic, for example, political authority is dispersed among a number of states or provinces; and laws, including criminal codes, will often vary from one to the next. This is one form of compromise that has evolved and which classical liberalism endorses as an important method of addressing and settling moral conflict, as well as checking central power.

It ought to be noted, however, that this method is not without its critics, and liberal critics in particular. The federal solution is what Ronald Dworkin has described as a "checkerboard" solution.[22] And to Dworkin, checkerboard laws are only acceptable when relatively unimportant matters are at stake: differences in zoning laws from one place to the next really do not matter. But not when those matters are matters of principle. It may seem, he notes, that "we have no reason of justice for rejecting the checkerboard strategy in advance, and strong reasons of fairness for endorsing it. Yet our instincts condemn it."[23] So hostile is Dworkin to checkerboard solutions that he says that, if there existed two alternative solutions, A and B, such that he thought that A was right in principle and B wrong in principle, he "would rank the checkerboard solution not intermediate between the other two but third, below both, and so would many other people."[24]

The reason Dworkin gives for taking this strong position is that he believes the only way in which we can make sense of "our" political ideals of justice and fairness is by recognizing another principle that stands directly in opposition to checkerboard solutions: "integrity." "Our instincts about internal compromise suggest another political ideal standing beside justice and fairness. Integrity. . . . The most natural explanation of why we oppose checkerboard statutes appeals to that ideal: we say that a state that adopts these internal compromises is acting in an unprincipled way, even though no single official who voted for or enforces the compromise has done anything which, judging his individual actions by the ordinary standards of personal morality, he ought not to have done."[25] Checkerboard solutions uphold "inconsistency in principle"; and this, integrity must condemn.[26]

From a classical liberal point of view, however, Dworkin's position is mistaken. There is nothing unprincipled about the kind of compromise implicit in checkerboard solutions. It only appears unprincipled if one adopts the starting point Dworkin does: one that claims that "we" need to work out what "we" think or feel or can in good conscience affirm. But, Dworkin's blithe references to "our" instincts nothwithstanding, the problem is that "we" disagree—and, on occasion, in fundamental ways. In such a situation, one principled solution is to agree to differ, and to allow different substantive solutions to prevail in different regions.

Indeed, we should go further and recognize that "integrity" is not the ideal that should guide our reflections if what it points to is an aspiration to bring about a kind of social unity that is altogether beyond reach in an ethically plural society. We might be able to agree to differ; but it looks much less likely that we will ever be able to agree *not* to differ.

In this respect, one kind of solution to the issue of physician-assisted suicide that would be endorsed by classical liberalism is one of the sort that might have arisen in 1995 with the passing in the Northern Territory of the Rights of the Terminally Ill Act, permitting assisted suicide under prescribed conditions. This act, which came into operation on 1 July 1996, made the Northern Territory the first jurisdiction in the world to permit a doctor to end the life of a terminally ill patient at the patient's request. The law survived an attempt at repeal in the Territory Parliament in August 1996 and a legal challenge in the Northern Territory Supreme Court, before leave was sought to challenge the act in the High Court of Australia. In September 1996, however, a Private Member's Bill designed to override the act was introduced in the Federal Parliament, and the passage of the Euthanasia Laws Bill by the Australian Senate on 25 March 1997 brought the experiment to an end. In the public and parliamentary debates surrounding the bill, it became clear that, while the majority of Australians favored permitting physician-assisted suicide, there were important (though not unexpected) divisions between different groups. The Doctors Reform Society and HIV/AIDS support groups favored the Northern Territory legislation, while the Australian Medical Association, many Aboriginal groups, and the churches opposed it. From a classical liberal point of view, however, the Rights of the Terminally Ill Act could be defended in at least one respect: that there is no reason why all jurisdictions have to conform to a single ethical standard, particularly when the ethical issue is one over which people are deeply divided.

Ironically, the Northern Territory legislation was overturned precisely because the classical liberal perspective on this matter was rejected. Had the legislation been enacted by any state in the Australian federation, the Commonwealth Parliament would have been powerless to intervene. The Northern Territory, however, is not a state but a territory; and although self-governing (with its own parliament and chief minister), it remains within the control of the Commonwealth. On this occasion, the Commonwealth chose to exercise its capacity to override—persuaded, perhaps, that integrity was too important to allow a black square to turn up on the checkerboard. Perversely, in this instance, the pursuit of integrity allowed a minority viewpoint to triumph, and to close off debate and the possibility of reform for the foreseeable future. One lesson, at least, that might be drawn from this episode is that there is little reason to assume that the pursuit of "integrity" need get us any closer to what "we" think about anything—let alone about justice.

CITIZENSHIP

A question that obviously arises now is, What are we to make of citizenship in a classical liberal regime? After all, if a doctrine has so little sympathy with social unity and legal and political integrity, can it really take citizenship seriously? Moreover, can it sensibly handle disagreements or disputes about the rights and duties of citizenship—disputes that might include questions about the obligation to undertake national service, or about the rights of women to take part in or shape fundamental institutions; or the right (or duty) of the state to educate children for citizenship?

The truth is that citizenship is not something that classical liberalism holds in especially high esteem. There are a number of reasons why. One, which has not been much mentioned thus far, is that as a political doctrine classical liberalism is fundamentally an internationalist creed. Because its interest is fundamentally in individual liberty, it has little commitment to states or nations, which are regarded only as agglomerations of individuals, or of associations of individuals. While the breakdown of states may be an evil because of the destruction that may bring, the existence, survival, or perpetuation of particular states is of no special ethical significance.

Because it takes this attitude, classical liberalism does not place especial importance on citizenship because it does not see any virtue in building up institutions that would make for a stronger or deeper form of social unity. An emphasis on citizenship generally comes out of a concern to build a political society in which the divisions that mark that society are overcome. The freedom that is emphasized in such a conception of the good society is the freedom that comes with the development of a virtuous citizenry, committed to a shared understanding of the common good. Citizenship is for republicans and, to some extent, for nationalists.[27] Classical liberals are more likely to favor open borders, or at least freedom of movement to a degree that might compromise efforts to build a sense of nationhood.[28]

For this reason, classical liberalism places more importance on the capacity or freedom of people to exit or dissent or withdraw from public institutions than on their duty to participate in them. Thus, for example, it does not put any emphasis on education for citizenship: it is not the purpose of education—public or otherwise—to create a virtuous citizenry that shares particular values or commitments to a national agenda, or a common understanding of the good of the state, or a shared view of democratic legitimacy. Every type of regime *will* produce its own kind of person(s), to be sure; and classical liberal regimes are no different. But however much that may be the case, classical liberalism values most the importance of freedom to dissent. It is, in a way, at one with Benjamin Constant in favoring not ancient liberty but modern liberty— a form of liberty that values freedom from politics as much as freedom in politics.

In such a regime, then, there would always be opportunity for conscientious objection. In any polity, the state will always pursue its interests; and it will take what measures it needs to in order to achieve its ends: this is a part of the logic of the state. In a classical liberal order, however, there will be opportunities for individuals or groups to avoid the domination of the state—to avoid being drawn into its projects. Thus, for example, it will be possible for individuals to object to national service; or to decline to be involved in the welfare system (as do the Amish people); or even to opt for different systems of punishment than that offered by the state.[29] In a classical liberal regime, it will be possible to a considerable degree for people to live untouched by the state, which will take no interest in their interests, and demand that they take no greater interest in its own concerns than they wish.

In this regard, the classical liberal view cares less about citizenship and ensuring that people are brought into the political fold so that they might be a part of a cohesive whole, than it does about leaving them free to exit from arrangements they find uncongenial, if not altogether intolerable or unconscionable. The difficulties this issue poses are brought out in a particularly clear way in current discussions of multiculturalism and the politics of cultural diversity. For someone like Will Kymlicka, who is the most significant thinker today writing on these issues, multiculturalism poses an important challenge because it appears at odds with the requirements of citizenship and an obstacle to social unity. If cultural communities, such as those formed by indigenous peoples and other ethnic minorities, may assert collective rights in virtue of their particular memberships, how can there be any commitment to citizenship of a modern state?[30] His own solution to this dilemma is to develop a theory of "differentiated citizenship" explaining how, "In a society which recognizes group-differentiated rights, the members of certain groups are incorporated into the political community not only as individuals, but also through the group,"[31] although he also concedes that, at least to date, liberal (egalitarian) theory has not been able to explain how social unity can be made consistent with the other ideals of the democratic multination state.[32]

From a classical liberal point of view, however, social unity is not so important except to the extent that it might be necessary for the preservation of order. And citizenship is not a substantial good or ideal of which too much can be made. It favors the freedom of people to come and go: to exit one community and enter another, or to form new associations altogether. But it takes no especial interest in any particular association, and attaches no great value to the quality of belonging in any of them.

One consequence of this aspect of the classical liberal outlook is that it is, in some ways, not very good at handling issues that involve questions of the quality of citizenship, and the duties of citizens. It does not, for example, have a theory of education for citizenship. Yet this is a weakness only to the extent that society and the modern state persist in taking an interest in matters classical liberals think beyond the scope of political authority. The state takes an interest in education because it has an interest in producing citizens who will accept the legitimacy of the state. For classical liberals the state has no legitimate role in education. That it will arrogate to itself the power to shape citizens and the citizenry is something not to be denied, but not either to be applauded.

NOTES

1. "Of Parties in General," in David Hume, *Political Writings*, ed. S. Warner and D. Livingston (Indianapolis: Hackett, 1994), pp. 161–62.

2. For recent treatments of the idea of classical liberalism, see Norman Barry, *On Classical Liberalism and Libertarianism* (London: Macmillan, 1986); David Conway, *Classical Liberalism: The Unvanquished Ideal* (New York: St Martin's Press, 1995); Charles K. Rowley, ed., *Classical Liberalism and Civil Society* (Cheltenham: Edward Elgar, 1997), especially the essay by Douglas B. Rasmussen and Douglas J. Den Uyl, "Liberalism Defended: The Challenge of Post-Modernity."

3. Modern exponents of the classical liberal tradition include, at one end of the spectrum, libertarian anarchists such as Murray Rothbard and David Friedman, and, at the other end, minimal-welfare-state liberals such as F. A. Hayek and Milton Friedman, as well as minimal-state libertarians such as Robert Nozick and constitutional contractarians such as James Buchanan. Moreover, in ethics, classical liberals have appeared in a variety of stripes: utilitarians, Kantians, Lockean natural rights theorists, Hobbesians, conservatives, and skeptics.

4. See, for example, David Boaz, ed., *The Libertarian Reader: Classic and Contemporary Writings from Lao-Tzu to Milton Friedman* (New York: Free Press, 1998).

5. 6 For example: John Locke, Adam Smith, James Madison, Montesquieu, Edmund Burke, Benjamin Constant, and John Stuart Mill.

6. Among their number the most important would include, after Montesquieu: David Hume, Adam Smith, Anne Robert, Jacques Turgot, James Madison, Alexis de Tocqueville, and, in modern times, F. A. Hayek.

7. Tom Paine, *Common Sense*, in Michael Foot and Isaac Kramnick, eds., *The Thomas Paine Reader* (Harmondsworth: Penguin, 1987), p. 67.

8. Acton, "Nationality," in *Selected Writings of Lord Acton*, vol. 1: *Essays in the History of Liberty*, ed. J. Rufus Fears (Indianapolis: Liberty Classics, 1986), p. 425.

9. Ibid., p. 432.

10. I have discussed federalism at greater length in C. Kukathas, D. Lovell and W. Maley, *The Theory of Politics* (Melbourne: Longman, 1990), chap. 2.

11. See Isaiah Berlin, "Two Concepts of Liberty," in his *Four Essays on Liberty* (Oxford: Oxford University Press, 1979).

12. On "perfectionism," see Steven Wall, *Liberalism, Perfectionism and Restraint* (Cambridge: Cambridge University Press, 1998).

13. Pierre Bayle, *A Philosophical Commentary on The Words of the Gospel, Luke XIV. 23: Compel them to come in, that my House may be full*, translator unknown (London: J. Darby and J. Morphew, 1708).

14. See on this Deborah Fitzmaurice, "Autonomy as a Good: Liberalism, Autonomy and Toleration," *Journal of Political Philosophy* 1, 1 (1993): 1–16. Fitzmaurice maintains that, according to liberalism, the conditions of autonomy are necessary for respectful moral relations. In these terms, she argues, the requirement to sustain individual autonomy becomes the moral basis of "our political relations with non-liberal minorities. No independent principle of toleration is required." (p. 16).

15. F. A. Hayek, *The Constitution of Liberty* (London: Routledge and Kegan Paul, 1976), p. 85.

16. "It is neither because it assumes that people are in fact equal nor because it attempts to make them equal that the argument for liberty demands that government treat them equally. This argument not only recognizes that individuals are very different but in a great measure rests on that assumption. It insists that these individual differences provide no justification for government to treat them differently. And it objects to the differences in treatment by the state that would be necessary if persons who are in fact very different were to be assured equal positions in life." Ibid., pp. 85–86.

17. See Gerald F. Gaus, *Justificatory Liberalism: An Essay on Epistemology and Political Theory* (Oxford: Oxford University Press, 1996), esp. pp. 184–91.

18. *Theologico-Political Treatise*, in Benedict de Spinoza, *A Theologico-Political Treatise* and *A Political Treatise*, trans. and introd. R.H.M. Elwes (New York: Dover, 1951), pp. 258–59.

19. See the essays in Martin Duberman, Martha Vicinus, and George Chauncey Jr., eds., *Hidden from History: Reclaiming the Gay and Lesbian Past* (New York: Meridien, 1989). See especially the essay by George Chauncey Jr., "Christian Brotherhood or Sexual Perversion? Homosexual Identities and the Construction of Sexual Boundaries in the World War I Era," pp. 294–317.

20. There is an interesting parallel to be drawn between this judgment and Lord Acton's assessment of the outcome of the American Civil War. On the positive side was the ending of slavery (even though that had been no part of the North's original purpose); on the negative side was the expansion of the power of the national government, and the loss of the power of the states to supply a "check on the absolutism of the sovereign will." See Acton's correspondence with Robert E. Lee, in *Selected Writings of Lord Acton*, vol. 1: *Essays in the History of Liberty*, pp. 361–67, esp. p. 363.

21. The most comprehensive treatment of these issues from a classical liberal perspective is H. Tristram Engelhardt Jr., *The Foundations of Bioethics*, 2d ed. (New York: Oxford University Press, 1996). Although a Christian who holds suicide and abortion to be moral evils, Engelhardt argues that, in the face of ethical diversity, the state can only adopt a secular, post-Christian morality in which what is privileged is not the correct understanding of the good but individual consent.

22. Ronald Dworkin, *Law's Empire* (London: Fontana, 1986), pp. 178–86.

23. Ibid., p. 182.

24. Ibid.

25. Ibid., p. 184.

26. Ibid.

27. See, for example, the argument of David Miller, *On Nationality* (Oxford: Oxford University Press, 1995).

28. Though, to be sure, some liberal egalitarians also advocate open borders. See Joseph H. Carens, "Migration and Morality: A Liberal Egalitarian Perspective," in Brian Barry and Robert E.Goodin, eds., *Free Movement: Ethical Issues in the Transnational Migration of People and of Money* (University Park: Pennsylvania State University Press, 1992), pp. 25–47.

29. A dramatic example of this may be found in the Northern Territory in Australia, where Aboriginal tribal law has coexisted with territory criminal codes. On occasion, judges have allowed Aborigines convicted of serious crimes to return to their communities unpunished so that they might accept the (invariably more severe) punishments to be meted out by their own peoples—including beatings and spearings. An account of this is in Paul Sheehan, *Among the Barbarians: The Dividing of Australia* (Sydney: Random House, 1998), pp. 8–18.

30. See Will Kymlicka, *Multicultural Citizenship: A Liberal Theory of Minority Rights* (Oxford: Oxford University Press, 1995).

31. Ibid., p. 174.

32. Ibid., p. 192.

Ethical Pluralism and Classical Liberalism

James Tully

INTRODUCTION: TWO SCHOOLS OF CLASSICAL LIBERALISM IN DIALOGUE

In "Ethical Pluralism from a Classical Liberal Perspective," Chandran Kukathas presents a clear and compelling analysis of how one school of classical liberalism copes with ethical pluralism. He points out that classical liberalism is a diverse, contested, and evolving tradition of political theory. He does not attempt to present a survey of the entire tradition but to concentrate exclusively on one school or "view of what classical liberalism amounts to" within the tradition. The strand of classical liberalism he explicates with great skill, "negative" or "minimal" liberalism, tolerates ethical pluralism, if it happens to exist, and sees a consequential good in its existence—the dispersion of concentrated power. It does not try to bring about ethical uniformity, but neither does it seek to foster, protect, or promote ethical pluralism. Whether different ethical ways of life, cultures, nations, and even political associations survive or die out is a matter of indifference. Minimal liberalism approaches the existence and conflicts of ethical pluralism like an "umpire," in a disinterested and uninterested manner as it seeks to protect individual liberty and political order.

Kukathas contrasts minimal liberalism with egalitarian liberalism. However, as he also mentions, one of the major reasons that the tradition of classical liberalism is diverse and internally contested is that many liberal philosophers have responded to ethical pluralism in a different way from both minimal and egalitarian liberalism. Benjamin Constant, J. S. Mill, Alexis de Tocqueville, T. H. Green, and Charles Taylor argue that ethical pluralism should be seen as a liberal public good, and Lord Acton, John Rawls, and Will Kymlicka argue that it should be seen as a necessary condition of a public good, such as liberty or self-respect. Constant, Hegel, Mill, Tocqueville, and Acton all place at the heart of liberalism a concern with combating the powerful processes of ethical uniformity and homogenization in modern commercial societies, and they see minimal liberalism as part of the problem. Since the early nineteenth century, the tradition of classical European and North American liberalism has consisted of a dialogue between the members of Kukathas's school, egalitarian liberals, and the members of this third school, now called "deliberative liberalism" or "plural liberalism," over how to respond to ethical pluralism.[1]

This brief comment is a presentation of the other side of the liberal dialogue on diversity. It sets out the responses of deliberative liberals to the difficulties of pluralism where these responses are different from those presented by Kukathas's liberals. One of the best examples of this other strand of classical liberalism today is John Rawls's "political liberalism," a view of liberalism founded on the ideal of the exchange of public reasons among ethically plural citizens.[2] Of course, both types of liberal share a great deal and most are members of both schools under some descriptions. However, important differences remain and their continuous contestation within liberalism make this a living and evolving tradition. The aim of this comment is thus to supplement Kukathas's excellent account by bringing in these other liberal voices where they dissent from the views of the minimal liberals on pluralism.

Two Liberal Orientations to Ethical Pluralism: Indifference versus Acknowledgment

Kukathas's strand of classical liberalism is, first, a single-value theory, built exclusively on the value of liberty. He does not deny that many classical liberals were value pluralists but sets these aside for the sake of argument. Second, even with respect to the single value of liberty, he sets aside the various aspects of liberty, emphasized at different times by different liberals, and singles out an aspect of liberty, individual, negative liberty, what Constant calls "the liberty of the moderns."[3] As a result, as Kukathas underscores, minimal liberals are indifferent to "the liberty of the ancients," the democratic liberty of citizens to participate, and indifferent to citizenship in a democracy itself.

This second feature distinguishes Kukathas's minimal liberals from the school that has sought to combine the liberty of the ancients with that of the moderns—the coequal principles of popular sovereignty and the rule of law—as, for example, one sees in John Locke, Rousseau, Hegel, Constant, Mill, Habermas, and Rawls.[4] In this deliberative stream, classical liberalism is internally (not just contingently) related to democracy and to a degree of citizen participation and deliberation. As Rawls points out, there is no difference on this point between classical liberalism and classical republicanism: "The safety of democratic liberties requires the active participation of citizens who possess the political virtues needed to maintain a constitutional regime."[5] The difference comes when participation is seen as a duty or as "the privileged locus of the good life," a position Rawls associates with "civic humanism" and opposes.[6] In contrast, as Kukathas argues, minimal liberals do not distinguish between classical republicanism and civic humanism in this way, and they oppose both. One of the major reasons for the defense of citizenship rights of participation within deliberative liberalism is to foster a better awareness of, and mutual respect for, the reasonable ethical differences of fellow citizens. Participation involving public deliberation is not only seen as good in itself, generating the "enlarged" understanding championed by Kant, Mill, and Tocqueville, but also as the means to enhance "positive" toleration, trust, and solidarity across class and ethical differences for the sake of stability in diverse societies, as Constant and Rawls both argue.

Third, as Kukathas explains, minimal liberals are opposed to the social and economic rights advanced by egalitarian liberals. However, many classical liberals promote so-called third-generation social and economic rights because, among other benefits, they provide the necessary precondition of individuals living an ethical life at all, or sustaining a viable minority ethical life. If a liberal polity protects only negative liberty and formal equality, as Kukathas recommends, many citizens would be unable to exercise their negative liberties in practice because they would lack the social and economic preconditions for participation in the ethical life they value, as classical liberals from Hegel and T. H. Green to T. H. Marshall and Eleanor Roosevelt have argued.[7] Egalitarian liberals and plural liberals thus often join hands on this issue but just as often disagree on the way to reconcile equality rights and pluralism in particular cases.[8]

ETHICAL PLURALISM AND THE PROBLEM OF "NON-POLITICAL" FORMS OF ASSIMILATIVE POWER

The negative liberty at the center of classical liberalism includes the freedom of individuals to "live by their own religious beliefs," the "liberty of conscience," and "freedom of association." In general, "there should be a presumption in favor of the toleration of differences." Accordingly, a "negative" kind of toleration of ethical pluralism, insofar as such pluralism exists, follows from negative liberty, even though, as Kukathas notes, it does not appear to be central to the tradition. Indeed, as he explains, many classical liberals such as Locke, Thomas Paine and Mill were intolerant of some ethical forms of life. They sought to phase out what they called "inferior" ethical ways and to inculcate the "superior" or "civilized" ethical ways of modern commercial societies, an abhorrent tendency that continues today in some liberal circles.[9] In contrast to this assimilative tendency in liberalism, minimal liberalism does not use political power to exclude or to assimilate ethical differences for the sake of uniformity and unity. Rather, it "tolerates" the differences it encounters in "society."

As a consequence, minimal liberalism is indifferent to the ways nonpolitical forms of power—such as social, economic, cultural, and media power—function in modern societies to homogenize ethical differences, to entrench a dominant ethical or cultural way of life, to discriminate against ethical minorities of various kinds, and to foster a "veneer" or "Benetton" pluralism. Furthermore, these forms of power often inculcate harmful ethical practices: for example, the eating disorders and lethargy associated with images of female thinness; poor health and death associated with smoking, drinking, and drug abuse; ethical degradation, sexual harassment, and violence associated with pornography; and the undermining of self-respect caused by nonrecognition and misrecognition. These are destructive of individuals and the social fabric, leading to problems of alienation and disintegration.[10]

The reasons why the "umpire" stance of minimal liberalism is relatively powerless in the face of these forms of assimilative power in relation to ethical pluralism are twofold: these forms of assimilative power are protected, rather than opened to public scrutiny, by the value of negative liberty standing alone; and they are taken as given, as part of an independent and prepolitical "society," in the social theory embraced by minimal liberals such as Hayek and summarized by Kukathas. To address these insidious forms of ethical harms classical liberals have to appeal to other values, such as self-respect, and to an alternative social theory, which addresses the social, economic, and educational preconditions of equality of participation in the public and private institutions of modern societies. On these normative and sociological bases they seek to govern democratically such powerful institutions and to educate the population to govern themselves in relation to them. Yet, these are precisely the sorts of political power minimal liberals are unable and unwilling to employ due to their social and moral theories, including their assumption that citizens are merely following their own wishes and desires, when in fact their desires are often constructed by these forms of power.[11]

ETHICAL PLURALISM AND THE POLITICS OF RECOGNITION: TWO CLASSICAL APPROACHES

The final problem minimal liberalism has with ethical pluralism is that, although it seeks to avoid recognizing any particular ethical way of life, it ends up giving state support to some ethical way of life or another and thus discriminates against others. The examples of sexual practices and practices related to life and death discussed by Kukathas both illustrate this problem of negative liberalism in practice. First, minimal liberalism ought to be indifferent to the sexual practices and life-and-death practices of citizens as much as this is compatible with the commitment to negative liberty and the toleration of dissent. As Kukathas fully acknowledges, however, this is impossible because modern political institutions are deeply involved not only in the recognition and regulation of sexual practices, practices relating to life and death, and other welfare and ethical practices, but also in the very construction and reproduction of these practices.[12]

The public institutions of a modern society have to operate with some definition of the "family," to use Kukathas's example, in a wide variety of contexts of social regulation. Minimal liberals accept this and try to tolerate indifferently various ethical views of the family. Yet this is often impossible. Recognition of one mainstream view of the family is unavoidable. This compromise is acceptable as long as those citizens who adhere to different ethical practices of family organization, such as same-sex families, are permitted to disengage from mainstream society—to dissent and live in their own counterculture. This form of dissent is "negative" and "nonpolitical." It is "negative" in the sense that the alternative forms of family life do not receive any public recognition and entitlements, as the mainstream family does. It is "nonpolitical" dissent in the sense that the proponents of alternative forms of family life are not empowered or encouraged to exercise their citizen rights of participation to deliberate the publicly supported family in various fora and to so to have a say over the public definition of a family, as in deliberative liberalism. The exception Kukathas mentions is the use of federalism in some cases. Deliberative liberals also use a wide variety of federal arrangements to protect minority groups and nations. In this example, however, federalism displaces rather than confronts the problem of treating minority ethical practices on a par with the majority's practice that concerns deliberative liberal pluralists. Federalism is used to set up another political structure that recognizes and entitles one ethical orientation and leaves the ethical minorities within its jurisdiction in the same position of nonrecognition and nonentitlement.

The problem with this response to ethical pluralism from the perspective of deliberative liberalism is that it recognizes and entitles the dominant ethical practices while leaving the others to fend for themselves. The mainstream family receives benefits not available to others, and it becomes the norm in public education and in hiring and promotion in the public sector. Moreover, the dominant ethic, as we have seen, is supported, partly constituted, and disseminated by the other forms of assimilative power that minimal liberalism ignores: the exercise of economic power in hiring practices, cultural power in the media, social power in forms of exclusion, discrimination, heterosexism, and so on. Finally, the asymmetrical nonrecognition and nonentitlement of other ethical orientations serves to undermine the ability of their members to protect and to live their ethical life on this biased playing field. The result is often that members of nonmainstream ethical communities are disempowered from exercising even their negative liberties unless they assimilate. The tendency of such societies over generations is either assimilation to the publicly established ethical practices or alienation of the dissenters who hold out.

Deliberative liberals respond to this problem of partiality and instability in the following way. They argue that one can participate on a par with others in the private and public institutions of modern societies if and only if there is a threshold of mutual public recognition and respect for the reasonable ethical differences of free and equal citizens. This generates the basic level of 'self-respect," in Rawls's sense, or "self-esteem" in Axel Honneth's sense, required to acquire and exercise the capacities to participate in the private and public institutions of modern societies on a par with others.[13] To achieve this, citizens of minority ethical communities have rights of democratic participation to contest the public recognition and entitlement of one dominant ethical group at the expense of all others and to enter into deliberations over a form of recognition that is even-handed. Also, they may exercise this right not only in the public sector but also across the private sector, in challenging biased hiring, promotion, and pension practices, as well as the bias of advertising and products, and in negotiating equity and diversity policies.

These citizens, then, have the participatory rights to present public reasons for and against appropriate forms of public recognition and accommodation of linguistic, cultural, religious, and other forms of ethical diversity in the public and private institutions of their society when it is impossible to be neutral. They also have the social and economic rights necessary to underpin their rights of participation. Furthermore, unlike minimal liberals, deliberative liberals are not in principle opposed to group rights if they serve to protect the members of the group from assimilation and empower them to participate in the larger society on a par with the members of the majority.[14] Deliberative liberalism does not have a theory on the correct answer to the question of what forms of mutual recognition and accommodation of ethical pluralism are appropriate. Rather, for a number of reasons, this is left up to citizens and their representatives, exchanging public reasons together in various deliberative bodies (the public sphere, representative institutions, the court system, and in the workplace itself), reaching agreements and compromises, and reviewing these in turn.[15] One of the central reasons for this commitment to citizen deliberation within an ideal of public reason is that the very participation in these debates over the recognition or nonrecognition of ethical practices is that citizens gain the level of respect and acknowledgment they require to sustain their ethical commitments. They also become aware of, and learn to accept, the variety of ethical practices in their society, and this awareness of reasonable pluralism is itself seen as a good by classical liberals.[16]

None of these remedies is available to minimal liberals because, as we have seen, they detach classic liberalism from democratic citizenship. As Kukathas concludes, they are not very good at handling questions of the qualities of citizenship. Deliberative liberals respond by attaching liberalism to citizenship—the rule of law to popular sovereignty—and employing this conjunction to deal in a different way with the challenges of ethical pluralism. Minimal liberals respond in turn by warning of the dangers of elevating citizenship participation and public support for ethical communities to a "privileged locus of the good life": that is, of ceasing to be liberals and becoming civic humanists.[17] The broad tradition of classical liberalism responds to ethical pluralism in this ongoing, dialogical way, as Kukathas and I have tried to exemplify.

NOTES

1. For presentations of this deliberative and pluralist school of classical liberalism and its approach to reasonable pluralism, see Anthony Laden, *Reasonably Radical: Deliberative Liberalism and the Politics of Identity* (Ithaca: Cornell University Press, 2001); Richard Bellamy, *Liberalism and Pluralism: Towards a Politics of Compromise* (London: Routledge, 1999); Avigail Eisenberg, *Reconstructing Political Pluralism* (Albany: State University of New York Press, 1995); and Will Kymlicka, *Multicultural Citizenship* (Oxford: Oxford University Press, 1995). I am indebted to these studies for the contrasts I draw to minimal liberalism. For the objections of egalitarian liberals to deliberative liberalism, see Brian Barry, *Culture and Equality: An Egalitarian Critique of Multiculturalism* (Cambridge: Polity Press, 2000). Of course, there are liberal defenders of public deliberation who are not defenders of pluralism, but this strand of liberalism can be set aside for another time.

2. John Rawls, *Political Liberalism* (New York: Columbia University Press, 1996), and "The Idea of Public Reason Revisited," in *The Law of Peoples* (Cambridge, Mass.: Harvard University Press, 1999), pp. 129–80. For a defense of Rawls against the common objection that his treatment of pluralism is inadequate, see Laden, *Reasonably Radical*.

3. Benjamin Constant, *The Liberty of the Ancients Compared with that of the Moderns*, in Biancamaria Fontana, ed., *Political Writings* (Cambridge: Cambridge University Press, 1988), pp. 308–29.

4. The fundamental status of both popular sovereignty and the rule of law in classical liberalism is discussed by John Rawls and Jürgen Habermas in their 1995 exchange. See Rawls, "Reply to Habermas," *Political Liberalism*, pp. 396–420, and Habermas, "Reconciliation through the Public use of Reason," in Ciaran Cronin and Pablo De Greiff, eds., *The Inclusion of the Other* (Cambridge, Mass.: MIT Press, 1998), pp. 49–74.

5. Rawls, *Political Liberalism*, p. 205. His understanding of classical republicanism draws on the work of Quentin Skinner.

6. Ibid., p. 206.

7. T. H. Marshall, "Citizenship and Social Class," in *Citizenship and Social Class and Other Essays* (Cambridge: Cambridge University Press, 1950).

8. The disagreement between Brian Barry and Will Kymlicka is a classic example. See Barry, *Culture and Equality*, and the forthcoming response by Kymlicka in David Held, ed., *Culture and Equality Reconsidered* (Cambridge: Polity Press, forthcoming).

9. See Kymlicka, *Multicultural Citizenship*, pp. 49–74.

10. See Laden, *Reasonably Radical*, and Charles Taylor, "The Politics of Recognition," Amy Gutmann, ed., *Multiculturalism* (Princeton: Princeton University Press, 1994), pp. 25–74, where he introduces a distinction between two types of liberalism similar to minimal and deliberative liberalism.

11. The classic liberal presentation of this argument against minimal liberalism is G.W.F. Hegel, *The Philosophy of Right*, trans. T. M. Knox (Oxford: Oxford University Press, 1967). Its influence on contemporary liberalism is discussed by Laden, *Reasonably Radical*, and Charles Taylor, *Hegel and Modern Society* (Cambridge: Cambridge University Press, 1985).

12. This feature of modern liberal societies has also caused many deliberative liberals to question the social theory underlying minimal liberalism, of a "society" and "economy" existing independently of the political "umpire." See Bellamy's objections to Hayek's social theory and minimal liberalism, *Liberalism and Pluralism*, pp. 17–41.

13. Axel Honneth, *The Struggle for Recognition*, trans. Joel Anderson (Cambridge: Polity Press, 1995).

14. For liberal views of group rights, see Will Kymlicka, ed., *The Rights of Minority Cultures* (Oxford: Oxford University Press, 1995).

15. See Bellamy, *Liberalism and Pluralism*, pp. 91–140.

16. In Rawls's terms, to accept the reasonable ethical pluralism of one's fellow citizens and to engage with them accordingly is to accept "the burdens of judgement."

17. See text accompanying notes 5 and 6. For a defense of the tradition of civic humanism or "civic activism" against this objection, see Charles Spinosa, Fernando Flores, and Hubert Dreyfus, *Disclosing New Worlds* (Cambridge, Mass.: MIT Press, 1997), pp. 69–115.

PART III

Natural Law and Ethical Pluralism

John H. Haldane

GENERAL CONSIDERATIONS

The One and the Many

Plato, Aristotle, and other philosophers in the ancient world were much concerned with the general metaphysical problem of the "one and the many"—that is to say, the question of the relationship between a universal or common nature, such as horseness or triangularity, and its many instances, the multitude of horses or triangles. They would ask, for example, whether each particular horse possessed a part or the whole of horseness or horse nature, and if triangularity was itself a triangle. Such abstruse questions are very much the stuff of philosophers' philosophy, and they continue to occupy metaphysicians today.

Equally ancient, equally philosophical, but of much wider concern is the particular question of the relationship between human nature and its many instances as these exist at different times and places. In part this issue is indeed metaphysical, but its interest and importance go beyond the general problem of universals. There is, for example, the matter of how far any common nature might extend.

At one extreme it might be supposed that in all significant respects human beings are constituted in exactly the same ways, with the same physiological, psychological, and sociological natures, so that we can generalize from the study of cases in one time and place to the nature of those from history and from other cultures. At the other extreme it may be held that apart from broad physical similarities attributable to common ancestry, human beings vary enormously in all sorts of respects. On this account humans may share no more of a common nature than do buildings. Certainly, the latter are very broadly similar with features such as walls, floor, and roof (though not all buildings have even these), but the developed variety now existent is far greater than any underlying unity.

A second set of philosophical questions concerns the ethical implications of human nature and of its unity or diversity. Morality and politics are concerned with wide ranges of values, virtues, norms, requirements, and prohibitions. Perhaps the central and certainly the most fundamental philosophical issue concerning these is that of their foundation. What is the basis of goodness? Why is justice a virtue and why is virtue to be sought for? What are requirements and prohibitions founded? And so on. As well as the very many disagreements about moral and political issues that characterize contemporary debate, particularly in advanced, technological, liberal societies, there are deep theoretical disputes about the foundations of ethics and politics.

Natural Law

Arguably the oldest accounts of these foundations are those provided by natural law theories. These originated in the ancient world, and basic versions of them can be found in the mythopoetic texts of the Near East that predate philosophy as it is generally understood. In these mythic writings (use of the term "myth" does not prejudge their basic truth or falsity) such as the narrative of the Epic of Gilgamesh or the early books of the Hebrew Bible, various episodes are related in which good and evil feature significantly. Whether or not their occurrence is attributed to the action of human or supernatural forces, the main point is that certain states of affairs are identified as having positive or negative value, and the question arises as to what the basis for this identification might be. Generally, the answer is that the author or authors are working with a reflective understanding of the situations they describe that has built into it notions of what is harmful or beneficial for human beings as such.

This suggests two ideas that have come to be associated with natural law theory: first, that of moral objectivity, as grounded in rationally discernible facts of nature, facts concerning what is good or evil for rational animals; and, second, that of ethical universality. Right and wrong, on this account, is not a matter of mere opinion or sentiment, nor is it a relative or local matter like custom. On the contrary, social customs and practices may be, and often are judged by reference to universal moral norms such as those of "natural justice."

These ideas can be found in developed forms in various philosophical writings of the ancient Greeks, particularly those of Aristotle, but they also feature in pagan Roman thought and in the writings of medieval Jewish, Islamic, and Christian theologians. By way of example consider the following two important statements of natural law thinking. The former is taken from Cicero's *De re publica* (written in the first century B.C.E); the latter from Aquinas's *Summa Theologiae* (composed in the thirteenth century C.E.). First Cicero (106–43 B.C.E.):

> True Law is Reason, right and natural, commanding people to fulfil their obligations and prohibiting and deterring them from doing wrong. Its validity is universal; it is unchangeable and eternal. Its commands and prohibitions

apply effectively to good men and have no effect on bad men. Any attempt to supersede this law, to repeal any part of it, is sinful; to cancel it entirely is impossible. Neither the Senate nor the Assembly can exempt us from its demands; we need no interpreter or expounder of it but ourselves. There will not be one law at Rome, one at Athens, or one now and one later, but all nations will be subject all the time to this one changeless and everlasting law.[1]

To the natural law belong those things to which a man is inclined naturally, and among these, it is proper to man to be inclined to act according to reason. Now it belongs to reason to proceed from what is common to what is proper as stated in [Aristotle's] *Physics*. I. Speculative reason, however, is different in this matter from practical reason. For, since speculative reason is concerned chiefly with necessary things, which cannot be otherwise than they are, its proper conclusions, like universal principles are invariably true. Practical reason, on the other hand, is concerned with contingent matters, about which human actions are concerned, and consequently, although there is necessity in the general principles, the more we descend to matters of detail, the more frequently we encounter deviations. . . . Accordingly, in matters of action, truth or practical rectitude is not the same for all in respect of detail but only as to the general principles, and where there is the same rectitude in matters of detail, it is not equally known to all.[2]

The second passage is especially relevant to the subject of this essay. First, because Aquinas (1225–74) was highly influential in the development of natural law theory, particularly, but by no means exclusively, within the tradition of Roman Catholic Christianity. But second, because Thomas expresses an appreciation of the fact that the options of unqualified universalism or of unrestricted diversity may not be the only ones, and that the truth may lie somewhere between them. Furthermore, he allows that, as one moves from general principle to detailed application, the scope for doubt and error, and hence for one kind of ethical disagreement, increases.[3]

Natural Law and Religious Ethics

These points are important for the task of addressing pluralism and we shall return to them in due course. For now, however, it is worth emphasizing what is often not appreciated, namely that not all advocates of natural law have been theists; that not all natural law theists have been Christian (Moses Maimonides [1135–1204] is an important Jewish example); and that within Christianity natural law is by no means the preserve of Catholicism. These facts may be news to some readers but the third is likely to be the most surprising, for in the twentieth century especially, the term "natural law" has generally come to be associated with the moral teachings of the Roman Catholic Church.

As mention of Aquinas suggests, that association is long-standing. It became widespread, however, following publication in 1968 of the encyclical *Humanae vitae* in which Pope Paul VI reaffirmed traditional Catholic opposition to artificial contraception. Whereas conservative Protestant views on sexuality are nowadays primarily (and often exclusively) scripture-based, Catholic teaching invokes styles of argument in which certain kinds of action are proscribed on grounds of violating a natural norm. This marked difference of approach is, however, a somewhat modern development and is connected with the fragmentation of Protestantism into a multitude of different groupings and with the trend, as theological differences increased in depth and number, to go back to scripture as a basis for doctrine.

In earlier centuries, by contrast, natural law was widely appealed to by non-Catholic Christian thinkers. Indeed, some of the greatest writers in the natural law tradition have been non-Catholics. Examples of these are the Anglican Richard Hooker (1554–1600), who wrote *The Laws of Ecclesiastical Polity*, and the Dutch Protestant Hugo Grotius (1583–1645), author of the *Law of War and Peace*. In the eighteenth century, versions of natural law were espoused by the largely Presbyterian Scottish philosophers of "common sense," most famously Thomas Reid (1710–96), and advocated by the English legal theorist Sir William Blackstone (1723–80) in his *Commentaries of the Laws of England*. From Britain and continental Europe these passed to North America and the rhetoric, if not always the substance, of natural law features in the Philadelphia Constitutional Convention of 1787.[4]

A Common Mistake

In the popular mind, however, the association of natural law with Catholicism has been strengthened by the continued reference to it in the widely discussed encyclicals of Pope John Paul II, especially *Veritatis splendor* (1993) and *Evangelium vitae* (1995). One common feature of this association, particularly as it dates from *Humanae vitae*, is the belief that opposition to contraception on the basis of natural law amounts to the claim that it is "not natural." Because the context is one where "artificial" contraception is at issue, this further suggests that Catholic ethics, and natural law ethics more generally, revolve around a contrast between what happens in the ordinary course of events (nature) and what might occur as a result of human interference (artifice).

This ill-informed impression has had some interesting consequences. Initially the view attributed to Catholic moral theology was criticized on the basis that it is absurd, cruel, and superstitious to confine actions and policies to ones that do not interfere with natural processes. Medicine, for example, is precisely designed to interfere with a course of events and to reverse or redirect them. If that is acceptable, how can interfering with other processes so as to avoid conception be intrinsically wrong?

This argument rests on a mistake about the way in which appeal to nature features in the anticontraception argument, but before commenting on that let me say something about a recent trend in public thinking, which, ironically as it turns out, might seem to support what is often taken to be the Catholic view. This is the rise of environmentalism, and more generally of "nature holism." Within a decade of the storm of criticism that surrounded *Humanae vitae* a movement had begun, the main claim of which was that techno-industrial consumer societies have become polluters and corrupters of nature. On this account environmental degradation, species exploitation, and human physical and mental illness have all resulted from an attempt to secure false goods by interfering with long-standing natural processes. Eco-activists, new-age travelers, and holistic healers represent one broad strand of this movement, with commercial and state environmental policies falling into line in the general campaign to "get back to nature."

As with the critics of Catholic teaching mentioned earlier, opponents of environmentalism and nature holism are quick to point out that human activity is unavoidably interventionist and that many of the processes and products that "naturalists" favor themselves are or result from interference in the course of events. Organic farming, homeopathy, and species conservation are all forms of intervention and in that respect are contrary to nature.

At more or less the same time, therefore, we find progressive sentiment criticizing traditional Catholic teaching for restricting liberty and inflicting misery on the grounds that it is wrong to interfere with nature, and the same sentiment criticizing techno-industrial society for treating nature as something that can be overridden in order to secure material goods and affluent life-styles. In short, and somewhat paradoxically: Catholic ethics is bad for insisting on respect for the natural order, and capitalism is bad for failing to respect it. This combination echoes something of the sound heard in recent years of traditional sexual morality voiced in unison with feminist criticism of pornography. And just as there is now an alliance between conservative and radical critics of the commercial exploitation of sex, so too there are signs of an alliance between old and new advocates of nature's ways.

However interesting and suggestive as this may be, it is also deeply confused. The appeal in Catholic moral theology to the idea of acting "in accord with nature" is not a recommendation of general noninterference,

or of letting what will happen happen. For apart from running into contradiction (implementing noninterference will itself constitute interference), such a policy stands in need of some account of "what happens
anyway." Setting aside the bare idea of an unchosen causal process, the
notion of "the naturally occurring" or of "what happens normally" remains ambiguous between what is in keeping with a statistical pattern,
and what is in accord with a value-protecting or value-promoting norm.
And, of course, the idea of natural law concerns the latter. That is to say,
it concerns the natural as *that which ought to be*, not merely that which
happens to be. In the traditional view, then, therapeutic medical interventions are warranted because they are aimed at protecting or restoring normal functioning; while contraceptive intervention is improper because it
is intended to inhibit or destroy proper functioning.

Recognition of this point should bring with it the realization that there
is nothing essentially religious about natural law thinking. Apart from the
consideration that the very possibility of there being natural norms depends upon purposeful creation, one could advance a natural law theory
without invoking the law of God.[5] Indeed one might hold that religious
ethical teachings that appeal to a natural law foundation actually go further than can be supported on that basis. This, indeed, is exactly what
some Catholic moral theologians of broadly natural law persuasion do
maintain with regard to their church's teachings on contraception and
divorce. According to such critics, natural law reasoning may establish
the good of marriage and procreation, but it does not show them to be
absolute in the sense associated with traditional teaching.

Reducibility and Plurality

Without engaging in the debate about artificial contraception, it may be
useful to illustrate something of the general character of natural law by
considering its bearing on the issue of sexuality in general. This will also
be relevant to the theme of the final section.

In a recently published book *Ethics and Sex*[6] the Israeli philosopher
Igor Primoratz contends that there is no distinctive sexual morality, that
is, no values or norms specific to this sphere of human life. That is now
a very common view, and it is often matched by similar rejections of the
idea that the major departments of life are governed by specific values or
virtues. Setting aside general moral skepticism, which involves the rejection of the cogency of *any* moral reasoning, even those who think that
something rational can be made out of morality usually contend that particular moral claims derive from a nonspecific, general ethical rule.

The two leading candidates for the ultimate principle from which particular claims derive are (in some or other version) the principle of utility

and the principle of pure practical reason. An action or policy is permitted, required, or prohibited in relation either to the maximization of preference-satisfaction, or to conformity with universal prescriptivity. For example, an action will be permissible according to the former principle if performing it creates no less (total) happiness than other available options, and according to the second if it is of a type that one can consistently prescribe both for oneself and for others.

Given these accounts and their current dominance one can see why contemporary moral philosophy can find no place for department-specific values, virtues, or norms. If there is anything wrong with telling a lie, or having casual sex, or taking goods from a shop without paying for them, or killing someone, it will have to consist in an intentional violation of the basic principle. Accordingly, that will be the only morally relevant description of it. More strictly, it will be the only nonreducible moral description, for, as a matter of convenience, one might mark out in other terms actions liable to violate the principle, say for purposes of training children.

In rejecting the idea of irreducibly distinct values, each proper to different areas of life, these moral philosophies disallow the possibility of at least one kind of ethical pluralism. Rather than it being something to think twice about, however, to advocates of these views this is likely to seem inevitable and quite proper. For it has often been supposed that ethical pluralism is equivalent to ethical relativism, which in turn is taken to be the thesis that reason cannot show some action or policy to be right or wrong as such. That then leaves us with either moral skepticism (in the strict sense, i.e., things may be intrinsically right or wrong but that fact cannot be known) or moral subjectivism (there are no moral facts). In short, moral rationalism excludes moral pluralism inasmuch as the former asserts and the latter denies that universal reason can determine unqualifiedly true moral claims.

There are those, however, who reject the assumed equivalence of pluralism and relativism. One such group includes figures in the British moral intuitionist tradition, especially Moore, Ross, and Pritchard.[7] Another related group comprises philosophers from the Austrian value-phenomenological school.[8] Common to both groupings is the idea of moral reflection leading to conclusions about what is good or bad. From this perspective there is no a priori reason to suppose that all moral phenomena will turn out to be instances of the one value, any more than it is rationally determined that the proper sensibles—color, flavor, odor, sound, and texture—be reducible to some foundational "perceptible quality." On this account, then, there is scope for the idea that right conduct in the area of sex is not reducible to conformity with a single, general ethical principle, but consists in respect for particular sexual values and virtues such as those of modesty, chastity, and fecundity.

Recognition of the possibility of real plurality is, I believe, commendable. However, what is called for philosophically is a legitimation of experience, and an explanation of how what is diverse can be so and of how variety might yet be unified. At one extreme stand the rational monists for whom all moral value must be one; and at the other the phenomenologists for whom things float free in their evaluative diversity. Traditional natural law walks a via media between these positions. It recognizes that life has departments, and thus that there are activity-specific values and virtues. On the other hand it sees that departments can only be viewed as such when seen as parts of a greater whole. That greater whole is human life. Mere material aggregates have no principle of dynamic unity; non-living compounds are sustained through a balance of attractive and repulsive forces; but life involves the integrated operation of vital functions. Not every human good must be an expression of *the* human good, but every such good must be intelligible as part of human life. By rooting value in animate nature, and by recognizing that a species-nature involves a plurality of functions, this most ancient variety of ethical theory combines plurality of values with unity of foundation.

Just as one and the same plant has roots, stem, branches, leaves, and flowers and functions associated with each, all subserving the well-being of the whole, so human nature has many parts and functions, each subject to particular norms, yet each integrated within a whole. In this sense there is a dimension of the ethical corresponding to each distinct voluntary activity. And so there are sexual norms as well as communicative ones. It should be clear that such a doctrine of moral pluralism has nothing to do with relativism as that is nowadays understood.

Nature and Right Action

Before turning to questions of application, it will be as well to clarify further the claim of natural law and to note important points of difference and disagreement between its present-day advocates. Among contemporary theorists, particularly in North America, there is an important debate between two prominent parties: first, those who maintain that what qualifies a position to be a natural law one is simply the claim that right and wrong are objective, universal, and naturally knowable; and, second, those who go further by insisting that it is part of the theory that what makes something right or wrong is its relation to natural human good (or the good of other animals). More precisely, the latter view is that the moral character of actions derives from their contribution as means toward, or as constituents of, well-being. In philosophical circles in which there is little if any historical knowledge of natural law traditions, this second view is better known as "objectivist naturalism," or more commonly as "naturalism." The first position by contrast, has no commonly used title but for purposes of contrast we might term it "naturalist objectivism."

Both views regard moral knowledge as naturally available—that is, as not depending on divine revelation or on some mystical power of ethical intuition. The difference between them concerns the role of nature in providing the *content* of morality. Besides disputing which is the best position philosophically speaking, advocates of these two views argue about the correct attribution of them to historical figures such as Aristotle and, most especially, Aquinas. Given the latter fact it will perhaps come as no surprise to say that this debate is largely confined to Catholic moral philosophers.[9]

This is not the place to enter into these disputes, let alone to try and resolve them. But it is appropriate that I should indicate where my own view lies. To some extent, in fact, I think that the opposition is overstated but to the extent that it exists my sympathies lie with the objectivist naturalists.[10] Such a view, I believe, provides a powerful way of thinking about the objectivity of value and practical reasoning. In the twentieth century moral objectivism has often been challenged with the claim that what we now know of reality leaves no scope for the existence of nonnatural values, let alone of "free-floating" requirements and prohibitions. On this account objectivism faces the task of showing how there could be such "objects" as moral facts and values. This has proved to be a *real* difficulty. At the same time, however, the subjectivist reduction of value to preference and sentiment has seemed contrary to experience and liable to undermine commitment to right action.

A better response is to reject the idea that moral objectivism requires moral "objects." The approach of objectivist naturalism draws from the writings of Aristotle and Aquinas (at least on its interpretation of them) the idea that right action is best understood in terms of the exercise of dispositions—virtues—the having and practice of which serve to advance natural human well-being. Virtues such as prudence, temperance, justice, and courage are as necessary as health and sanity in order to achieve and maintain a good life. Its goodness is not to be understood in terms of the presence in or around it of "values" in the sense of metaphysical objects. Rather it consists in the integrated and balanced operation of various natural functions, including physiological, psychological, and social ones. Goodness in human life on this view is metaphysically neither more nor less mysterious than goodness in the life of plants.

MacIntyre and the Challenge of Relativism

One might now ask whether this account of value is too good to be true. Ironically grounds for doubt arise from within the family of ethical naturalists. Forty years ago, in an essay whose importance for modern English-language moral theory could hardly be exaggerated, the British philosopher Elizabeth Anscombe advanced several bold and very interesting theses.[11] Among these is the claim that the basic moral vocabulary of requirement and of prohibition: "ought," "ought not," "must," "must not," and so on, is a cultural remnant of an earlier religious way of thinking in which morality consists of a series of divine commands. Because people in general no longer subscribe to such a view (indeed, it is uncommon even among moral theologians), Anscombe proposed that it be abandoned in favor of the language, and the philosophy, of human virtue and flourishing.

Twenty years later a second British philosopher, Alasdair MacIntyre, took up both this historico-conceptual analysis and the option for virtue. In *After Virtue* he argued that modern ethical language is an incoherent assemblage of disordered fragments left over from earlier moral systems.[12] However, whereas Anscombe focused exclusively on the remains of divine law and proposed the readoption of a traditional Aristotelian approach, MacIntyre argued that as things stand contemporary, secular liberal consciousness is no better placed to make sense of virtue talk than it is of the strongly prescriptive vocabulary of the Judeo-Christian moral law. In both cases what we lack are the historical and cultural contexts that give meaning to these ways of evaluating and commending character and conduct.

A further point of important difference between Anscombe and MacIntyre is that whereas she seemed to believe that we could reconstruct the philosophical anthropology by which Aristotle was able to prescribe a natural end for human kind, MacIntyre regarded this sort of quasi-philosophical anthropology as committed to a form of ahistorical, acultural "metaphysical biology," which he then believed was no longer tenable. In keeping with the general character of Aristotelian moral psychology, however, he still argued that the value, and indeed the moral meaning, of actions flows from habits whose standing as virtues derives from their orientation toward ends constitutive of good human lives. Like Anscombe and other neo-Aristotelians, therefore, MacIntyre hoped to restore coherence to morality by relating it to an account of life as teleologically ordered. In part for the reasons mentioned, and in part because of conclusions drawn and retained from his earlier studies in Marxism and sociology, however, he viewed that order in terms of social practices rather than of culturally invariant natural functions. In asking the question, What ought I to do? one is, in effect, asking a question about the kind of person one should be. The unit of moral assessment is not, strictly, individual actions but the form of life from which they issue and the agent's overall character. Furthermore, this character is formed and developed in a social context, out of participation in practices whose meaning is given by their traditional goals.

In summary, to understand the moral identity and value of individual actions one has to relate them to the agent's life, and through this to the practices and social forms of his or her culture. The very obvious problem presented by modernity, therefore, is that there is no single unifying culture and hence no shared set of values and virtues by reference to which actions may be interpreted: "The rhetoric of shared values is of great ideological importance, but it disguises the truth about how action is guided and directed. For what we genuinely share in the way of moral maxims, precepts and principles is insufficiently determinate to guide action and what is sufficiently determinate to guide action is not shared."[13]

The considerable interest of MacIntyre's explorations of these issues is testified to by the attention his work has attracted. Yet his thoughts also raise a problematic question about the claim to objectivity. If the standards of moral assessment are not given by extra-moral and uncontested values, or by ahistorical principles of practical reason, but are entirely immanent within the particular social traditions and practices in which agents are situated, then how is relativism to be avoided? If what is right is determined by virtues whose form and content is specific to a tradition, how can it even make sense to raise questions about the morality of conduct from a perspective outside that tradition? Because the diagnosis of modernity, and a fortiori of "post-modernity," is that there is no single moral order, the threat of relativism is not merely speculative, it is real.

Back to Nature

MacIntyre's concern with the question of competing moral traditions is reflected in the title of the book that followed *After Virtue*, namely, *Whose Justice? Which Rationality?*[14] In this, and in the sequel *Three Rival Versions of Moral Enquiry*,[15] he developed a dialectical account of how one tradition of reflection can establish its rational superiority over another. In broad outline it maintains that a tradition may run into philosophical difficulties and recognize this fact without having the resources to solve the problems. It might yet, however, be able to appreciate that another, rival tradition does possess the means to diagnose and to resolve these difficulties. Acknowledgment of these facts therefore amounts to recognition of the superiority of the rival. Thus, while styles and principles of inquiry may be tradition-specific, the ultimate goal of moral enquiry, namely goodness, is tradition-transcendent.

But if virtue and moral reasoning are necessarily formed in interpersonal contexts, can this really be squared with claims to transcendent objectivity? MacIntyre believed himself to have provided the basis for a positive answer but his critics have maintained the charge that his position is a version of relativism—be it a very sophisticated one. While MacIntyre has always denied this, in recent writings he retracts his earlier rejection of Aristotelian appeals to nature.

No doubt he still maintains that we must recognize the diversity of times and circumstances and acknowledge culturally situated histories but he no longer takes the acceptance of these requirements to be incompatible with a naturalistic philosophical anthropology. In the past he has emphasized "deep conflicts" in our cultural history over what human well-being (and hence human nature) consists in. Now he points to the fact that an understanding of value has to be placed within an account of human animality and of what befits its flourishing. He writes:

> In *After Virtue* I had attempted to give an account of the place of the virtues, understood as Aristotle had understood them, within social practices, the lives of individuals and the lives of communities, while making that account independent of what I called Aristotle's "metaphysical biology." Although there is indeed good reason to repudiate important elements in Aristotle's biology, I now judge that I was in error in supposing an ethics independent of biology to be possible . . . no account of the goods, rules and virtues that are definitive of our moral life can be adequate that does not explain—or at least point us towards an explanation—how that form of life is possible for beings who are biologically constituted as we are, by providing us with an account of our development towards and into that form of life.[16]

If as MacIntyre now accepts, the rejection of universal human anthropology was unwarranted, he is surely right to emphasize the importance of second nature: what time, place, and community add to what God or evolution has established. Our movement toward self-realization is in no small part as beings nurtured and formed by the communities of our birth, adoption, education, or career. What this suggests, though, is not that Aristotelian anthropology is redundant but only that it must needs be attendant to historical and cultural diversification. As MacIntyre himself has come to emphasize, there need be no opposition between *historicism* understood as the claim that reason has a variety of cultural and historical starting points, and *realism* conceived as the view that truth is something objective and transcendent of these perspectives.[17]

APPLICATIONS

Problems of Pluralism

While this reconciliation may be theoretically satisfactory, it would be facile to suppose that it can easily be invoked to resolve deep moral disagreements. Recall again the words of Aquinas:

> [S]ince speculative reason is concerned chiefly with necessary things . . . its proper conclusions, like universal principles are invariably true. Practical reason, on the other hand, is concerned with contingent matters, about which human actions are concerned, and consequently, although there is necessity in the general principles, the more we descend to matters of detail, the more frequently we encounter deviations. . . . Accordingly, in matters of action, truth or practical rectitude is not the same for all in respect of detail but only as to the general principles.

The conclusion of the previous section was that according to natural law, most clearly in the interpretation that associates it with objectivist naturalism, the plurality of human values is located within the broad unity provided by a common human nature. If the various points and arguments are found cogent, it will be agreed that moral questions admit of objective answers, though not necessarily of exclusive ones.

But several issues now arise. First, to what extent do the relevant facts prescribe particular policies? Consideration of what pertains to human nature may be insufficient to determine a unique course of action, just as the knowledge that it would be good to apply color to a wall leaves open the question of precisely what color to apply. Second, even where it is determined what would be good, the context of action may be such that the effort required to realize this, and the collateral damage of doing so, would be too great to warrant it. For example, it would be good if all parents treated their children with loving care and refrained from any psychological or physical abuse of them. Given this fact, a community might seek to encourage norms of good parenting and intervene in cases where these norms are violated. However, the effort required to eliminate parental abuse would be enormous, and the social and familial effects of surveillance and intervention might be immensely destructive and themselves violate rights of privacy. Where prevention or cure may be more harmful than the disease, prudence may need to temper idealism. This is not to say that nothing should be done but only that social regulation has to take account of a range of values and be mindful of the costs of coercion and restraint. Third, it is one thing to defend the coherence and even the plausibility of natural law theory and to suggest what its stance on various ethical questions might be; it is yet a further task to show how it might deal with a situation in which not everyone shares that perspective; in which, indeed, some reject both it and the particular judgments it gives rise to. The second and third of these considerations are particularly relevant to the business of managing ethical pluralism.

Citizenship and Social Regulation

In and of itself the mere idea of natural law does not prescribe any particular form of social life or political organization. How it may be appropriate for human beings collectively to live, and what constraining and enabling structures it may be just to impose, depend in no small part upon one's understanding of the extent and modes of human sociability. Here is one point at which the relation of natural law to philosophical anthropology becomes important. If, for example, one's account of human nature conceives of persons as constituted independently of any social relations into which they may enter, then the argument for an individualist politics looks strong. If on the other hand one views human beings as essentially social, as did Aristotle and Aquinas, then one will look to the political order to realize the goods of community. For the most part contemporary theorists who are drawn to natural law have taken inspiration from the Aristotelian-Thomistic tradition and have favored communitarian accounts of political society. There are, though, distinguished exceptions who combine an appreciation of Aristotle with forms of liberal individualism.[18]

Given the "social animal" anthropology now most commonly associated with natural law theory, the good of citizenship (or, more generally, of membership in a community) is both instrumental and constitutive. Collaboration makes possible the achievement of projects and benefits not otherwise attainable; and social life provides the necessary context for the realization of certain aspects of human nature. It is not merely, as any individualist might be willing to grant, that collective action is an effective means to the achievement of ends that, as a matter of fact, no individual could attain by themselves. Rather, collective endeavor is a form of group activity through which bonds of community are strengthened and by which goods may be secured for members of society that *logically* could not be available to them as individuals. These latter benefits are what, strictly speaking, constitute "common goods."

To clarify this point it may be useful to distinguish and then illustrate several ways in which values can be possessed or enjoyed:

1. As *individual goods*: attaching to individuals independently of the states of well-being of others, for example, physical comfort.
2. As *collective goods*: as sets of individual goods, for example, aggregate wealth.

3. As *common goods*: as ones attaching to collectivities and thus only available to individuals as members of groups—for example, the happy mood at a social gathering.
4. As *private goods*: the possession of which by one party prevents their possession by another, for example, food.
5. As *public goods*: the possession or enjoyment of which by one party does not preclude similar benefit to others, for example, fresh air.

The state of happiness felt by those at a social gathering may be and typically is something other than the addition of the separable states of happiness of each. It is something emergent that comes into being through social interaction and is enjoyed by each participant derivatively through membership of the group and not directly as an individual. By way of chemical analogy, the resultant of interaction is not a "linear combination" or additive sum of antecedent quantities. Common goods are neither individual goods nor mere collections of such goods; they are irreducibly communal. Notice, however, that the distinction between private and public goods is tangential to this, inasmuch as not every public good is possessed commonly and not every individual good is a private one.

Part of the considerable importance of Aquinas in the development of natural law is his insistence on the social nature of human beings; his explicit identification of the existence of common goods (or as he says "the common good" [*bonum commune*]); and his claim that in order for this to be realized and protected it is necessary that a community should have leadership with the authority to regulate the activity of its members. All three points are present in the following short passage from his treatise on *The Governance of Rulers* (*De regimine principum*):

> When we consider all that is necessary to human life it is clear that man is naturally a social and political animal, destined more than all the other animals to live in community. . . . The fellowship of society being thus natural and necessary to man, it follows with equal necessity that there must be some principle of government within the society. For if a greater number of people were to live, each intent only upon his own interests [individual goods], such a community would surely disintegrate unless there were one of its number to have a care for the common good: just as the body of a man or of any other animal would disintegrate were there not a single controlling force sustaining the general vitality in all the members . . . the particular interest and the common good are not identical.[19]

Citizenship in this account serves to complete human social nature and is a common good. It is clear, then, that Aquinas and anyone following him is committed to some form of communitarianism as against individualism. Popular political opposition between these views is sometimes drawn in terms of alternative values and ideals of social life. Only among theorists, however, is the opposition cast in terms of conflicting metaphysical accounts of persons. Yet, as the passage from Aquinas suggests, the two contrasts are not unrelated: for the priorities of political governance have to take account of the essential nature of the governed. Unsurprisingly, therefore, philosophical individualists who believe that social relationships belong to persons *per accidens* and not *per se*, are willing to see the state act so as to limit interference with the lives and liberties of individuals, and are resistant to the idea of coercion for the sake of common goods or of society as a whole. By the same token, philosophical communitarians are often suspicious that an emphasis on individual liberty has behind it an antisocial disposition, and they favor the idea of collective action as an end in itself or as a practice part of whose benefit is intrinsic to it.

Rationality features twice over in determining the content of natural law theory. It is *by* the use of reason that we determine our good and the routes to it; and it is *because* we are rational animals that our good has the form it does, embracing intellectual, moral, and spiritual aspects as well as material ones. These are universal features of human nature and hence the goods of citizenship should be open to all. Any attempt to restrict them on the basis of race or gender is liable to be unjust, and members of civil society have a responsibility to ensure that the goods of community are not denied to those who have a human right to them. Within pluralist societies there are groups whose historic culture does discriminate on such grounds. For the sake of civil order, and mindful of the value of autonomy, a society might tolerate minor injustices but at the level of fundamental natural rights, entitlements flowing from one's human nature, there can be little if any room for compromise within a society. Happily, natural law's commitment to the rationality of human beings gives grounds for optimism that a change of view can be effected by argument. Typically, this will take the form of showing that the basis on which one individual or group claims for himself, herself, or itself the status and privileges of citizenship is also possessed by those to whom they would deny this benefit. This argument to consistency is one of the oldest and most commonly used methods in political debate and has had notable (if less than complete) successes, such as the end of slavery and the emancipation of women.

While the communitarian account imposes constraints on policy, it nevertheless allows considerable scope for the variety of arrangements that might realize social goods. In considering conflicts, for example, what have to be balanced are, first, the demonstrable need of an individual or group to pursue projects that are recognizably variants of the general human good; second, the impact of this on the similar need of others;

and, third, the resulting effect of the combination of arrangements on the common good. Natural law on this account sees social regulation not as an undesirable necessity but as an expression of communal existence, which is itself a basic good. However, it must also recognize that the circumstances of social life, particularly in contemporary developed societies, involve immense diversities of life-style, considerable ranges of values, and no little amount of conflict. To some extent it can treat pluralism as a desirable consequence of the fact that basic values, such as those of intellectual or physical activity, can be realized in different but equally good ways. However, not every difference is benign. Where there is conflict, the advocate of natural law must deploy moral reasoning and prudence in order to determine whether the harms or evils resultant from conflict, or from the pursuit of goals that are, on its account, disvaluable, are so great that they must be ruled against, or whether they are such that the effort and measures required to act against them would themselves cause more harm than good. These issues are best pursued by considering examples, and not merely speculative ones but those which represent some of the deepest and most conflicted divisions within our societies, namely, matters of life, death, and sex.

Life-and-Death Decisions

Because all human values are instrumental toward, or constitutive of, the actualization of human nature in individual persons, these lives are the primary loci of value and hence must be respected. Unlike certain other traditions that separate morality and politics, natural law sees these as necessarily related, political values being a subset of moral ones. Accordingly, for natural law no policy that provides resources for, let alone promotes, the intentional and direct destruction of human life will be morally acceptable. One only has to write or read such a claim, however, to recognize that for all its initial plausibility it faces a number of challenges.

First, there is the fact that communities are vulnerable to attack both from within and without and consequently have need of protection. Where the attacks are life-threatening the means of defense against them may themselves pose mortal threats. Government rules society using the apparatus of the state, itself the organized institution through which the community is regulated and protected. For this reason it has been characteristic (and in some accounts definitional) of the state to claim for itself a monopoly of the legitimate use of coercive power. Combining this prerogative with the need to protect their citizens, states have established and maintained police and military forces with the means and the entitlement to use lethal force. This is qualified in various ways but the fact remains that the killing of human beings is provided for within common justifications of the state. For the natural law theorist this derives from the right of self-defense.

Typically, however, natural lawyers have gone on to say that what this right provides for is not the intentional and direct destruction of human life, but only the use of force, which it is conceived may result in death, *though that end is not intended*. Although this distinction (of "double effect") is open to abuse it is a coherent and morally significant one, as is brought out by the following "counterfactual test." Suppose an agent acts in his own defense, or in the defense of those he is charged to protect, in such a way as results in the death of an aggressor. Now consider whether, had his action been equally successful but not lethal, he would have regarded this as a failure or as a success. If the former, then his intentions were murderous; if the latter, they were not.

Capital punishment is a more difficult issue, for this certainly does involve the intentional and direct destruction of human life (as the counterfactual test shows: if the condemned survives the executioner's actions, that is regarded as a failure of the process). It may nevertheless be argued that such killing is justified by the fact that society has a right to protect itself and to exact due penalty for the most serious crimes. This claim is highly controversial and cannot be explored here beyond noting the following. Most philosophers and political leaders in societies in which natural law theory has had an influence are against capital punishment, and yet most ordinary people tend to favor it. At least they do so when asked for their opinion, and that is usually at times when some brutal murder has been in the news. However, when at other, less emotional times the point is made that not all who have been executed have been guilty, and they are then asked whether they would prefer a situation in which someone whom they think might deserve to die escapes that fate, or one in which mistakes having been made the innocent are put to death, they tend to favor the former option. Interestingly, given its association with natural law, the Catholic Church in the form of its Catechism and the pronouncements of John Paul II has moved toward the conclusion that in stable and civilized societies capital punishment cannot be justified.

If liberal intellectual opinion and Catholic moral teaching find themselves in agreement on this life-and-death issue, they are deeply opposed on those of abortion and euthanasia. More than proponents of any other ethical theory, advocates of natural law tend to be opposed to abortion. Their argument is straightforward, combining the general prohibition on the taking of innocent human life with the claim that a fetus in the womb is an innocent human being. Equally and for parallel reasons they tend strongly to oppose non- and involuntary euthanasia—that is, those cases in which a patient is constitutionally incapable of giving, or has not given consent to having themselves killed. The matter of voluntary euthanasia and assisted suicide is more complex but again the preponderance of natural law opinion is probably against it.

Unlike certain increasingly prominent versions of political liberalism that hold that it is not the business of the state to advance or protect any conception of the morally good life but only to provide a safe and procedurally just sphere for individual activity, natural law holds the laws of the state *should* reflect moral values and requirements. Accordingly it can hardly take a neutralist stance on questions of killing where it believes this killing to be unjustified. Consider in this connection the following passage drawn from a recent statement on abortion issued by the Vatican Congregation for the Doctrine of the Faith:

> The inalienable rights of the person must be recognised and respected by civil society and the political authority. These human rights depend neither on single individuals nor on parents; nor do they represent a concession made by society and the state. . . . Among such fundamental rights one should mention in this regard every human being's right to life and physical integrity from the moment of conception . . . a consequence of the respect and protection which must be ensured for the unborn child from the moment of conception, the law must provide appropriate legal sanctions for every deliberate violation of the child's rights.[20]

There is scope for argument even in natural law terms about the blanket opposition to abortion and euthanasia. For example, the claim that the fetus is an innocent human being carries greater weight than does the claim that the immediate product of conception is such. Additionally it may be recognized that respecting the rights of autonomy, which natural law regards as integral to human self-realization, gives scope for tolerating error and wrongdoing at certain levels and to certain extents. However, anyone who believes that the laws of the state should embody fundamental moral principles and who also believes that certainly abortion and probably euthanasia are gross violations of such principles has little option but to resist legislative changes in the direction of liberalizing these practices, and to strive to repeal such legislation once it has been enacted. At the same time, concern for the overall good of society and acceptance of the fact that many seriously and sincerely hold a different view on such issues must limit the forms of opposition. In this and in other matters the following balanced compromise may be reasonable: while one may certainly not give support to legislation that provides for or permits what one holds to be evils, one may yet accept the constitutional right of the state to enact such legislation and thus confine one's opposition to legally permissible forms. Necessarily this formulation is qualified by the phrase "may yet accept"; for the evils might be so great that one then has no moral option but to break the law and, at the limit, to regard lawful government as having ceased to exist. If this seems extreme it is worth recalling that precisely this situation has faced the citizens of more than one state during the course of the twentieth century. Put another way, there is a limit to how much ethical difference a society can withstand.

Human Sexuality

Along with abortion, sexuality has become one of the main issues of contention between traditional natural law morality and politics, and the moral and social philosophy of "liberal pluralism." Although a range of matters are in contention, the most prominent is the issue of homosexual practice (by which I include lesbianism) and its legitimation by the state. It is only relatively recently that homosexual relations have been decriminalized in many societies, and in some they are still illegal. Yet in many of the states where homosexual activity was once prohibited there are now moves to bestow legal rights on homosexual partners and even to extend the institution of marriage to them.

For those liberals who uphold the moral neutrality of the state this latter prospect can be perplexing. For on the one hand while they do not believe that it is for the state to proscribe sexual practice on moral grounds, nor do they believe that it should endorse, let alone prescribe, forms of sexual union as expressions of moral values. Yet this latter is precisely the basis on which some gay activists seek the extension of marriage to homosexual partners. In this respect at least they share with the traditional defenders of heterosexual marriage a common belief in the value of publicly recognized partnerships.

Once again what the natural law theorist has to say will depend on what he or she believes about human nature and the goods that perfect it. What is generally, and unsurprisingly the case, however, is that most proponents of natural law take a "conservative" position. According to traditional natural law ethics, judgments as to the moral acceptability of sexual practices must be keyed to an understanding of the proper role of sex in human life. Sexual organs are defined by function and their (primary) function is that of reproduction. What follows is that the definitive use of sexual organs is intersexual, that is, between male and female, and for the sake of procreation. This is not to say that the only function of sex or of the sexual organs is to reproduce. Sex obviously gives pleasure and serves to express and deepen emotional bonds; but these features are located within the boundaries of its primary, reproductive function.

Suppose, then, that the natural law theorist believes homosexual practice to be contrary to nature, and thus at odds with right reason. What should follow so far as policy is concerned given the fact that this opinion is now widely contested? Here it may be useful to relate a real case in which moral and political views on just these issues have been in heated conflict. In 1988 under the Conservative administration of Margaret Thatcher a piece of legislation was enacted in the United Kingdom regulating local government. This contained within it the following clause, known universally as Section 28: "A local authority shall not (a) intentionally promote homosexuality or publish material with the intention of promoting homosexuality; or (b) promote the teaching of homosexuality as a pretended family relationship."[21]

This clause was introduced in legislation designed to curb what were viewed as doctrinaire policies then being advanced, and sometimes implemented, by far left activists particularly in London. The general legislation was contested by the parliamentary opposition, and the clause was viewed with some disquiet by others, but it was presented as part of a general block to policies for which the public certainly had no sympathy. Then, as now, the dominant feeling was probably one of wishing not to know what people do in private so long as it is not contrary to the well-being or interests of others.

Since the removal from power of the Conservatives in 1997 and the election of New Labour, a move has been made to repeal Section 28 and that now seems likely to happen. However, this proposal has met with considerable opposition from various quarters including many leaders of Christian, Jewish, and Islamic faiths—all traditions in which natural law has had an influence. On the other side the proponents of repeal divide into three broad groups: first, liberals of the sort who do not believe that it is the business of law either to promote or to prohibit behavior on moral grounds; second, advocates of alternative sexualities who insist that the state has a responsibility to encourage attitudes and actions favorable to these sexualities, not in the sense of teaching people to adopt them but of teaching them to affirm or even to celebrate them; and, third, moral conservatives who, while not favoring the neutral state, are unhappy about the way in which matters of sexual morality are now dealt with.

There is certainly ground for complaint that the clause is discriminatory in singling out one particular sexual group. So far as public opinion is concerned, it is hard to suppose that those who maintain the moral superiority of heterosexual over homosexual activity would be happy to have local authorities promote sadomasochism or fetishism. And if that is not the case, then the charge of homophobia commonly leveled against opponents of repeal does indeed begin to look justified.

What is in fact the case is that most people do not want local authorities or schools to promote, recommend, or celebrate any particular form of sexual activity though they would, I suspect, be happy and indeed wish to see heterosexual marriage, or at least stable, domestic heterosexual family life presented as a desirable norm. Clearly, though, this would be unacceptable to sexual radicals. Moreover, they will regard mere social toleration of homosexuality (or of other alternatives) as insufficient, noting (correctly) that toleration is compatible with moral disapproval. But approval cannot be coerced, and it is evident that the majority do not regard all forms of sexual activity as "equally valid." If pressed as to why, they will usually speak in terms of what is "normal" or "natural."

Such replies are now regularly countered by the suggestion that, while homosexuality or fetishism may be statistically abnormal, it occurs in nature and hence cannot be objected to as unnatural. Whether by accident or design, however, such rejoinders confuse the two senses of the terms identified earlier. "Normal" may mean usual (i.e., according to a pattern), or it may mean conforming to an appropriate standard. Likewise "natural" may mean not artificial or according to design or proper function. In each case it is the latter meaning that is intended by the critic of alternative sexualities, and his or her position is untouched by pointing out that these occur "in nature." So too do inclinations to obsession and addiction, but that is hardly a basis for maintaining equivalence between these and the human norm.

Of course, such natural law reasoning is unlikely to persuade those who maintain the moral equivalence of all forms of sexual life-style. And against this background of fundamental moral disagreement the liberal idea of state neutrality may have some appeal. But it is neither practical nor consistent with the natural law view of the state. In such a view morality does and should constrain the public sphere insofar as policies bear upon basic rights and interests. The state exists in part to promote the common good and, more fundamentally, to protect its members' interests from harm or injury arising from the actions of others. On this at least moral conservatives and radicals are likely to agree.

How then to proceed? On the one hand, discrimination in law on the basis of private sexual practice cannot be justified. On the other hand, society has a right to expect its commonly shared interests to be protected, and these include the norm of heterosexual marriage, particularly as that bears upon the needs and formation of children. With that in mind one might see some wisdom in the search for a middle way between repeal and retention. When the matter was debated in the Westminster Upper Chamber—the House of Lords—Lord Brightman drafted the following replacement clause:

> Subject to the general principle that the institution of [heterosexual] marriage is to be supported, a local authority shall not encourage or publish material intended to encourage the adoption of any particular sexual lifestyle. This section does not prohibit the provision for young persons of sex education or counselling services on sexual behaviour and associated health risks.[22]

In the event this was not put to the vote and the issue remains to be brought back to Parliament, but the proposal has merit. Reasoning about what policy it is rational for an individual or a government to pursue has to be related to the question of what burdens and harms arise from the effort to encourage or to enforce any given option. Here it may be useful to recall the distinction between value-promoting and value-protecting policies. Natural-law-based legislation will seek to protect the good of heterosexual union open to procreation and it will not promote forms of union other than this. Equally, however, where there is strong demand for alternatives, it will consider the cost of opposing this, and where that seems too great in its impact upon civil order and the common good, it may elect to tolerate what it cannot endorse.

Conclusions

Having quoted severally from Aquinas, the principal medieval author of natural law ethics and politics, I end with a quotation from one of the leading twentieth-century contributors in the same tradition, Jacques Maritain. In his classic work, *The Person and the Common Good*, Maritain writes as follows:

> [T]he common good of political society is not only the collection of public commodities. . . . It includes the sum or sociological integration of all the civic conscience, political virtues, and sense of right and liberty, of all the activity, material prosperity and spiritual riches, of unconsciously operative hereditary wisdom, of moral rectitude, justice, friendship, happiness, virtue and heroism in the individual lives of its members. For these things are, in a certain measure, communicable and so revert to each member, helping him to perfect his life of liberty and person.[23]

This is an inspiring conception of the life of a civil and political community and it should serve to win friends if not converts to the view it represents. But anyone reviewing the degree of ideological and moral diversity and conflict exhibited today, half a century after Maritain wrote these words, must wonder how feasible in countries such as the United States is the project of a civil society and political culture based on natural law. Lying behind the foregoing applications of natural law theory has been the question of the social preconditions of the possibility of protecting or promoting certain fundamental values. This raises the interesting though somewhat unsettling thought that an advocate of natural law, who for that reason is likely to be a moral and social conservative (a nonlibertarian communitarian), may find himself or herself in a situation in which the diversity of opinions and the plurality of positions within society is so great that there is no possibility of ordering the institutions and policies of the state according to natural law reasoning. In that circumstance the conservative may be persuaded that the best option is to urge the dismantling of the state. If a polity cannot be well ordered, then better, *perhaps*, that it be abandoned. It is for this reason that natural law ethics and practical politics (conceived as the art of the possible) may not always go hand in hand.

NOTES

1. Cicero, *De re publica* I, 43 as translated by Michael Grant in *Roman Readings* (Harmonsdworth: Penguin, 1958). The complete text—Latin and English facing—can be found in Cicero, *De re publica* and *De legibus*, trans. C. W. Keyes, Loeb Classical Library (London: Loeb, 1977).

2. Aquinas, *Summa Theologiae*, 1-2, q. 94, a. 4 *responsio*. The translation is based on that of the Fathers of the English Dominican Province (London: R & T Washbourne, 1915). The relevant sections of the *Summa* (1-2, 22, 90–97) are given in Latin and in English translation together with commentary in R. J. Henle, *Saint Thomas Aquinas: The Treatise on Law* (Notre Dame, Ind.: University of Notre Dame Press, 1993).

3. Two interesting accounts and discussions of Aquinas's thought in relation to natural law and the ethical foundations of politics are provided by Anthony J. Lisska, *Aquinas's Theory of Natural Law* (Oxford: Oxford University Press, 1996), and John Finnis, *Aquinas: Moral, Political, and Legal Theory* (Oxford: Oxford University Press, 1998).

4. For an excellent account of political thought from antiquity to the Renaissance, which situates natural law throughout this period, see Janet Coleman, *A History of Political Thought*, vol. 1: *From Ancient Greece to Early Christianity*; vol. 2: *From the Middle Ages to the Renaissance* (Oxford: Blackwell, 2000). For an introduction to and selections from the writings of moral and social philosophers of the modern and Enlightenment periods, see J. Schneewind, ed., *Moral Philosophy from Montaigne to Kant*, 2 vols. (Cambridge: Cambridge University Press, 1990). For a general history of moral philosophy, see Alasdair MacIntyre, *A Short History of Ethics*, 2nd ed. (London: Routledge, 1998).

5. Such, in a sense, is the case with Cicero, as quoted earlier. For while he writes of attempts to supersede the law as being "sinful" and refers to "God" as its author, these references are regularly set aside as rhetorical and nontheistic. On the other hand, however, in his dialogue *On the Nature of the Gods* composed around 45 B.C.E. but set some thirty years earlier, Cicero has one of the interlocutors, the Stoic philosopher Lucillus, speak as follows: "The point seems scarcely to need affirming. What can be so obvious and clear, as we gaze up at the sky and observe the heavenly bodies, as that there is some divine power of surpassing intelligence by which they are ordered?" *The Nature of the Gods*, trans. P. G. Walsh (Oxford: Claredon Press, 1991), 48. The parallel between this and the following from Saint Paul's *Letter to the Romans* is striking: "What can be known about God is plain to men for God has shown it to them. Ever since the creation

of the world his invisible nature, namely his eternal power and deity, has been clearly perceived in the things that have been made." (Romans 1:19–20).

6. Igor Primoratz, *Ethics and Sex* (London: Routledge, 1999).

7. For a brief account of the ideas of these figures, see Jonathan Dancy "Intuitionism" in Peter Singer, ed., *A Companion to Ethics* (Oxford: Blackwell, 1991), pp. 411–20.

8. This is now an unduly neglected group. For an introduction to the main figures and their ideas, see J. N. Findlay, *Axiological Ethics* (London: Macmillan, 1970).

9. For representations of these positions, see (1) on the side of naturalist objectivism: John Finnis, *Natural Law and Natural Rights* (Oxford: Oxford University Press, 1980); Robert George, "Natural Law and Human Nature," in Robert George, ed., *Natural Law Theory: Contemporary Essays* (Oxford: Clarendon Press, 1992), reprinted in Robert George, *In Defence of Natural Law* (Oxford: Clarendon Press, 1999); and Patrick Lee, "Is Thomas's Natural Law Theory Naturalist?" *American Catholic Philosophical Quarterly* 71 (1997): 567–87; and 2) on the side of objectivist naturalism: Russell Hittinger, *A Critique of the New Natural Law Theory* (Notre Dame, Ind.: University of Notre Dame Press, 1987); Lloyd Weinreb, *Natural Law and Justice* (Cambridge, Mass.: Harvard University Press, 1987); and Mark Murphy, "Self-Evidence, Human Nature, and Natural Law," *American Catholic Philosophical Quarterly* 69 (1995): 471–84.

10. For further discussion, see John Haldane, "Thomistic Ethics in America," *Logos,* 3 (2000): 150–68, and for some historical background, John Haldane, "Medieval and Renaissance Ethics," in Singer, *Companion to Ethics,* pp. 133–46.

11. G.E.M. Anscombe, "Modern Moral Philosophy," *Philosophy* 33 (1958): 1–19 reprinted in Anscombe, *Ethics, Religion and Politics: Collected Papers,* vol. 3 (Oxford: Blackwell, 1981), pp. 26–42.

12. Alasdair MacIntyre, *After Virtue* (London: Duckworth, 1981).

13. Alasdair MacIntyre, "The Privatisation of Good," in C. F. Delaney, ed., *The Liberalism-Communitarianism Debate* (Lanham, Md.: Rowman & Littlefield, 1994), p. 6.

14. Alasdair MacIntyre, *Whose Justice? Which Rationality?* (London: Duckworth, 1988).

15. Alasdair MacIntyre, *Three Rival Versions of Moral Enquiry* (London: Duckworth, 1990).

16. Alasdair MacIntyre, *Dependent Rational Animals: Why Human Beings Need the Virtues* (Notre Dame, Ind.: University of Notre Dame Press, 1999), p. x.

17. I discuss the character and coherence of MacIntyre's account of the structure of rational inquiry in John Haldane, "MacIntyre's Thomist Revival: What's Next?" in J. Horton and S. Mendus, eds., *After MacIntyre* (Cambridge: Polity Press, 1994), pp. 91–107. For MacIntyre's reply see the same volume, pp. 294–96.

18. See Fred D. Miller Jr., *Nature, Justice, and Rights in Aristotle's Politics* (Oxford: Oxford University Press, 1995); also, Michael Novak, *Free Persons and the Common Good* (Madison, Wis.: Madison House, 1989).

19. Translated as "On Princely Government" by J. G. Dawson, in A. P. D'Entreves, ed., *Aquinas: Selected Political Writings* (Oxford: Blackwell, 1959), p. 3.

20. From *Donum vitae* (1987) as quoted in the *Catechism of the Catholic Church* (London: Chapman, 1994), part 3, section 2, paragraph 2273.

21. *Local Government Act* (London: Her Majesty's Stationary Office, 1988), section 28.

22. Lords Hansard for 7 February 2000 (London: Her Majesty's Stationary Office, 2000).

23. Jacques Maritain, *The Person and the Common Good*, trans. John Fitzgerald (New York: Scribner, 1947), pp. 52–53.

Natural Law Reflections on the Social Management of Ethical Pluralism

Joseph Boyle

John Haldane has provided a wide-ranging and insightful essay on natural law and ethical pluralism. His essay usefully details the manifold relationships between natural law and ethical pluralism and hints at many of the deep and interesting theoretical and practical issues these relationships generate. Although I disagree with Haldane about some details of natural law analysis and have a somewhat different conception of how best to formulate what is fundamental in natural law, these disagreements and differences are not likely to be of wide interest outside the debates of natural law thinkers, and do not affect the subject of this book. Consequently I will criticize Haldane only implicitly or in passing and will undertake an independent look at several issues central to this volume from my own perspective, which, although very similar to Haldane's, is shaped by my own concerns in moral theory and political philosophy.[1]

The core idea of natural law, as a thesis about morality, law, and other forms of social authority, is that some action-guiding thoughts and statements, that is, some precepts or practical principles, are natural in the sense that they are not dependent for their validity on human decision, authority, or convention. Because of their independence of these factors, natural precepts and principles must be generally accessible to human reason; the critical reflection that is not dependent upon but potentially critical of any particular social enactment or practice is the work of common human reason. I take this immediate implication concerning the accessibility of moral truth to human beings generally to be part of the core idea of natural law.

Yet this component of the core idea of natural law seems to render it a most unpromising candidate for throwing light on how the ethical diversity of modern life is to be managed. For any natural law conception implies that people commonly do know, or should know, or readily can know moral principles capable of overcoming this diversity and leading to common moral understandings and judgments. And that, of course, is at odds with both the facts of moral existence as seen through the prism of the moral pluralism of modern, multicultural societies and the widely accepted social norms that give to that pluralism a kind of normative status. It might appear that if natural law is the correct view of morality, then ethical pluralism would not exist and, therefore, that its existence refutes natural law claims.

This suggests that, before seeking to articulate natural law political and social norms for managing ethical pluralism, it is worth exploring how natural law understands and accounts for the phenomenon of ethical pluralism.

Natural law theorists from ancient times to now have recognized and plausibly explained a number of the facts about moral diversity.

First, differences in moral outlook between societies separated by time and/or geography are accepted as factual and have been explained in more or less moralistic terms. For many, differences in custom and law among different societies are compatible with a common recognition of moral principle. The different circumstances of societies in different geographical or historical conditions can lead to different social choices, which are completely reasonable in the circumstances, although they implement moral principle in very different and even apparently contrary ways. For example, the property regulations in a simple society of hunter-gatherers are reasonably quite different from those of an agricultural society, and those from comparable regulations in highly industrialized and postindustrialized societies.[2]

Second, differences in moral judgment in difficult cases calling for careful casuistry to assess a host of conflicting moral considerations are also not taken by natural law theorists to be problematic, but to be expected given the complexity of these cases.[3]

Third, natural law is not embarrassed by the diversity of humanly good ways of life but, indeed, as Haldane has noted, has a theoretical framework that allows their full recognition. The diverse excellences that comprise a good human life are such that the complete set of them cannot fully exist in a single life; for example, the particular excellences of the life of a religious celibate and of that of a father or a mother are both components in the aggregate of human perfection, yet they cannot exist in a single life. Many other forms of human fulfillment are similarly exclusionary of others in practice, if perhaps not so starkly as a matter of simple logic. The virtues of the judge are not necessarily opposed to those of the general, but often enough a person must choose to cultivate one or the other.

These standard natural law responses to the phenomenon of ethical pluralism, which are well rehearsed by Haldane, are certainly important parts of its attempts to recognize its reality and explain its possibility. But contemporary moral pluralism seems to include stronger claims than those the tradition can easily accommodate. First, moral diversity and conflict do not exist only in far distant societies. For the pluralism under discussion nowadays surely exists within the same societies and polities.

Differences among individuals and groups, some holding and some rejecting the first-order moral views of traditional natural law, which Haldane usefully brings to the fore, are not cross-cultural, but occur within virtually every modern city, state, province, or nation and often within the same families, professions, ethnic groups, and religions.

Second, differences in moral judgment characteristic of modern pluralism are not differences simply about hard cases but apparently also about general norms, basic principles, and moral perspectives. For example, however much public debate about abortion may focus on the hard case of abortion to deal with rape or incest, or on the hard case of partial birth abortion, the underlying judgments of people in disagreement about the hard cases usually reflect a substantial disagreement of moral principle.

Third, what are now thought of as incompatible but equally or incommensurably good ways of living do not easily fit into a common moral framework, as diverse property regimes can be or as the plural excellences of diverse but not morally opposed ways of life can be. There is moral opposition, not simply difference, between the political views of those who oppose and those who support legal and social permission for physician-assisted suicide. Similarly, the defenders of marriage as traditionally understood in the Western societies influenced by the Bible and Saint Augustine can hardly accommodate same-sex marriage as socially and morally acceptable.

The challenge to natural law from modern ethical pluralism is, in a word, somewhat different and more radical than that posed by the common forms of moral diversity and disagreement. Haldane's chronicling of Alasdair MacIntyre's evolving views on the tradition-based character of morality is an instance of the kind of response natural law theorists must make to this challenge.

Still, it seems to me that defenders of natural law need not accept at face value the common formulation of ethical pluralism as involving moral disagreement at the most basic level. Of course, there are some facts here, and natural law must acknowledge these. It is a fact that people who interact within the institutions made possible by modern polities differ and disagree about moral matters in ways such people likely have not done before. Whatever the difficulties of historical comparisons, this diversity and disagreement appears to be more pervasive and deeper than in other ages and in other social arrangements. For now, at least within polities and within their wider societies of the economically developed world, diverse groups of people interact, mostly peacefully, and cooperate with others with whom they have profound moral and cultural disagreements.

It is not an incontrovertible fact, however, that this diversity and disagreement goes all the way to the foundations of people's moral perspectives. For, although philosophers' formulations of basic moral principles plainly are contradictory, the merits of these different formulations can be and are rationally debated, and the possibility that philosophers introduce false assumptions into these formulations is real.[4] Consequently, the existence of such philosophical disagreements does not in itself refute natural law claims about universal awareness of common principles. For those claims are not about the adequacy of the articulation of common basic moral awareness but its reality. And the very fact that such disagreements lead to further discussion suggests that philosophers think they can reach common understandings.

More practically, the possibility of overcoming moral diversity and especially disagreement by means other than manipulation, force, or compromise is underwritten by natural law claims of the universal accessibility of moral principle. Aspirations to agreement about moral principle are hardly rational if all possibility of rational moral agreement among people in moral conflict is excluded. Moreover, these aspirations seem sometimes to have been fulfilled. As noted earlier, people in ethically pluralistic societies do have enough in common to exist together in peace and to cooperate in rather robust ways. Those common interests seem to include some norms for existing togther in peace and some norms for fair cooperation. A noninstrumental conception of these norms as commonly agreed upon moral principles is surely possible. Natural law theorists will defend such a conception against a more Hobbesian conception of the grounds for social cooperation and tolerance. Finally, there is moral argument and moral reasoning in what Michael Walzer has called the "moral world."[5] That argumentation is not simply ideological conflict carried out verbally but rather is careful reasoning, ordinarily of a casuistical character, dealing with moral issues, such as warfare, that affect the interactions between communities. That casuistry can and sometimes has led to agreements about moral matters that are not simply opportune but are common practical judgments based upon this kind of moral reasoning. In short, there seems to remain, even in our morally fragmented world, some elements of what scholastic theologians and international lawyers have called "the *jus gentium*," the common customs of humankind that provide some guidance to regulating, among other things, the relationships between communities.[6]

In short, the modern recognition of moral pluralism does not provide evidence that contradicts those widely recognized aspects of moral life and practice that are nonlocal and not plausibly understood as arising from the particular choices, history, and values of some communities. These aspects of moral life certainly seem to point toward some common acceptance of moral principle. Of course, natural law is not the only form of ethical universalism. Hobbesian social philosophy has universalist elements as do the various forms of consequentialism. But differences among universalist approaches to morality do not obscure their common rejection of morality as purely local and community-based.

The preceding has been a sketch of some elements in a natural law account of ethical pluralism. I have sought to elaborate aspects of a natural law understanding of ethical pluralism that are not emphasized by Haldane but important for showing that natural law is not dialectically incapacitated by its very existence. I now turn briefly to the task of elaborating natural law's norms for dealing socially and politically with ethical pluralism.

I will make use of Aquinas's moral theory as the entrée into this set of issues. He put forth an extensive, complex, and interrelated set of precepts governing private and public life.[7] He held that these precepts were implications of general moral principles, which he characterized as the principles of the natural law. Not surprisingly he formulated what he took to be the most basic of these principles in several ways: most notably as the prescription to act in accord with right reason, or to act in accord with its basic moral deliverance, namely, to love God above all things and one's neighbor as oneself.[8]

The precepts of the second tablet of the decalogue are the immediate implications of the principle that one is to love one's neighbor as oneself. These precepts—prohibiting killing, stealing, lying, and adultery and requiring respect for parents—are taken as providing the normative shape for social life. In most cases they indicate moral limits beyond which a person or group must not go if decent social existence is to be maintained. But this hardly amounts to a complete political morality. Until the shape of such a political morality is plain, the implications of practical reason for individuals, families, and voluntary associations concerning how they should deal with individuals and groups who do not accept their judgments about what is practically reasonable are not obvious. Therefore, the commitment to the universal truth of the precepts of the decalogue and other general moral norms does not by itself settle the natural law position concerning how polities should deal with ethical pluralism.

The normative core of Thomistic natural law contains the basis for a further step in that direction. A component of the second love commandment itself—the Golden Rule—provides a principle that does more than delineate outer moral limits for social life. The Golden Rule provides a rational basis for scrutinizing the bias that our feelings can generate in favor of ourselves and those with whom we identify. So it provides a moral ground for scrutiny of actions that are compatible with the precepts of the decalogue. The Golden Rule also underlies Kantian and Rawlsian devices, such as universalizability and the veil of ignorance, for securing fairness or morally significant impartiality. In these and other ways, this principle serves as a consideration in the justification of duties and rights, and in the reasoning that settles ranking duties and sometimes overriding rights. So the Golden Rule is an essential working principle in social and political morality. Still, the conjunction of this principle with the precepts of the decalogue does not provide determinate answers to many questions of political philosophy including many of those concerning moral pluralism.

To deal with these questions, we seem to need, in addition to strictly moral principles and precepts, some way of understanding the conditions for common action and cooperation. Thus, because the human actions by which communities respect or do not respect a variety of moral views and ways of life are the purposeful acts of communities, only when the character of such actions is clarified will we be able to articulate the moral norms that should govern them.

Thomistic natural law makes use of two interrelated ideas to understand common human action and cooperation: the notion of the common good and a conception of practical authority. The notion of the good, as what is desirable for humans because of its capacity to perfect or fulfill the human person, both individually and in community with others, is the analytical foundation of practical reasoning, including moral reasoning. The goods that motivate human beings are intelligible: they provide reasons for action.[9] This feature of human goods allows the same goods to be pursued by groups of people: life by a survival community; health by a health care team, including professionals, patients, and family supporters; victory and excellence in performance by a team of athletes; good relations with God or the gods by a religious congregation; and so on. When the same good is pursued by a group of people that good is common to them.[10] When that good grounds the pursuit by different people of the same concrete goal, they are unified not only in seeking the same kind of good, but also in pursuing the same concrete objective. They are after the very same thing. That is, a goal is common in this way if each of those who pursue it understands his or her actions as a means toward the realization of that goal. But even aiming at the same goal, such as the defeat of a common enemy by communities completely out of touch with each other, is not sufficient for common action.[11]

At least one further condition is needed if common action is to exist, that is, some form of coordination of individual action toward the common goal. This coordination of action toward a common goal occurs if each participant's contribution to the achievement of the goal is understood by him or her as dependent for its success in the project on the success of actions of other parties—coordination toward a common goal includes the idea of taking account of the contribution of others to the project and adjusting one's actions accordingly.

I think these two conditions for common action are together sufficient for an action's being, morally speaking, a common action. If a person acts for a goal he or she thinks is common and makes relevant choices by taking into consideration actions of others for that goal, then that person's actions are joined to the actions of the others. He or she does what is possible to realize a goal understood to be others' goal as well and to take into account their actions for its realization.

These conditions can be met when there is a very considerable unanimity within a group of people, not only about the common goods and common goals to which they are committed, but also about each person's contribution to realization of the common goal by his or her choice of the appropriate action to pursue it. Absent that kind of unanimity, practical authority is needed for the coordination of individual action necessary for common action. Practical authority is recognized by a person's willingness to allow his or her choices to be settled not by his or her own preferences or practical judgments but by the decision of another person—the one accepted as having practical authority. This surrender of discretion to a person or group intent on the common goal has the same effect as unanimity: it allows the actions of the obedient to be integrated into the project of realizing the goal.[12]

The notions of the common good and of authority introduced here are formal notions that apply, mutatis mutandis, to all communities and to all common actions. But I think this brief account of basic natural law categories makes plain that the question of managing ethical pluralism, as distinct from the natural law position about the substance of issues about which there exists pluralism, is fundamentally a question of the authority of political society (or of any other community that would seek to manage it), and therefore of the extent of the common good of that kind of community.

Unless the common good of political society is all-encompassing, embracing not simply the public aspects of any human activity but all aspects of life, there will be limitations on the authority of political leaders. But classical natural law theorists, for example, Aquinas, have been understood as holding that political society, because of its responsibility to promote human good, is justified in enforcing any moral position it judges true and is broadly capable of enforcing through political means.[13]

Natural law theorists who accept this all-encompassing conception of the political common good admit, of course, that political society's capacity to act for the human good is limited by many factors, including the virtue and culture of its members. They emphasize that the judgment of what is concretely possible to do by political means is a matter of wise judgment, and that, as Haldane suggests, allows for considerable discretion by political leaders about the extent to which morally based political action is reasonable, all things considered. The same kinds of reason that justify the toleration of evil by individuals and families have application in political life: one can do something to prevent or remedy an evil, yet the cost is high, the promise of success dubious, and other duties call out. So natural law theorists generally recognize the virtues of sometimes tolerating evils one could do something about.

But there will be more principled limits on the action of political society in dealing with moral pluralism to the extent that such moral disagreements fall outside the common good of political society. Some of these differences seem to have little connection with the common life that people of a region share because of their common membership in a polity: aspects of child rearing and sexual behavior, the use of food and alcohol, religious practice, and so on seem to be largely private and outside the realism of direct political interest. These, of course, include many of the aspects of life pursued differently by various people and in dispute within multicultural societies.

There is a development particularly within Catholic twentieth-century natural law reasoning that seems to set such principled limits to political action in the moral lives of communities and individuals living within it. This development has emphasized the instrumental role of the common good of political society in relation to the actions and welfare of individuals, families, and voluntary associations. On this conception the common good is the set of conditions of social life that allow social groups and their members relatively thorough and ready access to their fulfillment.[14] Although this instrumental conception does not imply that good citizens find no part of their perfection as social beings in political life, it supports the idea that the fundamental moral undertaking of leading a good life is not political but personal and familial. The role of political society is supportive, and in extreme cases corrective and preventive; it is never to be the main agent of a person's moral living.

The Second Vatican Council's reasoning about religious liberty suggests some of the implications of this conception of the common good and political authority in respect to moral pluralism. Religious pluralism to be sure is distinct from moral pluralism, but the two phenomena are plainly related. The reasoning laid out by the council contains not only religious support for a significant liberty of individuals and groups to act in religious matters, but also a strictly moral argument that is labeled natural law reasoning. The heart of this argument is that there are human goods, specifically those of a religious nature, whose proper pursuit requires conscientious personal inquiry, judgment, and choice as well as uncoerced cooperation with others. These demands of the goods themselves exclude legal enforcement not only as counterproductive but also as harmful to those regulated and incompatible with respect for their human rights.[15] Although this important bit of natural law reasoning (which I believe correct not simply because I am a Catholic) by no means determines the entire set of natural law answers to the questions ethical pluralism poses to political society, it makes unmistakable that from this—objectivist and universalist— moral perspective there are morally important and humanly significant goods whose value is not definable independently of personal judgment and commitment. The fundamental commitments of people as members of the religious, ideological, ethnic, and other communities that are so central to our conception of ethical pluralism seem to be goods of this kind. These deep convictions, therefore, are not simply to be tolerated by political communities; they are to be respected as central to the business of moral life into which political society should not directly enter. So, even if political society is required to control some actions following from a group's way of life, it must be within this respectful context.

To sum up: those guided by a natural law conception of morality and its precepts have much to add to the discussion of how political societies should seek to regulate moral pluralism. The very universalism that makes natural law initially seem so unfriendly to moral pluralism provides a basis for discussion and rational argument across the boundaries of ethically disagreeing individuals and communities that is not readily available to those holding for purely local conceptions of moral knowledge and practice. Moreover, the recent developments and applications of analytical categories by which natural law theories have sought to understand and direct social life suggest reasons for restraint and caution in using the instruments of governmental power and the law directly to support even correct moral deliverances of practical reason. That said, natural law judgments on such issues as abortion and euthanasia are likely to remain part of public controversy; the natural law view is that in many respects these and related issues involve matters of justice, clearly within the responsibility of political society.

NOTES

1. I hold the version of Catholic natural law theory, which Haldane dubs "naturalistic objectivism" and rejects. My overall interpretation of natural law as a broad normative and metaethical approach focuses more on biblical and Stoic roots than does Haldane's Aristotelianism. On this account Kant's moral theory can be seen as part of a broader moral tradition that includes some biblical and rabbinic sources and reasoning, Saint Paul and Cicero as well as Saint Thomas Aquinas and the Catholic theorizing he started. For this construal of natural law and his idea of "common morality," see Alan Donagan, *The Theory of Morality* (Chicago: University of Chicago Press, 1977), pp. 1–31.

2. The classic text of Aquinas's dealing with the natural law account of moral diversity and disagreement is *Summa Theologiae*, 1–2, q. 94, a. 4, which Haldane correctly highlights. The question Aquinas addresses here is whether the natural law is the same for all. It is formulated against the background of his claims that fundamental principles are known to all without argumentation. He addresses two questions: whether the moral truth is variable and whether people's moral awareness is variable. To both questions he gives a qualifiedly affirmative response, but one consistent with universal awareness of moral principle. Aquinas's position on variations in moral awareness attributes it to "bad custom." Aquinas's position on property is that it is not a matter of natural law but human decision; see 2–2, q. 66, a. 2. I take this to mean not that there are no natural moral principles underlying property but that the details of property arrangements include reasonable discretion for social choice.

3. See Aquinas, *Summa Theologiae*, 1–2, q. 100, a. 2: "Certain judgments are such as to require a great consideration of diverse circumstances, the consideration of which is not for everybody but only for the wise; just as the consideration of the detailed conclusions of science does not belong to everybody but only to scientists [*philosophos*]."

4. For some development of these points, see my "Natural Law and the Ethics of Traditions," in R. George, ed., *Natural Law Theory: Contemporary Essays* (Oxford: Oxford University Press, 1992), pp. 23–25, and "Aquinas, Kant and Donagan on Moral Principles," *New Scholasticism* 58, 4 (1984): 391–408.

5. Michael Walzer, *Just and Unjust Wars* (New York: Basic Books, 1977), pp. xii–xvi.

6. See my "*Just and Unjust Wars*: Casuistry and the Boundaries of the Moral World," *Ethics and International Affairs* 11 (1997): 83–98.

7. Aquinas devoted a large volume, the second part of the ethical treatise in his *Summa Theologiae*, to detailing the complex normative picture of individual and social life that he inherited from canonists, theologians, and Greek philosophy. These norms are plainly meant to be related to, and in some way derived from, the general ethical considerations in the first part of his ethical treatise, which contains his famous treatment of civil and natural law. But the connection is neither tight nor explicit. Because ethics composes the second part of the *Summa Theologiae*, the first part of the second part, dealing with ethical theory, is distinguished in references from the second part of the second part, which deals with precepts.

8. See *Summa Theologiae*, 1–2 q. 100, a. 3, body of the article and ad 1 (reply to the first objection), for a classic Thomistic statement of the primacy of the love commands and of the role in moral reasoning in this and other "primary and common" precepts. The twofold love commandment has obvious similarities to other prescriptions thought to be fundamental in moral life, most notably, to several of Kant's formulations of the categorical imperative: actions respecting rational nature as an end in itself surely express something of the love of neighbor that Aquinas thought implied in the precepts of the decalogue. Kant's kingdom of ends seems a secularized version of the human community shaped by compliance with the love commandments.

9. See *Summa Theologiae*, 1–2, q. 94, a. 2; for commentary, see John Finnis, *Aquinas: Moral, Political and Legal Theory* (Oxford: Oxford University Press, 1999), pp. 79–102.

10. See Finnis, *Aquinas*, pp. 111–17.

11. The preceding paragraphs are my own analytical reconstruction of the natural law account of the common good and common action. My distinction between common goods and common goals is tacit in the tradition. For the reasons given, it is essential to the story. For the basis of the distinction, see Germain Grisez, Joseph Boyle, and John Finnis, "Practical, Moral Truth and Ultimate Ends," *American Journal of Jurisprudence* 32 (1987): 103–5.

12. The classic exposition of the natural law conception of authority is Yves Simon, *Philosophy of Democratic Government* (Chicago: University of Chicago Press, 1966), pp. 1–71; see also John Finnis, *Natural Law and Natural Rights*, (Oxford: Oxford University Press, 1980), pp. 231–59.

13. See Finnis, *Aquinas*, pp. 219–54, for a discussion of the relevant Thomistic texts and a refutation of the widely held view that Aquinas held for an unlimited and all-encompassing view of the political common good.

14. This view of the common good of political society is often associated with the political philosophy of Jacques Maritain. See *The Person and the Common Good*, trans. John J. Fitzgerald (Notre Dame, Ind.: University of Notre Dame Press, 1966), pp. 49–89 (which includes the quotation with which Haldane ends). My formulation is adapted from that of Vatican Council II, Decree on the Church and the Modern World (*Gaudium et spes*, paragraph 26). For commentary, see Germain Grisez, *The Way of the Lord Jesus*, vol. 2: *Living a Christian Life* (Quincy, Il.: Franciscan Press, 1993), pp. 846–51.

15. This text is important enough to quote in full. It is most of paragraph 3 of *Dignitatis humanae*, The Declaration on Religious Freedom, in Walter Abbott, ed., *The Documents of Vatican II* (New York: Herder, 1966), pp. 690–91 (in the context of Catholic teaching the references to the divine law, conscience, and "every man," label this reasoning as a natural law argument):

> Man has been made by God to participate in this law (the divine law), with the result that, under the gentle disposition of divine providence, he can come to perceive ever increasingly the unchanging truth. Hence every man has the duty, and therefore the right, to seek the truth in matters religious, in order that he may with prudence form for himself right and true judgments of conscience with use of all suitable means. Truth, however, is to be sought after in a manner proper to the dignity of the human person and his social nature. The inquiry is to be free, carried on with the aid of teaching or instruction, communication and dialogue. In the course of these men explain to one another the truth they have discovered, in order to assist one another in the quest for truth. Moreover as the truth is discovered, it is by personal assent that men are to adhere to it.
>
> On his part man perceives and acknowledges the imperatives of the divine law through conscience. In all his activity a man is bound to follow his conscience faithfully, in order that he may come to God, for whom he was created. It follows that he is not to be forced to act in a manner contrary to

his conscience. Nor on the other hand is he to be restrained from acting in accordance with his conscience, especially in matters religious.

For of its very nature, the exercise of religion consists before all else in those internal, voluntary, and free acts whereby man sets the course of his life towards God. No merely human power can either command or prohibit acts of this kind.

However, the social nature of man itself requires that he should give external expression to his internal acts of religion; that he should participate with others in matters religious; that he should profess his religion in community. Injury, therefore, is done to the human person and to the very order established by God for human life, if the free exercise of religion is denied in society when the just requirements of public order do not so require.

There is a further consideration. The religious acts whereby men in private and in public and out of a sense of personal conviction, direct their lives to God transcend by their very nature the order of terrestrial and temporal affairs. Government, therefore, ought indeed to take account of the religious life of the people and show it favor, since the function of government is to provide for the common welfare. However, it would clearly transgress the limits set to its power were it to presume to direct or inhibit acts that are religious.

PART IV

Confucian Attitudes toward Ethical Pluralism

Joseph Chan

THE CONFUCIAN TRADITION

As a tradition of thought, Confucianism began life in China more than 2,500 years ago. Although its core ideas can be traced back to the teachings of Confucius (551–479 B.C.E.), this tradition was never thought to be wholly created by Confucius himself. In fact, the original Chinese term of Confucianism, *ru-jia*, makes no reference at all to Confucius. It rather refers to a school of *ru*, "a type of man who is cultural, moral, and responsible for religious rites, and hence religious."[1] Confucius himself stressed that he was not an inventor of any radically new vision of ethics or ideal society, but only a transmitter of the old tradition—the rites and social values developed in the early Zhou dynasty (traditionally, mid-eleventh century to 256 B.C.E.). Nevertheless, it was Confucius who most creatively interpreted the tradition he had inherited, gave it a new meaning at a time when it became stifling, and expounded it so effectively that his views have influenced a great number of generations of *ru* to come. *The Analects*, a record of his ideas and teaching compiled primarily by his disciples and later scholars, is the most fundamental text in the Confucian tradition. However, Confucius handed down no systematic philosophy, nor is *The Analects* a treatise on ethics. *The Analects* left a number of basic questions undeveloped, such as those about human nature, the metaphysical grounds of ethics, and the proper organization of the state. It was Mencius (approx. 379–28 B.C.E.) and Xunzi (approx. 340–245 B.C.E.) who filled in the details more systematically and developed the tradition into new, and different, directions. The thoughts of these three thinkers together constitute the classical tradition of Confucianism.

Confucianism has continued to evolve ever since its inception, in part as a response to the political needs of the time (as in Han Confucianism), and in part to the challenges of other schools of thought (as in Song-Ming Confucianism). Han Confucianism had made Confucian ethics and politics rigid and hierarchical, placing the father and ruler at the center of absolute power in the family and polity respectively. Song-Ming Confucianism, on the contrary, turned its inquiry inward into the human mind in order to meet the challenges of Buddhism, and constructed robust theories of the inner life of human individuals. No matter what innovations were made in these later developments, however, classical Confucianism, especially the Mencius strand, has been recognized as the canon of the tradition, something that later thinkers claimed only to appreciate, vindicate, and enrich, and this was exactly the kind of moderate claim made by Confucius himself regarding his attitude toward the tradition before him. In this sense, a deep respect for tradition—thinking that it was the sages in the past who had got things right—has always been a salient mark of Confucianism.

But what are the core ideas in Confucianism? And how much influence has it had? Most simply put, Confucianism holds that people should cultivate their minds and virtues through lifelong learning and participation in rituals; they should treat their family members according to the norms of filial piety and fatherly love, respect the superiors and rulers, and show a graded concern and care for all; learned intellectuals above all others should devote themselves in politics and education to promote the Way and help build the good society. Even this brief characterization enables us to see that the Confucian vision of human life has fundamentally shaped the Chinese culture and the basic structure of society in the past 2,000 years or so. Its vision, however, has extended far beyond the Chinese borders and has penetrated deeply into its neighboring countries. Today, those East Asian societies that have been influenced by Confucian culture, namely, Korea, Japan, Singapore, Taiwan, Hong Kong, and mainland China, have undergone modernization and are exposed to the powerful forces of global capitalism, which have eroded their Confucian cultural traditions to a considerable extent. But Confucian values such as the importance of the family, the respect for learning and education, and the emphasis on order and harmony remain significant in these societies.

CONFUCIAN ETHICS: STRUCTURE AND SUBSTANCE

The Perfectionist Structure of Confucianism

Like such other major ancient traditions as the thoughts of Plato and Aristotle, Confucianism contains profound reflections on ethics, society, and politics. These ancient traditions of thought developed conceptions of the good life, the good society, and ideal politics. Although these conceptions differ importantly in their substantive content, their structural features are strikingly similar. They are what I would call perfectionist theories of ethics, society, and politics. On ethics, these traditions of thought base ethical judgments about values, virtues, and norms—or, in short, conceptions of the good life—on their understandings of human nature or principles of nature (I call this ethical perfectionism). On society, these theories regard social groups as important sites where people develop ethical capacities and skills necessary for the good life (social perfectionism). On politics, these theories hold the view that one of the major aims of the state is to help people pursue the good life by means of law, education, provision of resources, and coordination of social groups and their activities (political perfectionism).

The issues that this book addresses concern the proper role of society and the state in dealing with disagreements over ethical judgments. The views of Confucianism on this set of issues are determined in part by its substantive content and in part by its structure as a perfectionist theory. The substantive content of Confucianism will be discussed in detail shortly. Here we can briefly lay out the typical responses of perfectionist theories, of which Confucianism is an instance, to this set of issues. As a theory of ethical perfectionism, Confucianism is inclined to view ethical disagreements as something regrettable, or something that is a result of human errors that can be overcome through proper ethical or rational training. As a theory of social and political perfectionism, Confucianism is inclined to suggest that disagreements should be removed as much as possible, and that the state should be led by the wise and the ethically better informed so as to resolve those conflicts and equip people with appropriate mental and ethical capacities.

This perfectionist perspective has a certain attractiveness but it also faces serious challenges posed by the conditions of modern society, which John Rawls calls "reasonable pluralism." There are at least two challenges to perfectionist theories. First, the legitimacy of a perfectionist state would seem to be undermined if it promotes a conception of the good life that can be reasonably disputed by people who do not hold that conception. Second, even if the conception of the good life is correct and beyond reasonable doubt, there is a danger for a perfectionist state to paternalistically or moralistically impose its favored conception on people who fail to see its correctness. What ideas within perfectionism can prevent a perfectionist state from sliding into authoritarian rule? These two challenges are hard questions for Confucianism, because, first, it does not have the modern notion of personal autonomy to counter state paternalism or moralism,[2] and, second, its conceptions of the good life and ideal society have become increasing problematic in modern society. These difficult questions cannot be adequately dealt with here. Rather the main aim of this chapter is primarily descriptive and reconstructive. I describe traditional Confucian conceptions of the good society and the good life, and see what attitudes Confucians may hold toward ethical disagreements and social regulation.[3] Through this analysis we can begin to understand the difficulties confronting contemporary scholars who try to develop a new Confucian perspective relevant to the needs and aspirations of people in modern society.

The Substantive Content of Confucian Ethics

We need first to describe the substantive content of Confucian ethics before examining the question of ethical uniformity or pluralism in society. In doing this, it is important to bear in mind the historical character of Confucianism.[4] As said in the previous section, Confucius basically inherited the order of rites and social values developed in the early Zhou dynasty. What, then, are the core aspects of Zhou's system of rites that Confucius had inherited? The central core of the system of rites in Zhou was a system of relationships of differentiated roles and duties. The central principle as summarized in the *Book of Rituals* is: respect and obey those who are in a superior social position (the emperor and the noble lords); show filial piety to one's parents; show respect to the elderly in one's family; and maintain the distinction between men and women. The *Book of Rituals* says that, whereas many social conventions and norms can and should change, these basic principles of human relationship should never change.

These principles were endorsed by Confucius, as well as by Mencius, Xunzi, and the later generations of Confucians. The *Book of Rituals* recorded a conversation between Confucius and the duke of Lu. The duke asked, Why do gentlemen give high regard to rites? Confucius replied that rites are the basis of human life. Without rites, we have no directives to guide us in religious ceremony; without rites we would not be able to differentiate between the ruler and the minister, the superior and inferior, old and young, man and women, father and son, and elder brother and younger brother; and without rites we would not be able to determine the intimate and the distant in social interaction.[5] Confucius thus accepted the basic social order developed in Zhou. For him, there was nothing wrong with this system of rites. Equally, the political institutions and laws developed on the basis of this system of rites were basically sound. Yet, the once prosperous and stable Zhou dynasty could not escape the fate of decline and was disintegrating into several states that were under constant threats of internal power struggles and external aggression. Confucius's reflection on the problems of social and political disorder led him to conclude that the root of the problems was the weakening of rites and ethical norms because powerful feudal lords were generally unwilling to be bounded by rites—people, especially those in power, became self-centered, arrogant, undisciplined, and corrupted.[6] His solution is therefore to revitalize Zhou's system of rites, by giving it a new ethical foundation, by showing its attractiveness to common people and the elite alike, and by arguing that a return to this system was the key to order and harmony in society. In his attempt to solve the problem, Confucius advocated an ingenious conception of rites, which treats rites as not merely external rules constraining people's behavior and distributing powers and duties, but essentially as a necessary part of a conception of an ideal moral person—the man of *ren*, an inner requirement of morality founded in humanity. Rites are based on and required by a deeper ethical foundation, *ren*.

The moral ideal for each individual is the attainment of *ren*—the highest and most perfect virtue. *Ren* is a human quality, an expression of humanity. It can be manifested in different virtues, from personal reflection and critical examination of one's life to respect, concern, and care for others. On the personal dimension of *ren*, Confucius says, "to return to the observance of the rites through overcoming the self constitutes *ren*."[7] On the interpersonal dimension, he says that *ren* is to "love your fellow men [*ai ren*]."[8] In dealing with others, the ideal of *ren* requires us to practice the art of *shu*, an ethics of sympathy and reciprocity, which can be expressed positively or negatively. Positively, it tells us to seek to establish and enlarge others insofar as we seek also to establish and enlarge ourselves.[9] Negatively, it tells us not to impose on others what we ourselves do not desire.[10] In another place, Confucius says that the method of *ren* is the ability to understand sympathetically the needs of others in light of the needs of oneself as a human being. "Now the man of [*ren*], wishing to be established himself, seeks also to establish others; wishing to be enlarged himself, he seeks also to enlarge others. To be able to judge *of others* by what is nigh *in ourselves*; —this may be called the [method of *ren*]."[11]

These attitudes and qualities of self-examination, sympathetic understanding, and caring for others are essential to the spirit and vitality of rites. Confucius says, "What can a man do with the rites who is not benevolent? What can a man do with music who is not benevolent?"[12] Rites in Confucius's time stressed the hierarchy of social relationships and the differentiation of roles and duties according to one's status in those relationships. Without the spirit of *ren*, these aspects may easily lead to, at best, mechanical observance of rules without a humanistic concern for others or, at worst, selfish domination of the stronger party over the weaker one. *Ren* thus serves to instill a strong humanistic spirit into rites, providing an ethics of sympathy, reciprocity, and care into an otherwise essentially hierarchical system of social relationships. In more concrete terms, the superior party in a hierarchical relationship should always show concern to the inferior. For example, the ruler should show benevolence to the people, the father should show fatherly love to the son, and the husband should show respect to the wife.[13] Harmony is easier to achieve in a relationship in which *ren* is the guiding spirit.

On the other hand, it is important to note that to Confucius *ren* is still expressed through the system of rites, which differentiates human relationships into varying degrees of intimacy and varying degrees of inequality of status. The ideal of love expressed by *ren* is constituted by reference to rites, and this makes love a graded concern for others rather than a pure impartial concern for all. While one's love can be extended to anyone in the world, one's parents and other family members should always have a priority in one's love for others. In the same vein, the ideal of harmony is meant to coexist side by side with hierarchy. The son is expected to show filial piety to his parents, and the people are to respect and be loyal to the emperor. *Ren* not only harmonizes the rites but makes them more pervasive and stable. In short, they complement and restrain each other at the same time. The marriage of *ren* and rites helps contain an unequal relationship in harmony; it also helps people practice the ethics of benevolence to everyone without failing to give special respect and concern to those in special relationships.

THE CONFUCIAN CONCEPTION OF IDEAL SOCIETY: STRONG EMPHASIS ON UNIFORMITY

The Importance of Uniformity

Confucian ethics was a response to the disintegration of the Zhou's polity and the decline of its rites. The solution of Confucius, as discussed earlier, was to revive the rites by founding them on a deeper ethical ideal of *ren*. Confucius and Mencius believe in the powerful effect of rites based on *ren*. If men learn to cultivate *ren* and follow rites, there will be social and political stability and harmony.

> It is rare for a man who has the virtues of filial piety [*xiao*] and brotherhood [*ti*] to have the inclination to be rebellious against his superior.[14]

> Mencius said, "If only everyone loved his parents and treated his elders with deference, the world would be at peace."[15]

Adherence to *ren* and rites by members of a community is essential to the stability and harmony of that community. For Confucius, however (and on this matter for Mencius and Xunzi as well), it is those in the political establishment who have a specially strong duty to practice *ren* and rituals. If they can behave according to *ren*, these classical masters believe, they will practice a kind of benevolent politics that puts people's well-being in first priority, attract voluntary submission of the ruled, motivate people to follow the way and practice *ren*, and achieve a well-ordered society with harmonious social relationships.

In order to help people to cultivate *ren* and to understand clearly and to follow the norms in accordance with their roles in social relationships,

Confucius proposes that people should adhere to a commonly shared set of names and vocabularies that have significant social functions. This is the famous doctrine of "rectification of names." Uniformity in naming and in understanding the ethical meaning of names is indispensable to the harmony of society.

> Duke Jing of Qu: asked Confucius about government. Confucius answered, "Let the ruler be a ruler, the subject a subject, the father a father, the son a son."[16]

> Zilu said, "If the Lord of Wei left the administration of his state to you, what would you put first?" The Master said, "If something has to be put first, it is, perhaps, the rectification of names. . . . When names are not correct, what is said will not sound reasonable; when what is said does not sound reasonable, affairs will not culminate in success; when affairs do not culminate in success, rites and music will not flourish; when rites and music do not flourish, punishments will not fit the crimes; when punishments do not fit the crimes, the common people will not know where to put hand and foot."[17]

These passages suggest that essential to an ideal society is a high degree of uniformity, or shared social consensus, in the naming of social roles and positions, the specification of the responsibilities that fall upon the people occupying these roles and positions, and the identification of the appropriate norms according to which others should treat the people in those roles and positions. In this sense, the Confucian social ideal aims for ethical uniformity. Failing to rectify names, and failing to set up clearly a set of ethical standards about roles and responsibilities for people to follow, would result in mistaken judgments and wrongful actions, leading ultimately to nothing but moral and social disorder.

How rigid and exhaustive is this ideal of ethical uniformity? To what extent does it allow different or conflicting ethical judgments? The answer depends on how rigid or flexible are the contents of *ren* and rites that define the basic structure of society. This is an important issue, for it determines directly the Confucian position on the further question of what kinds of ethical disagreement are acceptable and what are not.

The central core of rites that define the appropriate duties and norms of conduct are stated in very similar ways by the classical Confucian thinkers.

> Confucius: Let the ruler be a ruler, the subject a subject, the father a father, the son a son.[18]

> Mencius: Love between father and son, duty between ruler and subject, distinction between husband and wife, precedence of the old over the young, and faith between friends.[19]

Xunzi: The relationships between lord and minister, father and son, older and younger brothers, husband and wife, begin as they end and end as they begin, share with Heaven and Earth the same organizing principle, and endure in the same form through all eternity.[20]

These relationships, and the accompanying principles governing them, then, constitute the core substance of rites. They are supposed to be unchanging, for the Way or the Principle of Heaven and Earth, upon which these relationships are based, never changes. They are not only moral principles but also social and political. The spirit of these principles is to make distinctions between different social roles and positions and, with the guidance of *ren*, to maintain a hierarchical system of human relationships in the spirit of reciprocity and harmony. Unlike the liberal conception of society and politics, Confucianism sees no separation between public and private morality. The rites at once govern political, social, familial relationships, with the latter being the most basic foundation of all others. Society and politics are closely knitted together under a single ideal.

Any view that rejects these basic principles of human relationship, or any action that violates them, would be regarded by Confucians as fundamentally wrong. This can be seen by Confucians' rejection of Mohism, which preaches an impartial, universal love of all human beings. Mencius heavily criticized this doctrine as not respecting the special relationship between father and son. It denies filial piety. Mohist doctrine therefore was regarded by Mencius as entirely unacceptable and unreasonable. I shall come back to this debate between Mencius and Mohism. The main aim here, however, is to show that the core substance of *ren* and rites set the moral limits to people's conduct.

Room for Plurality of Judgments and Ethical Disagreements

Insofar as the framework of *ren* and rites remains unchallenged, Confucians are often ready to accept a plurality of diverse or contradicting ethical judgments. Many occasions and circumstances allow for individual moral discretion and choice, and for revision of social norms. Here legitimate differences in ethical judgments or courses of action may arise. In what follows, I mention two types of situation of this kind.

The first concerns the application of rites and the importance of moral discretion. Rites as norms of conduct and virtues sometimes cannot give precise guidance to people when they make concrete moral decisions. There may be novel situations, borderline cases, and hard cases (where some rites are in conflict with each other) that call for interpretive judgment and moral discretion. As a result, Confucians often emphasize the importance of discretion (*quan*),[21] flexibility (*wu gu*),[22] and timeliness (*shi*)[23] in making moral decisions in particular circumstances.[24] These are important qualities that a gentleman ought to develop, and Confucius was praised for being timely in action, instead of stubborn and inflexible:

> There are four things the Master refused to have anything to do with: he refused to entertain conjectures or insist on certainty; he refused to be inflexible or to be egotistical.[25]

> Confucius was the sage whose actions were timely.[26]

If after careful and conscientious deliberation, two persons equipped with *ren* come up with two different or contradictory judgments and courses of action, Confucians would tell us to respect both of the judgments.

> The Master said, "How straight Shi Yu is! When the Way prevails in the state he is as straight as an arrow, yet when the Way falls into disuse in the state he is still as straight as an arrow. How gentlemanly Qu Boyu is! When the Way prevails in the state he takes office, but when the Way falls into disuse in the state he allows himself to be furled and put away safely."[27]

This is an example in which two men find themselves in similar circumstances (living in an unjust state) but take contradictory courses of action (one chooses to pursue the Way in politics and the other withdraws from it), yet Confucius respects and praises both of them and their chosen course of actions.[28]

The second type of situation concerns revision and selective use of rites. While endorsing the basic system of Zhou's rites, Confucius did not dogmatically believe that all rites as norms of proper conduct cannot change. Although the essence of filial piety or respect for the superior are constant, ways of expressing these norms may change. For instance, the essence of filial piety consists in caring for and supporting one's parents and respecting them, but the concrete ways of expressing caring and respect may change (Confucius protested against the extravagant burial practices of the age). Second, some rites may seem inappropriate when judged with a deeper ethical perspective or lose their attractiveness in a new circumstance.

> The Master said, "A ceremonial cap of linen is what is prescribed by the rites. Today black silk is used instead. This is more frugal and I follow the majority. To prostrate oneself before ascending the steps is what is prescribed by the rites. Today one does so after having ascended them. This is casual and, though going against the majority, I follow the practice of doing so before ascending."[29]

> The Master said, "Follow the calendar of the Xia, ride in the carriage of the

Yin, and wear the ceremonial cap of the Zhou, but, as for music, adopt the *shao* and the *wu*."[30]

These passages suggest two things about the Confucian attitudes toward rites. First, one should not blindly follow the rites as endorsed by society or the majority. Rather, one should adopt a reflective moral attitude to examine the ethical reason behind a rite and to determine whether that rite is appropriate. Second, a rite can and should change if the circumstance changes. Confucius himself stresses that we should critically learn and select appropriate rites developed in different periods and places.

To conclude, the ideal society in Confucianism is one of a high degree of ethical uniformity. The uniformity is based on the ethical ideal of *ren* and rites, which sets the bounds for morally permissible behavior. However, the application of the ideal of *ren* and rites often requires individual moral judgment and discretion. Also, some rites may change, and should change, if social circumstances change. Confucians would allow a plurality of judgments on concrete interpretation and application of the ideal in situations where the ideal does not have clear, determinate implications.

POLITICAL REGULATION

We should distinguish between ethical disagreements within the bounds of Confucian conceptions of *ren* and rites and those which violate those bounds. The first are family disputes, in which case Confucians would respect a person who exercises his ethical capacities and deliberates carefully but reaches a decision different from that of others. However, for those views which present an ethical perspective seriously at odds with the very core contents of *ren* and rites, Confucians would be inclined to reject them as unreasonable. In the face of fundamental ethical disagreements, it is unlikely that Confucians would say, "while I believe my views are correct, your views are not unreasonable either." For Confucians, when a debate comes down to ethical fundamentals, there is little room for reasonable disagreements. There is no substantial middle ground between, to use Thomas Nagel's words, "what it is unreasonable to believe and what it is unreasonable not to believe."[31]

How would Confucians deal with serious disagreements? Would they invoke the state to ban what they regard as unreasonable views or actions? Here Confucians have two different sets of reasons leading to opposite recommendations. The first set of reasons pushes for governmental banning and is derived from the kind of ethical, social, and political perfectionism that Confucianism endorses. The second set of reasons favors a noncoercive approach, which is derived from the Confucian faith in morality and dislike of the use of coercion. Let me now turn to the first set of reasons.

We have seen that Confucians based their ethical theory on the Way, the Heaven, or human nature. They also seem to be confident that their basic ethical beliefs correctly capture the Way and the principles of the Heaven. The Confucian ethical ideal is to be achieved through transformation of individual moral life and through implementing the basic social relationships in society and politics. The emperor and ministers are expected to behave according to the ethical requirements and to act benevolently and righteously so as to promote the material and ethical well-being of the common people. There is no fundamental separation between the familial, the social, and the political spheres. All parts should be ordered in mutually supportive ways to achieve the ethical ideal. This ideal, if achieved, can at once solve problems of individual morality, social harmony, and political stability.

As a theory of ethical perfectionism, Confucianism would likely treat with great suspicion ethical perspectives that are at odds with the core substance of the Confucian ideal. It tends to see these perspectives as "heresies." As a theory of social perfectionism, Confucianism would be worried about the harmful effects of heresies on social harmony and stability, which are important values in the Confucian scheme. Finally, as a theory of political perfectionism, Confucianism would expect the political rulers to help maintain or restore the Way in the face of heretical challenges.

One telling example of this tendency is Mencius's attitude toward two schools of thought in his time. The egocentric philosophy of Yang Zhu (fourth century B.C.E.) is regarded by Mencius as "denial of one's prince" and the philosophy of Mozi (fourth century B.C.E.), which preaches universal love, is "a denial of one's father." "If the way of Yang and Mo does not subside and the Way of Confucius is not proclaimed, the people will be deceived by heresies and the path of morality will be blocked."[32]

However, from a logical point of view, all this does not necessarily lead to the use of coercion by the state to maintain uniformity and combat heresies. If Confucians believe, as J. S. Mill does, that the best way to combat false doctrines and opinions is by better arguments, then they would not necessarily endorse governmental suppression of speech. In addition, if Confucians believe that the best way to correct ethically wrong actions and promote virtues is by education and socialization, then no coercive punishment would necessarily follow. Do Confucians hold these two views? I believe they do explicitly hold the second but not so clearly the first. This leads to the second set of reasons mentioned earlier.

A Noncoercive Approach

It is well known that Confucians do not favor the use of legal coercion to foster virtues or prevent people from indulging in the bad or debased. The reason for this has to do with the nature of moral life. Confucians reckon that legal punishment cannot change one's heart or soul; only moral education and rites can. As Confucius says, "Guide them by edicts, keep them in line with punishments, and the common people will stay out of trouble but will have no sense of shame. Guide them by virtue, keep them in line with the rites, and they will, besides having a sense of shame, reform themselves."[33] One cannot be compelled by force to be virtuous. To live a genuinely virtuous life, the agent must see the point of that life—he or she must endorse the virtues, be motivated to live by virtues, and enjoy that life. "One who is not benevolent cannot remain long in strained circumstances, nor can he remain long in easy circumstances. *The benevolent man is attracted to benevolence because he feels at home in it.*"[34] The cultivation of virtues is done through education and practice in rites—it is rites, not physical force, that make people feel at home with virtues. This point has significant bearing on personal freedom as absence of coercion. To act virtuously, we must act for the right reason. Avoidance of punishment is not a right reason for virtuous action. The law is thus not a good instrument of moral edification. Anyone recognizing this point would want to limit the scope of criminal law. Neither should punishment be used to prevent the bad from influencing the good, for Confucius thinks that the best method is still moral edification by example, and he urges the rulers to set a good example.

> Lord Ji Kang asked Confucius about government, saying, "Suppose I were to kill the bad to help the good: how about that?" Confucius replied: "You are here to govern; what need is there to kill? If you desire what is good, the people will be good. The moral power of the gentlemen is wind, the moral power of the common man is grass. Under the wind, the grass must bend."[35]

Confucius puts demanding standards of moral behavior on the rulers and gentlemen, not the common people. This is consistent with the general spirit of tolerance in Confucianism—"to set strict standards for oneself, and make allowances for others."[36] Confucian tolerance is not grounded on liberal values like personal independence or sovereignty or any notion of a moral right to wrongdoing. It is grounded on sympathy, on the view that coercion is ineffective in promoting *ren*, and on a particular approach to moral edification.[37]

However, it is important to note the limits of this argument. The argument focuses on the person who is ethically wrong. The idea is that coercion offers little help to his moral life. But if our concern is for people who would be adversely affected by his ethical wrongdoing rather than the wrongdoer himself, then the argument has nothing to reject any suggestion to prevent coercively the wrongdoer from affecting others. For instance, consider a certain type of unethical deed so influential that it subverts the basic structure of a Confucian society. If the use of force is proved to be the best among all options or the least of all evils in preventing this from happening, there seems no fundamental tenet in Confucianism that would prevent it from using coercion.

Having discussed unethical deeds, we now turn to the issue of unethical or heretical thoughts. The Confucian argument against the use of force in suppressing unethical or wrong beliefs is even less explicit than the argument against deeds. Perhaps we can go back to the example of Mencius's criticism of Yang Zhu and Mohism. While Mencius uses very strong words to condemn the two schools of thought, he does not advocate the use of political weapons to ban them. Instead, he says whoever can combat them "with words" is a true disciple of the sages. "I wish to follow in the footsteps of the three sages in rectifying the hearts of men, laying heresies to rest, opposing extreme action, and banishing excessive views. I am not fond of disputation. I have no alternative. Whoever can, *with words*, combat Yang and Mo is a true disciple of the sages."[38] Mencius does not explain why he asks people to combat heresies with words. One possible reason for this is perhaps the view that only through thorough exposition and criticism of those doctrines can doubts and mistaken thinking be completely dispelled; and only by this means can people have a stronger confidence in the Way. Confucians would not object to this Millian reasoning, although we are not sure how far they can go along this line of argument. Confucians do put much stress on the need of moral learning, understanding, and deliberation in the cultivation of virtues. Confucius's education emphasizes not only learning, but also thinking and examining.[39] Similarly, Mencius also underscores the importance of understanding and inquiry in one's moral life.[40] Human life-situations are varied and complex. Confucius asks us to find out the mean and make the best decision in the midst of many half-truths and extreme views. If a person does not have any opportunity to be exposed to contrary views and falsehood, he will not be able to develop the ethical and mental capacities to make the best judgment or hit at the mean in many practical situations of human life. In short, an oppressive environment does not help people to develop the reflective understanding and deliberative capacities essential to a successful moral life.[41]

Nonetheless, this argument shares the same limitation of the argument against using coercion to prevent or punish unethical deeds. The argument is an instrumental one, and both the harmful effects of wrong ethical beliefs and one's critical and ethical capacities admit of degree. If there is a situation where coercion or suppression can prevent a heresy from spreading its harmful effect on people's minds and at the same time only constitutes a slight impediment to the chance for people to develop their mental and ethical capacities, then Confucians would find no principled reason against doing so.

To conclude, we have seen two tendencies of thought in Confucianism. The first tendency is to favor governmental regulation and control of ethical beliefs or deeds that violate the basic bounds of *ren* and rites. This tendency is based on the special nature of Confucian perfectionism that stresses moral uniformity, social harmony, and political stability. Confucianism does not accept a liberal separation of morality into the public and private spheres—the first sphere of morality is enforceable by the state while the second belongs to the business of civil society only. Unlike the antimoralistic and neutralist strands in liberalism, Confucianism regards the ethical content, or the morality or immorality, of an action always as *one* relevant reason for the state to promote or prohibit it. But this reason has to compete with other reasons, which may or may not outweigh the first. These competing reasons come from what I call the second tendency of thought regarding political regulation. The second tendency favors noncoercive means (education and rites) to deal with this problem. It is based on the Confucian beliefs on the proper way to moral cultivation, on the importance of moral thinking and deliberation, and on the ineffective nature of coercion in promoting virtues. It is also based on an approach of moral socialization that puts a much greater moral demand on rulers rather than the common people. While the second tendency always serves to restrain the use of coercion, it does not constitute an absolute restraint. In each particular case, a Confucian would have to weigh the possible consequences and consider all relevant reasons in that case before he makes up his mind on the need for governmental coercion. Xunzi has exactly this advice: "When one sees something desirable, he must consider whether or not it will lead to detestable consequences. When he sees something beneficial, he must carefully consider whether or not it will lead to harmful consequences. All these consequences must be weighed together in any mature plan before one determines which desire or aversion, choice or rejection, is to be preferred."[42] In this spirit the following issues of ethical disagreement will be examined.

CITIZENSHIP

In Confucianism, there are no citizens, only subjects and rulers. Yet subjects do have legitimate *opportunities* that they can reasonably expect from society and *duties* that they are legitimately expected to perform in turn. In this sense we can talk about the status—legitimate opportunities and duties—of women as subjects in society. The status of women in Confucianism is largely discussed in connection with the relationship between husband and wife, which is one of the most important human relationships to be governed by *ren* and rites. Thus the issue of women is part of the core of the Confucian ideal of human relationships. Confucianism would take a clear position on this question and would allow little room for permissible disagreements. Confucianism would require the state to regulate the basic duties and opportunities that women ought to have according to whatever conception of gender relationship it believes to be the ethically correct one.

Like most other parts of the world in ancient times, women in traditional China occupied an inferior status to men. Women were excluded from serving in the government. Female children could not receive education in schools. Women's main roles and responsibilities were domestic. Not only did Confucianism not challenge gender inequality, it implicitly or explicitly endorsed it. Today, we can still see a significant degree of gender inequality in countries like South Korea and Japan over which Confucianism still has a relatively strong hold. However, is there any deep Confucian reason to support its endorsement of the subordination of women? Let me first describe some Confucian positions on the role of women in society, and then examine whether these positions can find strong support from within Confucian ethics.

The Mencius characterizes basic human relationships in the following way: "love between father and son, duty between ruler and subject, *distinction between husband and wife*, order between the elder and the young, faith between friends."[43] "Distinction" (*bie*) is used to describe the husband-and-wife relationship. While the word itself does not say what is to be distinguished, it is generally believed that it refers to the functional distinction between the roles of men and women inside and outside of a family. The common traditional saying that "males are primary in the external, females are primary in the internal" confirms this understanding. Men in the family are expected to take care of external affairs, and women domestic affairs. This, however, does not imply that men have no final control of family affairs. The distinction refers to duties, not authority. The husband is expected to make final decisions on important family matters and to set a good moral example to his wife and children. "The *Book of Odes* says, 'He set an example for his consort, and also for his brother, and so ruled over the family and the state.' "[44] The distinction between internal and external duties is thus primarily meant to limit the involvement of women's activities in the household.

In a recent essay, Chan Sin Yee argues that some implications seem to follow from this division of labor. "First it would imply excluding a woman from serving in the government if her role is merely domestic and she should never speak about the external affairs. This exclusion is an important deprivation for it would lead to the exclusion of women from the ideal of a morally cultivated person, *juinzi*."[45] That these implications do follow seems to be confirmed by both history and textual evidence. As a matter of history in classical China, women were indeed excluded in politics, although there were a few exceptions, particularly the female family members and relatives of emperors. One passage in *The Analects* interestingly shows how Confucius reacted to the case of a woman's participation in government. "Shun had five officials and the Empire was well governed, King Wu said, 'I have ten capable officials.' Confucius commented, 'How true it is that talent is difficult to find! The period of Tang and Yu was rich in talent. With a woman amongst them, there were, in fact, only nine.' "[46] That Confucius casually discounted the woman from the list of talented officials shows his stance that women ought not to take part in government.

It follows from the exclusion of women from serving in the government that they are also excluded from having the opportunity to receive formal school education that prepares people to become gentlemen, *junzi*, whose typical duty is to participate in and contribute to politics. Women had to stay at home and receive whatever education their families could afford or would be willing to provide. Typically, women received a narrower range of knowledge than men, and they were taught the proper rituals and duties for females in the household.[47]

However, the Confucian attitude on the role of women does not fit comfortably with other major elements in Confucian ethics. The first Confucian element that may challenge gender inequality is that females and males are regarded in early Confucianism as being equal in terms of their inborn moral instincts and capacities. Unlike Aristotle, who thinks that women are biologically inferior to men in rational capacities, Mencius is of the view that the most important feature that defines a human being, namely, *ren* as an inborn moral instinct and potentiality to be fully realized, is equally distributed among males and females. The second element is Confucius's famous principle that education should be open to all.[48] He was proud of the fact that, as a teacher, he has never "denied instruction to anyone who, of his own accord, has given [him] so much as a bundle of dried meat as a present."[49] Ironically, Confucius never had a female student. Perhaps he was never approached by any woman for education, given the prevailing norm in his time was that women should receive their special type of education at home. But if there were one woman approaching Confucius for education, it would be difficult for him to refuse her, given the nondiscriminatory ideal of education he advocates.

These two elements combined together will produce some significant implications. Because women have the same moral potentiality as men, if they are given the same education as men, they could equally develop and cultivate the moral capacities as men do that are necessary to political participation. In other words, women can become gentlemen, *junzi*. This leads to the final element that may challenge subordination of women. Confucians hold a meritocratic view of distribution of political offices. Offices ought to be held by people who have appropriate ethical and rational capacities, irrespective of their class background or ethnic origin. The famous competitive examination system for recruiting officials in traditional China was conducted on this meritocratic basis. Now, if women could perform just as well as men in ethical and rational capacities, there seems no Confucian reason to bar them from taking part in the examination except the earlier doctrine of the functional division of labor between men and women. But it is precisely this doctrine that lacks deep Confucian justification. It does not cohere well with the Confucian view of the equal moral nature of human beings, the Confucian ideal of education, and its meritocratic criterion for distribution of political offices.

We may ask, then, why Confucians held strongly to gender inequality? I suspect the real reason is sociological rather than ethical. In a primitive, labor-intensive agricultural economy, the most efficient division of labor in the family is that men work outside to make a living and women stay at home to nourish babies and take care of children and the elderly. A stable set of patriarchal norms and principles is important for the maintenance of this division of labor and power, which in turn is essential to the survival of the family which is the most important economic unit in an agricultural society. Now we live in a modern industrial society where there is no strong sociological ground for the necessity of this division of labor. In fact, contemporary Confucians today typically favor the modern view that women should enjoy the same basic civil and political opportunities as men. I think such a change of attitude can be justified by appealing to the three elements in Confucianism identified here.

LIFE AND-DEATH-DECISIONS

Legalization of assisted suicide is a contemporary issue, which has received no discussion in the traditional Confucian discourse. At the risk of overspeculation, we may try to draw some relevant implications from within the tradition. I believe this issue is one for which we can expect a plurality of views even within the bounds of Confucian ethics.

Confucians value human life, but they put moral life higher than biological life. Suicide is sometimes morally justifiable. In a recent paper, Ping-cheung Lo argues that for Confucians there are two general circumstances in which people can, and sometime should, choose death in order to preserve a higher moral life.[50] First, sometimes one can, or should, sacrifice one's life in order to uphold *ren* and *yi* (righteousness), which are supreme values in the Confucian ethical thought. We have the Confucian teaching of "to die to achieve *ren*" (*sha shen cheng ren*) and of "to lay down one's life for a cause of *yi*" (*she sheng qu yi*). Confucius said, "For Gentlemen of purpose and men of benevolence while it is inconceivable that they should seek to stay alive at the expense of benevolence, it may happen that they have to accept death in order to have benevolence accomplished."[51] One can choose to die for the sake of the country, or to save the lives of one's family members or other people. This is what we may call altruistic suicide. In addition, one can also choose to die for one's self, for the sake of preserving one's honor and dignity. To choose suicide in face of humiliation by one's enemy, or to choose suicide in order to avoid the indignity of being unfairly tried in court, would be met with approval.

However, these two morally justifiable circumstances of suicide do not lend immediate help to the morality of assisted suicide. Let us discuss the case of altruistic assisted suicide first. An aged mother with terminal illness might want to hasten her death in order not to become a heavy burden on her family members. This motivation certainly expresses an attitude of benevolence, and in itself it would not be disapproved by Confucian ethics. However, such a move would be strongly dissented by her family members, especially her children who have a strong and clear moral duty to look after their parents. Any person with a sense of filial piety would not want to endorse a law that allows parents to undergo assisted suicide just for the sake relieving the burden of family members.

How about self-regarding assisted suicide? Again, the proceeding discussion does not lend immediate help. For one thing, Confucianism approves suicide primarily when it serves strong moral causes. In this case, it is the possibility of losing one's *moral* honor or dignity in face of humiliation that justifies suicide. It does not entail the approval of the act of killing oneself when one's life is threatened by terminal illness and intense pain. In addition, Confucianism does not recognize the liberal value of personal autonomy or individual sovereignty, which is often claimed to imply a moral right to terminate one's own life as and when one sees fit. Confucianism would not appeal to any notion of a general moral right to suicide concerning the issue of assisted suicide.

While the above Confucian views on suicide do not give direct support to assisted suicide, there is no clear and strong ground in Confucianism to reject it either. Confucianism values human life, but it is not clear that it entails a negative attitude toward assisted suicide in the case of terminal illness. Some might argue that according to Confucianism a human life has a great value even if it is immobile and full of pain, and even if the dying person does not want to bear with this pain any more. However, some others might argue that for Confucianism, the value of life lies primarily in human activity, in the cultivation of virtues and excellence, and in interacting with others and contributing to the well-being of them.

Thus it is not clear that Confucianism would accept the idea of "sanctity of life" even in a situation where a person can only spend the rest of his life on his deathbed suffering from immense pain. So there seem to be disagreements over the exact meaning and implication of the Confucian view of the value of life regarding the terminally ill. But whatever the interpretations, assisted suicide for the terminally ill does not violate the more basic moral content of *ren* and rites. It does not seem to constitute a violation of *ren* if one chooses to terminate one's life is this situation. Here we seem to have reached the zone of permissible differences. The act of terminating one's own life in the case of terminal illness with great pain is neither required by *ren* nor opposed by it. It lies in the area where different people should be allowed to make different choices.

Moreover, as far as people other than the one suffering from terminal illness are concerned, there is one reason, though not a conclusive one, for them not to oppose assisted suicide. Confucianism emphasizes the importance of compassion and benevolence. If a dying relative or friend of a person requests death in order to avoid the tormenting pain that no palliative treatment can help to relieve, that person, if moved by compassion, would be inclined to agree to assisted suicide. I would even argue that from a Confucian perspective, the person's own controversial interpretation of the Confucian view on the value of life is less important than his duty to show compassion to the suffering of others.

However, one Confucian concern has not been addressed thus far. While Confucians may agree that assisted suicide is morally permissible, they would be concerned about the role of the patient's family in making the ultimate decision concerning assisted suicide. For Confucians, familial relationships are the most important personal or social relationships an individual has and are central to his or her well-being. Members of a family are supposed to care for each other, and to take each other's well-being as part of one's own. This is of course not to suggest that the family should have absolute authority over its members—even the father has no such absolute authority over the son if what the father does violates the bounds of morality. Rather, the point is that in a closely nested Confucian family, one would not think one is the sole sovereign over one's own life or the sole caretaker of one's well-being. How one should live, and die, should be a matter of the entire family's concern. What this means in the case of assisted suicide is that the patient who requests assisted suicide should consult with his or her family members, be sensitive to their feelings and concerns, and try to reach a decision that the family as a whole thinks is the best. Of course, other members of the patient's family are expected to show care and compassion to their dying member, and put the well-being of the latter in first priority. But it would be wrong, from a Confucian point of view, if the other members are left out in the consultation process between the patient and the doctor or in the process in which the medical decision is made.

It seems that this emphasis of family involvement in medical decisions is still very common today in East Asian countries that have a Confucian heritage. One such observation is made by the Japanese medical ethicist Kazumasa Hoshino, who writes:

> Japanese people are not accustomed to making medical decisions regarding their own diseases by themselves without consulting the family. This is because of their deep regard and respect for the opinions and feelings of the family. When one member of the family becomes sick, it is the responsibility of the entire family to look after him . . . The family knows that the care of the sick member is a family matter. In these circumstances, it seems rather natural for the family to first decide on the best medical procedures and to care for him . . . Eventually, decision-making for medical procedures and care for the patient may be done with the mutual consent of both himself and the remaining members of the family.[52]

Ruiping Fan, a Chinese medical ethicist, concurs with this observation and further argues that the practice of family involvement in East Asian societies "has been shaped by the Confucian understanding of the nature of the family and individuals . . . It is a Confucian moral requirement that one should take one's family as an autonomous unit from the rest of society, flourishing or suffering as a whole. Hence the injury, disease or disability of one family member must be taken as a problem of the entire family, and thereby the medical decision should be made by the family as a whole."[53]

To conclude, from a Confucian point of view, the request of a terminally ill person for assisted suicide violates no principles of *ren*, and it belongs to the legitimate sphere of personal choice. Also, compassion and benevolence supply people a reason not to refuse such a request. But Confucians would stress that the family of the patient should be involved in the decision making as to whether the option of assisted suicide ought to be taken up by the patient. Thus far we have only discussed the moral dimension of assisted suicide. There are many consequentialist reasons for and against the legalization of the practice that we should consider but cannot here. Also, the principle of family involvement can create problems in its implementation. What should be done if the family cannot reach a consensus? Should all members of a patient's family, or only some representatives, be involved in the medical consultation and decision? These are taxing questions that require careful consideration, and inevitably there would be reasonable disagreements on what the best policy, all things considered, would be. Confucians would have no firm commitment to the legislation of assisted suicide if these difficult issues are not settled.

Human Sexuality

Early Confucian masters had a positive attitude toward sex. *The Mencius* in particular affirms that human desire for sex is part of human nature. It is not something that we need to despise or repress.[54] The *Book of Rituals* (book 9) also says that appetite and sex are the major desires of human beings. However, "sexual desire" in the traditional Confucian discourse refers to heterosexual desire or sexual attraction between the male and female. There was no explicit discussion on homosexual preferences, and there was no affirmation or condemnation of homosexuality. Homosexuality was not uncommon in traditional China, however. There are historical records of emperors having homosexual relationships with young ministers and mates, and ministers and the upper class having affairs with young men and male prostitutes. The descriptions of these homosexual behaviors were not cast in a negative light. On the other hand, as far as I know, there was no socially approved homosexual marriage or union of any kind in China.

Given the lack of discussion of homosexuality in the Confucian texts, any attempt to find out a "Confucian" attitude on homosexuality is highly speculative. I myself would speculate that while Confucians might regard homosexuality as a kind of deviance, it may not be immoral as such— especially if some people are *born* a with homosexual tendency. Moreover, as explained earlier in this chapter, Confucians generally do not favor the use of coercion in trying to change people's conduct. Hence Confucians would tend not to support criminalization of homosexual behavior. However, if the focus of discussion is on homosexual marriage, I believe Confucians would find it harder to accept, for the following reasons. Confucians regard heterosexual union as natural, reflecting the order of nature. Classical Confucian texts all share the belief that the sexual union of man and woman gives life to all things, just as the constant intermingling of the Heaven and Earth gives shape to all things. The *Yi-Jing* regards the male (*Yang*) and female (*Yin*) as complimentary parts of a natural whole. Mencius says that "a man and woman living together is the most important of human relationships."[55] The union of man and woman is not only natural but has the socially important function of procreation. It makes possible other human relationships. The *Book of Rituals* says that without marriage there will be no father and son, nor emperor and minister.[56] This leads to the next point about the social importance of (heterosexual) marriage.

Confucians in the classical time understood marriage not simply as a private business between a man and woman, but between two families. A man marries a woman not for his own sake alone but for his family's sake. In the words of the *Book of Rituals*, marriage has to do with serving one's family and ancestors and continuing the family line by procreation.[57] Marriage is not the creation of a new family but an expansion and continuation of the husband's. (Family is also understood to be made up of heterosexual union with a view to procreation.) Marriage is thus intimately linked to filial duties. One of the main duties of filial piety is to produce children so as to continue the family tree. Having no heir is regarded as the worst way of being a "bad son."[58] A filial son is expected to get married and produce children. The two acts go together in filial piety.

This traditional Confucian understanding of marriage and family still to a certain extent shapes the values of the Chinese in Hong Kong and mainland China, to give just two examples. According to the findings of a recent research that interviewed gays in Hong Kong, many gays told the same story that when they disclosed their sexual orientation to their parents, what their parents worried and were upset about the most was that their gay sons would not get married and produce children. This was especially true when the son was the only offspring in the family.[59] Similarly, in Mainland China the problem with homosexuality is not mainly in the sexual activity itself but with its inconsistency with the family relationships that are at the heart of social structure in China. There are now a fair number of people in China who have gay and lesbian relationships; but most of them feel an overwhelming pressure to enter into a heterosexual marriage that produces children. Sometimes they continue their homosexual relationships while being married; but usually they have to give them up (with much pain and sorrow) at the point of being married.[60]

If we use this traditional understanding of marriage and family as a criterion to assess homosexual marriage, then it is clear that Confucians would not recognize it as a legitimate form of marriage, for it violates the very basic meaning and function of marriage as understood by Confucians. However, some might argue that such a traditional Confucian perspective of marriage faces serious challenges from the changing norms and expectations of marriage in modern society. Wouldn't this traditional perspective lead us to reject not only homosexual union but those heterosexual couples who get married on the basis of mutual affection and romantic love, who do not want to procreate, and who intend to form a nuclear family independent of the parents' families? As the number of heterosexual couples holding these attitudes is steadily increasing in China and other East Asian societies, wouldn't Confucians today condemn these heterosexual couples and take away their right to marry as well?

These questions raise a serious problem about the contemporary relevance of the traditional Confucian conception of marriage and family. This conception would alienate a great number of people, heterosexual

and homosexual alike. If a contemporary version of Confucianism is prepared to revise its conception of marriage so as to accept the decision of
married couples not to procreate, then why can't it also allow homosexual
marriage? However, if its new conception of marriage allows homosexual
marriage, what is so specifically Confucian about this conception? I raise
these questions not in order to answer them, but only to show the difficulty of searching for a social and political perspective that is attractive
to modern men and women and yet sufficiently connected with traditional
Confucianism to be worthy of the name "Confucian."

NOTES

I would like to thank Daniel A. Bell, Richard Madsen, Peter Nosco, Tracy
Strong, and Lee Yearley for helpful comments.

1. Tang Chun-I, *Essays on Chinese Philosophy and Culture* (Taipei: Students
Book Co. Ltd, 1988), p. 362.

2. However, as I argued elsewhere, there is a conception of moral autonomy
that supports to a certain extent civil and personal liberties understood as absence
of coercion. But beyond a certain point it lends no further support to them. Confucianism requires the modern notion of personal autonomy to give a stronger
justification for liberties. For detailed arguments for this view, see my "Moral
Autonomy, Liberties, and Confucianism" (unpublished manuscript 1999). I thank
Lee Yearley for drawing my attention to the notion of moral autonomy in Confucianism.

3. This process requires, as Lee Yearley suggested to me, both elaboration and
emendation of the Confucian tradition. Needless to say, the interpretation, elaboration, and even emendation given in this chapter are controversial.

4. My description of Confucianism is based on classical Confucian texts, as
they form the most important basis of the Confucian tradition. The texts that I
use are mainly *Confucius: The Analects*, trans. D. C. Lau (London: Penguin
Books, 1979), and *Mencius*, trans. D. C. Lau (London: Penguin 1970), although
I also occasionally refer to *Xunzi: A Translation and Study of the Complete Works*
Vol. 2: *The Book of Rituals*, trans. J. Knoblock (Stanford: Stanford University
Press, 1990)—reference to this is from the original Chinese text; an English trans-
lation can be found in *Li Ching: Book of Rites*, trans. James Legge (New York:
University Books, 1967).

5. *The Book of Rituals*, book 27: 1.

6. Ibid.

7. *The Analects*, book XII: 1

8. Ibid., book XII: 22.

9. Ibid., book VI: 30.

10. Ibid., book XII: 2, book XV: 24.

11. Ibid., book VI: 30. This translation is taken from "Confucian Analects,"
trans. James Legge, in his *The Chinese Classics, vol. 1.* (Hong Kong: Hong Kong
University Press, 1960), p. 194.

12. *The Analects*, Book III: 3.

13. On the notion that the husband should respect the wife, see *The Book of Rituals*, book, 27.

14. *The Analects*, book I: 2. See also, 2: 21.

15. *Mencius*, Book IV: 12.

16. *The Analects*, book XII: 11.

17. Ibid., book XIII: 3.

18. Ibid., book XII: 11.

19. *Mencius*, book III, part A: 4.

20. *Xunzi*, book IX: 15.

21. *The Analects*, book IX: 30.

22. Ibid., book IX: 4.

23. *Mencius*, book V, part B: 1.

24. For a good discussion on this point, see A. S. Cua, *Moral Vision and Tradition: Essays in Chinese Ethics* (Washington, D.C.: Catholic University of America Press, 1998), p. 257.

25. *The Analects*, book IX:4, see also XVIII: 8

26. *Mencius*, book V, part B: 1.

27. *The Analects*, book XV: 7.

28. For a similar view, see *Mencius*, book II, part A: 2.

29. *The Analects*, book IX: 3.

30. Ibid., book XV: 11.

31. Thomas Nagel, *Equality and Partiality* (New York: Oxford University Press, 1991), p. 161.

32. *Mencius*, book III B: 9; see also book II A: 2.

33. *The Analects*, book II: 3.

34. Ibid., book IV: 2, (italics added).

35. Ibid., book XII: 19, translation from S. Leys , *The Analects of Confucius* (New York: W. W. Norton, 1997).

36. Ibid., book XV: 15.

37. The above discussion draws on my "A Confucian Perspective on Human Rights for Contemporary China," in Joanne R. Bauer and Daniel A. Bell, eds., *The East Asian Challenge for Human Rights* (Cambridge: Cambridge University Press, 1999), pp. 232–33.

38. *Mencius*, Book III, Part B: 9 (italics added).

39. See *The Analects*, books II: 15, XIX: 6, VII: 8, and IX: 8.

40. *Mencius*, book VII, part A: 5.

41. For a more detailed discussion of this point, see my "Moral Autonomy, Liberties, and Confucianism."

42. *Xunzi* book III; translation is taken from Cua, *Moral Vision and Tradition: Essays in Chinese Ethics*, p. 260.

43. *Mencius*, book III, part A: 4; (emphasis added).

44. *Mencius*, book I, part A: 7.

45. See Chan Sin Yee, "Gender and Relationship Roles in Confucius and Mencius," (unpublished manuscript, 1998), pp. 8–9. The analysis of the early Confucian views on gender inequality here is heavily indebted to this essay.

46. *The Analects*, book VIII: 20.

47. See Wm. Theodore de Bary, *Asian Values and Human Rights: A Confucian Communitarian Perspective* (Cambridge, Mass.: Harvard University Press, 1998), Chap. 7.

48. *The Analects*, book XV: 39.

49. Ibid., book VII: 7

50. Ping-cheung Lo, "Confucian Views on Suicide," Occasional Paper Series, (Centre for Applied Ethics, Hong Kong Baptist University, 1997). At the end the paper draws out some implications of the Confucian views on suicide regarding the issue of assisted suicide. The following discussion on suicide is indebted to this paper, although I draw a different conclusion on assisted suicide.

51. *The Analects*, book XV: 9; see also *Mencius*, book VI, part A: 10.

52. Kazumasa Hoshino, "Bioethics in the Light of Japanese Sentiments," in Kazumasa Hoshino, ed., *Japanese and Western Bioethics* (Dordrecht: Kluwer Academic Publishers, 1996), pp. 16–17. This quote is taken from Ruiping Fan, "Self-determination vs. Family-Determination: Two Incommensurable Prinicples of Autonomy," *Bioethics* 11 (1997): 316. The point of view developed in this and the last paragraph is indebted to Fan's article.

53. Fan, "Self-Determination vs. Family-Determination," p. 317.

54. *Mencius*, book VI, part A: 4 and book V, part A: 1.

55. Ibid., book V, part A: 2.

56. Book 44: Rites of marriage: 3.

57. Book 44: 1.

58. *Mencius*, book IV, part A: 26.

59. S. Y. Ho, "Politicising Identity: Decriminalisation of Homosexuality and the Emergence of Gay Identity in Hong Kong" (Ph.D. thesis, University of Essex, United Kingdom, 1997).

60. See Robert B. Geyer, "In Love and Gay," in Perry Link, Richard P. Madsen, Paul G. Pickowicz, eds., *Popular China: Unofficial Culture in a Globalizing Society* (Boulder, Colo.: Rowman and Littlefield, 2002). I thank Richard Madsen for drawing attention to this paper.

Two Strands of Confucianism

Lee H. Yearley

Professor Chan's essay is rich, clear, appropriately critical, and (when warranted) appropriately appreciative. I aim in what follows only to sketch out a few separable but related comments that may aid our understanding of his essay and the important issues he treats. My comments are made, then, in what I take to be the spirit of a comment from *The Analects* of Confucius on the subject of who can be taught: "If I give out one corner and they don't come back with the other three corners, then I don't go on."

Let me begin with a methodological point—or, put in a less stuffy way, a point about approaches to topics like the ones Professor Chan considers. Those who are allergic to methodological inquiry may wish to skip to my next point. But I take the time to present these ideas because I believe they are relevant not only to the essay but also to the larger enterprise of the book of which it is a part.

I have found helpful a distinction between two kinds of development that occur when we ask new or different questions of a tradition: elaboration and emendation. Both draw on the results of modern scholarship and reflection, and although they need to be delineated for the sake of clarity, they often relate very closely. Elaboration utilizes modern historical and textual scholarship to understand the language and context of texts, and it is especially important with ideas that appear in forms that either make them easily misunderstood or allow their challenge to be easily overlooked. Emendation utilizes modern theoretical analyses and formulations to clarify, test, and reformulate the ideas the texts present, and it involves complex decisions about what is and is not fundamental to the tradition. The examples Professor Chan treats obviously exemplify this process. But much of his essay necessarily is also involved in it (which he graciously acknowledges), as when he quite properly asks at various places both what has been characteristic of the tradition and what resources it may have to meet new challenges.

A word more on these two processes. Elaboration can either be a benign scholarly activity close to philology or be so close to emendation as to be virtually indistinguishable from it. Simple elaboration is, however, often needed to penetrate the density of traditions as alien from most of us as is Confucianism and thereby to bridge, if not always diminish, their distance from us. An example is the Confucian version of the basic Chinese conception of *wu-wei*, often translated as "inaction" and said to refer either to an action unguided by thought or to a kind of passive withdrawal. In fact, however, the conception refers to a complex picture of what human agency can be, one that is as far from passivity as it is from feckless spontaneity.

The actual process of emendation is a complicated and, at times, dangerous, activity. Emendation, that is, might so change the original that a disinterested observer could well wonder what role the traditional text played. The text can seem only a device to jog the interpreter's reflections or, worse, to give him or her an authority he or she otherwise would not have. The dangers here are serious and involve substantial decisions. For example, is the apparent denial of many powers to woman in classical Confucianism a distortion of the fundamental position or a basic implication of it? Throughout the process, then, we need to remain alert to the possibility that in some cases no genuine emendation is possible. When this occurs, we face ideas that have their attractions but are finally unacceptable.

The processes operating here involve us in dealing constantly with two demands that initially may appear to be incompatible or even only to generate conflict—what I call the demands of being both credible and appropriate. To meet the demand of being credible is to formulate Confucian ideas about ethical pluralism in a way that is credible to (meets the conditions of plausibility found in) our common contemporary experience, informed as that experience is by modern scientific explanations, historical consciousness, and ideas about the rights of all humans. To meet the demands of appropriateness is to formulate those Confucian ideas in a way that is appropriate to, shows appreciative fidelity toward, their meaning as judged by the most basic norms found in the tradition. Meeting both demands a kind of balancing act, and it may in some cases— such as ethical pluralism—not be possible.

The distinctions noted here (especially perhaps the warnings about emendation) inform my second point, which I will frankly describe as an exaggeration in the direction of truth. I would argue there are two major strands in the Confucian tradition (although elements of each strand appear in many Confucian thinkers), and the distinctions between them are important for us because they can lead to very different postures on issues about ethical pluralism. The most influential and sophisticated proponents of the respective strands are Xunzi and Mencius, and I use those two thinkers as labels for each strand.

The differences between the two strands can be stated in terms of the cosmogonies that underlie them, the role past sages play in them, and the distinctive moral emphases they produce. In the Mencius strand, Heaven gives each person a nature, and therefore anyone can become a sage, a fully flourishing, benevolent person. In the Xunzi strand, past sages best understood Heaven's plans and provided highly differentiated social forms that need to be followed if humans are to be perfected. In the former the sages are grammarians of human nature; in the latter they are legislators to human beings. In the former virtues like benevolence and righteousness are highlighted. In the latter virtues like ritual (*li*) and loyalty are highlighted.

It is fair to say, I think, that in much of the Confucian tradition (and Professor Chan's essay reflects this) the Xunzi strand has been more prominent, and therefore notions of, for example, hierarchical rules and ritual have been dominant. (In one of those complex ironies that traditions often exhibit, the intellectual and governmental elite expressed a commitment to Mencius—as they understood him—even though their practice often more closely followed the strand represented by Xunzi.) The Mencius strand has also been present, however, and when it is in ascendancy, notions of discretion, such as those Professor Chan notes, are highlighted and tensions between righteousness or benevolence and ritual are pronounced.

With both strands but especially with what became the dominant form of the Mencius strand, metaphysical commitments underlie their respective positions. It may be that any perfectionist picture (and Professor Chan rightly characterizes Confucianism as perfectionist) has such commitments, but these two strands surely do. The commitments are, however, quite different in form, importance, and possible contemporary viability. Each strand, of course, might be emended in order to fit into a pluralist frame. But the emendations needed, and the difficulties involved in making the emendations, take very different forms depending on which strand is being treated.

Put telegraphically, the Xunzi strand has a development model, and the later form of the Mencius strand, which I call a Neo-Confucian model, has a discovery model. (The distinction also reflects a temporal dimension—that is, between Confucianism before it encountered Buddhism and after it encountered Buddhism.) In a developmental model, a common model in many traditions, human nature has an innate constitution that manifests itself in processes of growth and culminates in specifiable forms. That fulfillment occurs, however, only if the organism is both uninjured and properly nurtured. The basic conceptual model is, then, relatively simple and it draws on a biological framework. A basic set of capacities exist and their unhindered, nurtured development generates qualities that lead to specifiable actions or characteristic forms. Those, in turn, provide the standard that allows observers to determine a being's nature and to judge whether any specific action represents its nature in normal, exemplary, or defective fashion. In such a model, processes of cultivation, social and individual, are absolutely crucial.

In a discovery model, in contrast, human nature exists as a permanent set of dispositions that are obscured but that can be contacted or discovered. People do not cultivate inchoate capacities through appropriate social forms. Rather they discover a hidden ontological reality that defines them, whatever may be the reigning social forms. The two models differ, then, both in the character of the ontological ideas they rely on and also in the ways in which their notions of human perfection depend on those ideas.

The ideas of perfection in a discovery model are much more deeply embedded in specific ontological ideas than are the ideas of perfection in a developmental model; Neo-Confucian ideas fundamentally rely on, that is, a distinctive metaphysical picture. The level of embedding is important because I think it is very difficult to defend, to make plausible, a Neo-Confucian ontology and the discovery model it manifests. Most directly relevant here, I also think it is considerably more difficult to imagine a discovery model generating a lively notion of pluralism. Difficult but not impossible I should add: the issue is structurally similar to what is involved in generating notions of pluralism from certain kinds of theistic or Platonic pictures.

Allow me to end by briefly commenting on two other points in Professor Chan's essay. First, a prominent motif at several points is the role of "good argument" in the Confucian tradition. I would suggest that one feature of this subject is important not simply for the Confucian tradition but for the more general issue of ethical pluralism.

I would like to distinguish the persuasively presented from the "well argued" when ethical inquiry is the subject, and to suggest that the Confucian tradition has usually emphasized the former—and has had very good reasons to do so. (Indeed, many Confucian texts are excellent instances of reasoned attempts to doubt the value, when the subject is ethics, of many kinds of reasoned arguments.) "Persuasively presented" is a considerably wider category than is "well argued," and examining it necessarily involves us in the treatment of issues about the character of rhetoric and those subjects that follow in its wake. Confucians recognize, for example, just how dangerous rhetoric can be and yet they also attempt, both in their interpretive theory and in their practice, to display how rhetorical language presents realities that can be made evident or compelling in no other way

Most important to us, perhaps, is the question of how well a focus on persuasive presentation can fit with pluralistic ideals. That question spawns various other ones, and to most of them Confucianism has given detailed if controversial responses. A practical one, for example, concerns who is to control those institutions that can teach rhetoric and disseminate persuasively presented ideas. A theoretical one concerns what exactly is implied by the central Confucian claim that most forms of ethical presentation are not the shadowgraphs of ideas: that is, that the language we use is not the mere adornment of an idea but is constitutive of the idea, is not just a device to persuade the recalcitrant or intellectually inept but is what makes possible any appropriation of an ethical position.

My second and final point concerns the issue of the place of autonomy inside the Confucian tradition, an issue Professor Chan quite rightly focuses on at points and also has treated in other work. Our disagreement may be slight, especially given different possible meanings for the notion of "autonomy" and our agreement that a modern Western sense of autonomy is not present in traditional Confucianism. I do think, however, that a distinctive sense of autonomy is present (especially in the Mencian strand of Confucianism) and discussing how it could fit into a pluralistic view might be productive.

Crucial inside much of the Confucian tradition is the distinction between semblances of virtue and virtue. Semblances of virtue generate activities that resemble the activities of real virtue but lack important elements in it, and the notion appears in a central Confucian notion, the idea of the village honest person (*xiangyuan*). Such people are called the thief, not the epitome of virtue because their apparently virtuous actions arise from an imperfectly virtuous character. Such people do a virtuous act not for itself but for consequences that a nonvirtuous people would desire. Or they choose it not for their own reasons but because of some second-hand support such as custom, unexamined authority, or the inertia provided by accepted, routine reactions.

My suggestion, then, is that we may find in Confucianism a sense of autonomy that, although different from a modern Western one, is both full-blooded and worth considering for its pluralistic implications. It may, for example, rest on the notion that truly fine human behavior has not only acquisitive but also expressive motives. That is, especially laudable people choose a virtuous action not only because it contributes to goods they want to acquire but also because it expresses their conception of the good.

PART V

Islam and Ethical Pluralism

Dale F. Eickelman

The Qur'an offers a distinctly modern perspective on the role of Islam as a force for tolerance and mutual recognition in a multiethnic, multicommunity world: "To each among you, We have ordained a law and assigned a path. Had God pleased, he could have made you one nation, but His will is to test you by what He has given you; so compete in goodness" (5:48).[1] Other verses reinforce the concepts and practices of tolerating religious difference: "Had your Lord willed, He would have made mankind one nation: but they will not cease differing" (11:118). Another reads: "O mankind! We created you from a male and a female and made you into nations and tribes, that you may know one another" (49: 13).

The contextual interpretations of these verses are multiple, but in contemporary Muslim discussion and debate, the point of departure is increasingly the Qur'an itself and not the many layers of scholarly interpretation that have accumulated over the centuries. It would be incorrect to say that there is a single, dominant view among Muslims concerning religious and ethical pluralism. As Khalid Masud argues in the next essay, modern Muslims proclaim with pride that there is no "church" in Islam, no prevalent "official" or "authoritative" view. He writes that there have always been several moral traditions in Islam, some of which—as in other religious traditions—are more tolerant and open to alternative ethical positions.[2] As part of this use of reason, however, many Muslim voices call for return to understanding the Qur'an and Prophetic tradition in their historical context. For example, Sohail Hashmi argues that Muslims must "disentangle Islamic ethics from medieval Islamic law" and treat the Qur'an as "a complete ethical system" in order to elaborate new principles for Muslim participation in international society.[3]

Had this chapter been completed entirely prior to the events of 11 September 2001, its main theme would have been that increasing levels of education, greater ease of travel, and the rise of new communications media are rapidly developing a public sphere in Muslim-majority societies in which large numbers of people—and not just an educated, political, and economic elite—want a say in religion, governance, and public issues. The consequent fragmentation of religious and political authority challenges authoritarianism. This can lead to more open societies, just as globalization has been accompanied by such developments as Vatican II and secular transnational human rights movements. These movements show the positive side of globalization, in which small but determined transnational groups work toward goals seen to improve the human condition. The leaders of such movements, including religious interpreters, sometimes lack theological and philosophical sophistication. They can, however, motivate a minority and persuade a wider public of the justice of their cause, changing implicit, practical understandings of ethical issues in the process.

There is, however, a darker side to globalization: the fragmentation of authority, and the growing ability of large numbers of people to participate in wider spheres of religious and political debates and practical action. This darker side is epitomized by Osama bin Laden and the al-Qa'ida terrorist movement. The movement is not noted for its theoretical sophistication. In quality of thought, Bin Laden and his associates, such as the Egyptian physician Ayman al-Zawahiri, are no match for Thomas Hobbes or Martin Heidegger. They have, however, demonstrated a public relations genius that, combined with massive and dramatic terrorist acts, have caught the world by surprise.

As James Piscatori argues, the Bin Laden/al-Qa'ida view of world politics is powerfully timeless—appealing to unity and faith regardless of a balance of power against them, attributing the evils of this world to Christians and Jews, and to "Muslims" who associate with them and thus pervert the goals of the *umma*, the worldwide community of true believers. Does not the Qur'an say that polytheists should be fought until they cease to exist (Q. 9:5) and that those who do not rule by God's law are unbelievers and, by implication, should be resisted (Q. 5:44)?[4]

These interpretations of scripture are highly contestable. Only a tiny but lethal minority has been inspired to action by such interpretations. As Piscatori explains, the "theology" of this group is basically an update of that of the Egyptian Islamic Jihad group, best known for its assassination of Anwar al-Sadat. Some elements of its message, including that of injustices perpetrated against the worldwide Islamic community—in Palestine, Chechnya, Kashmir, and elsewhere—capture the imagination of wider numbers of people, although their accord with some elements of the al-Qa'ida view of world politics and repression by state authorities does not get translated into action.

This essay highlights the circumstances and potential of voices and practices in the Muslim world that contribute to more open societies and religious interpretations. We must accept that there will always be ideas available to justify intolerance and violence, and there will also always be ways for terrorists to manipulate open societies for their own nefarious ends. Countering radical ideologies and theologies of violence is not easy. Yet the proliferation of voices arguing in open debate about the role of Islam in the modern world and in contemporary society contributes significantly to defusing terrorist appeals. Because the advocates of ethical pluralism are less well known outside of the Muslim world than, for instance, the views of Solidarity activists in Poland or the advocates of liberation theology, this essay is focused on them. Even if challenged by much less tolerant views from what is sometimes called the "street," the courage of those who advocate toleration, or who practice it without articulating their views in public, merits more attention than it has received to date.

Islam's "Remarkably Modern" Origins

Writing in the 1960s, sociologist Robert Bellah argued that Islam in its seventh-century origins was for its time and place "remarkably modern . . . in the high degree of commitment, involvement, and participation expected from the rank-and-file members of the community."[5] Its leadership positions were open, and divine revelation emphasized equality among believers. Bellah argues that the restraints that kept the early Muslim community from "wholly exemplifying" these principles of modernity underscore the modernity of the basic message of Qur'anic Islam, exhorting its initial audience in seventh-century Arabia to break through the "stagnant localisms" of tribe and kinship.[6] Indeed, Bellah argues that "the effort of modern Muslims to depict the early community as the very type of equalitarian participant nationalism is by no means entirely an unhistorical ideological fabrication."[7]

Of course, these "stagnant localisms" offered powerful resistance to the Qur'anic vision of community in the seventh century. Another often-cited Qur'anic verse emphasizes that there is "no compulsion in religion. Whoever . . . believes in God has grasped a firm handhold of the truth that will never break" (2:256). Other verses nonetheless appear to justify coercion and severe punishment for apostates, renegades, and unbelievers who break their agreement with the prophet Muhammad (e.g., 4:89, 9:1–16).

Some commentators conclude that such coercion is specific to the context of the early Islamic community and grounded in "emergency conditions." In this view, coercion was needed to emphasize such "basic moral requirements" as keeping promises and treaties, and protecting a community's "basic welfare and security against aggression."[8] The overall emphasis is on voluntary consent to the will of God, "which is prompted by the universal guidance that is engraved upon the human heart." The Qur'an advises even the Prophet Muhammad to show tolerance toward his opponents: "If it had been your Lord's will, they would all have believed, all who are on earth. Would you [O Muhammad] then compel mankind against their will to believe?" (10:99).[9]

More specifically, as Fazlur Rahman argues, the prophet Muhammad "recognized without a moment of hesitation that Abraham, Moses, Jesus, and other Old and New Testament religious personalities had been genuine prophets like himself." Their different messages, coming to different peoples and nations at different times, were "universal and identical."[10] Indeed, Muhammad is made to say in the Qur'an, "I believe in whatever book God may have revealed" (42:15), because "God's guidance is universal and not restricted to any nation or nations."[11] The idea of "book" (*kitab*), as Rahman points out, is a generic term in the Qur'an, "denoting the totality of divine revelations."[12]

WHAT HAPPENED IN HISTORY

The modern era has accelerated the intensity and pace of interaction among believers in different religious traditions. However, as the preceding Qur'anic verses indicate, intense awareness of and interaction with other faiths have been present in the Islamic tradition from its inception and are not characteristics unique to the modern era. For much of Islamic history, Muslim societies have been remarkably open to the outside world, incorporating through bricolage many preexisting and coexisting elements. Indeed, the vast expanse of the Muslim world inevitably meant that it came to encompass a variety of civilizational and cultural forms. By the tenth and eleventh centuries, the Muslim-majority world showed a remarkable variety of institutional forms from North Africa to South Asia, up to and including the hinterland of the Chinese empire, and soon thereafter emerged as a dominant force in Southeast Asia.[13] Likewise, the Mediterranean, far from being a barrier between civilizations in the early modern era, facilitated sharpened awareness of differences and similarities among both Muslim and non-Muslim "others." As Masud points out, the Islamic tradition incorporated many pre-Islamic tribal values. The "literary moral tradition" called *adab*, to which he refers, derives its ethical values from multiple sources, both Muslim and non-Muslim. The same is the case for philosophy and the Sufi moral tradition. Even legal ethics (*fiqh*), incorrectly (in Masud's view) excoriated by some Islamic modernists as rigid and fixed, developed out of multiple customary legal traditions. Even before the advent of the modern state, Muslim jurists resisted the efforts of political rulers to reduce this pluralism, regarding it as an attack on their freedom to interpret. Moreover, most jurists were acutely aware that local customary laws continued to prevail in rural and tribal areas, even non-Muslim laws in the case of Mughal India and parts of the Ottoman empire.

Pluralism was also encouraged by the fact that the boundaries of the Muslim world were not sharply delineated. It was not only the boundaries between the Mediterranean Muslim world that were fluid and indistinct but also those of other areas of the Muslim world. In India, the great Mughal ruler Akbar (1542–1605) ruled over Muslims, Christians, Jains, Sikhs, Parsees, Jews, and others. It was only by the end of the sixteenth century that the intellectual and material conditions for a symbolic duality between the West and the Muslim "Orient" began to take hold. It reached full form by the seventeenth and eighteenth centuries, when it conveyed the idea that the Muslim world was "distinct" from Europe and the West. Even after this period, however, an awareness of the "other" continued to be available to the elites and many ordinary people of the Muslim-majority world, from Indonesia to the Maghrib.[14]

Contrary to the tolerance and awareness of other religions set forth in the Qur'an, the record of Muslim attitudes in history toward other religions and different interpretations of Islam is as uneven as that of the followers of other religious traditions. A nadir of intolerance within the Muslim community was the inquisition (*mihna*) of 833–848. In its fifteen years, four successive caliphs supported the views of some jurists that the Qur'an was created, in spite of intensely held popular support for the traditionalist view that the Qur'an had always existed. This authoritarian imposition of doctrine through state violence and torture met fierce resistance, and the effort was abandoned after 848. A lasting result of this episode, however, was that later caliphs and other temporal rulers intervened only with caution in religious disputes.

Muslim awareness of the other was not always neutral and tolerant, but neither was it unremittingly hostile. Indeed, when the Christian rulers of the Iberian Peninsula broke the treaties they earlier signed allowing freedom of worship, expelling the Jews from Spain in 1492 and in Portugal ordering their forced conversion to Christianity in 1497, the majority took refuge in Morocco and the other North African principalities.[15] Likewise Morocco's Muhammad V protected Jews of Moroccan nationality during World War II from the threat of deportation by the Vichy French. Jews with French nationality had no such protection.[16]

The basis for openness to different religious interpretations within the Muslim tradition and for other religious traditions antedates European modernity. In Andalusia, for example, the jurist Abu Ishaq al-Shatibi (d. 1388) advocated the centrality of human reason for interpreting Islamic law and applying it to specific social, economic, and political contexts.[17] Such a formulation recognized the possibility of multiple and co-existing interpretations. In India, Akbar the Great developed Islamic institutions but also advocated the "cult of reason" (*rah-i 'aql*), insisting on open dialogue and free choice among religions.[18] At one point he even sponsored a universalistic cult called "Divine Religion" (*Din-i Ilahi*), with himself as master of a religious order synthesizing Islam and Hinduism.[19] Indian villagers often fused Hindu and Muslim religious practices, but Akbar used reason to represent himself as a ruler whose government and values transcended specific religious traditions. He deliberately set about creating an empire in which the followers of various religions could coexist. Akbar argued that "morality can be guided by critical reason" and that "we must not make reasoning subordinate to religious command."[20]

The historical antecedents for tolerance and the use of reason to achieve it facilitate understanding Islam in history and how Muslims interpret, accommodate, and explain differences in religious belief and practice. The historical experience of al-Shatibi in jurisprudence and Akbar the Great in governance also indicate that the multiple paths to "modernity" do not necessarily depend on replicating or emulating the European historical experience. The modernization theories of the mid-twentieth century assumed that "the cultural program of modernity as it developed in modern Europe and the basic institutional constellations that emerged there would ultimately take over in all modernizing and modern societies."[21] A concomitant of this assumption was that religion had no place in the "modern" public sphere. In the words of philosopher Richard Rorty, outside of circles of believers, it usually functions as a "conversation stopper."[22]

Rorty's observation reminds us that any discussion of religion and tolerance involves three dimensions: tolerance within the various currents of a religious tradition, tolerance among religions, and the tolerance of religion itself.[23] As Masud notes, sectarian violence in Pakistan, and religious and ethnic violence in Indonesia, Kosovo, Bosnia, northern Nigeria, the southern Sudan, and Northern Ireland are only some of the more obvious indications that religiously based intolerance persists. The so-called headscarf dispute in France in 1989, mirroring the unease of the Turkish republic with religion in the public sphere, suggests intolerance for the public expression of some religious identities.[24] Indeed, the intolerance of some of Turkey's secular elite for any form of public religious expression serves as a reminder that elements of the secular tradition can be highly intolerant.

There are significant antecedents for religious tolerance and for the use of reason to interpret religious traditions in the premodern era, and in the next chapter Masud persuasively sets out the evidence, sometimes ignored by Islamic modernists themselves, that supports this view. However, the trend over the past two centuries has been for a heightened awareness of religious difference. It is seen both in how intellectuals talk about religious belief and practice and in the ordinary, taken-for-granted language by which we perceive the world. It was only in the early nineteenth century that the notion of "religions" to reflect different religious systems came into common use in English, with a parallel development taking place in other languages, including Arabic. The naming of specific "religions"—such as Hinduism, Buddhism, and Taoism—came into common currency only by the 1840s.[25] This was also when the idea of "religion" as separate from other aspects of life—in other words a de facto secularization—became general.

CONTEMPORARY UNDERSTANDINGS

In the Muslim world, as elsewhere, the spread of printing in vernacular Muslim languages in the nineteenth century accelerated the process of large numbers of people thinking of their religion as one set apart from other traditions in doctrine and practice.[26] Since the mid-nineteenth century, with the dramatic rise in mass higher education, the greater ease and rapidity of travel, and the proliferation of means of communication enabled large numbers of people to raise questions such as "What is my religion?" "Why is it important to my life?" and "How do my beliefs guide my conduct?" This interest in such basic, abstract questions of doctrine and faith by large numbers of people, as opposed to a small elite, is new. The result, at least for the Muslim world, has not been a homogenization of faith but rather an intensified, multipolar struggle over people's imaginations—over the symbols and principles of "Islam." Many different voices assert that they speak for "Islam," and not all these voices offer a vision of tolerance and mutual understanding, either among Muslims themselves or between Islam and other religious traditions.

Some contemporary Muslim intellectuals argue that Islam offers a timeless precedent of "peace, harmony, hope, justice, and tolerance, not only for the Muslims but also for the whole of mankind," and that tolerance is a problem only for "those who belong to other than the Islamic faith."[27] Others, such as Masud, shift between sociologically and historically aware perspectives of the social and political contexts in which ethical ideas are shaped, reformulated, and practiced. As he writes in the following chapter, "pluralism derives its legitimacy and acceptance by justifying universal values in local contexts. Ethical pluralism [in Islam] is thus a concept that is constantly negotiated between universal and local ethical values." Or, as an Arabian peninsula intellectual argues, the notion of *shura* (consultation), the Qur'anic equivalent to democracy, expands and develops over time and remains incomplete. He makes an explicit analogy with the American democratic experience—an analogy certainly not part of the standard analogies of an earlier era. The essentials of the American democratic experience, he argues, were expressed at the founding of the republic, but the principles of equality and of voting rights were elaborated and expanded over time and continue to develop to this day.[28]

Similarly, Islamic concepts of conduct are subject to elaboration and expansion over time. As Robert Wuthnow argues, all religious traditions have a "problem of articulation."[29] If their ideas and practices do not articulate closely enough to their social settings, "they are likely to be regarded by their potential audiences of which these settings are composed as irrelevant, unrealistic, artificial, and overly abstract." But if they "articulate too closely with the specific social environment in which they are produced, they are likely to be thought of as esoteric, parochial, time bound, and fail to attract a wider and more lasting audience."[30]

Any system of ethics acquires legitimacy as supposedly "timeless" moral presuppositions interact with, and are interpreted by, specific moral experience. Charles Taylor refers to the background understandings of person, authority, and responsibility on the basis of which explicit systems of beliefs and practices are formulated as the "social imaginary."[31] In ideology, Islamic law (the *shari'a*—a concept much wider than legislated jurisprudence) is eternal and enduring. In practice, however, it is the Muslim world's equivalent of the social imaginary. Even judges in contemporary Saudi Arabia practice a de facto, if not a de jure, form of case law, even as they deny that they do so.[32] Likewise, most Muslims assume that their accepted local practices are part of the shari'a.

Even when Islamic thinkers advocate a separation of Islamic thought and practice from other traditions, including European colonialism and economic domination, they encourage the elaboration of habits of thought and practice that facilitate introducing new elements and practices. Thus activist thinkers such as Sayyid Qutb (1906–1966) wrote of Islam as a "system" or "program" (*minhaj*), an open, manifest, and clear system of thought and practice that could be distinguished from other systems of belief, including nonreligious ones. For Qutb, as for other activists, it is not sufficient simply to "be" Muslim and to follow Muslim practices. One must reflect upon Islam and articulate it. When activists declare that they are engaged in the "Islamization" of their society, the sense of thinking of religious beliefs as an objective system becomes explicit. Such thinking is increasingly reflected at the popular level by the proliferation of catechism-like "new" Islamic books, the printed sermons and audio cassettes of popular preachers, and books "proving" the compatibility of modern science and medicine with the Qur'an.[33]

A Religious Movement in Turkey

Turkey is an especially pivotal Muslim-majority country because it is where debates about secularism and modernity, and Islam and the West, have become most public and spirited. A salient indication of the ways in which the pervasive trend toward the systematization of belief and practice and the advocacy of conscious reflection on faith can be used to pave the way to a greater openness toward other religious traditions is Turkey's Nurculuk movement. It began in Turkey in the early twentieth century and today has followers in Germany, California, Central Asia, and elsewhere. The teachings of its founder, Bediüzzaman Said Nursi (1873–1960)—originally written and passed on by hand because of government hostility in republican Turkey—have been collected in pamphlets with titles such as *The Miracles of Muhammad, Belief in Man,* and *Resurrection in the Hereafter.*[34] These pamphlets have "the function of explaining, in accordance with the understanding of the age, the truths of the Qur'an."[35] Nursi insisted that books, not people, "have waged a battle against unbelief."[36]

Nursi stressed the importance of direct contact with texts and encouraged his followers to adopt his own approach, which emphasized exploring multiple combinations of knowledge, including those outside the Islamic tradition. In 1910 a policeman in Tiflis, asking Nursi about his plans for building a religious school, said that it was hopeless to envision a unity of the "broken up and fragmented" Muslim world. Nursi replied: "They have gone to study. It is like this: India is an able son of Islam; it is studying in the high school of the British. Egypt is a clever son of Islam; it is taking lessons in the British school for civil servants. Caucasia and Turkestan are two valiant sons of Islam; they are training in the Russian war academy. And so on."[37] In 1911, a half century before the Second Vatican Council urged Christians and Muslims to resolve their differences and move beyond the conflicts of the past, Nursi advocated such a dialogue, and his successors have taken significant steps to engage in interfaith discussions.[38]

Another element in Nursi's writing sets him apart from earlier religious intellectuals such as Muhammad 'Abduh (1849–1905) and Jamal al-Din al-Afghani (1838/9–1897). As much as these two predecessors appealed to the learned classes throughout the Muslim world and sought to popularize their message, their primary audience remained the educated, urban cadres. They, like other religious modernists, distanced themselves from popular belief and rhetorical styles. Nursi, in contrast, never lost his rural roots and often employed the metaphors and imagery of Turkey's rural population.

Although familiar with the structure and content of modern scientific knowledge, Nursi recognized the value of fable and metaphor in shaping his message. His use of them facilitated understandings of his message in different social and historical contexts. Thus in the early part of Nursi's career, his writings and messages were listened to by audiences as they were read aloud, either directly by him to his disciples or by "persons who had already acquired religious prestige." Moreover, in spite of the "official terror and persecution" carried out against those caught reading and teaching books in the old (Arabic) script in the 1920s and 1930s, the practices continued.[39] The *Risale-i Nur*, the collection of Nursi's principal writings, was first disseminated by "thousands" of women and men, young and old, who made copies by hand, and by 1946 or 1947 through the use of duplicating machines.[40] After 1956, when Nursi's books were taken off the banned list and published in modern Turkish, his audience broadened to include those whose primary engagement with the *Risale-i Nur* was through reading it, and not necessarily the face-to-face or hand-to-hand contact of an earlier era.[41]

The *Risale-i Nur* is modern in the sense that its texts encourage reflection on ideas of society and nation. In countries other than Turkey, religious intellectuals also spoke of constitutionalism, justice, and the relation of Islamic belief to modern science, morality, public responsibilities, and the application of faith to public life and spiritual development. Moreover, after 1923 Nursi made a distinctive contribution to the sense of public space. The Syrian translator of Nursi's writings, Saïd Ramadan al-Buti, remarks on the disjunction in Nursi's career between his early political activism and his post-1923 writings and activities. After 1923, Nursi encouraged reasoned reflection and action based on core ethical and religious values without prescribing particular, context-specific political action.[42] Nursi's message, more than that of many of his contemporaries, was accessible not only to religiously oriented educated cadres but also to the less educated, who saw in his message a means of integrating faith with modernity, nationalism, and social revitalization.

The other defining feature of his message, especially in the earlier part of this century, was its success in speaking to the conditions of Turkish society, especially rural Turkish society, when the hold of local leaders was rapidly giving way to an increasingly effective state apparatus, improved communications, and centralization. His message was sufficiently adaptable in structure and content, however, so that it subsequently spoke to the Turkey of later eras and, increasingly, to an international audience. Produced at first in manuscript form and faithfully copied by disciples despite long-standing official prohibitions, Nursi's work is now communicated in multiple languages and publications and through a multilingual website (*www.nesil.com.tr*).

Nursi's style is readily accessible to these multiple audiences, and women are taking an increasingly active role in promoting the message. For some readers, the specifics of Turkish historical development help explain the nuances of certain passages and the context for which they were originally intended. For others, however, the rich metaphors and imagery offer a point of departure for religious understanding that requires only minimal familiarity with the specifics of the times and places in Turkey where the various elements of the *Risale-i Nur* first came into existence.

In the current era, the Nurculuk movement has succeeded in attracting significant followers from all social classes in Turkey. Especially as articulated by one of Nursi's leading contemporary disciples, Fethullah Gülen (b. 1938), Nursi's interpretation of Islamic values offers a union between religion and science, and tradition and modernity, stressing the compatibility of Islamic ideas and practices with Turkish nationalism, education, and the market economy.[43] His followers control a complex web of businesses and significant broadcast and print media in Turkey and in Central Asia. The movement has over 300 schools in Turkey and the countries of the Commonwealth of Independent States, especially Central Asia. Within Turkey, the only religious classes are those prescribed by the Turkish national curriculum. The schools do not explicitly promote a particular interpretation of Islam but rather instill a morality and sense of discipline intended to pervade personal conduct and public life. This teaching advocates a public role for women in society. As Gülen has stated, to the consternation both of conservative Muslims and Turkey's secular elite, the wearing of the headscarf by women is a matter of personal choice. It is not prescribed by faith.

The businessmen, teachers, journalists, students, and others to whom his message appeals stress the combination of knowledge and discipline to empower Muslims and, at least within Turkey, the Turkish state. Less a centralized network than loosely affiliated clusters of organizations, those inspired by Gülen's ideas stress discipline and dialogue.[44] The disciplined use of reason and acquisition of knowledge are stressed within Turkey itself, and are combined with highly publicized and sustained dialogues with Christian and Jewish religious leaders, which stress tolerance, electoral politics, moderation, and participation in a market economy.

In spite of efforts of some elements of Turkey's militantly secularist elite to consider all those who advocate a public role for religious expression as antidemocratic "fundamentalists," most Turks consider Islam an integral part of their social identity. Indeed, the "background" understandings of Islam appear to be on the side of Gülen and others who see Islam as a religion of dialogue, tolerance, and reason. In this respect, rising educational levels, strengthened ties between Turks living in Turkey and in Europe, and the proliferation of media and the means of communication not necessarily mediated by state elites favor these more open interpretations. For example, in 1992, 1993, and 1994, a sample of rural and urban Turks (N–1,363) was asked whether Turkey was "Muslim," "European," or "both"; roughly the same number, 20–21 percent each year, said "European." The number who said that Turkey was primarily Muslim, however, declined from 37 percent in 1992 to 25 percent in 1994, while the number who answered "both" increased from 25 percent to 36 percent.[45] More recently, in a survey conducted by TESEV, a Turkish think tank,

> 97% of those questioned identified themselves as Muslim, 92% said they fasted during the holy month of Ramadan, and 46% claimed to pray five times a day. But 91% also said different religious beliefs should be respected, and clear majorities thought it did not matter if Muslims consumed alcohol, failed to fast or pray or, if they were women, went outside without covering their heads. Only 21% called for an Islamic state, and once the implications were pointed out to them, some were not so sure.[46]

The Turkish experience does not represent the entire Muslim world, but it serves as a reminder of the diversity of the Muslim experience, both among intellectual formulations of Islamic thought and among the practical, implicit shared understandings of large numbers of people.

TOLERANCE TODAY

Many Muslim thinkers interpret the Islamic tradition as enjoining a continuous dialogue over meaning, one that explicitly enjoins tolerance among Muslims and among Muslim and other religious traditions. For example, Morocco's Said Binsaid, speaking out against the intolerance of some Muslim fundamentalists in the early 1990s, wrote that religious radicals, by coercing their opponents into silence, seek to "worship God in ignorance." He argues that a proper understanding of the principles of Islam enjoins dialogue, a willingness to understand the opinions of others, and a disposition toward good relations (*husna*) with them. This dialogue entails adaptation and the continual renewal of religious understandings within a framework of civility.[47] Said Binsaid in Morocco, Syria's Muhammad Shahrur, Turkey's Fethullah Gülen, Iran's Muhammad Khatami, and Indonesia's Nurcholish Madjid are but a few prominent Muslim thinkers who advocate this ongoing "internal" dialogue of reason among Muslims, often paralleled by discussions with both secularists and the followers of other religious faiths.

In a similar vein, Syria's Muhammad Shahrur, whose *The Book and the Qur'an: A Contemporary Interpretation*, became a best seller throughout the Arab world since its publication in 1990, argues for the use of reason in interpreting Islamic doctrine. He advocates religious tolerance both from Qur'anic precedent and "in its spirit."[48] On inheritance laws, for example, which some scholars argue are fixed for all times, Shahrur suggests that the various Qura'nic verses have been interpreted in such a way as to give women lesser shares in most instances. Shahrur argues that jurists in earlier eras reached wrong conclusions based on the limitations of the human knowledge of their time. Using the more sophisticated understandings of mathematics available in the current era, for instance, he argues for new interpretations of Islamic law concerning inheritance.

Such arguments will not win Shahrur friends among most jurists, but legal scholars such as Wael Hallaq state that of all contemporary reformers, Shahrur is the most persuasive.[49] Shahrur also argues that the *hadd* punishments, which include penalties such as stoning and the amputations of limbs for certain offenses, are not prescriptive but rather serve as the "outer limits" permitted by divine law, and which invite modification as societies mature. Indeed, Shahrur's thinking is imbued with the idea of the evolution of human societies. He argues that implicit in Qur'anic thought is the idea that humankind is now beyond prophecy and revelation, and is now prepared to "go it alone" in the spirit of divine precept. Shahrur's solution for the multiplicity of religions is that we are all Muslims— Muslim-Christians, Muslim-Jews, and "believing Muslims" (*al-muslimun al-mu'minun*, those who accept the prophecy of Muhammad), and that all must be treated equally, even atheists and apostates. It is God's responsibility alone to judge human conduct.[50]

Shahrur shares a common feature with many other contemporary Islamic thinkers. Scholars trained in the Islamic religious sciences remain important, but authoritative religious interpretations, once the monopoly of religious scholars who had mastered recognized religious texts, is now replaced by direct and broader access to the printed word. More and more Muslims take it upon themselves to interpret the textual sources— classical or modern—of Islam. Hasan al-Turabi (b. 1930), the Sorbonne-educated leader of the Muslim Brothers in the Sudan and a former attorney-general, forcefully makes this point: "Because all knowledge is divine and religious, a chemist, an engineer, an economist, or a jurist are all *'ulama'*"[51] Turabi implicitly builds on an Islamic tradition that affirms the authority of those who possess religious knowledge (*'ilm*) over the faithful., He expands the idea of valued knowledge, however, to include any scientific endeavor.

The approach to authoritative knowledge articulated by Turabi captures the public imagination throughout the Muslim world. Indeed, the more unfettered broadcast media, such as Qatar's al-Jazeera satellite TV, which has a wide audience throughout the Arab world, finds that its discussion programs dealing with religious issues are highly popular.[52] Such arguments proceed not from traditional jurisprudence, the form used by most *madrasa*-trained clerics, but by expounding directly from the actual Qur'anic text, linking it to contemporary issues and approaches and drawing on many other sources.

Thus powerful arguments can be elaborated from the Qur'an to show how its divine message forms the basis for a complex moral language that encompasses all mankind, not just Muslims. In Shahrur's words, Islam (*islam*, or submission to God) is a covenant "between God and the whole of humanity," and the specifically Islamic faith (*iman*) "is a covenant between God and the believers who specifically follow Muhammad's prophecy."[53] Thus for Shahrur and others, religious and ethical pluralism is divinely approved.

Some Iranians now write of a "post-Islamic" Iran. Iranian anthropologist Fariba Adelkhah, for example, writes that a "religious public sphere" (*espace public confessionel*) has emerged in Iran in which politics and religion are subtly intertwined, and not always in ways anticipated by Iran's established religious leaders. In this post-Islamic society, vigorous and increasingly public debates center on such issues of the role of religious leaders in politics, women in public spaces, and other vital issues influencing daily life.[54]

Qur'anic interpretation and the Islamic tradition can be used to elaborate a notion of civil society and a public sphere in which Islam can play a role, alongside other religious and secular perspectives, free from coercion and guaranteeing individual dignity and personal liberty. The idea of citizenship as a bundle of rights and obligations to the state is firmly incorporated into the social imaginary, even in regions where authoritarianism prevails. Counting Muslims in India (about 200 million, nearly double the number of Muslims in the Arab Middle East) and Indonesia (the most populous Muslim-majority country), many Muslims live under democratic rule. Masud points to a prominent twentieth-century Muslim intellectual, Muhammad Iqbal, who even defined Islam as a civil society. Many Muslims may live under authoritarian rule, but this is not due to any inherent link between Islam and authoritarianism.

The Islamic Republic of Iran, in which elections are assuming increasing significance, suggests the contours of the ongoing dialogue concerning religion and democracy. The substantive clauses of the Iranian constitution display the coexistence of two contrasting notions of sovereignty. Principles 2 and 56 affirm the conventional concept of the absolute sovereignty of Allah, but elsewhere the constitution accommodates the very different idea of popular sovereignty in acknowledging the people's right to determine their own "destiny" (Principle 3:8), and allowing for occasional referenda (Principle 59) and a popularly elected assembly (Principle 62).[55] The constitution of Pakistan shows a similar dual sovereignty, and in many countries, the status of the *shari'a* versus legislated law remains unresolved.

Islam as a moral tradition, as Masud argues, favors ethical pluralism both because it appeals to human reason and because the value of pluralism is widely accepted. The opportunity and scope to apply reason to solving ongoing practical problems, such as human sexuality, decisions over life and death, organ transplants, gender relations, and international relations is uneven. This unevenness is itself an indication of pluralism. Throughout the Muslim-majority world, there is a patchwork of incremental practical decisions that affect issues of tolerance both within and among religious traditions. In Indonesia, for example, legal decisionmaking related to issues of family law and other issues of civil society are no longer confined exclusively to religious jurists.[56] Likewise, there is an overall trend, although not without resistance, for women to play increasingly public roles in society.

Attitudes toward homosexuality and same-sex unions indicate the challenges facing greater openness toward individual choice and responsibility in personal issues. At one level, homosexuality meets with profound religious disapproval, as is also the case in the orthodox Jewish tradition and among many Christians. At another level, however, as Masud points out in the next chapter, there is a long history of de facto tolerance for homosexuality. Only contemporary Turkey has a public tolerance for homosexuality, and hosts an openly gay website. In Europe, however, debates among Muslims over the legitimacy of homosexual life-styles have become increasingly common. In spring 2001 a highly publicized homophobic statement by the Moroccan *imam* of a mosque in Rotterdam, in response to the Dutch legalization of same-sex unions (voted for by all three Muslim members of parliament) set off a national debate over the role of Muslims in Dutch society. It also, however, led to the creation of a support group for gay Muslim youth. States in the Middle East, such as Egypt, are wary of any societies or organizations not under state supervision.

From the perspective of some states, homosexual and women's rights organizations are as much of a threat as human rights groups and nongovernmental organizations that advocate the monitoring of elections.[57] The overall trend toward the fragmentation of religious and political authority favors greater openness and toleration in all spheres of social action. In sexual politics as in other forms of expression, however, the road ahead is uneven and rocky. Some will argue that such practices should not be condoned, but leave judgment to God, not human justice. In some U.S. jurisdictions, laws against sodomy were only removed from statutes in recent years, and only two states allow same-sex unions.

The fact that decisions and debates on issues of personal status are made on a country-by-country basis indicates the absence of a pan-Islamic or doctrinal consensus. Local cultural practices often allow for a spectrum of de facto autonomy on decisions that affect private life, including the expression of sexual orientation.[58] The prevalent practical approach in many societies is "Don't ask, don't tell," but in some respects the lack of open debate on all issues of personal choice can pragmatically allow for a greater liberty by denying extreme conservatives the opportunity to silence minority voices.

The prevailing secularist bias of many theories of society has alternatively marginalized and demonized religious forces and religious intellectuals. The Muslim world has been characterized as especially resistant to "modernity" and intolerant of other religious traditions. Yet the Muslim-majority world is as open as that of any other civilizational domain. We live in a world in which an Islamic leader such as Fethullah Gülen meets popes and patriarchs, advocating diversity and tolerance in the public sphere more than many of those who are secular. Far from compromising the public sphere, religious movements and religious intellectuals in the Muslim majority world can advocate compromise and a mutual agreement to persuade by words rather than by force. Religious intellectuals may claim strong links with the past, but their practice in the present conveys significantly different and more open ideas of person, authority, and responsibility.

NOTES

1. Quotations from the Qur'an are based on Ezzidin al-Hayek, *Approximate Translation of the Meaning of the Qur'an* (Damascus: Dar al-Fikr, 1996).

2. All references to Khalid Masud, unless otherwise noted, are to his essay, "The Scope of Pluralism in Islamic Moral Traditions," in this volume.

3. Sohail H. Hashmi, "Islamic Ethics in International Society," in Sohail H. Hashmi, ed., *Islamic Political Ethics: Civil Society, Pluralism, and Conflict* (Princeton: Princeton University Press, 2002), pp. 148–72.

4. I am grateful to James Piscatori for generously sharing with me an unpublished paper in progress concerning the Bin Laden/al-Qa'ida view of world politics.

5. Robert N. Bellah, *Beyond Belief: Essays on Religion in a Post-Traditional World* (New York: Harper & Row, 1970), pp. 150–51.

6. Ibid., p. 160.

7. Ibid., p. 151.

8. David Little, "The Development in the West of the Right to Freedom of Religion and Conscience: A Basis for Comparison with Islam," in David Little, John Kelsay, and Abdulaziz A. Sachedina, eds., *Human Rights and the Conflict of Cultures: Western and Islamic Perspectives on Religious Liberty* (Columbia: University of South Carolina Press, 1988), p. 30.

9. This is the argument of Abdulaziz A. Sachedina, "Freedom of Conscience and Religion in the Qur'an," in Little, Kelsay, and Sachedina, *Human Rights*, pp. 68, 74.

10. Fazlur Rahman, *Major Themes of the Qur'an* (Minneapolis: Bibliotheca Islamica, 1980), p. 163.

11. Ibid., p. 164.

12. Ibid., p. 164.

13. Paul Wheatley, *The Places Where Men Pray Together: Cities in Islamic Lands, 7th–10th Centuries* (Chicago: University of Chicago Press, 2000).

14. See Dale F. Eickelman and James Piscatori, "Social Theory in the Study of Muslim Societies," in Dale F. Eickelman and James Piscatori, eds., *Muslim Travellers: Pilgrimage, Migration, and the Religious Imagination* (Berkeley and Los Angeles: University of California Press, 1990), pp. 3–25.

15. Mikhaêl Elbaz, "La diáspora Sefardí a través del Meriterráneo y el Maghreb tras la expulsión de España en 1492," in Bernabé López García, ed., *Atlas de la inmigración magrebî en España* (Madrid: Ediciones Universidad Autónoma de Madrid, 1996), p. 18.

16. Robert Assaraf, *Mohammed V et les Juifs du Maroc à l'époque de Vichy* (Paris: Plon, 1997).

17. See Muhammad Khalid Masud, *Shatibi's Philosophy of Islamic Law* (Islamabad: Islamic Research Institute, 1995).

18. Iqtidar Ali Khan, "Akbar's Personality Traits and World Outlook—A Critical Appraisal," in Irfan Habib, ed., *Akbar and His India* (Delhi: Oxford University Press, 1997), p. 95.

19. Ira M. Lapidus, *A History of Islamic Societies* (Cambridge: Cambridge University Press, 1988), p. 456.

20. Amartya Sen, "East and West: The Reach of Reason," *New York Review of Books*, 20 July 2000, p. 33.

21. S. N. Eisenstadt, "Multiple Modernities," *Daedalus* 129, 1 (Winter 2000): 1.

22. Cited in John Keane, "The Limits of Secularism," *Times Literary Supplement*, 9 January 1998, pp. 12–13.

23. This distinction is noted by Muhammad Khalid Masud, "Religions and Tolerance: Islam," paper presented at a symposium on Religions and Tolerance, 8–10 May 2000, Potsdam and Berlin, Germany, p. 2 (cited here with permission).

24. Ibid., pp. 1–2. See also Dale F. Eickelman and James Piscatori, *Muslim Politics* (Princeton: Princeton University Press, 1996), pp. 3–4.

25. See Wilfred Cantwell Smith, *The Meaning and End of Religion: A New Approach to the Religious Traditions of Mankind* (New York: Macmillan, 1963), pp. 48–50, 60–62.

26. Francis Robinson, "Technology and Religious Change: Islam and the Impact of Print," *Modern Asian Studies* 27, 1 (January 1993): 229–51.

27. Syed Othman Alhabshi and Nik Mustapha Nik Hasan, introduction to Syed Othman Alhabshi and Nik Mustapha Nik Hasan, eds., *Islam and Tolerance* (Kuala Lumpur: Institute of Islamic Understanding Malaysia, 1994), 1–2.

28. Sadek J. Sulaiman, "Democracy and *Shura*," in Charles Kurzman, ed., *Liberal Islam: A Sourcebook* (New York: Oxford University Press, 1998), pp. 96–98.

29. Robert Wuthnow, *Communities of Discourse: Ideology and Social Structure in the Reformation, the Enlightenment, and European Socialism* (Cambridge, Mass.: Harvard University Press, 1989), p. 3.

30. Ibid.

31. Charles Taylor, "Modernity and the Rise of the Public Sphere," in *The Tanner Lectures on Human Values*, vol. 14 (Salt Lake City: University of Utah Press, 1993), p. 213.

32. Frank Vogel, *Islamic Law and Legal System: Studies of Saudi Arabia* (Leiden: E.J. Brill, 2000).

33. See Yves Gonzalez-Quijano, *Les Gens du livre: Édition et champ intellectuel dans l'Égypte républicaine* (Paris: CNRS Éditions, 1998), pp. 171–98.

34. Bediüzzaman Said Nursi, *The Miracles of Muhammad*, trans. Ümit Şimşek (Istanbul: Yeni Asya Yanıları, 1985); Nursi, *Belief and Man*, trans. Ümit Şimşek (Istanbul: Yeni Asya Yanıları, 1985); and Nursi, *Resurrection and the Hereafter*, trans. Ümit Şimşek (Istanbul: Yeni Asya Yanıları, 1985).

35. Bediüzzaman Said Nursi, *Nature: Cause or Effect?* trans. Ümit Şimşek (Istanbul: Yeni Asya Yanıları, 1985).

36. Cited in Şerif Mardin, *Religion and Social Change in Modern Turkey: The Case of Bediüzzaman Said Nursi* (Albany: State University of New York Press, 1989), p. 4.

37. Sükran Vahide, *The Author of the* Risale-i Nur: *Bediüzzaman Said Nursi* (Istanbul: Sölzer Publications, 1992), pp. 89–90. For a further discussion of the structure of Nursi's ideas and their appeal to different audiences, see Dale F. Eickelman, "Qur'anic Commentary, Public Space, and Religious Intellectuals in the Writings of Said Nursi," *Muslim World* 89, 3–4 (July-October 1999): 260–69, from which part of this section is adapted.

38. Thomas Michel, "Muslim-Christian Dialogue and Cooperation in the Thought of Bediüzzaman Said Nursi," *Muslim World* 89, 3–4 (July-October 1999): 325.

39. Vahide, *Bediüzzaman Said Nursi*, p. 217.

40. Ibid., p. 219.

41. Mardin, *Religion and Social Change in Modern Turkey*, p. 6.

42. Muhammad Said Ramadan al-Buti, "Bediüzzaman Said Nursi's Experience of Serving Islam by Means of Politics," in *Third International Symposium on Bediuzzaman Said Nursi: The Reconstruction of Islamic Thought in the Twentieth Century and Bediuzzaman Said Nursi, 24th–26th September 1995, Istanbul*, vol. 1, trans. Şükran Vahide (Istanbul: Sözler Publications, 1997), pp. 111–21. Al-Buti is a prominent Syrian religious scholar who broadcasts a popular weekly television program in Damascus.

43. For an excellent overview of the significance of the movement, see M. Hakan Yavuz, "Towards an Islamic Liberalism? The Nurcu Movement and Fethullah Gülen," *Middle East Journal* 53, 4 (Fall 1999): 584–605. See also Bülent Aras, "Turkish Islam's Moderate Face," *Middle East Quarterly* 5, 3 (September 1998): 23–29.

44. Yavuz, "Towards an Islamic Liberalism?" p. 600.

45. Sources: PIAR Gallup, polls conducted November 1992, November 1993; DAP/Yankelvitch poll, Turkey, August–September 1994. N–1,363. I wish to thank the United States Information Service, Washington, for providing me with these polls in February 1996.

46. Cited in "Fundamental Separation," in special supplement: "Ataturk's Long Shadow: A Survey of Turkey," *Economist*, 10 June 2000, p. 11

47. Said Bensaid, "Al-Hiwar wa'l-fahm la al-qat'iyya wa'l-jahl" (Dialogue and understanding, not alienation and ignorance), *Al-Sharq al-awsat* (London), 7 July 1993, p. 10.

48. Muhammad Shahrur, *Al-Kitab wa'l-Qur'an: Qira'a Mu'asira* (The Book and the Qur'an: A contemporary interpretation) (Damascus: Dar al-Ahali, 1990).

49. Wael B. Hallaq, *A History of Islamic Legal Theories* (Cambridge: Cambridge University Press, 1997), p. 253.

50. See Muhammad Shahrur, *Proposal for an Islamic Covenant*, trans. Dale F. Eickelman and Ismail S. Abu Shehadeh (Damascus: Dar al-Ahali, 2000). This book is also available online at <*www.isim.nl/isim/publications/other/shahrur*>. For an introduction to Shahrur's thinking, see Dale F. Eickelman, "Islamic Liberalism Strikes Back," *Middle East Studies Association Bulletin* 27, 2 (December 1993): 163–68.

51. Hasan al-Turabi, "The Islamic State," in John L. Esposito, ed., *Voices of Resurgent Islam* (New York: Oxford University Press, 1983), p. 245.

52. See John F. Burns, "Arab TV Gets a New Slant: Newscasts Without Censorship," *New York Times*, 4 July 1999, pp. A1, A6.

53. Shahrur, *Islamic Covenant*.

54. Fariba Adelkhah, *Being Modern in Iran* (New York: Columbia University Press, 2000), pp. 105–38.

55. Islamic Republic of Iran, "Constitution of the Islamic Republic of Iran" (ratified 2–3 December 1979), *Middle East Journal* 34, 2 (Spring 1980): 181–204.

56. John R. Bowen, "Legal Reasoning and Public Discourse in Indonesian Islam," in Dale F. Eickelman and Jon W. Anderson, eds., *New Media in the Muslim World: The Emerging Public Sphere* (Bloomington: Indiana University Press, 1999), pp. 80–105.

57. For an argument on personal liberty linking gay rights to the right of female students to wear headscarves, see Bahar Öcal Düzgören, "Neyim Ki, Kimim Ki Ben?" *Sözleşme*, 9 July 1998, pp. 47–49. For ethnic Turkish homosexual organizations in the Netherlands ("Strange Fruit"), Moroccans ("Ipoth"), and Arabs in general ("Yusuf"), see Oussama Cherreibi, "Imams d'Amsterdam: À travers l'example des imams de la diaspora marocaine" (Ph.D. diss., University of Amsterdam, 2000), pp. 164–67.

58. See Stephen O. Murray and Will Roscoe, eds., *Islamic Homosexualities: Culture, Homosexuality, and Literature* (New York: New York University Press, 1997).

The Scope of Pluralism
in Islamic Moral Traditions

Muhammad Khalid Masud

Dale Eickelman argues in the preceding essay that the Qur'an offers a modern perspective of a multiethnic and multicommunity world. Despite the fact that over time localisms have resisted the full realization of this Qur'anic perspective, Muslim societies have nevertheless continuously demonstrated their belief in this principle, as illustrated by the thought of the jurist Abu Ishaq al-Shatibi in fourteenth-century Spain, the Mughal ruler Akbar in sixteenth-century India, and the Nurculuk movement in twentieth-century Turkey. Eickelman has very significantly noted that on various Islamic issues, the point of departure in contemporary debates is the Qur'an itself, not the interpretations of the 'ulama in the past or present.

I fully support Eickelman's thesis, especially the point that modern Muslims do not support the concept of an "official" or "authoritative" view. They often proclaim with some sense of pride that there is no church in Islam. Inevitably, this claim implies accommodating pluralism. In my remarks, I would like to present an overview of the several moral traditions in Islam and also comment, with specific reference to the issues of social regulation, citizenship, life-and-death decisions, and human sexuality, that Muslim ethical positions may differ from others', and these differences should be regarded as part of ethical pluralism on the global level.

Modern Muslim writings on pluralism are clearly apprehensive of the possible anarchy and schism to which it may lead, threatening the unity of the Muslim *umma*.[1] They particularly stress that pluralism in Islam is conceived within a framework of unity. This apprehension reflects the distinct attitude of these Muslim thinkers toward prioritizing society over the individual.

In my view, pluralism is a part of the project of modernity that favors the freedom of the individual. Pluralism does not stress multiplicity per se as much as it is concerned with questioning the traditional monopoly of certain persons, groups, or institutions on prescribing ethical values authoritatively. In this sense, pluralism is not against the idea of unity and universalism on the basis of rationalism and humanism. It aims also at the growth of these values on the transnational and global level. This does not, however, mean that pluralism should ignore local or religious values.

In fact, pluralism derives its legitimacy and acceptance by justifying universal values in local contexts. Ethical pluralism is thus a concept that is constantly negotiated between universal and local ethical values.

ETHICAL TRADITIONS IN ISLAM

Islam as a moral tradition has never been monolithic.[2] Quite early in its history, it developed several approaches to moral issues. These approaches vary in their sources of authority, methods of interpretations, and emphasis. They sometimes oppose one another but often continue to function side by side, even complementing each other. It is therefore appropriate to review, even if briefly, these various moral traditions in Islam.

The *hadith* literature reflects a very significant moral tradition. It offers the prophet Muhammad and his companions as models for moral behavior. This tradition developed a very comprehensive ethical system of the *sunna* (norms) of the prophet Muhammad. The tradition frequently refers to the pre-Islamic tribal sunna, even if it is only to elaborate its assimilation or rejection into the Prophetic sunna. The definition of the sunna not only included the sayings and the practice of the Prophet, but also the practices to which the Prophet did not raise any objection.

The outstanding aspect of this ethical tradition is that it is essentially oriented to issues of religion and authenticity. The fact that this tradition produced dozens of compendia, however, each of them accepted as authoritative, stresses the principle of ethical pluralism within the tradition itself.

Pre-Islamic tribal values such as manliness, honor, forbearance, and tolerance were part of the Arab sunna that operated at the level of custom and usage in the literary moral tradition called *adab*. The adab tradition represents a humanist moral approach to morality. Most probably, writings in this tradition were initiated by Ibn Muqaffa' (d. 756), and carried on by several other well-known writers like Ibn Qutayba (d. 889), al-Mawardi (d. 1058), and al-Qalqashandi (d. 1418). The tradition expresses itself in the literary genre that comprises guidebooks for rulers or civil servants, laying down principles of model behavior for them. This tradition is more open than hadith, as it derives its ethical values from various sources: pre-Islamic Arabic as well as Persian literature, the Qur'an, Islamic history, ancient Persian history, and Greek and Indian literature. Ibn Muqaffa' translated into Arabic *Kalila wa Dimna*, a book of moral stories that originated in India. The adab tradition continues in arts and literature, but also as etiquette literature that provides a code of ethics for various professions, such as musicians.[3]

The philosophical tradition in Islam dealt with ethical issues on a more abstract level than the adab tradition. One of the essential questions with which this tradition was engaged was that of ethical obligation and its origins. The issue was whether it was only religion that defined rights and obligations, or whether human reason on its own could also differentiate between ethically good and bad. The Muslim philosophers explored the nature of prophethood, revelation, the role of reason, and other such themes. From Ibn Sina (d. 1037) to Ibn Rushd (d. 1198), the Muslim philosophers generally argued that there was no conflict between reason and revelation. The most interesting examples of the discussion of this problem are the treatises entitled *Hayy bin Yaqzan* (The Living, Son of Awake) by Ibn Sina and Ibn Tufayl (d. 1185).[4] Ibn Tufayl's story presents Hayy as a human child growing up on an island among animals without any contact with humans. By instinct and experience, he develops a moral code for himself. Later, he finds out that his moral values are no different from the religious values in the neighboring island inhabited by humans. Jurist-philosophers such as Shatibi[5] and Shah Waliullah (d. 1762)[6] also hold that human reason reaches similar conclusions during the absence of revelation.

The philosophical tradition developed a system of practical or applied ethics that came to be known as *akhlaq*. It received its recognition as a system of Islamic ethics proper as early as the eleventh century. It is a synthesis of pre-Islamic Arab moral values and Qur'anic teachings, and has Persian, Indian, and Greek elements. Miskawayh's (d. 1030) *Tahdhib al-akhlaq* offers a comprehensive and systematic treatment of ethical values in this tradition. It is obviously influenced by Greek ethical literature. Miskawayh explains that Greek ethics is more in accord with Islamic teachings than is pre-Islamic Arab morality. Jalal al-Din al-Dawwani (d. 1501) and Nasir al-Din al-Tusi (d. 1274) followed Miskawayh in their writings on ethics. Their books, popularly known as *Akhlaq Jalali* and *Akhlaq Nasiri*, respectively, were used as textbooks in the religious institutions.

The Sufi moral tradition is more popular than the other Islamic moral traditions. The Sufis were critical of the literal and exoteric approach to obligations by the jurists and theologians. Al-Harith al-Muhasibi (d. 857) wrote *Kitab al-ri 'aya li huquq Allah* (The Book of Observance of the Rights of God). He treats ethical obligations as surrender to the will of God and speaks of moral values such as *taqwa* (fear of God), *tawba* (return to God), *mahabba* (love), and others. Muhasibi stresses the need to abide by the laws of prescription and prohibition in the Qur'an and sunna, but he also stresses a more conscious effort to control the self from its propensity toward evil. Al-Ghazali (d. 1111) also followed Miskawayh in his ethical writings. His books on ethics, namely *Ihya 'ulum al-din* and *Kimiya-yi sa 'adat*, have been more popular than his other works.

The Sufis became more and more critical of the legal and theological approaches to obligations in later local traditions. The folk literature stresses the inner and humanist meanings of obligations and emphasizes tolerance, love, and sincerity.

Kalam (theology) is another tradition that dealt extensively with moral questions. Looking at the theological debates in the second and third centuries of Islam, one cannot fail to notice the diversity of the opinions even on such questions as the nature of divine attributes and the scope of human reason. It took up very early the question of whether the ethical values of good and bad were known only by revelation and religion, or whether human reason can also discover them. The Mu'tazilite school maintained that ethical values are rational and that revelation never contradicts them. The Mu'tazilites developed an entire system of theology and jurisprudence on this basis. They believed in the principle of justice to the extent that they argued that it was an obligation even for God. Revelation, specifically the Qur'an, was not sempiternal because it conformed to the findings of human reason.

The theologians were also divided on the nature of divine attributes. On the question of divine knowledge, for example: Does it exist eternally with God, is it in the essence of God, or is it independent of His essence? Anthropomorphists had an easy solution: humans can understand God only in human terms. The divine attributes are like human attributes. The Mu'tazilites, as strict monotheists, rejected the anthropomorphist view. They also rejected the position of those theologians who held that the divine attributes had an eternal and independent existence apart from God. Such an idea, in their view, could not be reconciled with the idea of God's unity (*tawhid*). They explained the problem in linguistic terms: The attributes were like adjectives. They only denoted a quality that is part of the entity. God's knowledge is part of his essence. When we say God is all-knowing, we are only saying that knowledge is a quality of His essence.

The Mu'tazilites came into conflict with other Muslims, especially those championing hadith, such as Ibn Qutayba, who accused them of denying divine attributes.[7] The Ash'arites, another group of theologians, broke away from the Mu'tazilites, denouncing their theology of human reason. The Mu'tazilites eventually lost the caliphal support they had initially enjoyed, and other groups gained strength. Although a consensus developed within Sunni Islam, the kalam tradition was never monolithic; it continued to develop multiple voices. It was not pluralist in the strict sense, however, as each group claimed authenticity only for itself.

Finally, we come to the tradition of *fiqh* (legal ethics). Although it is the closest Islamic equivalent to Western positive law, fiqh is generally regarded as a tradition that created moral obligations more than legal rights. Snouck Hurgronje even defined Islamic law as a doctrine of ethics and duties.[8]

Regardless of whether it is law in the strict sense or merely a moral tradition, what is significant is that the fiqh tradition also evinces diverse origins and interpretations. In fact, fiqh developed initially as multiple local customary legal traditions. The plurality of views in the fiqh traditions is proverbial. The hadith tradition questioned the authenticity of fiqh traditions and described them as mere opinions (*ra'y*) as opposed to the hadith, which was based on scientific knowledge (*'ilm*). The fiqh traditions produced more than nineteen schools, all of them recognizing one another's validity. The multiplicity of views continues within the schools and is regarded as a blessing. The principle of legal reasoning (*ijtihad*) encourages differences of opinion, because the struggle of the jurist to derive the right ruling is considered religiously commendable even though he may arrive at an erroneous conclusion. Adherence to these different schools of law is reflected in the diverse personal laws in Muslim societies.

It is significant that the caliphs in early Islamic history were apprehensive about the conflicting views of the Muslim jurists that produced diverse court judgments. Several Abbasid caliphs, and later other Muslim rulers, tried to unify laws. Resistance to such attempts often came from the Muslim jurists themselves. They feared that such attempts would mean state interference in this tradition, and they wanted to preserve their freedom. They considered their rulings enforceable by the state, but they never agreed to codify them as state laws. As a result, Muslim societies continuously practiced legal pluralism before the advent of the modern state.

The rural and tribal areas continued their local customary laws, sometimes even non-Muslim laws—as, for example, in Mughal and Ottoman villages. In cities, as well, there were different types of courts. The courts of complaints (*mazalim*) differed from ordinary courts even in their procedural laws. Different state institutions like the police also had their own legal system and procedures. The *hisba* (public censor) courts had jurisdiction over business ethics in the market as well as over offenses against public morals.

Fiqh soon came to stand for *shari'a* (divine law) and defined moral as well as legal obligations. This position of fiqh came about mostly through the function of jurists as *muftis*. A mufti, even today, may be asked about any matter under the sun, and he is supposed to explain God's law on the points in question. Consequently, fiqh assumed a dominant position in Islamic ethical discourse. A mufti's response, called a *fatwa*, offers a social construction of shari'a, as most often it refers to a concrete social question. It evaluates a practice with reference to an ideal. Most often, we find muftis also adjusting ideals to practice in view of the prevailing social conditions. These practices are frequently assimilated into the tradition in such a way that they are sometimes hard to distinguish. In the following pages, we shall refer to some fatwas to illustrate this point.

To conclude this section, we may say that Muslim societies have in practice accommodated ethical pluralism. Modern scholarship, however, generally considers this phenomenon of pluralism a deviation from the ideal. The conservative 'ulama, while recognizing the validity of the different schools of Islamic law, nevertheless insist on *taqlid*, or adherence to one of them. They regard the ijtihad that produced these various schools of interpretation as an instrument of a bygone "golden age," but reject its exercise today because it would lead to anarchy and conflicting opinions. Even many of the reformist 'ulama criticize the plurality of customs and social practices as innovations (*bid'a*), that are contrary to the Qur'an and sunna.

Many Western scholars, among them Reuben Levy, Georges-Henri Bousquet, and Joseph Schacht, have also treated the pluralism in Muslim societies in terms of theory and practice. The theory or ideal is defined, for them, by the Qur'an, sunna, and fiqh. Muslim practices or customs (*adat*, *'urf*) that led to pluralism are defined as deviations. It is noteworthy that these Western scholars were studying this pluralism at times when colonialism or the centralizing nation-state stressed the unification of legal and ethical standards, and upheld it as the ideal. Similarly, Muslim societies also became more conscious of the plurality of societal practices during the reformist phases when unity of the umma was upheld as the ideal, and the ideal was defined in terms of unity of ethical standards.

In fact, I would argue, this "dichotomy" between theory and practice is more imagined than real because both are continuously readjusted in light of each other. The general or universal principles, which may determine the extent to which ethical pluralism is acceptable, are constantly redefined with reference to their local objectification.

Social Regulation

Muslim moral traditions evolved independently of state support. Each tradition expected the state to enforce the laws to ensure social regulations, but would never allow the state to arbitrate ethical differences. As we have mentioned already, the Mu'tazilites invoked the power of the state to regulate ethical differences. They failed. Such attempts on the part of the state were always resisted by society. IbnMuqaffa' in Baghdad and some Indian 'ulama in Akbar's court tried to win for the ruler the right to arbitrate in case of differences among scholars. The majority of scholars disagreed and did not allow the ruler even the right to choose one among their different views. To them, the basis of authority was *ijma'*, or consensus of legal experts. This concept of consensus required the gradual acceptance of an idea by the whole community. This type of consensus was called *ijma' sukuti* (silent approval) in contrast to *ijma' qawli* (verbal approval), which rarely occurred.

Invocation of the state's power in these matters is more frequent today than previously in Muslim societies. This is perhaps because the concept of the state has changed. The modern concept of the state is that of a nation-state, which implies identity and unity of the polity. The state today frequently brings with it a reform agenda. It is also more encompassing in its function and operation.

Citizenship

Islamic moral traditions obviously support the idea of civil society. Muhammad Iqbal, a twentieth-century Muslim thinker, even defines Islam as a civil society.[9] On the basis of this idea, Iqbal declared the necessity of a separate state for Muslims in the Indian subcontinent. In his view, the role of the state should be to provide facilities to promote an ethically based sense of rights and duties.

Modern political systems have introduced several new practices that did not exist in the past, and consequently some dissenting positions on these matters have emerged. One of the controversial issues is the civil status of women. It is significant to note that there is, for instance, no difference of opinion among most Muslim thinkers today on the education of women or their participation in elections. The 'ulama who oppose women's participation in these activities do so for other reasons. The following example illustrates the point.

In response to a long query by the government of Afghanistan about the civil status of women, the Indian mufti Kifayatullah explained in 1924 that there should be no objection to the education of women, as it is one of the essential Islamic obligations for both men and women.[10] The requirements of modern times make education of women imperative. Muslim societies are losing advantages and opportunities due to their lack of education. The point of controversy lies in the modes of education, which might disregard Islamic requirements of veiling and prohibition of the free mixing of the sexes.

In answer to various other questions about the status of women by several other inquirers, the mufti explained on other occasions that a Muslim woman could go outside the home to cast ballots in elections, provided she observed the veiling requirement.[11] He was, however, reluctant to allow women to contest elections because it would not be possible for them to observe all religious requirements. He did not explain what these requirements were. Apparently, he meant mixed gatherings, but in another fatwa he allowed a Muslim woman to address a gathering of men if she observed the veil.[12]

We can see that, as far as the civil rights of women are concerned, the areas of dissent do not lie in the rights themselves but in some cultural considerations, which these scholars regard as religious requirements. The particular ethical values of veiling and the separation of sexes are explained in view of the corruption of society in modern times. The time of the Prophet, the ideal time, was not corrupt and hence women frequented mosques and participated in social and religious events.

Life-and-Death Decisions

I discuss issues related to bioethics with reference to a recent study by Vardit Rispler-Chaim.[13] According to Tristram Engelhardt Jr., bioethics is an element of a secular culture and a product of the Enlightenment. In this sense, it forms a venture in secular ethics. Rispler-Chaim disagrees with this conclusion and argues that solutions to problems of life and death must be provided locally and independently in each society and religious community.[14] She explains that there can be no one ethical code for these decisions. Even within particular religious traditions, including Islam, there exist several trends.

According to Rispler-Chaim, the modern Western code of medical ethics is informed by an emphasis on the rights of the individual. It is closely associated with the study of human rights, privacy, personal dignity, and individual freedom of choice in life and death. Islamic ethics, on the other hand, evaluates individual rights in relation to those of society. Islamic ethics does not ignore human rights but it places more emphasis on society.

With regard to euthanasia, she finds a consensus emerging among Muslim scholars that the mercy killing of a terminally sick patient is forbidden in Islamic law.[15] Their justification is based not on a clear text but on analogy with suicide. They argue that a human being does not own a body, and therefore a person has no right to put it to death.

They also argue that killing oneself to escape suffering, even extreme pain, constitutes suicide. It is a sin because God alone causes death. It also defies the belief in God's ability to perform miracles and interferes with God's exclusive control over life and death.[16]

There is no clear prohibition of suicide in the Qur'an, especially in cases of extreme suffering. Qur'anic references to killing oneself do not always refer to suicide (e.g., 2:54 and 4:66). The jurists often explain the verse

"Do not kill yourself" (6:29) as prohibition against mutual fighting among Muslims. The hadith literature, on the other hand, provides clear prohibitions of suicide and regards it sinful to the extent that funeral prayers are not to be offered for such a person. Suicide is generally a rare occurrence in the history of Muslim societies.[17]

In his discussion of the nature of obligation, Shatibi goes into a detailed analysis of the concept of suffering. Distinguishing between suffering or hardship that is part of obligation and that which is not, he argues that hunger, thirst, sickness, bodily harm, and the like are not part of the concept of obligation. It is therefore obligatory to remove or prevent these types of hardships. He observes, however, that suffering caused by incurable illness is not included in this category. Its removal or elimination is not an obligation. It must be endured as the will of God.[18]

The recent controversy over the legitimacy of suicide attacks by Palestinians as a military tactic against the Israelis has added a new dimension to ethical perspectives on suffering. If Muslims find themselves in the position of extreme suffering and have lost hope of any solution, can they decide to commit suicide in a way that results in the death of other innocent persons? The shaykh of al-Azhar, Muhammad Sayyid al-Tantawi, has declared that suicide attacks against the Israelis are not a legitimate tactic or form of *jihad*. They are simply suicide. Islam does not allow killing civilians in this or any other direct way, in any city or country, even in Israel. Another prominent scholar, Yusuf Qaradawi, disagrees with the shaykh and considers such attacks against the Israelis as justified because all Israelis are involved in the occupation of Palestinian land and in the oppression of ordinary Palestinians.[19]

Human Sexuality

Several studies on sexuality in Islam have recently appeared.[20] Among the issues relating to this topic, homosexuality *(liwat)* attracts the most attention. In view of the Muslim jurists' position on this issue, it is difficult to say if they would ever allow same-sex unions as a form of marriage. Nevertheless, homosexuality has undoubtedly existed in Muslim societies. There is, however, a distinction between sexual relations and simple cohabitation, as well as between this practice as a perversion and debauchery and as an incurable habit.

The Qur'an refers repeatedly to the people of Lot and their practice of sodomy, leaving little doubt that they suffered divine punishment for this pervasive practice (e.g., 11:77–83). There are, however, fleeting references to *ghilman* (52:24) and *wildan* (56:17, 76:19), the "youth" in paradise, but these are not in an explicitly sexual context.

Sexual relations between members of the same sex are harshly condemned in the hadith. The opinions of the jurists, based on the practice of the Prophet's companions, are divided on the exact punishment for sexual offenses, and depend largely on the circumstances surrounding such relations. First, most jurists distinguish liwat (same-sex relations) from *zina* (fornication, adultery, or rape). Second, they also distinguish between a married and an unmarried person. Ibn Hazm (d. 1064) recommended lesser punishment for an unmarried person. Ibn Abdun recommended expulsion from the town instead of corporal punishment.[21]

The generally harsh view toward homosexuality is probably due to the fact that the practice appeared, in the minds of many early scholars, to be a corruption of Muslim society in the wake of prosperity during the Abbasid period. Al-Jahiz (d. 868) cites a poem glorifying homosexuality as a sign of sophisticated civilization; normal sex was a practice of the primitive.[22] It is significant to note that in the past Christians attacked Muslim culture particularly for the frequency of homosexual relations.[23] One should not, however, take such descriptions of Muslim culture literally. It is possible that the authors in fact wanted to condemn the Christian monks who took a lenient view toward this practice. It is also possible that the authors of these stories attributed this practice to Muslims in order to stress that it was un-Christian, and that the Christians should not indulge in it.[24]

If one believes the popular literature, the practice also existed among Muslim religious brotherhoods and educational institutions. These stories probably reflect the fact that because of the separation of sexes—stressed so much by Muslim ethical traditions—intimate same-sex relationships inevitably evolved. Such relationships may not necessarily have been sexual. Frequent references in poetry to what may be construed as platonic love show the general acceptance of this form of intimacy.

CONCLUSIONS

Islam as a moral tradition favors pluralism, first, because it appeals to human reason. The Qur'an attaches pivotal significance to individual rational choice and responsibility. To be a Muslim is a matter of rational choice and an admission of responsibility. "There is no coercion in religion. The truth stands out clear from error" (2:256). "By the soul, and the order given it, He has inspired it to its wrong and to its good" (91:7–8). "To each is a goal to which He turns it. Then strive for what is good" (2:178). "Say, 'The truth is from your Lord,' then believe who wills and deny who wills" (18:29). The emphasis here is not so much that ethical values are rational and scientific but that they are reasonable and understandable by all humans. Because the level of understanding may differ from person to person and from community to community, a multiplicity of views is inevitable.

The second basis for pluralism is social acceptance of Islamic values as understood by different persons and different communities. This basis also regulates the permissible scope of dissent from what are widely accepted social norms. For the Qur'an calls the "good" *ma'ruf* (that which is well known) and "evil" *munkar* (that which is rejected). Social dialectics develop and enforce the acceptable definition of ethical values.

NOTES

1. For instance, see Muhammad Ammara, introduction to *Al-Ta 'addudiyya: Al-Ru 'ya al-Islamiyya wa 'l-tahaddiyyat al-gharbiyya* (Cairo: Dar Nahdat Misr li'l-Taba'a wa'l-Nashr, 1997); Zaki al-Milad, *Al-Fikr al-Islami: Qira 'at wa muraja 'at, al-ta 'addudiyya . . .* (Beirut: Mu'assasat al-Intishar al-'Arabi, 1999).

2. See R. Walzer, "Akhlak," in *Encyclopaedia of Islam*, rev. ed. (Leiden: E. J. Brill, 1986), 1: 325–29.

3. Barbara D. Metcalf, ed., *Moral Conduct and Authority: The Place of* Adab *in South Asian Islam* (Berkeley and Los Angeles: University of California Press, 1984), especially Brian Silver, "The *Adab* of Musicians," pp. 315–29.

4. See A.-M. Goichon, "Hayy b. Yakzan," in *Encyclopaedia of Islam*, 3:330–34.

5. Muhammad Khalid Masud, *Shatibi's Philosophy of Islamic Law* (Islamabad: Islamic Research Institute, 1995), pp. 157 ff.

6. Shah Waliullah, *Hujjatullah al-baligha* (Lahore: Maktaba Salafiyya, n.d.).

7. Ibn Qutayba, *Al-Ikhtilaf fi 'l lafz wa al-radd 'ala al-Jahmiyya wa 'l-mushabbiha* (Cairo: Matba'a al-Sa'ada, 1930), p. 23. Ibn Qutayba argues, "There are others who examined the issue in depth. They presumed that by rejecting anthropomorphism (*tashbih*) of the Creator they were correcting the belief in His unity (*tawhid*). However, they denied the attributes like *hilm, qudra, jalal* and *'afw*, and so on. They said, 'We believe that He is *halim*; we do not believe in His *hilm*. We believe that He is all-knowing; we do not believe in His knowledge.' " See also Gérard Lecomte, *Ibn Qutayba (mort en 276/889): L'homme, son oeuvre, ses idées* (Damascus: Institut français de Damas, 1965), p. 220. For a detailed discussion of the problem, see Richard MacDonough Frank, *Beings and Their Attributes: The Teaching of the Basrian School of the Mu'tazila in the Classical Period* (Albany: State University of New York Press, 1978).

8. See for instance, Snouck Hurgronje, *Selected Works of C. Snouck Hurgronje*, ed. G.-H. Bousqet and Joseph Schacht (Leiden: E. J. Brill, 1957), p. 256. He says, "le droit musulman qu'on ferait mieux de désigner par le terme de déontologie (ou: doctrines des devoirs de l'homme)."

9. Muhammad Iqbal, *The Reconstruction of Religious Thought in Islam* (Lahore: Institute of Islamic Culture, 1986), p. 123.

10. Mufti Kifayatullah, *Kifayat al-mufti* (Multan: Imdadiyya, n.d.), 2:25–40.

11. Ibid., 9:371, 380.

12. Ibid., 2:41.

13. Vardit Rispler-Chaim, *Islamic Medical Ethics in the Twentieth Century* (Leiden: E. J. Brill, 1993).

14. Ibid., p. 142.

15. Jalaluddin Umri, "Suicide or Termination of Life," trans. S.A.H. Rizvi, *Islamic and Comparative Law Quarterly* 7 (1987): 136–44; and Muhammad Rajab al-Bayumi, "Qatl al-marid al-mayus 'anhu," *Majallat al-Azhar* 52 (January–February 1986): 674–78.

16. Rispler-Chaim, *Islamic Medical Ethics*, pp. 95–97.

17. F. Rosenthal, "Intihar," in *Encyclopaedia of Islam*, 3:1246–48.

18. Masud, *Shatibi's Philosophy of Islamic Law*, pp. 193–94.

19. See "Dr. Qaradawi criticizes the shaykh al-Azhar's fatwa forbidding suicide attacks in Palestine," 5 December 2001, at <*www.qaradawi.net*>, under "Fatawa wa Ahkam."

20. See for instance, G.-H. Bousquet, *La morale de l'Islam et son éthique sexuelle* (Paris: A. Maisonneuve, 1953); Salah al-Din al-Munajjid, *Al-Hayat al-jinsiyya 'inda al 'Arab* (Beirut: Dar al-Kutub, 1958); M. Abd al-Wahid, *Al-Islam wa mushkilat al-jinsiyya* (Cairo: 'Isa al-Babi, 1961); A. Bouhdiba, *La sexualité en Islam* (Paris: Presses Universitaires de France, 1975); Basim Musallam, *Sex and Society in Islam* (Cambridge: Cambridge University Press, 1983).

21. For references, see "Liwat," in *Encylopaedia of Islam*, 5:777.

22. Al-Jahiz, *Mufakharat al-jawari wa'l-ghilman*, in ibid.

23. Norman Daniel, *Islam and the West* (Edinburgh: Edinburgh University Press, 1960), pp. 141–45.

24. For a detailed analysis of this aspect, see Rebecca Joubin, "Islam and Arabs through the Eyes of the *Encyclopédie*: The 'Other' as a Case of French Cultural Self-Criticism," *International Journal of Middle East Studies* 32, 2 (May 2000): 197–217.

PART VI

Ethical Diversity, Tolerance, and the Problem of Sovereignty: A Jewish Perspective

Menachem Fisch

Like all religions of long standing, Judaism does not speak in one voice, and perhaps never did—certainly not on the issues under consideration. It is customary to distinguish three major streams or movements within contemporary Judaism in the West—Orthodox, Conservative, and Reform—each standing for a cascade of further divisions. The three movements differ primarily in their attitude to halakha, the code of Jewish Law. Whereas Orthodox Jews accept halakha as the first place of reference and sole arbiter of authority, Conservative Judaism sees halakha as a crucial source of value holding "a vote, but not a veto" in determining personal behavior. Reform Judaism, by contrast, insists upon the primacy and ultimacy of personal autonomy in grounding religious norm and individual conscience. Although all three are, sociologically speaking, relatively recent developments, Orthodox communities alone boast full allegiance to a code they consider dating back to at least the talmudic era of late antiquity. This paper is written from an Orthodox point of view, from that of halakha as it is understood and practiced today by the majority of Orthodox Jews. I do so for three reasons. First, in being an Orthodox Jew myself I prefer to "report" from a perspective I feel I can speak for and to deliberate questions that are real for me. Second, and more significant, bound by deep religious conviction to a strict and richly detailed system of ritual and social norms, Orthodox Jews are challenged far more seriously by problems of ethical diversity than their more liberally motivated conservative and reform coreligionists. Third, and for me most important, is the extremely potent reality of these problems for the state of Israel. Israel is unique in being the only modern society in which many observant, halakhically committed Jews not only serve as municipal and parliamentary representatives of their communities but partake actively in executive extracommunal governmental roles. It is here that traditional Orthodox Judaism is swiftly and uneasily awakening to problems akin to those put forth for discussion by the Ethikon Institute. I say "akin to" because they are not identical. Problems of ethical diversity loom large in this context but do not always manifest themselves in questions of citizenship, physician-assisted suicide, or even same-sex unions as acutely as they do from the perspectives of other ethical systems. I shall try in what follows to characterize the problem and a possible solution to it from the viewpoint of halakhic Judaism without straying too far from the guidelines we have been asked to follow.

IDEAL SOCIETIES

In one sense Orthodox Judaism's choice of ideal society is obvious. Owing to its built-in sensitivity to the right of all citizens to the culture, life-style, and religion of their choice, modern multicultural democracy is by far the form of host government most favored by Orthodox Jewish communities. The communal autonomy granted by such a state provides and protects the cultural, educational, and religious space needed for them to run their lives as they see fit. The price to pay, though, is as obvious as the choice, for by the same token, in such a state many whose cultural and religious choices promote or enable forms of conduct deemed sinful and heretical in the eyes of halakha will be equally provided for and protected. Preference for such a political setting requires (protest, civil action, and lobbying permitted by the law notwithstanding) undertaking in advance to live and let live within it. Ethical diversity is a necessary consequence of multiculturalism. To desire such an environment requires, at the very least, accepting as ethical a diversity that is sanctioned by the law of the land. Needless to say, the more decided and rigid one's own ethical system is, the greater the chance of finding within that permitted diversity systems diametrically opposed to one's own.

Setting aside the much-discussed question of how liberal a liberal government should be toward violations of liberalism among its autonomous communities, let us look at the same tension from the opposite direction. To what extent, let us first ask, can observant Jews, participating in a larger liberal society, silently put up with what they strongly consider to be sinful and heretic practices of neighboring communities? How far does halakha permit one to go in tolerating others for the sake of maintaining one's own autonomy? The question is one of ethical plurality—not at the managerial level, but of ethical plurality nonetheless.

Of course, the question of tolerance only arises for whom *intolerance* is a viable option. If a community is powerless to raise its voice and take action against the sinners and heretics outside its boundaries, its putting up with them means nothing. On the other hand, one does not actually have to be *in* power to take such action. The levels of protest, civil action, access to the media, and boycotting permitted in most modern democracies provide sufficient means for one community to make the life of another quite unpleasant. Today Orthodox Jewish communities in the Western world enjoy such power like any other and are fully capable of loudly voicing their views for and against the various ethical systems they encounter. For them, as never before, the decision to put up with sinful conduct outside the community has ceased to be a matter of necessity and become a matter of choice.

Let us be clear about the question we are asking: what is required of observant Jews in liberal democracies is not to rethink their notions of sin and heresy but to reconsider the appropriate *attitude* toward the sinful and the heretical required of them by their religion. Needless to say, the question does not arise with respect to all forms of conduct frowned upon by Jewish law but only with respect to those considered desirable by some, and at least permissible by state law. What is minimally required is not for Judaism to change, or even to relativize its ethics, only to be able, in meaningful religious ways, to justify passively turning a blind eye to the forms of sin and heresy legally practiced outside its own communities. On this, I argue, halakhic Judaism comes relatively well equipped.

But is the culturally autonomous community, keeping politely to itself within a wider liberal state run by others, all that contemporary halakhic Judaism aspires to politically? For many Orthodox Jews the answer is still a firm yes. Prior to the messianic era, they argue insistently, such an exilic existence is all God-fearing Jewish communities are allowed actively to pursue. On these grounds the vast majority of Orthodox rabbis vehemently opposed the newly formed Zionist movement at the turn of the century.[1] Since then things have changed, however. For the last hundred years, and especially since the establishment of the State of Israel in 1948, the comparatively small group of halakhically committed pro-Zionists[2] has grown steadily to the extent that today the vast majority of observant Jews living in Israel participate actively in state and municipal politics. They are organized in a number of religious parties—ranging from the religiously pro-Zionist to the religiously a-Zionist (i.e., politically indifferent), and excluding the relatively small group of religiously anti-Zionists—whose representatives occupy key positions at the municipal, parliamentary, and governmental levels. For them, I submit, the question of the ideal society for halakhic Judaism becomes exceedingly more difficult.

The reason is simple: at the managerial level turning a blind eye to the halakhically objectionable is no longer enough. To partake actively in running (as opposed merely to living in) a liberal democracy requires more than to tolerate passively those with whom one disagrees. Observant members of the Israeli government—the ministers of education, the treasury, or the interior, for instance—cannot get away with merely ignoring those they consider sinful and heretic. As managerial level executives of a multicultural society they are required to take active responsibility for the well-being and welfare of all communities—including those whose life-styles they consider blatantly objectionable. Jewish law distinguishes between passive toleration and active enabling. There is a clear halakhic line to be drawn between employing passive judicial restraint and abstaining from taking action against the halakhically objectionable, and going out of one's way to assist them. For halakhic Judaism the question of the ideal society is hence an extremely tricky one depending on the nature of the halakhic warrant sought.

Halakha as it stands permits Jewish rulers to grant considerably less freedom to their subjects than they would have liked their rulers to grant them as subjects. The discrepancy between looking at questions of ethical diversity from above and from below, as it were, becomes especially problematic in Israel where Orthodox Jewish communities find themselves for the first time in the modern era having to tackle the problem from both perspectives simultaneously.[3] In what follows I do my best to discuss the general question of ethical plurality, as well as the specific problems we have all been asked to address, from each of the two halakhic perspectives, with a view to highlighting the difference between the diaspora and Israeli case. I then conclude by suggesting a way of reconciling the two approaches within the world of halakhic discourse.

One last word of introduction: rather than discuss ideal, theoretical models of statehood that have been suggested from time to time in pre-modern halakhic writings, I concentrate in what follows on the two real latter-day contexts in which halakhically committed Jews now freely confront ethical diversity—namely, latter-day Israel and the other Western democracies. With the establishment of the state of Israel Jews regained full political sovereignty for the very first time since long before the first formative halakhic texts came into existence. For the best of two millennia self-rule was envisaged in halakhic writings, if at all, only in the most remote and idyllic terms, never as a realistic possibility. The few texts in which a more detailed conception of Jewish statehood is attempted were written long before the emergence of the modern nation-state.[4] Modern Israel is not of Orthodox Jewish making. It preserves an ethical diversity far wider than halakha is capable of accommodating prima facie. It poses a real, rather than a theoretical challenge to traditional modes of thought—perhaps the greatest challenge to halakha of the modern era, certainly the most urgent one. But first to the problem of ethical plurality outside of Israel.

Ethical Diversity from Below

Halakhic Judaism's capacity for passively tolerating objectionable ethical systems adhered to beyond the confines of the community is almost unlimited. In this respect, the question of ethical pluralism can be answered by halakhic Jews, by means of a healthy, pragmatic, halakhically motivated tolerance. "Ethical pluralism," in the normative sense of the word, is the wrong term to use in this context, however, and, I am tempted to say, so is "tolerance." Pluralists attach value to other systems of thought and welcome their existence. Halakhic Judaism, as it is currently understood by its practitioners, does not.

Toleration is different. To merely tolerate a person, an idea, or a form of conduct does not imply attaching intrinsic value to its existence. To tolerate per se is minimally to agree to put up with the objectionable, to suffer in silence its unwelcome presence. To merely tolerate a person, idea, or form of conduct implies not looking upon it favorably in any way, or being curious to find out more about it, but only a willingness silently and passively to accept its existence. Most existing ideas of tolerance come grounded in liberal assumptions on the nature of humankind. We tolerate other people's beliefs because one's beliefs are regarded one's private business, or because individual autonomy is held sacred. As it stands, Jewish law contains nothing comparable with the sanctioning of an individual's right to cultural freedom or of individual autonomy in modern liberal thought. Halakhic Judaism tolerates the objectionable not in respect of someone else's rights but in order to avoid unnecessary trouble. The halakhic principles employed to justify slackening halakhic standards (when applicable) out of a concern for social or political tension are *mipnei darkei shalom* and *mipnei darkei eiva*—that is to say, for the sake of peace or for the sake of avoiding hostility. In theory this boils down to a rather crude, ad hoc, and wholly practical version of Kant's categorical imperative—not: do not do to others that which you would not like others to do to you, but rather avoid from doing to others what the law would have otherwise required you to do to them for fear of them not appreciating your noble intentions and retaliating by doing the same or worse to you. Such reasoning is morally coarse to say the least, pragmatic in the bad sense of the term, but it is genuine, and, most important, it works admirably well.

Like most religions, Judaism discriminates in two different and largely independent ways. Halakha discriminates, on the one hand, between prohibited and permitted conduct and, on the other, between people: between members of the faith and those who are not. (I am ignoring here discrimination within the community—for example, between male and female members—on which something more is said later.) In a variety of situations, Jewish law discriminates against gentiles qua gentiles—sinful or not. (These situations range from the purely ritual [e.g., exclusion from certain ceremonies] to the worryingly ethical [e.g., a status lower than Jews in certain life-saving situations].) One may speak therefore of two separate forms of religious toleration: a willingness to put up with objectionable conduct, and a willingness to include the other where the other

would otherwise be excluded. Both are easily accommodated by the pragmatism of arguing "for the sake of peace." "In a city populated by Jews
and gentiles, Jewish and gentile administrators are appointed," states the
Talmud of Palestine, "taxes are collected [equally] from Jew and gentile,
[from which] the needs of the Jewish and gentile poor are [jointly] supplied." One does not discriminate between the Jewish and gentile sick,
the Talmud goes on to rule, one attends equally to the dead of each community (although strictly speaking Jews and gentiles should be allocated
different cemeteries), and pays equal respect to their respective mourn-
ers—all in the interest of peace.[5] According to this fundamental ruling,
halakha actually encourages forming shared, representative administra-
tions for "multicultural" societies, to risk an anachronism, rather than
insist on Jewish control. But that is a different issue.

In principle at least, observant Jewish communities encounter no problem refraining from taking the offensive action required of them by halakha whenever there is the slightest chance of retaliation. Though the
metaphysics that back them may not always be to everyone's taste (e.g.,
when looking for ways around the halakhic prohibition against desecrat-
ing the Sabbath to save the life of a non-Jew), overriding halakhic prohibition with principles like "for the sake of peace" is about all that is needed
for halakhic Judaism to live peacefully amid the sinful, the heretical, and
the non-Jewish.

An interesting point to notice is that while concern "for the sake of
peace" provides halakhically meaningful justification for not doing what
one would otherwise be required to do, it provides no justification for
remaining silent about it. Excluding situations where one prefers to keep
a low profile for the sake of peace, one would expect communities with
firm positions on controversial issues to at least participate in the public
debate where such debate is allowed. To agree to tolerate other positions
does not mean giving up your own. It is not as if orthodox Judaism's
views on the moral issues currently debated in the United States are uncomfortably extreme. Halakha may not always accord with the most liberal approach, but it hardly ever coincides with the other extreme. And
yet, outside Israel, one hardly ever encounters serious Orthodox Jewish
involvement in any of the public ethical debates. Such questions are frequently raised in sermons and in the lively responsa literature, and are
firmly, and to a great extent unanimously, ruled upon by Orthodox halakhists *without*, however, any visible proselytizing intention of causing
anyone else to improve their ways. Orthodox Jews have quite thoroughly
absented themselves from the public moral debate anywhere but in Israel—so much so that it seems inappropriate to describe their attitude to
the moral diversity that they encounter outside Israel as one of toleration.

Sheer indifference seems more like it. Orthodox communities in the West, though perfectly welcome as bona fide members of society, tend to keep to themselves politically, and appear to show extremely little if any interest in influencing the public sphere—other, of course, than to lobby for their own communal needs. It is not as if they would have liked to make a stand but refrain from doing so for the sake of peace. It is more as if they simply couldn't care less.

Paradoxically, the level of indifference exhibited by Jewish communities to the moral space facilitated by state law and to the moral choices made by others, changes as if it were a direct function of their degree of halakhic seriousness. The stricter one is, the more seriously one takes one's religious duties, the less, it seems in the Jewish case, is one concerned with how other individuals and communities live their lives. In place of the religiously meaningful mechanisms of judicial restraint and considered toleration made available by halakha (that serve in themselves to elevate the value of peaceful coexistence) diaspora Orthodox Jews largely display an attitude of unconsidered apathy toward the moral choices and life-styles of all but their very own. Apathy and moral indifference are not uncommon Western maladies. Latter-day philosophical relativism doesn't help on this count either. Although of a kind, the Orthodox Jewish case is different, however, and hardly a modern or postmodern phenomenon. An understandable result of centuries of oppression and persecution, it is the defense mechanism of the less emancipated exhibiting an instinctive, disengaging, almost austere, ethnocentric dismissal of the outside world. Typical of very many Orthodox communities throughout the Western world is a deeply entrenched sense of not belonging, of having no responsibility, and of having no desire to be responsible for anything or anyone outside the enclave of their own community.

The upshot for the problem of ethical diversity is clear enough. Whether for the sake of the peace, or out of sheer indifference, as long as state law does not require Jews to violate halakha, the fact that it permits others to do so, or even sanctions such violations, poses orthodox Judaism no problem at all. Observant Jews are by no means ethical pluralists, let alone ethical relativists. Their views on the problems under consideration (though not always identical) are firm and determined. Still, halakhically autonomous Jewish communities are ideal (if silent and inactive) partners to as widely diverse an ethical plurality as liberals would have. As long as they are allowed to keep to themselves, and their rabbis granted the authority to make their own decisions and issue their own rulings on such issues as abortion, physician-assisted suicide, and one-sex unions, ethical pluralism is not a problem for diaspora Judaism.

The situation in Israel, however, is another matter entirely.

MANAGING ETHICAL DIVERSITY: THE PROBLEM OF SOVEREIGNTY

As noted at the outset, there remains a minority of ultra-Orthodox Jews living in Israel who continue to view themselves "exiled by the hand of Israel."[6] Their hostility toward Israelis, Israeli society, and the Israeli government and legal system ranges from a furious tight-lipped scorn to passive disobedience. They refuse to engage. In particular, they exhibit no desire to form an opposition within Israeli society or in any other way influence anyone or anything beyond the locked gates of their own community. If one ignores their ideological hostility to the very idea of a (nonmessianic, secular) Jewish state, their attitude toward the ethical diversity existing outside the community is, in practice, much the same as that of their Orthodox brethren abroad—they too couldn't care less. In the past Jews were powerless to react. Today, in Israel as in other Western democracies, this is no longer the case, as Orthodox Jews know very well. And yet, as noted, many orthodox communities speak and act as if it were. They seem to prefer to be viewed and to view themselves as incapable of making a stand, than as having chosen not to. If diaspora Orthodox Jews can still be described as having not yet fully comprehended the fact that they are ruled by a genuinely benign and welcoming alien state, the same cannot be said of the Israeli ultra-Orthodox. Their insular exilic existence is consciously self-fashioned—far less a failure to adjust than a considered and largely self-constructed preference. They seem truly to prefer living inwardly devoid of civil or social responsibilities at the mercy of an oppressive alien state—not unlike ancient Israel's desire to return to Egyptian captivity rather than accept the responsibilities of freedom. Due to its self-imposed, exilic mind-set, the anti-Zionist, Israeli, ultra-Orthodox minority remains austerely indifferent to the ethical diversity of Israeli society, and hence unproblematic in terms of the issues under consideration. For the vast majority of observant Israeli Jews, however, the problems are real, and by no means as easily avoided.

By assuming municipal and governmental responsibilities, Orthodox Jews in Israel cannot remain indifferent to the moral choices of other Israeli communities, especially those supported by Israeli law. Nor are the halakhic justifications for passively tolerating the sinful for the sake of maintaining the peace of much avail. For it is one thing for an Orthodox community to turn a blind eye to idolatry or to systematic transgressions of the dietary laws or the Sabbath restrictions by neighboring communities "for the sake of the peace," but quite another for an orthodox Jew to take it to be his job to assist actively and systematically such sinful conduct.

The role of government and municipal executives in multicultural democracies differs decisively from that of communal leadership. Whereas the job of the latter, even when acting as representatives of their home communities or cultures, is primarily to look out for their own, the former, regardless of personal conviction, assume responsibility for the security and welfare of all. The Israeli ministers of education, religious affairs, the interior, tourism, and the like cannot perform their governmental duties by merely turning a tolerating, peace-maintaining blind eye to what their religion considers sinful. It is their job, in their designated areas of responsibility, to actively ensure the security, the welfare, and the capacity of each and every community to flourish according to its custom and conviction (insofar as, in doing so, nothing is done to harm other communities, or to prevent them from exercising their own, identical rights, of course). If halakha firmly forbids Jewish travel agents to assist actively or profit from Muslim and Christian pilgrims, for instance,[7] it similarly forbids Jewish governmental officials to do so. But to volunteer such active assistance is the very job of the Ministry of Religious Affairs, of Finance, and of Education to name but three. Not only is the Ministry of Education, for instance, expected to assist Muslim and Christian communities in planning and funding their annual school trips to the holy places of their respective faiths but also, as a matter of course, is constantly engaged in improving the system—that is to say, in rendering their halakhically objectionable activity all the more efficient and worthwhile. And the same goes for the gravely sinful behavior of un-Orthodox Jews. The very same ministry is responsible for the ongoing activities of the various Israeli schools and youth movements—some of which are decidedly and, in the latter case, even ideologically irreligious. Most of their out-of-town activity—field trips, camping outings, hikes—are scheduled for the days held most holy by halakha. And, again, personal convictions notwithstanding, it is the ministry's job not only to assist and fund such blatant and public desecration of the Sabbath and the High Holidays, but to study them year by year, learn from past mistakes, and render them all the more enjoyable, efficient, and effective! This is a far cry from grudgingly turning a blind eye to sin for the sake of peace.

Although it is obviously the most desirable form of government when viewed from below, as things now stand halakhically, the liberal, multicultural democracy is at the same time the form of government most awkward for observant Jews to manage from above. The discrepancy is not paradoxical, but it certainly premises a moral double standard that requires urgent attention. From the point of view of the current state of Jewish law, the discrepancy is unavoidable, and the problem of ethical pluralism acute. If they are to abide by their halakhic convictions, Orthodox Jewish legislators and members of government are powerless to do for others what they would have expected others to do for them. The social- turned liberal-democratic vision of statehood on which modern Israel has modeled itself, is one halakha, as it is currently conceived, is incapable of accommodating. From the administrative viewpoint of the sovereign, liberal democracy and Jewish law are to a large extent diametrically opposed.

In principle, Orthodox Israelis have three options, none of them easy. One is to relinquish all Jewish pretension for sovereignty at the metacommunal level. According to this view, dreams of Jewish independence should be limited to self-rule in the narrowest sense of the term. Judaism should be considered a purely communal affair, harboring no desire to rule or to manage the lives of members of other cultural or religious groups.[8] Needless to say, such a position is untenable for those who regard national independence and political sovereignty as possessing religious significance. Orthodox Zionists reject it completely. Those for whom modern statehood is a religiously viable option—not to say a religious duty—have two further options: they can remain faithful to halakha as they find it and reject Western democracy as an halakhically inappropriate model for Jewish statehood. Or they can attempt to make room, from the point of view of the state, for a religiously meaningful approval of ethical pluralism by rethinking halakha along lines akin to latter-day developments in political philosophy. There is no other option. As we have seen, in the role of sovereign, one cannot, in principle, remain loyal both to halakha and to the ideas of liberal democracy as each of them stands at present. One of them needs to be significantly modified.

The last option—that of refashioning halakha in ways capable of assigning religious value to actively assisting halakhically objectionable forms of conduct—is both the most desirable and prima facie the most unthinkable. I believe, however, that the formative texts of halakhic Judaism contain important resources for the meaningful construction of such a position—a thesis I briefly outline in the concluding section. The other two positions do not solve the halakhic problem but merely lower the ante: either by abandoning political sovereignty or by abandoning the most advanced (and highly desired from below) model of statehood. I pursue them in the present context no further.

SOCIAL REGULATION

Bearing in mind the fundamental ethical double standard I have pointed to between the two ideal social frameworks—that by which to be governed as opposed to that by which to govern others—let us turn to the first problem we have been set. The problem of social regulation arises, of course, for both. The issue here steers closer to the latter, however, in no longer being that of living in an ethical diversity, but that of stating normatively and in advance whether and, if so, when the power of the state should be invoked in order to determine the limits of ethical diversity. The difference between the situation in and outside of Israel is still striking in this respect, despite the fact that the question is a normative one.

Questions of social regulation are relevant to both the upper and lower limits of ethical pluralism: how much and how little should be permitted? From a given ethical point of view the law can be found wanting either for enabling forms of conduct considered objectionable by the system in question, or for ruling objectionable forms of conduct that are held by the system to be one's duty, or are at least considered perfectly benign. Concern for problems of the first kind—those to do with the law permitting too much—often reflects consideration for others, a concern for the moral standards of those with whom one disagrees. Taking a stand on such issues often bespeaks a sense of responsibility that extends beyond the boundaries of the community. Questions of the second kind, by contrast, normally premise a concern for one's own.

Not surprisingly perhaps, the only questions of social regulation that have exercised Orthodox Jewish communities outside Israel have been those to do with the Jewish community directly. Despite the fact that Jewish law contains several categories of prohibitions addressed explicitly to non-Jews[9] (and, of course, many, many more addressed to Jews qua Jews), I know of no Orthodox Jewish action taken with a view to impelling Western legislators to "emend the world" by setting the permissible limits of ethical diversity in accord with these norms. Whatever Orthodox Jewish protest exists in this respect is motivated, as far as one can see, solely by self-interest. Although all Western systems of law are excessively liberal by any halakhic standard, its promiscuity is challenged by Orthodox Jews only when they themselves are directly effected—as when certain forms of anti-Semitic rallying, art, and literature are permitted in the name of freedom of speech. Other than that diaspora orthodox Judaism remains largely indifferent to the upper permissible limits of the ethical plurality in which they live.

Challenges to the lower limits are more common, yet equally, if naturally self-centered. Ritual slaughter, *shehita*, is a good example. One of the basic Jewish dietary laws has to do with the way an animal is put down. Halakha requires that it be done by means of a swift and deft slitting of the throat performed by a specially trained *shohet*. Eating the flesh of an otherwise kosher animal or bird killed any differently is strictly prohibited. Swedish law, for example, requires that animals be put down by certain, painless methods only, and prohibits Jewish *shehita* on moral grounds. Requests for separating men from women on public transport in and out of ultra-Orthodox neighborhoods in New York City are systematically turned down as nonconstitutional, and the building of Succoth during the feast of tabernacles is known to violate municipal regulations in some cities. By the same token, although I know of none, one can imagine societies legislating against ritual circumcision for similar reasons (customarily performed publicly without an anesthetic). In cases such as these, Jewish attempts to impel legislators to allow the state to regulate cultural diversity more generously are not uncommon.

The paradox I pointed to at the outset is thus intensified. Despite the seriousness in which halakha is studied and followed by its practitioners, Orthodox Jewish communities remain generally unmoved by society's promiscuity toward forms of conduct they regard ethically or halakhically offensive (except when they themselves are affected). The law is, therefore, hardly ever criticized for being too liberal, but only for not being liberal enough. There seems to be no general (meta)ethical principle at work here beyond sheer ethnocentricity. If there was, one would expect Orthodox Jews to speak up in defense of other ethnic groups similarly constrained and on behalf of the morally depraved, for whom, in their opinion, the law is not strict enough. There is no sign of either. As long as exilic Orthodox Jews are allowed to practice their religion freely and to make their own ethical choices, they remain, it seems, all but indifferent to the limits of state involvement in setting the levels and regulating the boundaries of ethical diversity

The situation in Israel is very different. In fact it is almost wholly reversed. There exists a small measure of state-imposed banning of custom for ethical reasons, though not against Jews, and never of actual religious law. (The state, for instance, prohibits marriages between minors although they are customary [but not religiously required] among certain Muslim communities.) No authentic Jewish custom or ritual is banned by Israeli law. With regard to community life proper, observant Jews do not find themselves in conflict with Israeli law. Orthodox Israeli Jews, in other words, have no reason to complain about the law being too restrictive. Orthodox complaint, and there is much of it in Israel, concentrates exclusively on it being overly permissive.

Unlike anywhere else in the world, Orthodox Israelis campaign vigorously, and not unsuccessfully, for limiting what they take to be public violations of halakha proper and of what they take to be halakhic sensibilities and sensitivities. For the most part, the issues in question are more ritual than ethical, although the involuntary imposition of ritual constraints certainly constitutes an ethical problem. Paradoxically, this is not altogether a bad thing. The bright side is that here one encounters, for the first time, at least in the modern era, real, if perspectival, Orthodox concern for the moral and religious character of the other. When Israeli television was first introduced, there was a huge fight about whether broadcasting should be allowed by law on the Jewish Sabbath. The question had nothing to do with the integrity of religious life among the Orthodox—many of whom continue to avoid television altogether. To this day, by the sheer force of Orthodox parliamentary bargaining power, public transport is discontinued by law on Saturdays and during the Jewish festivals in almost all Israeli townships, and food in state-owned institutions and modes of transport is kept strictly kosher. And one could cite many more examples of this kind. Unlike diaspora Orthodoxy, and unlike the militant anti-Zionist ultra-Orthodox minority, Israeli Orthodox involvement regarding questions of ethical plurality are motivated by more than narrow self-interest. Theirs is a deep concern for the moral and religious character of the wider society and the nature of the public sphere. Like their coreligionists abroad, orthodox Israelis would prefer the ethical diversity in which they live severely limited; here, however, they are willing to do something about it.

And yet, energetic as the campaigning may become, at the metacommunal level the accepted rules of the game remain democratic. Once the majority has made its ruling, and the issue is settled legally, a grudging tight-lipped toleration kicks in naturally. There is bound to be some huffing and puffing, but by and large the rallying, lobbying, boycotting, and public protest remain well contained within the boundaries of perfectly acceptable civil action. As noted earlier, Jewish law comes well equipped when passive toleration is the order of the day. The problem for Israeli Orthodox Jews, I repeat, is far less that of living with parliamentary or municipal rulings they consider halakhically objectionable than that of taking active responsibility as governmental executives for their implementation, once they're accepted. Abiding by majority rule, even when in violation of the spirit or letter of halakha, is for halakhic Judaism the kind of *force majeur* they are fully capable of silently (if sullenly) living with, as long as it does not entail active violation of halakha on their part. Taking responsibility for implementing such rulings does, and it is here, I have argued, that the most pressing problems lie.

Still, Israeli orthodoxy has come a long way in taking civic responsibility for society at large and, allowing for the full range of legitimate protest and civil action, in accepting the democratic processes of decision making as the final arbiter. What it yet lacks is the capacity to view such diversity as religiously desirable, as something worthy of an enabling framework.

CITIZENSHIP

Although Jews have a long history of being denied the full rights of citizenship, it was normally not done on ethical grounds. Delineating the boundaries of nationhood and with them those of full-blooded citizenship is a problem the Western world has grappled with painfully until quite recently. The grounds for the debate, however, were hardly ever ethical. Israel too has its share of ethnic chauvinist extremists who, from time to time, question the right of non-Jewish Israelis to fully fledged citizenship and to determine the fate and national identity of the Jewish state. They demand that major national issues, ranging from questions of church and state to the sealing of peace treaties, require by law a "Jewish" or "Zionist" parliamentary majority. But, again, although the outcome is of major ethical consequence, the motivation of such groups is usually not.

Halakha has nothing to say on how civil society should handle ethically based disagreements about civil status, but from time to time halakhists have been exercised by certain questions of civil status and of the proper deployment of civil rights and duties. Let me briefly discuss one such issue by way of an example.

The question of the right of women to vote and to run for office was raised and debated in Palestine around 1920. The context was halakhic, but some of the main lines of argument utilized by both parties were ethical.[10] Rabbi Avraham Isaac ha-Kohen Kook, Ashkenazic chief rabbi at the time, ruled firmly against women's suffrage. He organized his reasoning under three headings as answers to three separate questions: (a) Regarding the law: is it permitted or prohibited by halakha? (b) Regarding the common good: which of the options better promotes the common good for Israel? (c) Regarding the ideal: which is better supported by our moral consciousness? He goes on to explain: "The exposition must take all these values into account, for I must relate to all ranks [of the public]: the completely faithful of Israel for whom the halakhic ruling is central, those for whom the nation's is decisive, and those whose main view is to the moral ideal in itself." Rabbi Kook's consideration of all three aspects clearly bespeaks, even at that early date, a real sense of social responsibility extending far beyond the world of discourse of the community of his immediate followers.

Regarding halakha proper, he keeps his reasoning brief and simple: in all our canonical writings, he asserts, "we hear one voice; namely, that the duty of fixed public service falls upon men, for 'It is Man's manner to dominate and not Woman's manner to dominate.'[11] Roles of authority, judgment, and testimony are not her domain, as all her honor is within [the confines of the home]." The pragmatic and moral arguments he offers follow suit. It is also in the common good not to allow women's suffrage, because the "best of the gentiles generally and the best of the British people particularly" in whose hands lies the fate of the Jewish people's claim to the land of Israel, expect of us to realize the values of the Bible, which they too hold sacred but lack the ability to live up to, and in which "the special feeling of respect towards Woman . . . is based and centered on domestic life." The moral reasons offered by Rabbi Kook focus on the holiness of the Jewish household and the centrality of domestic peace and tranquillity for the quality of national life. "The psychological cause of the call for women's right to participate in public elections in [other] nations," he states, "comes fundamentally from the unhappy position of the masses of women in these nations. Had their family's situation been as peaceful and dignified as it is generally in Israel, women themselves . . . would not demand what they term 'rights' of election for women in a manner that might ruin domestic peace." He concludes that "We dare not obliterate the splendor of our sisters' lives, and embitter them through the din of opinions and disputations of elections and political questions." For the sake of family harmony, politics, the business of men, should be banned from the private domain and duly confined to its proper place: the public sphere.

Despite Rabbi Kook's considerable standing among the orthodox community during those years, and the fact that he was joined in his ruling against women's suffrage by several other rabbinic authorities, his ruling went wholly unheeded. One reason for this was the sephardic Rabbi Ben-Zion Hai Uziel's very different ruling issued in response to Kook's. His conclusions were stated as firmly and as unequivocally as Kook's: "A woman has the perfect right of participation in elections . . . [and a] woman may also be elected by the consent and ordinance on the community." He offers an ethical argument in favor of his position, and an ethical rejoinder to Kook's ethical argument against it. "It is inconceivable" that women be denied the right to vote. "For in these elections we raise leaders upon us, and empower our representatives to speak in our name, to organize the matters of our *Yishuv*, and to levy taxes on our property. . . . How then can one simultaneously . . . lay upon [women] the duty to obey those elected by the people, yet deny them the right to vote in the elections?" His rejection of Kook's argument from domestic tranquillity is equally decisive: if women's suffrage is to be prohibited

> for the sake of preserving the peace at home . . . we must also deny the right of voting to adult sons and daughters still living in their father's home. For in all cases where our rabbis concerned themselves with preserving tranquillity, they gave equal treatment to the wife and to adult sons living at home (see Bavli, *Bava Metzia* 12a–b). . . . But the truth is, that differences of opinion will surface in some form or other, for no one can suppress completely his opinions and attitudes. Rather familial love based on mutual labor is strong enough to withstand such differences of opinion.

He proves that, in addition, women may be elected by showing that the prohibition against appointing a queen stems not from halakha deeming women ineligible in principle for the job but from a concern for the "dignity of the community." Public opinion is incapable of overriding considerations of the former kind, he argues but has everything to do with the latter. If a majority of the community votes for a women, it would be a violation of its dignity *not* to appoint her!

Rabbi Uziel won the day. Participation in the Israeli elections is still debated among the ultra-Orthodox, but even they make no halakhic distinction between men and women in this respect. For Orthodox Judaism, women's suffrage is no longer a problem. Furthermore, in two of Israel's five Orthodox parties women also run for office.

However, the question under consideration is not that of Orthodox Judaism's position on the issue of citizenship but that of its position on the way ethically based disagreements about citizenship should be handled. Let us imagine, then, that Rabbi Kook had won the day and ask what would have been his and his followers' reaction to the state allowing women who felt differently to vote anyway. Although the question was never raised, had it been, it would have brought us back to the point I have been making all along. Orthodox women, even in Israel, would have followed the rabbi's ruling and piously refrained from voting while grudgingly accepting the fact that other women do. They'd have no problem whatsoever with the fact that others might think differently, and be allowed to do so, as long as they themselves were able to live their lives as they see fit. Problems would only arise when an Orthodox Jew was put in charge of actively implementing the women's vote law. It would be halakhically problematic even if all his job amounted to was to inform women of their rights. As I have stated repeatedly, ignoring violations of Torah is one thing, actively promoting them is another.

LIFE-AND-DEATH DECISIONS, HUMAN SEXUALITY, AND BEYOND: VALUING ETHICAL DIVERSITY— RELIGIOUS POSSIBILITIES

I think it has now become clear that the case studies selected for discussion add little to clarifying the main issue for halakhic Judaism: namely that of accommodating ethical plural*ism* from a managerial position. The current halakhic debates on physician-assisted suicide and same-sex unions are as fascinating as they are pressing, but bear little on the main issue in question. Those interested will find engaging and accessible introductions to the two issues in Noam J. Zohar's "Jewish Deliberation on Suicide"[12] and Bradley Shavit Artson's "Enfranchising the Monogamous Homosexual" respectively.[13] Here too, the halakhic tradition, and the current debate have nothing to say about the proper way to manage second-order regulation and accommodation of contrasting systems. On both issues, orthodox communities outside of Israel, though firmly committed to the teachings of their rabbinic leaders, remain largely indifferent to the moral choices of other communities, as to the levels of legitimacy granted them by the law. The situation in Israel is quite different. Prior to voting, orthodox Knesset members will do everything in their power to secure a majority in their favor. Protest may be loud and the rhetoric heated but only until the vote is taken. Once it is, the situation will closely resemble other Western countries, but with the one exception I have stressed repeatedly: in Israel there will inevitably be Orthodox governmental officials with the impossible task of actively enabling and vouching for the successful violation of norms they hold sacred.

The problem, to repeat, is not that of having to share political and social space with communities who knowingly conduct their lives in violation of halakha, nor is it the problem of determining the cultural-religious character of the public domain; it is that of taking responsibility for implementing and managing the very sharing. What is needed for halakhically committed members of such a government is not tolerance, but some form of religiously justified pluralism (in the normative rather than in the descriptive sense of the word). But how is it possible to square pluralism with a system of thought and action that claims access to the ultimate Good based on transcendental truths? On what grounds can halakhically committed Jews possibly view forms of conduct that are decidedly rejected *within* their religious communities as worthy of active promotion beyond their gates?[14]

Such grounds exist, I believe, along lines similar to those proposed, say, in Karl Popper's *The Open Society and Its Enemies*. According to such an approach, the grounds for ethical diversity are primarily *not* to do with a moral duty to defend individual autonomy, or with a moral obligation to keep out of one's neighbor's hair. Popper's position *entails* such liberal visions of individual autonomy but ultimately *rests* upon epistemological rather than moral or metaphysical arguments. Ethical systems diametrically opposed to one's own are valued by members of the open society, not merely on moral or legal grounds, but out of a realization that the environment of a plurality of engaging, especially conflicting voices is the setting in which one's own system is best and most effectively articulated and developed.

The obvious advantage of grounding ideas in pluralism in this way is that it sidesteps the entire issue of fundamental rights, an idea halakhic Judaism for one has great difficulty accommodating as an a priori given. The acknowledgment of humankind's profound fallibilism especially in the public sphere, of the fundamental time-boundedness and context-dependence of ethical judgments, coupled to the almost built-in instability of those very contexts, premises little more than that life, especially social life, is exceedingly complex and unpredictable, and that the chances of us making a mess of things are enormous—with this few would disagree. The upshot is an epistemic hesitance, modesty, and openness and an awareness that we are poor critics of our own ethical choices, that things are best done piecemeal, and that other viewpoints are not merely to be tolerated but to be highly valued, not for their own intrinsic worth so much as for their capacity to challenge our own by highlighting its flaws and shortcomings.

Of course, the Popperian option need not *deny* the idea that people have fundamental rights to whatever belief system or inoffensive form of conduct they see fit. The liberal and Popperian options are independent of one another but are not mutually exclusive. Liberalism alone, however, provides little incentive for building and maintaining a society transcending the boundaries of one's own community. Acknowledging the other's right to the belief system of his or her choice offers, in and of itself, little reason for establishing frameworks for living with others. Liberal rights' talk provides sufficient grounds for tolerating others once they are around, but not for *wanting* to have them around. Acknowledging a person's right to his beliefs entails an obligation to tolerate him holding to them but, of itself, attaches to them no intrinsic value. The Popperian option does. One wants to surround oneself with people who think and live differently in order to enrich one's own beliefs and life-style. On this inherently pluralistic model the other is not merely tolerated but is valued for his otherness. The beauty of it is that although the Popperian option is capable of delivering more than the traditional liberal options, it need not premise fundamental rights at all (although it need not deny them). If only for that the Popperian option is an attractive alternative for religious systems whose capacity for accommodating a rights-based liberalism is severely limited. The argument from epistemic modesty is an argument for more than toleration. It is an argument for pluralism. Arguments from rights compel us to take seriously a person's ethical choices but, of themselves, attach no intrinsic value to what he or she chooses; arguing from epistemic modesty, by contrast, attaches great intrinsic value to the outcome of their choosing but, in itself, cares little about their liberty to do so.

Furthermore, and perhaps most important, by allowing one to sidestep the entire rights issue, the Popperian argument from epistemic modesty provides grounds for the type of two-tier thinking mentioned earlier. In fact, it justifies and encourages it. To recall, the problem of religious sovereignty is that of justifying religiously working at governmental level actively to ensure the security and thriving of forms of conduct held to be sinful in the eyes of one's own religion. It is that of viewing forms of conduct that are actively condemned within one's own community, as worthy of active support outside it. Now, the ideal Open Society comprises epistemically humble learners, rather than systematic agnostics. In a deep sense, the dynamic of Popperian enrichment is the more effective the greater the contrast between the various viewpoints, and the firmer they are initially held. Criticism—and subsequently the learning process that may come in its wake—is more effective the more there is at stake: the more serious the problems, the more cherished the solutions at hand. Ideally, a person or community prudently motivated by Popperian considerations of epistemic humility will seek partners to debate whose views are as seriously held as they are significantly different from their own. And when such considerations are applied to state politics, one, it seems, should regard as ideal a multicultural society comprising a plurality of relatively decided communities fairly confident in their views.

But is such an option available for halakhic Judaism? Elsewhere, I have argued at length for the existence, within the formative texts of halakhic Judaism, of a major school of thought whose self-conscious epistemic presuppositions closely resemble those of the Popperian school.[15] The approach to which I am referring is aptly described in the words of Rabbi Naftali Tzvi Yehuda Berlin, writing in 1865 or so, in the introduction to his monumental commentary on the Pentateuch: *Ha'amek Davar.*

> Just as it is not possible for the wise student of nature ever to boast knowledge of all of nature's secrets . . ., and just as there is no guarantee that what he has accomplished in his investigations will not be invalidated by colleagues in this generation or the next who elect to study the same things differently, so *it is not possible for the student of the Torah to claim that he has attended to each and every point that claims attention, and even that which he does explain—there is never proof that he has ascertained the truth of the Torah.*
> (emphasis added)

However, Rabbi Berlin did not intend his surprisingly Popperian analogy of Torah study to science to apply to halakha. The model he attributes to the development of halakha is cumulative rather than revolutionary (resembling mathematical, rather than scientific development).[16] Unlike the interpreter of Scripture, the halakhist, he urged, does not seek to invalidate and improve upon the efforts of his forbears, as does the exegete, but to build upon their rulings by concentrating exclusively on halakhic lacunae.

Berlin's two models of development differ in the treatment of their legacies. Halakhists, according to Berlin, are wholly bound and obligated by the body of law they inherit and are, therefore, limited in their legislative efforts to questions on which no ruling has yet been issued. Biblical exegetes, by contrast, motivated by a profound epistemic modesty, are encouraged to challenge and improve upon former interpretations. Owing to their different attitudes to tradition, I have dubbed the two approaches traditionalist and antitraditionalist respectively. Contrary to Rabbi Ber-

lin's depiction—a view widely shared by halakhically committed Jews—
I believe there is strong evidence for the presence, within the talmudic
literature, of a reflective and insistent antitraditionalist approach *to halakha*. As noted, I have made the case for this contention in a book-length
study of the talmudic literature. It is a prevalent voice, which is detailed
and valorized in a variety of talmudic texts and genres. One example will
suffice in the present context.

The dispute between the Houses of Hillel and Shammai—schools of
halakhic thought that dominated the world of Jewish learning prior to
the fall of Jerusalem in 70 c.e.—is regarded as the paradigm of halakhic
disagreement. The talmudic literature contains much legal and legendary
material concerning the houses and the two sages to whom they owe their
names. The dispute between them covers three hundred or so matters
of halakha. In thirty-four cases, the texts record debates between them
following the statement of their initial contrasting views. These allow the
reader a glimpse of the different and the shared discursive practices attributed by the texts to the two houses. One such difference is highly significant. In seven of the fifteen dialogues in which the Shammaites are accorded the last word, the Hillelites are on record as having changed their
initial view and "admitting" to that of their adversaries. In none of the
eighteen cases in which the Hillelites are accorded the last word do the
Shammaites change their mind. A willingness to retract and modify a
bona fide halakhic legacy in the face of counterargument is the hallmark
of antitraditionalism. Nothing better attests to such a view than evidence
of actual replacement of a former ruling. Unlike traditionalists, who are
obligated absolutely by their traditions (and are, therefore, unable to
abandon a ruling even in the face of a counterargument for which they
have no answer), antitraditionalists, motivated by perpetual self-doubt,
are constantly on the lookout for possible flaws and problems in the system. It is clear from this and a variety of other evidence[17] that the talmudic
redactors responsible for these texts envisaged the two houses—whose
disputes are formative of the talmudic enterprise—as apt representatives
of the two approaches I have been discussing. It is also evident that major
talmudic texts that comment on the houses' controversy viewed it in the
same terms. One such text asserts that the reason we follow the House of
Hillel in matters of halakha is because it was humble and accommodating,
and would not only give the Shammaite view a hearing, but went out of
its way to hear it before stating its own.[18]

The talmudic antitraditionalist is, what I have elsewhere termed, a constructive skeptic, who translates his personal intellectual modesty into a
powerful method of critical reasoning. The Hillelites' attitude toward the
Shammaites is more than mere toleration. They accord their adversaries
more than the right to an opinion, and freedom of speech. No, they des-

perately need them around, for the keen challenge they afford their own hesitantly held views. They disagree with the Shammaites bitterly, but value their presence not for the cozy security of agreement that they offer, but for the exciting, constructive effects of their criticism. They are valued for their profound otherness!

Of course, all of this is very much in-house, and there is much work to be done in order to be able to extrapolate from it to modern social multicultural environments. Still, the existence of a firm tradition of halakhic antitraditionalism in the canonical halakhic literature provides valuable resources for Orthodox Judaism to attend to the problems at hand. The most important of these resources are two: a legitimacy to rethink halakha on ethical grounds and, even more important for the present context, a healthy, religiously meaningful pluralism that allows one both to disagree keenly and to value deeply the existence of ethical systems opposed to one's own.

NOTES

1. For a superb survey and analysis of the variety of Jewish religious reactions to the Zionist idea, see A. Ravitzky, *Messianism, Zionism and Jewish Religious Radicalism* (Chicago: University of Chicago Press, 1996). For the Orthodox opposition to early Zionism, see pp. 40–78; for their latter-day outgrowths in Israeli society, pp. 145–80.

2. These roughly speaking comprised two groups who differed in their disagreement with the majority. Some joined the Zionist movement claiming contrary to the majority that the messianic era should be actively ushered in. Others ruled that seeking a political solution for the Jewish people should have nothing to do with messianism and be pursued regardless of messianic aspiration. For further details, see ibid., pp. 10–39, 79–144.

3. The problem I am pointing to is, of course, a general one, that is by and large confined to Israel in fact, not in principle. The most notable example of a non-Israeli politician facing similar circumstances is, of course, U.S. Senator Joseph Leiberman of Connecticut. Nor is the problem, in principle, an exclusively Orthodox Jewish one. Any governmental executive firmly committed to a system of norms significantly less tolerant than the law of the land is bound to face similar dilemmas.

4. See, for instance, G. J. Blidstein, "The Monarchic Imperative in Rabbinic Perspective," *AJS Review* 78 (1982–83): 15–39; M. Lorberbaum, "Politics and the Limits of Law in Jewish Medieval Thought: Maimonides and Nissim Gerondi," (Ph.D. dissertation, Hebrew University, 1992); A. Ravitzky, *Religion and State in Jewish Philosophy: Models of Unity, Division, Collision and Subordination* (in Hebrew) (Jerusalem: Israel Democracy Institute, 1998); and M. Walzer, M. Lorberbaum, N. Zohar, and Y. Lorberbaum, eds., *The Jewish Political Tradition*, vol.1: *Authority* (New Haven: Yale University Press), 2000, chap. 3, "Monarchy."

5. Yerushalmi, *Gittin*, v, 47c.

6. This was the official position of the vast majority of non-Zionist Jews even after the establishment of the state. Since then, however, most Orthodox communities have accepted the existence and political authority of the state (de facto at least), participate actively in the elections, and are keenly represented at the legislative and executive levels.

7. Some years ago Rabbi Eliyahu Bakshi-Doron, sephardic chief rabbi of Israel, was approached by an observant Jewish travel agent inquiring whether halakha permitted him to serve non-Jewish pilgrims to the Holy Land. The chief rabbi's response is short and decisive. Although one is not required to hinder Muslim and Christian pilgrims actively, halakha clearly prohibits actively assisting them, let alone profiting from them in any way. ("Let the person who raised the question be rewarded twice," the rabbi concludes, "once for his obviously genuine concern for peace, and again for concentrating hereafter on encouraging and assisting in bringing many, many Jews to The Holy Land.") With regard to private travel agencies Rabbi Bakshi-Doron's ruling poses no problem. It may sound awful, and terribly impolitically correct, but, in principle, can be lived with. Every religion has certain areas of seclusion from which nonmembers are barred. Such being the halakha (and as far as I can tell the chief rabbi's reasoning is halakhically impeccable), one can easily imagine separate travel agencies serving Orthodox communities to the ritual exclusion of others just as special kosher restaurants, bakeries, and wineries cater to the Orthodox. A serious problem arises, however, when the person seeking the rabbi's advice is not a private entrepreneur but an Orthodox member of the Israeli cabinet.

8. Incredibly, despite their full participation in state politics, this remains the official ideology of one of the two Israeli *haredi* parties, who consistently pay it formal, ritual lip-service by insisting that their representatives receive full ministerial authority but without assuming the title of minister. By only becoming deputy ministers they avoid having to take the ministerial oath. Yet with no minister above them to answer to (the prime minister technically assumes the ministerial role himself), they are able to assume responsibility without actually accepting it. To the best of my knowledge this has always been the case since the state was established in 1948.

9. These are known as the Noachian Laws: laws supposed by the rabbis to have been binding upon all of mankind prior to Sinai, and upon non-Jews thereafter. There is considerable disagreement in the talmudic texts as to the precise list of Noachian laws. Basing their exegesis on Genesis 2:16 and 9:4 some sources list the following: (1) not to worship idols; (2) not to blaspheme the name of God; (3) to establish courts of justice; (4) not to kill; (5) not to commit adultery; (6) not to rob; (7) not to eat the flesh cut from a living animal (Genesis Rabba 16:9, 24:5). Elsewhere (Bavli, *Sanhedrin* 56b) blasphemy and the establishment of courts are dropped in favor of the emasculation of animals and the pairing of animals of different species. Elsewhere still (Bavli, *Hulin* 92a) the list is much extended.

10. The two parties to the debate were Rabbis Abraham ha-Kohen Kook and Ben Zion Hai Uziel, who were both approached by concerned members of the religious labor movement, Misrahi, around the same time. For the two responsa,

see respectively A.I.H. Kook, *Ma'amre Ha-Re'ayah* (Jerusalem: Avner, 1984), pp. 189–94 and B. H. Uziel, *Piskei Uziel* (Jerusalem: Mossad Harav Kook, 1977), pp. 228–34. For excellent English-language renditions of the texts and commentary by David Novak, see M. Walzer, M. Lorberbaum, and N. Zohar, eds., *The Jewish Political Tradition*, vol. 2: *Membership* (New Haven: Yale University Press, forthcoming), chap. 13, "Gender Hierarchy."

11. Bavli, *Yevamot* 65b.

12. Dealing first with passive euthanasia and suicide, and finally with active euthanasia, Zohar skillfully traces the conflicting voices within halakhic discourse. (More on the polyphonous nature of halakhic discourse later.) Most agree that since God is piously regarded the sole bestower and taker of life, death, when imminent, should be allowed to take its natural course. Some conclude that "we are, therefore, forbidden to do anything to hasten death" and prohibit any form of human intervention (e.g., Rabbi Eliezer Waldenberg, *Tsits Eliezer*, vol. 8, "Ramat Rachel," section 29, 1965), whereas others conclude to the contrary that it is, for the same very reason, our duty *not* to prolong a dying person's life "artificially" (e.g., Rabbi Haim David Ha'Levi, "Disconnecting a Terminal Patient from an Artificial Respirator," *Techumin* 2 [1981]: 304). Suicide, strictly prohibited for the same reason ("No creature in the world owns a person's soul, not even his own"), also has its exceptions—even biblical exceptions. Martyrdom is, of course, one. More important for the question at hand is Saul's apparently justified suicide. The nature of the legitimacy of Saul's act is disputed by the rabbis, however. The most widely accepted position is that of Nachmanides, who opines that to accept "God as sovereign does not imply He is a Master without compassion." In extreme situations, such as Saul's, suicide is permitted. However, in such cases, argues Zohar, it hardly makes sense to prohibit helping one do so. Still this seems to be the position of all halakhists (as it is the situation in many non-halakhic jurisdictions.) See, for instance, Rabbi P. Toledano of London's recent "A Responsum on Issues of Medical Halakha," in J. Sacks, ed., *Tradition and Transition* (London: Jews' College, 1986), pp. i–xv. For further details, see N. J. Zohar, "Jewish Deliberations on Suicide: Exceptions, Toleration, and Assistance," in M. P. Battin, R. Rhodes, and A. Silvers, eds., *Physician Assisted Suicide: Expanding the Debate* (New York: Routledge, 1998), pp. 362–72. See also by the same author *Alternatives in Jewish Bioethics* (Albany: State University of New York Press, 1997), chap. 2, "Death: Natural Process and Human Intervention."

13. Artson's intriguing paper is written with a view to break new halakhic ground rather than summarize the halakhic situation. Unlike euthanasia, there is very little, if any, halakhic disagreement regarding homosexuality—which is flatly prohibited across the board. Artson sets out to meet the challenge, not by contesting former rulings, but by arguing that they were issued with a very different notion of homosexuality in mind than the type of relationship currently under discussion. Until recently, he argues, the very notion of a lasting, monogamous, sharing, single-sex union, of the type for which he seeks halakhic recognition, was unheard of. All known ancient forms of homosexuality, he claims, were short-lasting, forced, abusive, and purely sexual. Single-sex marriage, he suggests, should therefore be treated as an halakhic lacuna and dealt with irrespective of

former rulings. For a keen and detailed discussion of this theme, see B. S. Artson, "Enfranchising the Monogamous Homosexual: A Legal Possibility, a Moral Imperative," *S'vara*, 3, 1 (1993): 15–26; J. Roth, "Homosexuality and Halakhic Decision-Making," Ibid., pp. 27–34; B. S Artson, "Response to Rabbi Joel Roth," ibid, pp. 35–38.

14. This is a project very different from that of the halakhic rethinking of specific forms of conduct. The innovative halakhic moves suggested with respect to first-order problems such as women's suffrage or single-sex unions are of major importance in Judaism's ongoing confrontation with modernity. But they are of no significance to the problem of sovereignty, which asserts itself, I repeat, wherever the law supports violations of halakha. What is needed are not ways of viewing such ethical choices as *un*sinful but of viewing their existence as religiously valuable *despite* them being sinful.

15. M. Fisch, *Rational Rabbis, Science and Talmudic Culture* (Bloomington: Indiana University Press, 1997).

16. See, for example, his commentaries to Exod. 34:1, 27 and Lev. 18:5, his preliminary remarks to Deuteronomy, and most importantly his introductory essay to *She'iltot de-Rav Ahai Gaon*, entitled "The Way of Torah" (Jerusalem: Mossad Harav Kook, 1986), esp. pp. 5–12.

17. For further details, see H. Shapira and M. Fisch "The Debates between the Houses of Shammai and Hillel: The Meta-Halakhic Issue" (Hebrew), *Iyyunei Mishpat* 22, 3 (1999).

18. Bavli, *Eruvin* 13b.

Jewish Responses to Modernity

Adam B. Seligman

As Menachem Fisch notes at the outset, Judaism does not speak with one voice. Indeed, it never has. In fact, as much as anyone, Menachem's own work has shown how a polyphony of voices constitutes the core moment of the Jewish legal tradition. Furthermore, and in terms of our interest here, it is well to remember that Jewish Orthodoxy, which Menachem has decided to take up in his essay, emerged in the nineteenth century as a reaction to modernizing and pluralistic tendencies within Judaism. With the spread of emancipation and its deepening within society, Jews began to accommodate themselves to modernity and sought ways to re-shape tradition and its dictates. These moves were expressed in matters ranging from ritual slaughter, to the placement of the bridal canopy, to the length of time to wait before interring the dead, to the language of the rabbinic sermon, and just about every imaginable regulation and cus-tom in between.

The first Reform Rabbinic Assembly of 1844 (fifty-eight years after the death of Moses Mendelssohn) sought, in the words of the historian Jacob Katz "to create harmony between public behavior and the injunctions of the halakhah."[1] Less radical changes were instituted by the Neolog movement in Hungary which, together with the Reform movement in Hungary and Germany, attempted to give institutional form to the growth of nontraditional forms of worship and behavior among both academi-cally trained rabbis and their congregants. Orthodoxy arose in response and virulent protest to these movements and their agendas—going so far as to prohibit, not only attendance, but even entry into a Reform syna-gogue. (Jews, we should note, are permitted to pray in Moslem mosques.)

Of course, 150 years later the positions have somewhat changed, and movements such as modern orthodoxy have emerged which, under the banner of "torah and science" betray an openness to aspects of modernity inconceivable only a few generations ago. This "openness" continues however to be mediated in matters of pluralistic behavior and the accep-tance of any form of Jewish diversity. Thus we should recall the more contemporary version of the Hatam Sofer's prohibition on attendance in Reform Synagogues in the twentieth century; the Orthodox, Pesak Din (rabbinic court ruling) of the prohibiting membership in the (now de-funct) Synagogue Council of America or the New York Board of Rabbis. Participation seemed to imply recognition which remained an anathema.[2]

On the other hand, the recent rulings of the Reform Rabbinic Assembly to return to broader forms of ritual observance (following what is essentially the lead of the congregants) indicate a new appreciation of aspects of Judaism not necessarily recognized in the famous (or infamous) 1885 Pittsburgh banquet of Reform rabbis where shrimp and lobster (but not pork, it should be noted) were served.

I remind us of the historical background then, not for its immediate relevance to current positions but because it highlights the two poles of Jewish response to modernity: acceptance and rejection. At the heart of both are the different Jewish responses to the modern value of individual autonomy and pluralistic values inherent to the political agenda of liberal regimes. Clearly traditional Judaism did not wish to remain disenfranchised and powerless. But it also did not wish to pay the cost that entry into the broader community brought with it. That cost, necessarily, was the acceptance of those pluralistic assumptions rooted in modern doctrines of individual rights and moral autonomy. As Menachem's essay makes clear, resources for individual autonomy are not abundant within traditional Judaism, which, to this day, puts Orthodoxy in a rather difficult situation vis-à-vis liberal political dicta, especially in conditions of political sovereignty.

While Menachem's essay makes these issues painstakingly clear—indeed, brings to our awareness issues that I believe will become of greater global concern in the next century—he does not address the overwhelming theoretical and philosophical set of problems that Judaism has with issues involving both ethics and pluralism. It is these issues that I wish, however briefly, to highlight here. I hope thereby to provide a brief theoretical postscript to Menachem's elegant argument.

My own contention would be that a position of ethical pluralism presupposes a commitment to individual rights, Kantian autonomy, and liberal ideas of the self as a self-regulating and autonomous moral agent subject to dicta of a transcendental reason rather than those of a transcendent heteronomy. Only from such a set of presuppositions with their inherent distinction between public and private realms, selves and desiderata, can a principled acceptance of ethical pluralism be advocated and advanced.

The universalism of reason, upon which the transcendental edicts of the French *Déclaration de la droits d'homme et citoyen* or the American *Decleration of Independence* are predicated, serve to anchor citizen's lives in a shared experience of reason. The very sameness of interest, posited by Hobbes, or later Hume, provide a new basis for that very modern, liberal society that Menachem discusses in his essay. Thus the social bonds existing between people were characterized by Hume in this now famous quote:

Your corn is ripe today; mine will be so to-morrow. 'Tis profitable for us both, that I shou'd labour with you today, and that you shou'd aid me to-morrow. I have no kindness for you, and know you have as little for me. . . . Hence I learn to do a service to another, without bearing him any real kindness; because I foresee, that he will return my service, in expectation of another of the same kind, and in order to maintain the same correspondence of good offices with me or with others.[3]

And the adjudication of disputes between such self-regulating and autonomous agents was, in Adam Smith's words, achieved through appeal "to the eyes of the third party, that impartial spectator, the great inmate of the breast who judges impartially between conflicting interests." In Smith's terms:

We endeavor to examine our own conduct as we imagine any other fair and impartial spectator would examine it. If, upon placing ourselves in his situation, we thoroughly enter into all the passions and motives which influenced it, we approve of it, by sympathy with the approbation of this supposed equitable judge. If otherwise, we enter into his disapprobation and condemn it.[4]

Before we can make any proper comparison of opposing interests, we must change our position. We must view them from neither our own place nor yet from his, neither with our own eyes nor yet with his, but from the place and with the eyes of a third person, who has no particular connection with either, and who judges impartially between us.[5] In both Hume and Smith we find that orientation based on the autonomous, contracting individual engaged in exchange with other such individuals that constitute modern politics and society.

The practical problems that Menachem parses out in terms of contemporary Orthodoxy in Israel and elsewhere, all turn, in the end, on the only mediate (at best) acceptance of these philosophical positions within traditional Jewish thought. Note that even the Catholic Church, in the second Vatican Council, came to accept not the rights of error but the rights of those who erred. This was in marked reversal of the Church's prior position that "Error has no rights." As indicated earlier, Judaism—which recognizes individual responsibility and agency—does not privilege the type of modern, post-Hobbesian vision of the individual upon which a politics of rights may rest. Nor does it share, for obvious historical reasons, the Christian privileging of intentionality and *Innerlichkeit*, which provided important foundations for the modern doctrine of rights.[6] Again, then, the presuppositions of individual rights as a precondition of a principled position of pluralism is a difficult position to sustain from within a traditional Jewish conception.

The philosophical problem of pluralism, however, rests on the analytically prior problem of ethics, that is, on the acceptance of a realm of normatively desirable behavior that is independent from the realm of legal injunctions. The diremption of ethics from law, of conscience from obligation, is extremely problematic in Judaism, although it is central to Christian and most especially to Protestant consciousness. Not surprisingly, pluralism is a most American value, reflecting this society's roots in seventeenth-century sectarian Protestantism and the illuminism of the "inner light." From the apostle Paul's rejection of the law as the necessary vehicle of salvation for gentiles to Moses Mendelssohn's exposition on the centrality of the law to Judaism, it has always been recognized that what distinguished Jewish civilization from Christian civilization is precisely this small matter of the relation between legal obligations and ethical ones.

To be sure, Judaism has had its pietistic movements, such as the Musar movement of R. Israel Salanter in the mid-nineteenth century, but this was far from stressing any position of ethical pluralism or, indeed, of ethics separate from the law.

The philosophically intriguing question from the perspective of Jewish tradition is thus of the relevance and status of ethical dicta in relation to legal edicts. This issue has been explored more extensively in terms of the status of the dicta *lifnim mishurat hadin* (beyond the line of the law) upon which nearly all attempts to argue an ethical orientation autonomous of the law have rested. Just how extralegal or extra-halakhic (the corpus of Jewish law) the injunctions of *lifnim mishurat hadin* are, however has been a point of continuing controversy. Although this is not the place to enter into this controversy, we should note that, on the whole, Orthodox commentators have stressed the seamless web that binds the legal injunctions of the halakha with those of *lifnim mishurat hadin*, whereas liberal commentators have tried to use the concept in order to argue for an extra-halakhic standard by which the halakha itself could be critiqued.

However much I would like to support the liberal reading, I am afraid that I am unconvinced. We must note, for example, that none of the (nine) examples given in the Babylonian Talmud for *lifnim mishurat hadin* involve breaking the law to follow the dictates of conscience. All, in fact, turn on acts of supererogation and the forgoing of legal rights and waiver of benefits usually by rabbis of extraordinary piety and virtue. The concept of *lifnim mishurat hadin* thus sanctions certain acts that the law does not require, but never acts that the law does not permit!

Indeed, for Maimonides *lifnim mishurat hadin* represents nothing more or less than the standards of saintly behavior that are neither required nor even desired for the majority of the populace.[7] For Maimonides, we recall, natural morality was both incorporated and superseded with the Sinitic revelation. Indeed, so much has the unity of halakha and *lifnim mishurat hadin* been the majority view that even statements that would seem to point in other directions—such as R. Yohanan's lament that the Temple was destroyed because the populace only followed the law and did not "go beyond its limits"—have been interpreted to point to *a halakhically mandated* edict to "go beyond the law." Indeed, the writings of both Nachmanides and the Maggid Mishneh (commentator on Maimonides) have explained the presence of areas unspecified by law as existing only to permit casuistic interpretation of general principles, not autonomous or pluralistic directives.[8] The realm of independent ethics is, throughout, seriously circumscribed. As argued by one contemporary commentator: "The very character of halakha as both legal system and divine revelation . . . blurs the distinction between law and ethics. Ethical obligations, like all divine imperatives within the tradition will be understood as part and parcel of the halakha, that divinely revealed law that governs the ongoing life of Israel. Moreover, the close relationship in Judaism between ethics and piety, between doing the right thing and doing the holy or godlike thing, tends to blur the distinction between moral obligation and supererogation."[9] Again, heteronomous dictates as prescribing normatively binding action defines Judaism's attitude toward both the halakha as well as toward any behavior that may be adduced from *lifnim mishurat hadin.*

There are, however, other possible approaches to the issue of ethical pluralism in Judaism. One of these is noted at the end of Menachem's essay and turns on a certain humility or what he terms epistemological modesty toward our own truth-claims. Not possessing the means to ascertain ultimate truths, we must entertain the possibility that our own understanding is faulty. A road from here to a more principled pluralism can well be imagined and that is one that Menachem more than others has argued for. Interestingly this resonates with the argument put forward by Jean Bodin in his famous *Colloquium heptaplomeres de rerum sublimium aracnis abditis* (Colloquium of the seven about the secrets of the sublime), written in the later third of the sixteenth century.[10] This dialogue between a Catholic, a Lutheran, a Calvinist, a Jew, a Muslim, an advocate of natural religion, and a skeptic refuses to reconcile all differences of religion, in one single and unitary truth-claim. Bodin's *Colloquium* seems to value dialogue for dialogue's sake. Valued is not the art of discourse for the sake of achieving a single and unitary truth but, as it were, for itself. The exchange of diverse views is for itself valuable. Not the negation of difference but its very upholding is the point of dialogue. None converts. None is bested in the sense of having lost his argument. Nor do they agree that their differences are only in matters inconsequential, marginal, or inessential. Nor, yet again, do they adopt an argument of skepticism toward religious truths, or lack of faith or relativism (which would, of course, be the modern version of such a dialogue). All keep their faith or their belief in both the existence of truth as in their own version thereof. Yet, they *tolerate* difference and argument, even revel in it. In this Bodin's work is perhaps analogous to the Jewish notion of *torah l'shma* and very close to the polyvalence of Talmudic discourse found in the Babylonian Talmud that Menachem and others have emphasized as containing seeds of pluralist perspective.[11]

A rather different notion of epistemological modesty as sustaining not pluralism but at least a degree of tolerance can be culled from the writings of certain ultra-Orthodox thinkers. One such scholar, the Chazon Ish (R. Avraham Yeshiya Karelitz, d. 1958)—the main ideologue of ultra-Orthodoxy in contemporary Israel—argued that since we live in a time when the sources of revelation are occluded, there is no authority for implementing divine commandments. As explained by Shlomo Fischer, because the epistemological condition of exile sustains unbelief, adherents thereof cannot be held culpable.[12] Although such a position does not perhaps support a positively privileged pluralism, it does maintain a position of principled tolerance and restraint, which is a critical component of religious traditions not inculcated with Christian and most especially Protestant notions of individual moral autonomy.

Yet another possibility of gaining some pluralistic ground (assuming that such is a good thing, though I have my doubts) is through the idea of *dina d'malchuta dina*. This very important dictum states that the law of the land is the law and must, as such, be obeyed. Now the traditional intepretations of this dictum have understood it as a concession to political expediency and nothing more. Yet some recent work by R. Bleich and by Suzanne Last Stone on Rashi's (eleventh-century commentator on Bible and Talmud) understanding of *dina d'malchuta dina* stress his interpretation of its roots in the Noachite commandments as a non-halakhic yet substantive component of the Jewish legal system. In Stone's terms, "the Noachite command of *dinin* is a residual source of law for Jews."[13] This fascinating argument opens up the possibility of a legal pluralism based on a common human morality, akin to natural law, as foundational of all social order, including presumably that of Jewish collectivites.

Note, however, that here too the terms are of a *legal* pluralism, not necessarily an *ethical* one (regardless of which we may hold as a stricter standard). For, once again, the case for an ethics independent of law is a difficult one to make in Judaism. Having said this and assuming that ethical pluralism (or even talk of ethical pluralism) to be a desirable "good," I should perhaps reframe that "good" in broader terms, relevant to those cultures and traditions that did not participate in the Pauline revolution.

NOTES

1. Jacob Katz, *A House Divided: Orthodoxy and Schism in Nineteenth Century Central European Jewry* (Hanover, N.H.: Brandeis University Press, 1998), p. 45.

2. Schubert Spero, "Orthodoxy vis a vis the General Community: Does Participation Imply Recognition." *Tradition: A Journal of Orthodox Jewish Thought* 8, 4 (Winter 1966): 56–64.

3. David Hume, *A Treatise of Human Nature* (Oxford: Clarendon Press, 1960), p. 520.

4. Adam Smith, *The Theory of Moral Sentiments* (Indianapolis, Ind.: Liberty Press, 1982), p. 110.

5. Ibid., p. 135.

6. On this see, Benjamin Nelson, *On the Roads to Modernity* (Totowa, N.J.: Rowman and Littlefield, 1981); George Jellinek, *The Declaration of the Rights of Man and Citizens: A Contribution to Modern Constitutional History* (London: Nicholson, 1863).

7. Mishne Torah, Faith, 1:5.

8. Aharon Lichtenstein, "Does Jewish Tradition Recognize an Ethic Independent of Halakha?" in Marvin Fox, ed., *Modern Jewish Ethics, Theory and Practice* (Ohio State University Press, 1975), pp. 62–87.

9. Louis Newman, *Past Imperatives: Studies in the History and Theory of Jewish Ethics* (Albany: State University of New York Press, 1998), p. 43.

10. Jean Bodin, *Colloquium of the Seven about Secrets of the Sublime.* trans. and ed. Marion Leathers Daniels Kuntz (Princeton: Princeton University Press, 1975).

11. The theoretical basis of such argumentation can be found in Menachem Fisch, *Rational Rabbis, Science and Talmudic Culture* (Bloomington: Indiana University Press, 1997); Avi Sagi, *"Elu va-Elu": A Study on the Meaning of Halakhic Discourse* (Hebrew) (Tel Aviv: Hakibbutz Hameuchad, 1996).

12. Shlomo Fischer, "Intolerance and Tolerance in the Jewish Tradition and Contemporary Israel," paper presented at the ISEC Conference on Religious Toleration, Institute for Human Science, Vienna, April 1999.

13. Suzanne Last Stone, "Sinitic and Noahide Law: Legal Pluralism in Jewish Law," *Cardozo Law Review* 12, 3–4 (Feb.–Mar. 1991): 1211.

PART VII

Conscientious Individualism
A Christian Perspective on Ethical Pluralism

David Little

TERMS OF REFERENCE

Ethical Pluralism

There are several conceptual ambiguities about the term "pluralism" that need to be clarified. According to the dictionary, it is both a descriptive term, "the quality or state of being plural," and a theoretical or normative term, "the doctrine that there are more than one or two kinds of being or independent centers of causation"; "opposed to *monism* or *dualism*."[1] Accordingly, the phrase "ethical pluralism" might designate the simple existence of a diversity or plurality of ethical positions, or it might refer to a doctrine holding that ethics, as the systematic evaluation of human action, is *in its nature* incapable of being reduced to one comprehensive theory (whether monistic or dualistic). Isaiah Berlin, for example, is reputed to have held such a view (although a recent biography raises doubts about the coherence and consistency of Berlin's position).[2]

In respect to the normative usage, it may be helpful to distinguish between a "strong" and a "weak" theory of ethical pluralism. A "strong" theory is the one just stated; it would be committed to opposing monistic or dualistic theories. A "weak" theory would on normative grounds make room, up to a point, for diverse ethical positions and propose procedures for "living with" or tolerating them, without necessarily rejecting a monistic (or dualistic) theory. In any case, the weak theory is the version we shall be assuming in what follows. Some form of monism, occasionally in combination with a weak theory of ethical pluralism, would seem to be most consonant with Christian assumptions about unitary divine authority.

Christian Perspective

Christianity obviously encompasses a huge and highly complex range of material bearing on our subject. There exists within the tradition a wide diversity of views regarding how much and what sort of allowance should be made for different ethical beliefs and practices. Although there are strong reasons in the tradition for favoring at least a weak theory of ethical pluralism, and though some range of ethical diversity is usually permitted, important differences remain concerning the extent and character of that range of "pluralism" within and among Roman Catholicism, Eastern Orthodoxy, Protestant Christianity in its profusion, and the proliferation of unconventional sectarian and breakaway groups that have attended the Christian movement from its beginnings. As is well known, the differences have often been accentuated in blood. In a short essay, we cannot begin to examine the whole range of diversity.

Instead, we take up but one part—more accurately, one strand of ideas—from this vast tradition, attempt briefly to explicate and synthesize it, and then try to apply it constructively to the specific challenges to pluralistic thinking (social regulation, citizenship, life-and-death decisions, etc.) that have been laid before the participants in this project.

We refer to this strand of ideas as "conscientious individualism" and hold that it is, sociologically and historically at least, central to the Christian understanding of the place of human beings in the world. Furthermore, we suggest that the way this notion developed within the context of Christianity implies an interesting approach to the challenges of ethical pluralism.

THE CHRISTIAN CONTEXT OF CONSCIENTIOUS INDIVIDUALISM

It is not surprising that the idea of conscience[3] as a "private moral monitor"—in Greek, *syneidesis*—found its way into the experience of the early Christian Church, and thereby into the New Testament, or that the idea became thereafter a central and abiding subject of cogitation and dispute in the history of Christian moral theology. The idea as we know it was originally a product of the special conditions in which the Christian Church itself was born, and partly for that reason it has occupied a central place in Christian life and thought ever since.

> [The concept of] conscience [as we know it] only came into its own in the Greek world after the collapse of the city-state. The close integration of politics with ethics . . . was no longer possible: there was no sufficiently close authority, external to the individual, effectively to direct conduct. Consequently, . . . [people] fell back . . . on [individual] conscience as the only authority.[4]

The concept, *syneidesis*, does not appear much, if at all, in Plato and Aristotle, or in the Greek Stoics; when it does it is usually devoid of moral content, and simply refers to self-consciousness.[5] Roman Stoics, like Cicero and Seneca, do invest the Latin equivalent, *conscientia*, with moral significance, although that is not the primary emphasis; in any case, they are part of the same general milieu in which early Christianity appeared.

Individual conscience as a seat of religious and moral authority and deliberation is thus associated with a period of significant social disruption
and change, involving the emergence of what social scientists call "cross-
cutting cleavages" or "plural identities." Under such conditions, civil,
religious, familial, ethnic, and other institutions and authorities are differentiated from each other, sometimes quite abruptly. Consequently, the
individual, located at the point of convergence and encounter among the
distinct and often competing authorities, has to mediate and negotiate
among them, heightening the demand for personal moral and religious
innovation and responsibility. In other words, the idea of conscience, as
the Christian tradition came to embody it, correlates importantly with
"pluralism"—ethical and otherwise, at least in the *descriptive* sense mentioned earlier.

The differentiation of the civil and religious authorities had a particularly strong impact upon the rise of conscientious individualism. That is
primarily because of the implied distancing, if not complete separation, of
force and coercion, typically administered by the civil authority, from the
religious sphere, and to a certain degree from the moral sphere. *Ecclesia*,
the Greek word for church, itself means "called out," or "set apart," and
in its earliest and most formative expression, the Christian movement
"called out" new adherents by means of individual persuasion rather than
by civil coercion or by appealing to ethnic or other forms of group identity.

To be sure, the religious and moral spheres on occasion eventually fell
under the jurisdiction of an ecclesiastical authority, which typically assumed its own coercive techniques of discipline and organizational control. Sometimes these techniques, as is well known, came close to revoking
altogether the critical distinction between church and state. Sometimes,
too, Christianity did become entangled with ethnic and political identity.
But the underlying constitutive assumption—*that membership in this new
community must, in order to be valid, rest upon a personal and voluntary
determination and commitment for which each individual is ultimately
responsible*—continued to exert a profound influence on the tradition,
even during its most repressive phases.

The concept of conscience was one of the key ways in which that influence was conveyed and maintained, and it came to have, in fact, quite
revolutionary consequences. The central image, as formulated by Saint
Paul in his letter to the Romans and elaborated in his first letter to the
Corinthians, is a *forensic* one. The conscience is an internalized public
forum—a *forum internum*, as it came to be known. It is a kind of person-
alized, inner lawcourt and legislative assembly governing an individual's
thoughts and actions, which is possessed, according to Paul, by all human
beings, Jew and Gentile alike. When conscience is in session, individuals
experience "conflicting thoughts," as Paul says, "that accuse or perhaps

excuse them"; there is prosecution, defense, and a final judgment, all aimed at determining whether an individual in a given case has or has not broken the law that is written on every human heart.[6]

But the conscience, according to Paul, not only functions "judicially," in the sense of passing judgment on past actions,[7] as it was commonly understood to do in the period around the first century B.C.E. In Paul's hands it took on two new features: First, the conscience is seen to act "legislatively," in the sense of anticipating the future and deliberating about what ought to be thought and done before the fact;[8] second, it is understood, apparently for the first time, as capable of becoming, in Paul's words, "weak" and "defiled"—capable, that is, of being subject to error.[9] The idea that the conscience can be mistaken paved the way for a momentous development in the history of Christianity that contributed to the rise of religious liberty and, by implication, opened the door to certain versions of ethical pluralism. That was the formation of the doctrine of *erroneous conscience*, which over centuries of Christian reflection and dispute came to imply that an individual's conscientious beliefs, though in error, ought, under some conditions, nevertheless to be tolerated.

In the interests of brevity, I offer the following summary description of, and brief commentary upon, the idea of conscience as it has evolved in the Western Christian tradition. This summary is proposed as a synthesis and composite of several different variations, but it refers especially to the views of the medieval scholastics, Saint Thomas, Calvin and his Puritan descendants, and, among them, particularly Roger Williams.[10]

Conscience is a "private monitor" or *forum internum*—a center or seat of authority and deliberation inherent in each individual that calls for special deference and protection from the *forum externum* (the civil authority). As such, conscience is an aspect of personal consciousness that is a partly passive, partly active private operation involving cognitive, volitional, and emotional or affective elements, and that is to a certain extent subject to error, and thus to revision. It is "private" both in the sense of being experienced inwardly, and of applying only to activities over which the owner of the conscience has responsibility. It is activated by a thought or an action (performed or contemplated) that poses a particular challenge or dilemma for personal moral, religious, or other fundamental commitments. The response includes a review of basic commitments as they bear on the circumstances of the particular challenge or dilemma, and is to be conducted in accord with certain standards of operation (the traditional "intellectual" and "moral virtues"). The purpose of the response, or "verdict," is to convict or to exonerate the owner of the conscience in affirming the thought or performing the action in question, with the purpose of prompting the owner to think or act (retrospectively or prospectively) in accord with the dictates of conscience.

The operations of the conscience are "partly passive" in two senses. First, the operations depend, ultimately, upon a "law written on the heart," as Paul puts it—that is, upon a prior objective "natural" moral law, common to all owners of conscience, regardless of cultural, religious, or social identity. This law includes principles of nonmaleficence, benevolence, fidelity, veracity, fairness, and the like. Even though the conscience actively seeks to apply these principles to concrete dilemmas, the general principles themselves are "given." Second, the "verdict" of conscience manifests itself in the form of emotional or affective feeling-states—for example, "pangs of conscience" for guilty thoughts or behavior—that are mostly beyond the control of the individual. (Where conscience acquits or vindicates, there results a "clear conscience," which is marked by the *absence* of the "pangs" or negative feeling-states.)

On the other hand, the operations of conscience are "partly active" in the sense that they require initiative and performance on the part of the owner in compliance with certain cognitive and volitional standards, standards that, taken together, define what it means to be "conscientious." The *cognitive* standards call for "scrupulousness" or rigor, impartiality, and honesty in several respects:

1. reviewing and consistently accounting for one's basic commitments as they relate to the case at hand;
2. giving proper consideration to a fundamental universal moral law that underlies all consciences;
3. pursuing, evaluating, and applying all relevant factual data pertinent to the case;
4. clarifying all motives, flattering and unflattering, that might influence the verdict or its implementation.

The *volitional* standards require that the owner of the conscience implement or "take action on" the appropriate dictate of conscience. In traditional terms, the "intellectual" and "moral" virtues (wisdom, knowledge, understanding, prudence, justice, temperance, and fortitude) characterize the normative expectations associated with the cognitive and volitional standards of conscience.

If all the standards of conscientiousness are satisfactorily complied with, and the "pangs" are absent, there exists a "good" or "clear" conscience. However, if one or another of the cognitive or volitional standards is violated, or if the "pangs" are absent when they shouldn't be, conscience may be said to be deficient in one way or another. The most serious of possible violations is in regard to the second of the cognitive standards listed. If there is evidence that someone has systematically disregarded or is indifferent to a primary moral principle such as nonmaleficence, that person's conscience would be described as "evil." If, on the other hand, one complies with the cognitive but not with the volitional requirements, one may be said to have a "weak" conscience.

Or, one might make "cognitive mistakes." One might in a given case ignore or overlook a principle or rule one had publicly advocated; one might mistakenly think that certain ideals or practices promote good when they do not, or one might ignore or mistake relevant factual material. Finally, one might reason fallaciously in connecting principles to facts. In such instances, there is said to exist an "erroneous conscience," a category of deficiency we introduced earlier. Regarding that category, the important question is, whether such errors are committed negligently or carelessly, or whether they are committed innocently and are thus "honest mistakes." If the errors are based on negligence and carelessness, they are culpable; if not, they are inculpable (sometimes called "invincible ignorance"), and are thus excused.

As we mentioned earlier, the idea of "erroneous conscience" (in its *inculpable* version) had a powerful impact on the evolution of religious pluralism, and also has, as we shall presently try to show, some interesting implications for ethical pluralism, as well.

As to religious pluralism, even so fervent a uniformist as Saint Thomas took a potentially liberal line. He held that certain non-Christians might reject Christian belief conscientiously and thus blamelessly and should therefore be allowed without external constraint to act on their consciences. "Belief in Christ," he wrote, "is something good, and necessary for salvation. But if one's reason presented it as something evil, one's will would be doing wrong in adopting it."[11]

Saint Thomas appears to have appreciated variations in culture and upbringing that might account for the possibility of "honest" or "conscientious" rejection of Christian doctrine.[12] But he also invoked a second consideration related to our previous comments about individual responsibility and early Christianity:

> The argument is very simple. The act of faith is essentially a free act; without an interior, free choice of the will there is no valid act of faith at all. It is therefore not lawful to use compulsion in any way to force Jews or pagans to accept the Christian faith. With regard to making the initial act of faith, St. Thomas accepts St. Augustine's principle: "A person can do other things against his will; but belief is possible only in one who is willing." A man may sign a contract, join a firing-squad, pronounce an oath of allegiance, without any interior consent; but unwilling belief is an impossibility. The only valid

act of faith is that which proceeds from a free, interior choice. Therefore, no one is to be compelled to believe.[13]

There are two important implications. One is that there exists a *natural right* to conscience,[14] whereby the conscience is (up to a point) to be protected from coercive interference, whether by the state or other institutions, in order to permit the exercise of personal sovereignty in matters of religious belief. The basis for this judgment is not simply theological—"the only valid act of [Christian] faith is what proceeds from a free, interior choice"; it is also "natural"—"an unwilling belief [of any sort] is an impossibility." The second implication is the validity of religious pluralism based on the universal right of free conscience.

Now it is clear that however liberal these implications, Saint Thomas and many followers of his era were reluctant to take the full consequences of this position. The same might be said of Protestant reformers like John Calvin, as well as of some of his seventeenth-century English and American spiritual descendants, such as William Perkins, Richard Baxter, William Ames, and John Cotton, all of whom devoted extensive attention to the conscience, and did so under the partial influence, at least, of Thomism.

The story of the liberalization of conscience in the Christian tradition is complicated. The basic question at issue was always, and remains, *where exactly to draw the limits of tolerable conscientious difference*. In the epic struggle between John Cotton and Roger Williams in seventeenth-century Massachusetts Bay, Cotton argued that because the only proper conscience is a religiously orthodox one, the state does an individual a favor by enforcing essential doctrine and practice. "The fundamentals [of the Christian religion] are so clear," he wrote, "that a man cannot but be convinced of them after two or three admonition[.]" If after that he still rejects them and is then punished, he is not punished for following his conscience, "but for sinning against [it]."[15] For Williams such thinking subverted the very idea of conscience and unduly inhibited its proper functions. He advocated much greater latitude for religious and moral diversity and suffered expulsion from the "Holy Community" in Massachusetts Bay for his trouble. In that way, he shared the fate of some early Christian sectarians, Reformation Anabaptists, and radical English Puritans, among others, who also paid a high price for challenging the restrictive views of orthodox church authorities.

The doctrine of the freedom or sovereignty of conscience that emerged at the hands of radical Puritans in England and America like Roger Williams, and that had such an important influence on John Locke, is a plausible, if controversial, extension of the notion of conscientious individualism nurtured within the Christian tradition.[16]

ROGER WILLIAMS AND THE FREEDOM OF CONSCIENCE:
SOME IMPLICATIONS FOR PLURALISM

Roger Williams was unquestionably a maverick. He spoke of a "restless unsatisfiedness of my soul,"[17] which drove him from England to the New World, and then from church to church, in a radical spiritual quest. In reaction to what he believed were the perversions of Anglicanism, he joined first the Separatist Puritans in Massachusetts Bay, then the Baptists in Rhode Island, and finally withdrew altogether, believing that "Christians had lost their church, and there was no present way to recover it."[18]

But however perfectionist his view of the church, Williams was not socially indifferent or altogether inept in his political dealings, as has been claimed.[19] Having established the Providence township in 1640, Williams became "chief officer," and later "president of Rhode Island," and in these ill-defined roles struggled indefatigably to mold the new colony into a coherent, effective, and tolerant political community. He eventually secured a liberal charter and occasionally conducted creative and humane negotiations with native Americans in the area, in stark contrast to the predatory policies of most of his fellow Puritans of the time. That he was not completely successful as a politician was hardly his fault alone. He had to contend with a distracted British Parliament, duplicitous and unreliable neighboring governments, and local special interests that, under the circumstances, would have been difficult for anyone to handle.[20]

Williams's position may be summarized as an effort to expand the limits of religious pluralism on the basis of a radicalized version of the doctrine of erroneous conscience. Saint Thomas and the more conservative Calvinist Puritan thinkers interpreted the doctrine in a way that sharply restricted the range of permissible religious and moral disagreement and deviation. But Williams, in the spirit of the radical Puritanism of his time, began advocating, and, when he got the chance, undertaking in practice, to liberate the conscience to an unheard of degree. True to his vision, and accomplished at huge personal cost, he managed to establish "the first commonwealth in modern history to make religious liberty . . . a cardinal principle of its corporate existence and to maintain the separation of church and state on these grounds."[21]

Williams had his own strong, if deviant, Calvinist convictions. He did not agree with the religious views of many of his contemporaries. He had doubts about the American Indians or "pagans," as he called them, about the "Mohammedans," the "Papists," and many Protestants of his time, especially the Quakers. He frequently and fervently voiced his opinions regarding the errors of these groups. Nevertheless, to his way of thinking the groups were all made up of conscientious people who had *a right to their error.* "[C]onscience is found in all mankind, more or less [erroneously], in Jews, Turks, papists, Protestants, pagans, etc.," and it ought everywhere to be duly respected and granted its rightful freedom.[22]

In keeping with the tradition of Paul, Augustine, Thomas, Calvin, and various Calvinist Puritans, Williams builds his case on the distinction between the "inner forum" and the "outer forum," which are, as Calvin put it, "two worlds over which different kings and different laws have authority." For Williams, such is the contrast between the "laws of the spirit" and the "laws of the sword," and he exhibits the difference by showing (a la Augustine) the futility of confusing the weapons of enforcement peculiar to each sphere.

> [T]o take a stronghold, men bring cannons, . . . bullets, muskets, swords, pikes; and these to this end are weapons effectual and proportionable. On the other side, to batter down idolatry, false worship, heresy, schism, blindness, . . . it is vain, improper, and unsuitable to bring those weapons which are used by persecutors. . . . [A]gainst these spiritual strongholds in the souls of men, spiritual artillery and weapons are proper. . . . [Thus,] civil weapons are improper in this business, and never able to effect aught in the soul.[23]

In Williams's hands, the implications of the distinction between the "laws of the spirit" and the "laws of the sword," between a "religious" and a "civil-moral" sphere, were dramatic. It meant people might err religiously and nevertheless be capable of living as reasonably responsible members of the civil community—in Williams's words, as "peaceable and quiet subjects, loving and helpful neighbors, fair and just dealers, true and loyal to the civil government."[24] That is because there exists, he says, "a moral virtue, a moral fidelity, ability and honesty, which other men (beside Church-members) are, by good nature and education, by good laws and good examples, nourished and trained up in, so that civil places need not be monopolized into the hands of Church-members (who sometimes are not fitted for them), and all others deprived of their natural and civil rights and liberties."[25]

In other words, despite religious disagreement and diversity, people may nevertheless exhibit moral fidelity, ability, and honesty—may, that is, be *conscientious* citizens, neighbors, tradespeople, and civil officials. Such a doctrine threatened all forms of preferential rule, whether based on religion or gender. The Massachusetts Bay colony from which Williams was expelled assigned full citizenship rights only to orthodox church members in good standing. Williams dispensed with that arrangement and extended full rights of citizenship to all, regardless of religious belief or affiliation, to members of the wide variety of Protestant groups, Jews, and others, who were all welcomed to Rhode Island.

Massachusetts Bay, like other political systems of the time, discriminated on the basis of religion because it was assumed that the religiously unenlightened were spiritually and morally deficient, and ought therefore to depend on the superior wisdom of those considered enlightened. Only the orthodox had "mature" consciences; only they could be entrusted to make the right decisions and institute the correct policies in civil and religious affairs. Williams completely rejected such theories. In civil matters, for example, *all* the people, "naturally considered," are "the sovereign original and foundation" of the state, who through a process of "consenting and agreeing," ought to enjoy the right "to see [the state] do her duty, to correct her, to redress, reform, establish, etc."[26] This is an expanded theory of conscientious individualism: in the conduct of, and deliberation over, civil affairs, no preference is to be given to the consciences of the orthodox, for in the civil sphere every conscience is equal.

There is no conclusive evidence that Williams applied the theory in the same radical way to gender relations as he did to politics, although there are some interesting hints. For one thing, Williams gave aid and comfort to Anne Hutchinson, a notorious dissenter in Massachusetts Bay, who reflected the new spirit of women's liberation rampant in the sectarian circles of the time, and who, like Williams, was eventually ejected from the colony.[27] For another, he appeared to consent to a majority judgment by the citizens of Providence to expel "from our civil freedom" one Joshua Verein because he violated his wife's "liberty of conscience" by severely punishing her for attending too many religious meetings and neglecting her duties to him.[28]

What the Hutchinson and Verein instances illustrate is the influence of "new thinking" concerning women's rights to conscience, and the possible sympathy Williams had for such thinking. A conservative Puritan reprimanded Anne Hutchinson for having stepped "out of your place," for being rather "a husband than wife," "a preacher than a hearer," "a magistrate than a subject," and thereby for having tried "to carry all things in Church and Commonwealth as you would."[29] But Anne Hutchinson and Mrs. Verein were having none of it. Like other women of the period, they were emboldened to reject the conventional wisdom according to which women were thought to be incapable of being as conscientious as men. They denied categorically the idea that women were afflicted with "mentall and sex-deficiency," producing a "greater susceptibility to error," and because of which they were expected to submit to their male betters.[30]

Women like Hutchinson and Verein drastically challenged the authority of the husband as "lord over [a wife's] conscience" and, in the bargain, the father's authority as well. In the "family, as in the commonwealth, it was religion which had kept the subject in obedience." But to remove the religious sanction, as sectarians like Hutchinson and Williams were doing, and to advocate opportunities for reorganizing social and political life in accord with an expanded notion of conscientious individualism, were to threaten "the very foundations of the old patriarchal family," along with the established hierarchy in church and civil order.[31]

Clearly, Roger Williams, drawing and dilating upon the idea of conscience embedded in the Christian tradition, contributed enormously to the spread of diversity. He advocated and began, well ahead of his time, to implement religious pluralism of both a descriptive and normative kind. So far as religion goes, his position exemplifies a weak theory of pluralism. He is a monist who found reasons to welcome and tolerate a wide diversity of religious views. But, generally speaking, he also implemented political and social pluralism, which had strong ethical overtones in regard to accommodating new, more inclusive, patterns of citizenship, interreligious and intergender behavior, and so on. Under Williams's "leveling" influence in Rhode Island, the institutions of government, church, and family encouraged and became susceptible to a variety of new and divergent opinions and influences.

For our purposes, however, the important question is, Precisely what sort of impact did Williams's doctrine of conscientious individualism have upon ethical pluralism, understood as a normative theory? We know, roughly, how he went about accommodating a diversity of religious opinions. How far did he go in explicitly accommodating a diversity of opinions concerning social and civil behavior?

The short answer is that his tolerance for ethical diversity was more limited than it was for religious diversity, although there are some clues in his thought (and in the tradition he inherited) for liberalizing his approach. Williams has some interesting things to say about "social regulation," and "citizenship," which call now for comment. Alhough he did not directly discuss "life-and-death decisions," or questions of "human sexuality," it is possible to apply his method constructively, if conjecturally, to those matters.

Social Regulation

Williams would have agreed with Locke's dictum concerning the overlapping relationship between religion and morality:

> A good life, in which consists not the least part of religion and true piety, concerns also the civil government; and in it lies the safety both of men's souls and of the commonwealth. Moral actions belong therefore to the jurisdiction both of the outward and the inward court, both of the civil and domestic governor; I mean both of the magistrate and the conscience. Here, therefore is great danger, lest one of these jurisdictions entrench upon the other and discord arise between the keeper of the public peace and the overseers of souls.[32]

Points of tension might well arise between "the outward and the inward court" because their jurisdictions converge, and may possibly conflict, in regard to certain kinds of outward action, namely those that impinge on "public safety, order, health, or morals," to borrow the language of the international human rights instruments.[33] But, rather surprisingly, Williams didn't worry too much about such points of conflict, because he seems to have shared Locke's rather complacent attitude that "all difficulty in this matter" can be "easily removed," if only "the limits of both these governments" are duly attended to.[34]

To be sure, Williams's core convictions in this matter, like Locke's and those of all their predecessors in the tradition of conscientious individualism, are tied to a belief in natural law (the second cognitive standard) that is in certain formulations (in my opinion) significant and defensible.[35] That belief implied, straightfowardly, that there are some common, basic moral norms that are "given" and that conjointly ought to govern the outward and the inward forums. Anyone, anywhere who acted so as systematically to violate such norms could not, according to Williams, Locke, and the whole tradition, be said to be "conscientious." No matter who they were, they would have, as Saint Thomas had put it, an "evil," or thoroughly corrupted, conscience. Williams summarized his thinking here in a characteristically prophetic way:

> Adulteries, murders, robberies, thefts,
> Wild Indians punish these!
> And hold the scales of justice so,
> That no man farthing less.
> When Indians hear the horrid filths,
> Of Irish, English men,
> The horrid oaths and murders late,
> Thus say these Indians then.
> We wear no clothes, have many gods,
> And yet our sins are less:
> You are barbarians, pagans wild,
> Your land's the wilderness.[36]

Accordingly, Williams held that it was "the duty of the civil magistrate to punish anyone whose conscience led [that person] to undertake actions against public safety and welfare," as defined by the natural law. That would include the prohibition, by coercive means if necessary, of such things as human sacrifice, even though practiced for conscience's sake, as was the case, Williams pointed out, in Mexico and Peru. [37]

The problem was (and this is a problem for the entire tradition of natural law) that the list of "nonderogable" (unabridgeable) offenses was imperceptibly expanded from self-evidently punishable actions to ones that were less clearly so. Williams had no doubt that just as instances of gross arbitrary injury, such as were performed by his countrymen against Native Americans, ought to be forcibly restrained and punished, so governments had every right to impose tight regulations upon other forms of activity, as, for example, reading licentious material, or practicing offensive patterns of dress and speech found among certain religious groups, "as the monstrous haire of women, up[on] the heads of some men," or the use by Quakers of the familiar, and, to Williams, contemptuous, "thou" in addressing superiors. Beyond that, Williams believed magistrates might properly regulate public speech that demeaned civil or other authorities.[38]

It is one thing for the state to protect against violence and extreme forms of arbitrary injury, and another for it to restrict behavior that is offensive but otherwise harmless, or to shield public officials from rude or contemptuous criticism. Though the line is not always easy to draw, Williams undoubtedly obscured it from time to time. A consistent theory of conscientious individualism would appear to favor more tolerance and greater pluralism than Williams himself displayed in regard to the preceding examples, as well as on one other occasion, to be taken up next.

Responsibilities of Citizenship

As "president" of Rhode Island ("an office with no defined powers, of little dignity and no salary,")[39] Williams was faced with the need to organize a militia to provide defense for the colony. A number of the citizens of Providence, mostly Baptists, invoked Williams's avowed principles against him, claiming the right of conscientious objection to military service on grounds of religious scruple.

Surprisingly, Williams rejected the claim.[40] He likened the predicament of the citizens of Rhode Island to the situation of passengers on a ship at sea called upon to protect, when needed, "their common peace or preservation." While Williams denied (as would be expected) that the captain of the ship might force "Papists, Protestants, Jews, or Turks" among the passengers "to come to ship's prayers or worship," or compel them "from their own particular prayers or worship, if they practice any," the captain nevertheless "may judge, resist, compel, and punish" "if any refuse to help, in person or purse, towards the common charges or defense."

There is some uncertainty as to whether Williams here means simply to counter the claims of conscientious objection to military service or whether he is attempting to answer a broader and more ominous challenge to the very principle of civil government itself.[41] In any case, what is, for our purposes, most noteworthy about Williams's letter is that he never even entertains (here or anywhere else) the possibility of selective exemption from civil law or obligation on grounds of conscience. It would therefore seem fair to conclude that he, like Locke, did not perceive any serious conflict of duties between the internal and external forums, primarily because he possessed excessive confidence that these two jurisdictions are easy to compartmentalize.

CONSTRUCTIVE SUGGESTIONS

We may conclude by gathering up and applying to the four problem areas of ethical pluralism certain suggestions that, for the proponent of a Christian theory of conscientious individualism, would seem to follow from our analysis.

Social Regulation

On the composite theory sketched out here, "conscientiousness" presupposes devotion to "a fundamental universal moral law that underlies all consciences" (the second cognitive standard). That law, typically called "natural law" in the tradition, applies to both the internal and the external forum. Accordingly, there are understood to be certain sorts of violation that are intolerable, and thus are properly restrained and punished—coercively, if necessary—by the state.

Because anyone who, even in the name of conscience, culpably violated the "natural" prohibition against arbitrary injury, might be said to have "no conscience," or at least to have one that is severely deficient, *appeals to conscience do not apply*, and such action is rightfully restrained and punished by the civil order. It follows that in justifying social regulation of this sort, a (weak) normative theory of ethical pluralism that is consistent with conscientious individualism could not accommodate positions that advocated arbitrary injury (such as fascist justifications for genocide or ultranationalist justifications for "ethnic cleansing").

But while theoretically important to establish, this prescription does not carry us very far. What about harder cases, like justifications for policies of female genital alteration? Here a more comprehensive consideration of the standards of conscientiousness is required.[42] The second cognitive standard—concern (among other things) for the fundamental moral prohibition against arbitrary injury—is certainly relevant. Indeed, its relevance its underscored by the initial *suspicion* outsiders inevitably have, in hearing descriptions of practices of female genital alteration, that the prohibition against arbitrary injury is in fact being violated by such practices. But this standard is not the only one that is pertinent. In such cases, it will be necessary to consult some of the other cognitive standards of conscientiousness in order to determine whether such practices, however dubious or "erroneous" they may appear to the outsider, are nevertheless tolerable.

One such standard that needs to be (and is often) applied is the first cognitive standard—reviewing and consistently accounting for basic commitments as they relate to the case at hand. It is frequently pointed out, in assessing justifications for policies of female genital alteration, that appeals to Islam, which are widespread among proponents, are, in fact, not well founded. If there is reason to conclude that such appeals are irrational, as many Muslim scholars argue,[43] then one important supporting reason for the practice collapses.

The third cognitive standard (pursuing, evaluating, and applying all relevant factual data pertinent to the case) and the fourth (clarifying all motives, flattering and unflattering, that might influence the verdict or its implementation) must also be considered in assessing the "conscientiousness" (and thus the "tolerability") of the policy in question. As to the relevant factual claims, there would appear to be serious errors. Assertions about the need to restrain female promiscuity (in comparison with male promiscuity) by imposing such a procedure, as well as about the alleged harmless or even beneficial effects of the procedure, appear to be profoundly flawed.

All of this brings us to the last cognitive standard, to the matter of "clarifying motives." On inspection, there appears good reason to think that there are very important *undisclosed* motives driving the practice of female genital alteration, which are fairly described, in general, as "patriarchal" in character. (Shades of the complaints of the radical Puritans!) If that is true, then a proper assessment of the justifications for the practice would be inclined to conclude that the consciences of those advocating the practice are not only "erroneous" but "culpably" (rather than "inculpably") erroneous. It follows that the assessment would be disposed *against* tolerating practices of this kind and in favor of their "social regulation." In short, the assessment would appear to rule *against* tolerating such policies under a theory of ethical pluralism.

A final word on the subject: in undertaking this kind of assessment of "conscientiousness," the second cognitive standard is pivotal. If there is strong suspicion that a fundamental moral principle (like the prohibition against arbitrary injury) is being violated by a given policy, then the bar for "reasonableness" represented by the other three cognitive standards would appear to be raised all the higher and become all the more demanding. In a word, *reasons justifying policies that impinge closely on concerns protected by fundamental moral prohibitions have a much-reduced margin for error.*

Citizenship

In regard to the "dissenting views on the civil status of women,"[44] the low assessment of the conscientiousness of their opponents presented by the radical Puritans of the seventeenth century seems to me worthy of emulation. In brief, the feminists of the period called into question the factual beliefs about the inferiority of women, as well as the motives for supporting policies of male domination. On the strength of the principle just enunciated—that reasons justifying policies that impinge closely on concerns protected by fundamental moral prohibitions have a much reduced margin for error, seventeenth-century feminists and their supporters would appear to have made a convincing case against the discriminatory conventions of the time. Therefore, their conclusions in favor of equal citizenship (and social regulation toward that end) seem valid.

On the question of the responsibilities of citizenship, raised by the exchange between Roger Williams and the citizens of Providence, as to whether "conscientious objection" to certain common civil obligations is permissible, Williams, as I hinted already, took too restrictive a position.

Certainly, Williams is right that on a proper understanding of the tradition appeals to conscience cannot automatically trump just and duly authorized civil laws and policies. The constitutive assumption of the conscience, which assumes two relatively independent authorities—the internal and the external forum—excludes that. The question is whether there exist *any* areas of action, normally under the authority of the civil order, where it is reasonable to permit conscientious exemptions. When, in Locke's terms, "the jurisdiction" of "the outward" or "the inward court" "entrench[es] upon the other and discord arise[s] between [them]," may "the inward court" ever prevail?

It is interesting that James Madison, writing more than a century later, proposes just such an exemption regarding conscientious objection to military service. He suggests the following wording (not adopted) for what was to become the Second Amendment of the United States Constitution: "The right of people to keep and bear arms shall not be infringed; a well regulated militia being the best security of a free country: *but no person religiously scrupulous of bearing arms shall be compelled to render military service in person.*"[45] It is also interesting, in a contemporary setting, that the Human Rights Committee, which provides authoritative interpretation of the International Covenant on Civil and Political Rights, has ruled that a right to conscientious objection, on grounds broader than simply religious ones, can properly be inferred from Article 18 of the covenant, the article that guarantees freedom of thought, conscience, religion, or belief.[46] Incidentally, Madison's original proposal for the language of the first amendment would have opened the door to the more inclusive interpretation of the Human Rights Committee, since he specified protection of "the equal rights of conscience," in his words, which could by implication include religious or nonreligious appeals.

The possible reason for proposing special exemption for conscientious objection to military service may well be one that is actually close to Williams's own convictions: mixing conscience and force is highly problematic. Because force is such a profoundly inappropriate instrument in the domain of conscience, and accordingly must have very restricted access thereto, it is understandable that people reflecting in the name of conscience would find perplexing, if not self-contradictory, the prospect of being forced to use force. In any case, Madison and the Human Rights Committee surely assume some such argument in order to single out and give special consideration to conscientious objection to military service over a much broader array of imaginable appeals for conscientious exemption. The pluralism they recommend in this regard is a strictly limited one.

It should be noted, also, that even if such exemption were permitted (which appears to have growing support in international human rights circles), it will still be necessary to "test" the conscientiousness of the objector, as typically happens, under conditions of conscription. That process involves examining for "sincerity" (a synonym for conscientiousness), which of course is determined by testing the objector according to the various cognitive and volitional standards we have employed throughout this essay.

Human Sexuality

Claims against extending civil rights to homosexuals would, on the theory of conscientious individualism, be tested according to the standards of conscientiousness that have been invoked throughout the essay.[47] Moreover, there appear to be some suggestive parallels between the arguments of the radical seventeenth-century Puritans favoring women's rights and the arguments of advocates of gay rights in our time.

The argument against granting gay rights has been put forward by people like the Reverend Jerry Falwell.[48] On the basis of his reading of scripture, homosexuality is profoundly offensive to Falwell's conscience, and he strongly believes homosexuals ought not be treated as a "legitimate minority." His primary argument against legislation favoring gay rights is close to the position developed by Lord Devlin in his famous lectures, *The Enforcement of Morals*.[49] When it comes to determining the standards of public order and decency, and to protecting citizens from what is offensive, injurious, exploitative, and corrupting, the majority of citizens gets to decide. If, as Lord Devlin says, the "vast bulk" of the community is agreed on an answer, even though a minority resolutely disagrees, a legislator must act on the consensus of the "moral majority." "The community must take the moral responsibility, and it must therefore act on its own lights—that is, on the moral faith of its members."[50]

The major problem with this position, as Ronald Dworkin has argued,[51] is that it vastly oversimplifies the role of the legislator. "A conscientious legislator who is told a moral consensus exists must test the credentials of that consensus."[52] Interestingly enough, Lord Devlin, confessing second thoughts, admitted that he might have placed "too much emphasis on feeling and too little on reason." He proceeds, a la Dworkin, to agree that a legislator "is entitled to disregard 'irrational' beliefs," such as the conviction—however widespread—that homosexuality causes earthquakes.[53]

Dworkin takes the point from there. To assess the rationality of a moral consensus, rather than simply supporting it uncritically, implies that considerations of coherence and consistency of argument, along with respect for the rules of factual evidence, are therefore applicable to a legislator's decision. Indeed, in cases in which basic civil rights are at stake, such as the issue of gay rights, our previously stated principle—reasons justifying policies that impinge closely on concerns protected by fundamental moral prohibitions have a much reduced margin of error—raises the demand for applying the standards of conscientiousness.

For example, Falwell states that a person "is not born with preference to the same sex, but . . . is introduced to the homosexual experience and cultivates the homosexual urge. It is innocent children and many young people who are victimized and who become addicts to sexual perversion."[54] But this is not an argument but an assertion that is, in fact, empirically highly controversial. In the absence of evidence, Falwell's claims do not qualify as a "reason" for anything.

Moreover, Falwell writes: "If homosexuality is deemed normal, how long will it be before rape, adultery, alcoholism, drug addiction, and incest are labeled as normal?"[55] But this implied argument begs the question and assumes what it must prove. Whether and why homosexuality is in a class with the other acts is what must be demonstrated. Until that is shown, our conscientious legislator must ignore unsupported assertions like these.

Of course, this is not to say that majority opinion can be ignored altogether in legislating in accord with "public order, security, health, and morals." But it is to say that any such legislation must be *conscientiously* evaluated, and if proposals fail the tests, they must be discarded.

Life-and-Death Issues

We suggested earlier that Williams may have been insufficiently pluralistic by failing to make room for conscientious objection within the Rhode Island community.[56] Questions were also raised as to whether it was consistent with a doctrine of conscientious individualism to punish, as Williams allowed, patterns of speech and dress displayed by Quakers and others that were found offensive but otherwise harmless.[57] However, despite these inconsistencies and shortcomings, there can be no doubt that the overall effect of Williams's notion of freedom of conscience revolutionized the idea of civil punishment, thereby affecting some "life-and-death" issues in a critical way.

There is no evidence that Williams opposed the death penalty as such, though it is of interest that "he never listed precisely what crimes he thought were worthy of death."[58] What is clear is that, in reaction to the conventions of his time, he substantially reduced the number of crimes that might legitimately be punished by "the civil sword" and concomitantly provided a new frame of reference for thinking about the subject.

> [T]he laws, rewards and punishments of several nations vastly differ from those of Israel, which doubtless were unlawful for God's people to submit to, except Christ Jesus had (at least in general) approved such humane ordinances and creations of men for their common peace and welfare. . . . Mr. Cotton, and such as literally stick to the punishment of adultery, witchcraft, etc. by death, must either deny the several governments of the world to be lawful . . . and that the nature and constitutions of peoples and nations are not to be respected, but all forced to one common law, or else they must see cause to moderate this their tenent in civil affairs, as persecution in affairs religious.[59]

Such sentiments are consonant with Williams's fundamental belief that "now under Christ, when all nations are merely civil," the earthly government, "being of a material[,] civil nature, [only] for the defense of persons, estates, families, liberties of a city or civil state, and the suppressing of uncivil or injurious persons or actions by such civil punishments," "cannot . . . extend to spiritual and soul causes, spiritual and soul punishment, which belongs to that spiritual sword with two edges, the soul piercing . . . Word of God."[60]

If civil governments no longer have any direct authority over the conscience, over private matters of spirit and soul, and the function of punishment is severely restricted to questions of "a material[,] civil nature," and to be applied only in accord with the common or natural "civil-moral" law, then civil punishment must be reconceived as primarily *defensive* in regard to protecting the "outward" welfare of citizens against "uncivil or injurious persons or actions." Administering punishment in the name of God by executing people for "adultery, witchcraft, etc.," which Williams's New England neighbors characteristically assumed they had a right to do, was in Williams's mind forever prohibited in the light of the rights of conscience. The implication of Williams's point of view is that systems of civil punishment that go beyond what might be called this minimalist theory of "civil defense" are guilty of "cruel, inhuman or degrading treatment or punishment," to use contemporary human rights language.[61]

Consequently, the familiar objections to the death penalty under present-day conditions acquire special salience. As is often claimed, to take the life of an unarmed prisoner safely in captivity who no longer represents a direct threat to the community, when a significantly less severe alternative (extended imprisonment) exists that is capable both of neutralizing the threat and of imposing a significant penalty, seems a clear example of excessive government action, according to Williams's standards. Moreover, if the standard complaints about the administration of capital punishment in the United States are valid, there is an additional reason for rejecting the practice, namely, that it is manifestly inconsistent with the demands of equal justice entailed in the "common or natural 'civil-moral' law," as Williams understood it.

> Since at least 1967, the death penalty has been inflicted only rarely, erratically, and often upon the least odious killers, while many of the most heinous criminals have escaped execution. Moreover, it has been employed almost exclusively in a few formerly slave-holding states, and there it has been used almost exclusively against killers of whites, not blacks, and never against white killers of blacks. This is the American system of capital punishment. It is this system, not some idealized one, that must be defended in any national debate on the death penalty.[62]

These considerations suggest that the administration of capital punishment itself becomes an example of the very thing that, on Williams's account, civil punishment is supposed to defend against, namely, arbitrary injury. That no doubt explains the beginning, these days, of movement in international human rights discussion toward significantly restricting the death penalty, if not abolishing it altogether. On 2 April 1983 the "Sixth Protocol" to the European Human Rights Convention was adopted by the member states of the Council of Europe, declaring that the "death penalty shall be abolished. No one shall be condemned to such penalty or executed."[63] The only exception permitted in the document applies during time of war or the threat of war.[64] The issue remains highly contentious, though a certain amount of momentum appears to be gathering in support of the Sixth Protocol to the European Convention.

A word about two other "life-and-death" issues of considerable present-day salience—abortion and physician-assisted suicide—are in order. There is no evidence that Williams himself took a stand for or against abortion or self-regarding "mercy killing," and we are therefore left to apply for ourselves the approach to conscientious reflection we have been developing. In regard to both questions, we shall briefly attempt to open some space, within limits, for "conscientious individualism."

In its most elemental terms, the issue of abortion is posed because, arguably, two human lives stand in profound conflict with each other. In one setting, a mother is found to carry a prenatal life that, if allowed naturally to proceed "to term," would threaten death for the mother. Such circumstances entail a stark choice between allowing the prenatal life to live and the mother to die, or acting deliberately so as to protect the mother by aborting the prenatal life. In another setting, an act of sexual violation (rape or incest) results in an unwanted pregnancy with severe psychic consequences for the mother. Again, a choice results between requiring the mother to bear the "moral costs" of seeing the pregnancy through, or permitting a termination of the pregnancy. In the first case, the physical health of the mother is at stake; in the second, her psychic and "moral" health.

A critical point of contention in the issue of abortion is the status of the prenatal life. If, as some hold, the prenatal life is, from the point of conception, a "full human being," then it would appear to have a right to the same protection normally due any postnatal person. The idea that persons after birth might involuntarily be sacrificed for the good of others would be a flagrant violation of the principle against arbitrary injury. If, as we say, the prenatal life is equivalent in all pertinent respects, there would seem to be no grounds for an exception in its matter.

If, on the other hand, the prenatal life, as others hold, is at best "incipient life," physically interconnected with and dependent upon the mother, especially in the early stages of pregnancy, then the status of the prenatal life is exceptional in a variety of ways, including, it is claimed, the applicability of the principle against arbitrary injury. On this reading, some latitude for discretion, some "freedom of choice," in favor of the mother's physical and/or psychic health would be permitted, given the special intimacy of the relationship of mother and prenatal life, together with the morally objectionable prospect of legally prohibiting an opportunity for the mother to protect her life against a direct physical threat, or to escape the psychically destructive consequences of an extreme violation of her dignity and integrity.

But even if this second position is affirmed (as it is by me), and the door is thereby opened for tolerating ethically a "right to abortion," there are some remaining concerns. For one thing, there is the question of how extensive that right is, of how many "indications" for permissible abortion are to be allowed.

We have already claimed (in respect to the second option) that, given the special intimacy of the relationship between mother and prenatal life, the mother's physical and psychic health are allowable indications for abortion. On further reflection, there would seem to be no good reason to limit too narrowly the range of indications to the mother's imminent death or to her right to escape the destructive consequences of sexual violation. Questions of physical and psychic health are to an important degree matters of subjective conscientious determination. Is it reasonable to demand that a woman accept her pregnancy if the consequence is not loss of life, but loss of a leg or kidney, or is some form of severe psychic distress? Does it seem suitable that judges or legislators be authorized to make these highly personal decisions regarding what constitutes the physical or psychic health of an individual? Are there not, at least within some limits, grounds for extending to the mother considerable discretion, or as we might otherwise put it, for respecting the exercise of individual conscience in these questions?

At the same time, even "incipient life" is potential human life, and thus in need, it would seem, of appropriate protection against arbitrary injury. There is reason, therefore, for a certain degree of social regulation of abortion. The legal provisions afforded by *Roe v. Wade*, according to which the range of permissibility for abortion narrows as the prenatal life develops and comes increasingly to approximate postnatal human beings, is an acceptable compromise. It affords extensive latitude for maternal discretion in the early stages of pregnancy, and progressively reduces that latitude as the prenatal life matures and approaches the critical postnatal status in which equal protection against arbitrary injury is guaranteed.

Physician-assisted suicide poses similar problems, requiring a similar kind of compromise in regard to social regulation. The fundamental issue is whether competent and consensually informed individuals should be granted conscientious control over their own life or death under conditions of terminal illness, irreversibly associated with severe forms of degeneracy and/or suffering, that are certified by an authorized physician. Incidentally, those circumstances are narrowly restricted to rule out an unlimited "right to suicide," on the assumption, among other things, that individuals are members of communities and thus morally obligated to live up to the responsibilities of their membership, despite temptations to the contrary. In that sense, the principle against arbitrary injury applies to the way individuals treat themselves, as well as to the way they treat others.

The worry in this matter, and therefore the concern over social regulation, is the possibility for abuse in regard to the taking of human life, voluntarily or not. For one thing, the individual, driven to distraction by the circumstances of illness, might rush irrationally and prematurely to arrange to die. For another, relatives motivated by financial or other ulterior interests, might bring pressure on the patient to acquiesce in a decision to die. There is the additional concern that a physician, professionally committed to the preservation of life, might be charged with violating that fundamental commitment by engaging in assisted suicide.

So long as the procedures of authorization and patient protection, as well as the medical indications (severe and irreversible degeneracy and/or suffering) permitting a voluntary and informed decision to terminate life, are clearly defined and enforced, there would appear to be good reason to allow conscientious discretion on the part of the patient. As in the matter of abortion, it appears humane and compassionate to permit the person concerned to decide what degree of suffering and distress ought, under specified circumstances, to be borne. Nor, in the case of physician-assisted suicide, does such a conclusion necessarily conflict with the basic obligations of the physician. It is not morally self-evident that, when the choice is between death and suffering, suffering must automatically be preferred.

CONCLUSIONS

We have described and explicated a theory of conscientious individualism, as it has emerged from the Christian tradition, and especially as it was developed by Roger Williams, the seventeenth-century Puritan and founder of the Rhode Island colony. We have suggested this theory as one response to the challenge of "ethical pluralism." The theory was then applied to four areas of contemporary concern put before each of the participants in this colloquium: social regulation, the duties of citizenship, human sexuality, and life-and-death issues. Williams's own responses to some of these concerns, where relevant, provided a background for our reflections. The proposal is that the theory is richly applicable to present-day problems, even where it modifies or revises some of Williams's own positions. Given Williams's commitment to "search and trial," without which no one "attains . . . right persuasion,"[65] the arguments with him, such as we have had these pages, would, one suspects, have received his full approval.

NOTES

1. *Webster's New International Dictionary of the English Language* (Springfield, Mass.: G. & C. Merriam, 1928), p. 1659. See John Kelsay, "Plurality, Pluralism, and Comparative Ethics: A Review Essay," *Journal of Religious Ethics* 24, 2 (1996): 405–28, for an illuminating discussion of the distinction between the descriptive and normative use of the term.

2. Michael Ignatieff, *Isaiah Berlin: A Life* (New York: Henry Holt, 1998), esp. pp. 248–50, 284–86. "[Berlin] never claimed to have been the first to think about pluralism. But [he] had reason to believe that he was the first to argue that pluralism *entailed* liberalism—that is, if human beings disagreed about ultimate ends, the political system that best enabled them to adjudicate these conflicts was one which privileged their liberty, for only conditions of liberty could enable them to make the compromises between values necessary to maintain a free social life. Beyond the obvious circularity of the argument, the real difficulty, as John Gray has argued, is that a pluralist logically cannot put liberty first. Liberty is simply one of the values that must be reconciled with others; it is not a trump card. If so, why should a free society be valued above all? Berlin's later work opened up these questions, even though it failed to supply adequate answers" (p. 286). Moreover: "What Isaiah could affirm was that the century's experience of infamy had brought the European conscience back to its senses. . . . Since the Second World War there had been a return to 'the ancient notion of natural law'—sustained this time not by faith *in*, but fear *of*, mankind. . . . He hoped that Europe had learned from its journey into the abyss; he deeply believed that the concentration camps offered the most conclusive justification ever for the necessity of a universal moral law. But towards even his own moderately hopeful propositions, he remained what he had always been: a wise, watchful and incurably realist sceptic" (p. 250). It is not clear what we are to make of these comments about Berlin's position on a "universal moral law," and whether such a position is or is not compatible with the strong theory of ethical pluralism Berlin often claimed he held.

3. There appears in some philosophical circles to be an astounding lack of knowledge about the origins and development of the concept of conscience. In the entry on "Conscience" in the *Encyclopedia of Philosophy* (New York: Macmillan and Free Press, 1967), 2:189–91, the author, Charles A. Baylis, gives the impression that the idea did not arise until the eighteenth century, with the treatises of Francis Hutcheson, Samuel Clarke, Joseph Butler, Immanual Kant, and others. (The bibliographical references exclude any pre-eighteenth-century literature.) Such a description provides a truncated and distorted analysis of the tradition.

4. C. A. Pierce, *Conscience in the New Testament* (London: SCM Press, 1954), p. 76.

5. Ibid., pp. 11–28. Cf. Eric D'Arcy, *Conscience and Its Right to Freedom* (London: Sheed and Ward, 1941), pp. 5–8.

6. Romans 2:14–16.

7. Ibid.

8. See Paul's discussion of what to do in face of a potential "conflict of conscience" over eating food that has been offered to idols at I Cor. 10:23–33.

9. I Cor. 9:7, 10, 12.

10. In a fuller account, of course, the Lutheran and Anglican contributions to the subject of conscience, among others, would need to be consulted. The account here is rather skeletal but serves for our purposes.

11. *Summa Theologica*, 1–22, 19, a. 5; quoted in D'Arcy, *Conscience and Its Right to Freedom*, p. 156.

12. See D'Arcy, *Conscience and Its Right to Freedom*, pp. 133–41.

13. Ibid., pp. 153–54.

14. See Brian Tierney, "Religious Rights: An Historical Perspective," in John Witte, Jr. and Johan van der Vyver, eds., *Religious Rights in Global Perspective: Religious Perspectives* (The Hague: Nihjoff, 1996), pp. 17–45. By "natural right" I understand a subjective claim, regarded as inborn and unearned, that is antecedent to and independent of governmental authority, and that ascribes to individuals a legitimately enforceable title or warrant to constrain (or demand constraint) regarding such things as the exercise of conscience, political participation, control of property, and resistance to arbitrary authority.

15. John Cotton, "Massachusetts Does Not Persecute," in Irwin H. Polishook, ed., in *Roger Williams, John Cotton and Religious Freedom* (Englewood Cliffs, N.J.: Prentice-Hall, 1967), p. 72.

16. See David Little, "A Christian Interpretation of Human Rights," in Abdullahi An-Na'im and Francis Deng, eds., *Human Rights in Africa: Cross-Cultural Perspectives* (Washington, D.C.: Brookings Institution, 1990), pp. 59–103, for a fuller account.

17. Edward Gaustad, *Liberty of Conscience: Roger Williams in America* (Grand Rapids, Mich.: Eerdman's, 1991), p. 90.

18. Edmund S. Morgan, *Roger Williams: The Church and the State* (New York: Harcourt Brace & World, 1967), p. 53.

19. Robert Bellah has written (*America*, July 31–August 7, 1999, pp. 9–14) that "Williams was a moral genius but he was a sociological catastrophe. . . . Since [he] ignored secular society, money took over in Rhode Island to a degree that would not be true in Massachusetts or Connecticut for a long time. Rhode Island under Williams gives us an early and local example of what happens when the sacredness of the individual is not balanced by any sense of the whole or concern for the common good."

20. Gaustad, *Liberty of Conscience*, pp. 128–53.

21. Sydney E. Ahlstrom, *A Religious History of the American People* (New Haven: Yale University Press, 1972), p. 172.

22. *Complete Writings of Roger Williams*, 7 vols. (New York: Russell & Russell, 1963), 4:508.

23. Ibid., 3:148.

24. *Complete Writings of Roger Williams*, 3:142.

25. Ibid., 4:365.

26. Ibid., 3:249. The statement about seeing "her do her duty, . . . etc." is applied to the church. However, in the context Williams interchanges comments about the state and church. What goes for one appears to go for the other.

27. See Keith Thomas, "Women and Civil War Sects," *Past and Present* 13 (April 1958): 42–62.

28. See Timothy L. Hall, "Order and 'Civility,'" in *Separating Church and State: Roger Williams and Religious Liberty* (Urbana: University of Illinois, 1998), pp. 103–5.

29. Cited in Thomas, "Women and Civil War Sects," p. 49.

30. Ibid., p. 49.

31. Ibid., pp. 52, 54–55.

32. John Locke, *A Letter Concerning Toleration* (New York: Liberal Arts Press, 1950), p. 46. Locke undoubtedly stands in the tradition of conscientious individualism we have been outlining. In particular, as I and others have argued elsewhere, he was profoundly influenced by the radical Puritans of the seventeenth century in this and related matters. Incidentally, it is rather surprising, to say the least, to observe that John Simmons, in what is in many respects a fine book on Locke's theory of rights, completely ignores the place of a right to conscience, and the background and role of such a right, in Locke's thinking. A. John Simmons, *The Lockean Theory of Rights* (Princeton: Princeton University Press, 1992).

33. For example, International Convention on Civil and Political Rights, article 18.3.

34. Locke, *A Letter*, p. 46.

35. Such a defense would have to be provided by a proponent of a Christian theory of conscientious individualism. (For my part, I have tried to do that elsewhere.) An assumption about a universal moral law is important to what follows in respect to constructive reflection about the problems of ethical pluralism.

36. *Complete Writings of Roger Williams*, 1:227.

37. Morgan, *Roger Williams*, p. 134.

38. Ibid., pp. 134–35.

39. Perry Miller, *Roger Williams: His Contribution to ethe American Tradition* (New York: Atheneum, 1954), p. 224.

40. Williams, "A Letter to the Town of Providence, January 1655," in ibid., pp. 225–26.

41. Timothy Hall makes such a suggestion ("Order and 'Civility,'" p. 109). Apparently, some objectors had circulated a paper contending "That it is blood-guiltiness, and against the rule of the Gospel, to execute judgment upon transgressors against the private or public weal," which sounds like an anarchist argument. Also, in the letter, Williams explicitly criticizes those who "should preach or write that there ought to be no commanders and officers because all are equal in Christ, therefore . . . no laws nor orders, nor corrections nor punishments," which does seemed aimed at Christian anarchists, who were not uncommon in the seventeenth century.

42. I have spent considerable time on this problem, but because of the demands of time, I here only summarize my conclusions, without providing reference to all the details and relevant literature.

43. "[Female circumcision] may be out of place in a book on Islamic aspects [of gynecology and obstetrics], for the practice is neither Islamic nor ordained by Islam. . . . The procedure long antedates Islam, and its geographical distribution is different from the map of Islamic peoples." Hassan Hathout, *Islamic Perspec-*

tives in Obstetrics and Gynaecology (Cairo: Alamal-Kutub 1988)), p. 102; cited in Stephen A. James, "Reconciling International Human Rights and Cultural Relativism: The Case of Female Circumcision," *Bioethics* 8, 1 (1994): p. 10, n. 24.

44. I am considering in this section the "tolerability" of certain kinds of overt action, not ideas about action. A distinction needs to be made between tolerating ethical ideas and tolerating actions performed in the name of those ideas. Obviously, the "freedom of thought, religion, conscience or belief" needs to be protected, however permissible it may be to restrict overt action in the name of principle.

45. "Proposals to the Congress for a Bill of Rights, 1789," in Lillian Schlissel, ed., *Conscience in America: A Documentary History of Conscientious Objection in America, 1757–1967* (New York: E. P. Dutton, 1968), p. 47 (emphasis added).

46. According to the committee, the "Covenant does not explicitly refer to a right of conscientious objection, but the Committee believes that such a right can be derived from article 18, inasmuch as the obligation to use lethal force may seriously conflict with the freedom of conscience and the right to manifest one's religion or belief." Tad Stahnke and J. Paul Martin, eds., *Religion and Human Rights: Basic Documents* (New York: Center for the Study of Human Rights, Columbia University, 1998), p. 94. The opinion of the committee is more inclusive than Madison's proposal, because it links a right to conscientious objection not only to religious convictions, but also to "conscience" or "belief" (explicitly understood to cover nonreligious or even antireligious belief, so long as it is "fundamental," or occupies in the life and behavior of the objector the same status religious belief occupies for religious people).

47. This section draws on an earlier essay of mine, "Legislating Morality: The Role of Religion," in Carol Friedley Griffith, ed., *Christianity and Politics: Catholic and Protestant Perspectives* (Washington, D.C.: Ethics and Public Policy Center, 1976), pp. 39–53.

48. Jerry Falwell, *Listen, America!* (Garden City, N.Y., Doubleday, 1980), pp. 253ff.

49. Oxford: Oxford University Press, 1959; reprinted 1965.

50. A summary of Devlin's view by Ronald Dworkin is to be found in an excellent article, "Liberty and Moralism," in *Taking Rights Seriously* (Cambridge, Mass.: Harvard University Press, 1977), pp. 240–58.

51. Ibid.

52. Ibid., p. 254.

53. Ibid., n. 3.

54. Falwell, *Listen, America!*, p. 182.

55. Ibid., p. 184.

56. See the earlier section on "Citizenship" under "Constructive Suggestions."

57. See the earlier section on Williams's views of "Social Regulation."

58. Morgan, *Roger Williams*, p. 102.

59. *Complete Writings of Roger Williams*, 4:488.

60. Cited in Miller, *Roger Williams*, p. 133.

61. Universal Declaration of Human Rights, article 5.

62. Jack Greenberg, "Against the American System of Capital Punishment," *Harvard Law Review* 99 (1986): 1670.

63. Sixth Protocol to the Convention for the Protection of Human Rights and Fundamental Freedoms concerning the Abolition of the Death Penalty, in Albert P. Blaustein, Roger S. Clark, and Jay A. Sigler, eds. *Human Rights Source Book* (New York: Paragon House Publishers, 1987), pp. 477–79.

64. Ibid., article 2.

65. *Complete Writings of Roger Williams*, 3:13.

Pluralism as a Matter of Principle

James W. Skillen

David Little builds his case for a "weak theory" of ethical pluralism largely on the basis of what he calls "conscientious individualism." In response, I would like to argue that something broader and deeper than conscientious individualism is needed to account for both the diversity of ethical responsibilities that humans bear and the diverse, often incompatible ways they exercise those responsibilities. By enlarging and strengthening the normative basis, I believe it is possible to develop a strong, principled argument for pluralism, which is not the same as a defense of ethical relativism.

By a weak theory of ethical pluralism Little means that normative grounds can be found for welcoming diverse ethical positions without thereby rejecting a monistic theory. In the abstract, however, this sounds equivocal. How strong does a weak theory have to be to remain standing? How warm a welcome can be extended to contradictory, even fully contrary positions? And who does what kind of welcoming to whom—in the academy, in the political order, in churches and other religious bodies, and in other spheres of life?

As a point of entry into Little's argument and my own, consider his discussion of religious liberty in the thought and practice of Roger Williams. Williams established a political order that sought to respect and make room for the free (even if erroneous) conscience of every person. Standing in a long Christian tradition, according to Little, Williams distinguished between the "inner forum" of spiritual conscience and the "outer forum" of civil authority. The practical outcome was a *religious* pluralism under government grounded in the universal right of free conscience.

What does "pluralism" mean in this case? On the one hand, Williams accepted and worked with a distinction between inner and outer forums, yet he was building on more than simply freedom of conscience. Whether intentionally or not, he was also developing further the already familiar distinction between ecclesiastical and civil authority. He was affirming a plural structure of society, namely, that different institutional authorities bear different kinds of limited authority. This is more than the distinction between inner and outer forums.

Moreover, within the political sphere he was actually arguing for the establishment of a universal, nonpluralistic principle of freedom of conscience. A person's conscience may be mistaken, as judged from several vantage points, but as a citizen he or she should, nonetheless, enjoy the same public-legal protection as everyone else. In other words, what looks like (and is) religious "pluralism" from the perspective of the churches and individual conscience is, from the perspective of the civil authority, a definite ethical monism: the political-ethical principle of freedom of conscience is made to displace entirely the principle of church establishment or, more accurately, the principle of a religious qualification for citizenship. Clarifying the difference between two institutional communities—church and state—meant for Williams accepting at least two different points of view on religious life. What might be ethically legitimate in one sphere would *not* be ethically legitimate in the other and vice versa.

The most important "pluralism" for Williams, at least by implication, appears to have been the recognition of (at least) two different kinds of institutional jurisdiction in the "outer forum"—a political community of citizens and an ecclesiastical community of believers. A political community, he concluded, could not be justly constituted if it based membership on a religious confession. Yet he also surely held that a Christian church could not be a church if it did not base membership on religious confession. It would be ethically legitimate for a church to exclude non-Christians from membership, but it would be ethically illegitimate for government to exclude non-Christians from citizenship. What we might call Williams's strong affirmation of *structural* pluralism is on display in his distinction between church and state. At the same time, *within* each of those spheres he was not at all an ethical pluralist and certainly not an ethical relativist. His principles for each do not contradict one another, however, as long as the distinct institutional identity of each is accepted. Religious pluralism within the state, along with a variety of other pluralisms flowing from freedom of conscience and freedom of association, is the consequence of an agreed-upon identity of the political community itself. To put it another way, Williams, as political leader and founder, disagreed in principle with those who believed that a particular ecclesiastical qualification for citizenship should be established by the state. Thus, he would never have agreed that the state can support both freedom of conscience and an established church at the same time. That would be internally contradictory as a political stance—a relativism that would have led to political-ethical suicide. Williams' political-ethical monism appears in his decision to affirm religious freedom and to reject church establishment. Thus, he stood directly opposed to those Bay Colony monists who believed that confession or church membership was an essential criterion for citizenship.

Williams's contrary political-ethical monism becomes even clearer when we notice, as Little points out, that Williams was willing to "expel 'from our civil freedom' one Joshua Verein because he violated his wife's 'liberty of conscience' by severely punishing her for attending too many religious meetings and neglecting her duties to him." Clearly, a criterion for civic exclusion did exist for Williams. A citizen who violated a civil protection of another citizen's free conscience should be expelled. And undoubtedly Williams believed that churches could expel from church membership those who violated that church's laws. Williams was neither an ecclesiastical nor a political relativist. His "welcoming" of citizens who held erroneous religious beliefs did not signal that, as a church leader, he welcomed their religious error. However, having accepted the distinction between types of institutions and deciding that a political community should not be a community of uniform faith, he stuck to his universal, ethical-political principle for membership in the civic community.

Insofar as we are all heirs of Williams when we agree that citizenship should not be based on a confessional criterion, we have opened the door to the need for ever-increasing clarity about the normative criteria for determining institutional and organizational identities. What precisely should be the limits of the state's jurisdiction? And how many other institutional and organizational jurisdictions should be recognized if we are to do justice to the real diversity of society? These questions, it seems to me, cannot be answered by referring to individual conscience alone.

THE ORIGIN OF CRITERIA FOR MAKING DISTINCTIONS?

Conscientious individualism cannot, of itself, generate the criterion by which to distinguish church from state, or family from state, or business from state. There are some Christians and many Muslims and people of other faiths who conscientiously believe that citizenship should be based, at least in part, on confessional criteria. Likewise, there are many people in the world and some in the United States who believe that a husband has every right to demand that his wife attend to his needs even if that inhibits the exercise of her religious conscience. As we will see in dealing with other issues, the possibility of achieving clarity about what should be required and not required, allowed and not allowed, of citizens in a state depends on what we believe a state ought to be. The same can be said of church, family, education, corporate enterprise, and so on. Few, if any, ethical pluralists welcome all expressions of conscientious conviction in every sphere of life. Little, in fact, suggests that the historical emergence of "individual conscience as a seat of religious and moral authority" arose as a result of social disruption and change that caused the differentiation of society into a diversity of independent institutions. Yet, we must ask, what was the source of that societal differentiation process? Did it just happen? And if we now live in a highly differentiated society, is the only seat of moral authority the individual conscience?

Little addresses this problem, in part, by appealing to natural law, or at least indicates that Williams and other Christians have done so. The conscience, in other words, can function actively as "legislator" only because it is, in part, a passive receptor of and responder to "a prior objective 'natural' moral law." The conscience displays its passive nature by, among other things, feeling "pangs of conscience" when guilt or error are experienced. Such feelings "are mostly beyond the control of the individual." Little apparently agrees with those who argue that individuals are not and cannot be "autonomous" in the sense of being a law to themselves or originating all law from themselves. Individuals are somehow bound by something prior to conscience, a law that can elicit feelings of guilt from the conscience. This certainly sounds Christian in the biblical sense that God's commandments originate with God, not with the human beings whom God obligates by them. A strong Christian affirmation of conscience thus entails a simultaneous affirmation of the Creator's laws that bind conscience.

Yet this is precisely where the limits of conscientious individualism become most evident. In Christian terms, the individual conscience is not the ultimate seat of authority. The Creator and the Creator's moral law function as the authority and the normative standards for human beings. Yet, from a biblical point of view, God's moral law does not drop from the heavens to confront lone individuals or isolated individual consciences. God created humans with a diverse array of responsibilities, including institutional and communal responsibilities. Therefore, in order to know how "natural law" binds the conscience, we must make judgments about the different responsibilities appropriate to each distinct institution and relationship. Listing a few of the obligations of the moral law in the abstract, as Little does, such as "nonmaleficence, benevolence, fidelity, veracity, fairness, and the like," does not shed much light on the differentiated institutions and organizations of society or provide insight into the criteria for distinguishing between church and state, family and state, and so forth. This is, of course, not a peculiarly modern limitation. Even in the most primitive social order of Israel's clan structure, the Ten Commandments presupposed the institutions of marriage, family, clan, and property ownership. And if Israel did not know the separation of church and state, it *did* know the distinctions among prophet, priest, king, and clan elders. Biblically speaking, the commandments were not addressed to individual consciences but to persons in community, including those who held institutional authority as parents, priests, elders, judges, kings, and prophets.

We may laud the emergence of greater individual freedom in the West, leading to limits on the authority of both government and church to compel conscience. Yet if we approve of that enlargement of the sphere of individual conscience, and if we approve of the differentiation and limitation of the jurisdictions of church and state, we do so as ones who give moral approval to the differentiation of society and the diversification of spheres of human authority. Such approval or affirmation leads back to the question about the basis for such differentiation and normative pluralism. Conscientious individualism does not by itself clarify the criteria for distinguishing the types and limits of different authorities.

Structural Pluralism and Ethical Legitimacy

There are two kinds of identifications and distinctions that we find ourselves making or needing to make. The first kind concerns the diversities that belong to the legitimate differentiation of human society in this world, created by God. These are the different cultures, languages, and types of institutions and innovative human behaviors. We do not say English is the right language and French a wrong language; we say that many different languages are legitimate expressions of creational diversity, but within each language we distinguish its correct and incorrect use.

The second kind of identification and distinction has to do with this matter of the correct and incorrect use of a language, or the ethical and unethical types of behavior in each differentiated sphere of life. What are the criteria for judging between ethically legitimate and ethically illegitimate behavior in each different kind of institution or relationship that we consider legitimate? On what grounds, for example, do we affirm that parents should love and not destroy their children; that marriage is good and prostitution is bad; that governments should uphold justice by (among other things) protecting religious freedom and not require confessional uniformity; that teachers should convey truth, not error; that friends should be faithful, not unfaithful. Relativistic subjectivism offers no means of distinguishing between just and unjust acts, between logical and illogical judgments, between economic and uneconomic behavior. Ethical pluralism cannot stand as an "ethic" if it has no criteria for making judgments between good and evil, truth and error. Yet this type of ethical distinction presupposes a plural structure of society in terms of which we can recognize jurisdictions, competencies, and responsibilities. To judge that a state's discrimination against a particular religious group is unethical (unjust) derives from a prior judgment about what a state ought to be. And that takes us back to the first set of identifications and distinctions.

Let's take this a step further. If the distinction between church and state is legitimate, does it follow that churches should be free of all political interference in their decision, for example, to elevate or not elevate women to the highest offices of ecclesiastical authority? Two people might believe that women have the religious right to ordination and therefore believe that the denial of ordination to women is illegitimate—unethical—on the part of any church. Yet one of those persons may also believe that it is ethically *improper* for the state to intervene in the internal affairs of churches to force them to treat women and men equally, while the other person might believe that such intervention on the part of government or the courts is exactly proper and called for. Thus, the unavoidable question: is the ecclesiastical ordination or nonordination of women ultimately an ecclesiastical or a civil matter? This is the structural-pluralist question.

At every ethical juncture there are questions about multiple jurisdictions of authority in relation to multiple judgments of conscience. Or to put it another way, an individual's conscientious conviction that women should or should not have equal opportunity to hold any office of authority must go hand in hand with a conscientious conviction about who bears responsibility to act on this conviction in each of several different institutions. Those whom I call undifferentiated, political-ethical monists on this subject will ask the government to act in every way possible to require equality between men and women. They will seek political or legal action wherever possible to encourage or require egalitarian marriages, teaching of egalitarianism to children in all educational settings, and the imposition of egalitarianism in every business, church, and voluntary association. If the ethical principle of equality is right and true and universal, in other words, the political-ethical monist will argue that it ought to be enforced everywhere by the highest authority. Ethical universality leads to or requires political omnicompetence. Consequently, even in those churches where women are welcome to hold high office, the ultimate authority for such ordination would be the state's civil laws, not the church's laws.

On the other hand, another person who believes just as strongly in the equal treatment of women might believe, contra omnicompetence, that the diverse responsibilities of families, schools, churches, business enterprises, and governments ought to be respected and upheld by public law. No institution should be allowed to function with omnicompetent authority, not even the democratic state or federal Supreme Court. The state—or, better, the constitution of the state—should, universally, uphold societal or structural pluralism, a plurality of competencies and jurisdictions. The social-ethical perspective of this person will be pluralistic, not monistic, in regard to the struggle for women's equal treatment. Equal treatment of women in church office will have to be "fought out" in churches. The teaching of egalitarianism to children will have to struggled for in schools. The equal treatment of women as citizens will have to be won in the political arena through legislation and constitutional appeals.

CONSCIENCE IN CREATURELY CONTEXT

While I would affirm, with Little, the importance of individual conscience, I would not begin there but with the biblical witness to human identity as the image of God, created by and for the God who commissions us for a diverse range of services to one another and to all creation for the glory of God. Human respect for "erroneous conscience" is, from this perspective, grounded in God's own covenantal commitment to the creation and patience with sinners who continue to bear creaturely responsibility before God. It is also grounded in God's judging and redeeming purpose for creation in Jesus Christ. The Creator-Redeemer is the one who sends rain and sunshine on the just and unjust alike, upholding creation's responsibilities for all who have been created in the divine image. Conscience, then, is situated in the context of both divine norms for a differentiating creation order (a richer concept than natural law) and God's call for humans to fulfill multiple tasks in developing their diverse range of talents and capabilities. The differentiation of society, and human discernment of proper institutional distinctions, is thus seen as part of the context of our call to ethical responsibility. And in each sphere of life, we are called to obedience, to what is ethically right in contrast to what is disobedient and unethical. Making *political* room for religious and ethical error would, from this point of view, be justified not on the basis of religious and ethical relativism but as a matter of monistic ethical obedience to the political principle that government has limited authority in a political community and does not possess omnicompetent ethical authority.

The contest over institutional jurisdictions and competencies as well as over the distinction between moral and immoral behavior within each sphere of responsibility will undoubtedly continue for as long as human life continues in this age, because no human institution or person stands in the place of God. Yet Christians should always engage in these contests with the conviction that ethical clarity and resolution is possible.

FURTHER ILLUSTRATION OF THE COMMITMENT TO PLURALIST PRINCIPLES

The best way to continue this argument is by way of concrete illustration. I have already done that to some extent with regard to the distinction between church and state. Women's rights requires slightly more development. Given my Christian affirmation of the creational legitimacy of the differentiation of society, one of the consequences is the necessity of articulating the identity and obligations of the state and membership in it. Here I would contend for equal civil rights for all people under government. Women and men, adults and children, people of all faiths and colors should receive equal treatment as citizens. This reflects the universal ethical monism of nonexclusivity in any state. It also assumes (though there is not space to argue it here) that the political community exists to protect life and the common good of all, including all of the nongovernmental responsibilities that belong to people. Human beings, in other words, are always more than citizens, and thus equal civil rights entails government's equal, nondiscriminatory protection of every nongovernment sphere of life (friendship, family, church, education, and so forth), each of which has its own nonpolitical jurisdiction. Within the framework of government's protection of life, upholding of equal civil rights, and guarding the public trust—the common political good of all—humans should be free to exercise various kinds of responsibilities and authority. Consequently, I would stand on the side of those who say that the authority of women in diverse religious bodies should be decided by those bodies and not by the government.

What about the protection of children? When someone says that government has the authority to *interfere* in the internal affairs of the family in order to protect children, it seems to me that this is worded improperly. Government's responsibility is to protect the life of all citizens. If any person's life is threatened, regardless of whether that threat comes from parents or an employer or a church authority, the *danger to life is an internal political affair*—it belongs to the very responsibility of government. Thus, the state is not *interfering* in responsibilities that belong to family life when it acts to protect endangered children; it is simply fulfilling its own responsibility. This presupposes, of course, that the family's authority is not that of a mini-state. The same can be said for churches, businesses, and academic institutions. The authority to use force, even to take life as in war or capital punishment, belongs to the state's jurisdiction, not to families, churches, and other institutions. At the same time, by contrast, it is important to say that parental authority does not derive from state authority. It has its own direct creational integrity before God. Thus, the state has no legitimate authority—no right—to intervene to displace the exercise of legitimate parental responsibility and authority.

Governmental authority entails the monopoly of force and the right to use it to protect the innocent and to punish those who threaten the innocent. This is precisely what has become differentiated in the course of history and can be defended on Christian, creational grounds. No longer do we recognize parents, or church authorities, or feudal lords, or corporate authorities as having the right to take life. This is not a settled consensus, however. Some people will argue that their religious convictions or individual rights require recognition of personal, or parental, or ecclesiastical authority to make ultimate decisions about medical care or even the taking of life. Just as I would argue that the state does not have original jurisdiction over family life, education, science, human labor, and worship, I would argue with equal emphasis that government *ought* to have jurisdiction over all matters of life and death. That is why the just-war criteria have been developed by Christians over the centuries, and it is why I believe that abortion and euthanasia are ultimately matters of governmental jurisdiction.

From this point of view, the abortion debate over when the fetus becomes viable or whether it is a person is beside the point. Sexual intercourse leads to the propagation of human life—generation upon generation. Laws regarding the responsibility of parents for children, of physicians for medical care, and so forth, have been developed, and should continue to be developed, precisely to make clear the ways in which nongovernmental authorities and institutions have competence to nurture and enhance life but never to take it. The presumption of almost all such laws is and should be on the side of life and the generation of life. Government's responsibility is to protect human life and either to certify or to make the final judgment about death (through established public laws governing health, police forces, the judicial process, and the military). Every child born must be registered publicly; every death, even natural death, must be certified publicly. My point is that no authority other than government should be allowed, on its own authority, within its own jurisdiction, to take human life—at whatever stage of development.

This means that the presumption in favor of life protection, including the protection of life-generating human intercourse that leads to pregnancy, is an ethically monistic responsibility of government that cannot be delegated to any other institution or person, and no authority other than government should be allowed to make decisions about the taking of human life or interrupting the life-generating process. On this basis, I would approach the legitimacy of abortion somewhat the way I approach the matter of a government's justified entrance into warfare. Are there any circumstances in which the threat to life requires decisions by government that might lead to the destruction of one life for the sake of another? And can some of these circumstances be codified so that a doctor, or team of doctors, can be held responsible as public health official(s) to make publicly authorized decisions about the taking of life, much as the rules of policing and of warfare are codified so that police and military officers may, under certain circumstances, be authorized to make decisions about the taking of life. Yes, I think there are such circumstances, such as the danger of a pregnancy to the life of the mother and probably others, such as pregnancy due to rape or incest. But these circumstances merely validate the presumption in favor of life and that exceptions to that presumption should be determined by government, through public law.

This line of argument also holds for euthanasia. Life-taking, whether through suicide or the decision of a loving family member or doctor, must in principle be rejected because of government's responsibility to protect life. Although the wholly artificial prolongation of life is not required by this principle, I know of no circumstance in which government may legitimately relinquish its responsibility to protect life and say simply, in law, that private persons, doctors, or anyone else should be free to take their own life or someone else's life when they judge that the life is no longer worthwhile or cost-effective or desirable to another.

In keeping with this argument, I would agree that many aspects of the law that governs capital punishment should, indeed, be debated today. There are many grounds, including that of "arbitrary injury" (mentioned by Little), that should caution Christians against insisting on the death penalty. Another ground is that the very basis given for capital punishment in the Bible may not be recognized by people in our society, and Christians definitely may not defend the death penalty as an act of purely human retribution. Nevertheless, Little does not confront the question of the death penalty directly as a matter of Christian principle. What if our criminal justice system can be designed to avoid arbitrary injury? What if it can be made clear that such retribution is a divine commandment, not a merely human reaction? Isn't human life valuable precisely because we are made in the image of God? Isn't that why the willful destruction of another person requires just recompense—the divinely instituted act of retribution, which is capital punishment?

What about the identity of marriage, the family, and homosexual relationships? Let's enter this discussion by way of analogy from the distinction made earlier between church and state. The first challenge is to identify institutional and relational distinctions and then to determine accountability for moral and immoral behaviors within those institutions and relationships. If, for example, we agree that church and state should be distinguished from one another and separated, we thereby affirm that government holds no jurisdiction to determine correct faith, theology, or church governance for churches. However, in order for government to do justice to the independence of churches, it must have some criterion for recognizing a church (or equivalent religious body) and distinguishing it from a family or a business enterprise. Even settling on this criterion may prove politically contentious, but deciding how to identify a church or churchlike entity is different from deciding what should go on inside such bodies.

Now, if we return to the question of marriage and gay rights, the first public-legal question, it seems to me, is how to identity and distinguish different kinds of relationships. I would contend, on the basis of historical and contemporary experience, that there are several possible kinds of marriage relationship, including monogamous and polygamous forms, and that there are multiple kinds of friendship, including homosexual friendships. I do not see how, at the level of identification, a homosexual relationship can be called a marriage, chiefly because my biblically grounded, Christian-creational perspective identifies marriage with repro-ductive potential and responsibility, which a homosexual relationship can never have. Now, within the realm of marriage I am ethically pro-monog-amy and believe that polygamy expresses "erroneous conscience," just as in the realm of ecclesiastical organization I am pro-Christian and believe that atheism and other religions reflect an "erroneous conscience." But politically speaking, I would argue that those determinations of marital bonds and religious association should be left in the hands of marriage partners and religious bodies.

Likewise, within the realm of friendship, I am pro-chastity in regard to both heterosexual and homosexual friendships, but in the political realm I believe that the state should neither give special recognition to nor crimi-nalize any form of friendship. Thus, I would oppose granting the legal identification of marriage to gay relationships not because I want to use state power to deny the right of homosexual friendships. To the contrary, I believe the state should give equal treatment, including equal protection of life and the freedom of association, to all citizens. But whereas the logic of my position could allow for the legal recognition of polygamy as a form of marriage (even though I don't think it is an ethically obedient form), the logic of my position leads in the political sphere to rejecting the identification of homosexual relationships as a form of marriage.

CONCLUSIONS

Contentious issues of abortion and euthanasia, of gay "marriage" and the equal treatment of men and women, cannot be resolved, it seems to me, with an abstract or institutionally undifferentiated ethical argument. Whether one argues for conscientious individualism or for the priority of individual freedom, one must still confront the fact that any appeal to governmental or constitutional protection or empowerment presupposes the existence of a differentiated and limited state. Whatever the rights of majorities and minorities to "have their way" in the political arena, the deeper and prior question concerns the very identity and jurisdiction of the state. Most of us now believe the state's jurisdiction was mistakenly defined in Williams's time when a confessional requirement for citizenship existed, or, until recently, when a black person could be both denied civil rights and owned as another's property. Resolving today's disputes will require more than universal ethical appeals and political-legal crusades in favor of certain "good" things and against certain "evils." Jurisdictional distinctions among institutions and relationships must be made in order that, within each of them, arguments over good and bad, right and wrong behavior can be contended for. Clearly, one of my first principles is to recognize the plural structure of society and to oppose all individualistic or communalistic reductions of that plural structure. The basis for such argument is the biblical confession that this is God's creation—in all of its human and natural diversity—and that Jesus Christ is lord of all, the judge and redeemer of the very reality that was created in, through, and for him in the first place.

PART VIII

Feminist Attitudes toward Ethical Pluralism

Christine Di Stefano

Feminism is best approached as a political, rather than ethical, designation. Furthermore, feminism does not lend itself to description and assessment as a single and unitary tradition. References to feminisms in the contemporary literature underscore this point. Marxist feminism, liberal feminism, libertarian feminism, socialist feminism, social feminism, standpoint feminism, lesbian feminism, radical feminism, anarchist feminism, queer feminism, psychoanalytic feminism, black feminism, poststructuralist feminism, ecofeminism, Third World feminism, "third wave" feminism, postcolonial feminism, and global feminism are all shorthand (and, in the end, imperfect) labels for some of the varieties of feminism in our midst.[1] Feminism today is a plural and contested concept, whose various articulations nevertheless congeal around a number of descriptive and prescriptive claims about the social world. A feminist viewpoint sees women as a category of persons whose life chances are unjustly and adversely impacted as a result of practices and values that prescribe norms of conduct and treatment for persons classified as "women." Feminists typically identify some combination of some of the following factors in their analyses of the social construction and treatment of women: symbolic systems; cultural values; social norms and practices; economic, legal, religious, and political systems and institutions; and biologically based or socially constructed sex differences. Whereas some feminists construe life chances primarily in materialist terms having to do with physical security, bodily integrity, and economic and sexual well-being, other feminists are more inclined to focus on the cultural and psychosocial dimensions of women's lives, particularly as these affect self-esteem . Many, if not most, feminist analyses involve some combination of these elements. Some feminists argue that men as a group instigate, perpetuate, and benefit from arrangements that prescribe and proscribe women's activities and roles. Other feminists are rather more interested in how men as well as women are caught up in apparatuses of gender that produce and constrain all of their subject effects. Some feminists see men as conscious agents and wielders of power over women. Other feminists take a more structuralist approach to the phenomenon of male domination.

An important issue in the contemporary literature has to do with how to think about the categories of "male" and "female," "men" and "women." To what extent are these natural or constructed categories?

Feminists are inclined to agree that women, qua their status as "women" or "feminine subjects," are disempowered. Whether this status can be hived off from other dimensions of identity and experience such as class, race, religion, ethnicity, nationality, and sexuality is a major issue of discussion and debate. Most feminists today agree that analyses of women's condition and situation must be context-specific and -sensitive. In this respect, it is increasingly rare to find references to the figure of "woman" as a universal signifier in the literature; feminists are also far less interested in developing universal accounts of male dominance and female subordination than they used to be.

Feminisms, in all of their dazzling varieties, share a commitment to making the world more hospitable to women than it is.[2] This entails that women themselves be empowered to act in and on that world. And this is why feminism is first and foremost a *political* concept. While feminists disagree about the sources and dynamics of women's disempowerment, as well as about appropriate and effective paths to their empowerment, what makes their various endeavors identifiably "feminist" is a commitment to the empowerment of women. This commitment to the empowerment of women is fueled by the sense that women are not yet, but should be, self-governing. Whereas Carole Pateman has stressed that feminism from the late seventeenth century on has been concerned with the specific problem of the power exercised *by men* over women, this formulation seems to me to tell only part of the story.[3] For example, the feminism articulated by black American women beginning in the nineteenth century was centrally concerned with white racism, while the feminism developed by Marxist-feminists at the beginning of the twentieth century focused on capitalism as the key contributor to working-class women's disempowerment.[4]

The salient feature of feminisms in all of their multiplicity and diversity is, I believe, an underlying sense that women lack the requisite resources and opportunities for effective practices of agency. But specific feminists and feminisms offer very different appraisals of the sources of and reasons for this shortage of power resources. The theme of empowerment simply alerts us to the basic claim that women experience a deficit of power relative to other social actors. In the context of this particular discussion of feminism, "empowerment" should not be construed along the lines of its meaning in the contemporary social psychological literature—which is to say, as self-actualization. Political feminism is, in key respects, hostile to the notion of self-actualization precisely because it begs key questions concerning the construction and constitution of feminized selves. The practice of consciousness-raising, for example, was concerned with changing women's selves, rather than actualizing them. Furthermore, self-actualization, with its overtures to the figure of the utility-maximizing

individual, will not appeal to feminists who are critical of liberal individualism and who prefer to think of themselves as solidaristic members of
transindividual groups and communities.

Some feminists will disagree with my characterization of feminism as
entailing a basic commitment to the empowerment of women. Uma Narayan, for example, has argued eloquently on behalf of a feminism that is
geared toward the question of the outcomes of women's empowerment.[5]
She asks, Do we want to empower women so that they can become agents
of injustice against other persons, including women? Narayan's concerns
are shared by many feminists, but especially by those who are attentive
to relations of domination and inequality between women. For example,
in the contemporary international context, we observe vast differences
between women's basic living standards around the world; and it is difficult to avoid the conclusion that the affluent life-styles of women from
the "developed" economies are implicated in the substandard living conditions of their Third World sisters. Narayan's normative concerns, with
which I am in sympathy, specify an ethical orientation proper to feminism
as a whole that, to my mind, does not capture the full descriptive range
of feminisms. Nor do I believe that Narayan's ethical concerns may be
derived from feminism without assistance from other sources. As I argue
later, one is never simply a feminist. Feminist attitudes typically include
a complex mix of ideological, theoretical, aesthetic, philosophical, and
normative commitments that derive from sources other than feminism.
For the purposes of this project, the task of presenting a somewhat comprehensive and descriptive account of feminism requires a definition that
can accommodate the extensive variety of historical and extant feminisms, between which there is nothing approaching anything like a consensus regarding the normative commitments of feminism. It seems to me
that a minimalist definition of feminism as entailing a basic commitment
to the empowerment of women works for these purposes.

What follows from the feminist commitment to the empowerment of
women is neither obvious nor straightforward. Feminists have disagreed
about political strategies, intellectual and political allies and enemies, uto-
pian visions, public policies, and much else besides, including ethics and
epistemology. They also disagree about the purposes to which women's
empowerment should be put. In this sense, there is nothing like a "feminist ethics," although many feminists are interested in exploring and elaborating the ethical implications of their commitments to the empowerment of women.[6] What, then, can be said about the ideal society and
ethical pluralism from the perspective of feminism? In a nutshell, Gregor
McLennan has it right when he asserts that "contemporary feminist discourse expresses a series of dilemmas around issues of pluralism."[7]

In these introductory comments I have referred to feminism as a complex and diversified phenomenon and I have tried to capture—perhaps impossibly—what I think lies at the core of that designation, however variously that designation is articulated, interpreted, and applied in different contexts. Nevertheless, much of the following discussion in this essay focuses primarily on Western and mainly U.S. variants of feminism.[8] In short, what follows is only part of a much larger and more complicated account of feminist attitudes toward ethical pluralism.

GENERAL CONSIDERATIONS

Political and intellectual commitments to feminism tend to be adopted by persons who experience or observe, either firsthand or vicariously, that girls and women are the subjects of discrimination and injustice. To date, feminism is not the kind of strong or constitutive tradition on the order of religious traditions or political cultures into which individuals are born and in relation to which maturing and adult individuals will negotiate some kind of relationship, on a continuum ranging from acceptance to rejection. Rather, feminism is more likely to be adopted on the basis of some combination of experience and observation, as well as exposure to feminist ideas. Feminist orientations tend to be forged in experiential contexts of a pluralism of sorts—the differential treatment of persons that is justified on the basis of sex and/or gender differences. In short, repeated and various experiences of "difference" experienced as disempowerment are typically the stimulants to the adoption of a feminist perspective. Nevertheless, feminists have elaborated radically different responses to the phenomenology of "difference." For some feminists, the ideal society will have transcended sex- and gender-differences so that we are all "just persons." This brand of feminism is known as "equality feminism." For "difference feminists," on the other hand, justice requires the explicit recognition of sexual difference, along with the valorization of the "female" or "feminine" components of this difference, which, to date, have been subordinated to the hegemonic components of "masculine" difference, masquerading as "universal" or "humanist" descriptors and criteria.[9] For equality feminists, women and girls need to be brought under the purview of an impartial justice from which they have been too long excluded. They need to be treated as "persons." For difference feminists, discursive space and political opportunity—which women have been denied because their speech and actions fail to conform to the rules of these male-structured and -dominated arenas—should be allocated to women as women rather than as persons. In the United States, these diverse characterizations of feminism have been translated, albeit simplistically, into two different orientations to feminist political ethics. The "justice orientation" draws our attention to procedural issues and to the goal of impartial fairness accorded to all persons as individuals. The "care orientation," by contrast, urges attention to the particular needs of particular persons who are embedded in context-specific relationships.[10]

Each of these orientations, it seems to me, is broadly compatible with ethical pluralism, although each envisions a different understanding of the basis for such pluralism. To the extent that equality feminism is a version of classical political liberalism, sexism according to this account diminishes the pluralism of a society by suppressing the individualism of half of its population.[11] On this view, ethical pluralism rests on the uniqueness of each individual who must be as free to pursue her view of the "good" as is compatible with the basic requirements for fairness to others and social order. Difference feminism, on the other hand, envisions its contribution to pluralism as a challenge to the "sexual indifference" of a patriarchal culture. On this view, ethical pluralism rests not on the irreducible difference of individuals but rather on the irreducible difference of sex difference.[12] Until this difference is acknowledged, society is not even partially pluralist; it is a gray-on-gray masculinist monoculture.

In another version of "difference feminism," feminist discourse is critically scrutinized for its facile invocation of "women" as a unified and relatively undifferentiated cohort, who presumably share the same values and interests.[13] Feminist theory and politics are judged to be insufficiently attentive to the differences among "women" and therefore complicitous with preexisting power differentials among women who are not only sexed and gendered, but also classed, racialized, sexualized, ethnicized, nationalized, globalized, and transnationalized. According to these critics, the failure to pluralize "women" is implicated in the production and reproduction of power differentials among women. Hence, we should not expect women or even feminists, for that matter, to agree about everything; a feminism that fails to acknowledge the plurality of interests, needs, and goods among women is politically as well as ethically problematic. Whether this existing plurality of interests and goods is envisioned as part of the ideal society, however, is not always made clear. To the extent that this plurality has been forged in the context of systemic oppressive practices such as racism and economic exploitation, feminists hope for the eradication of certain forms of difference (on analogy with the Marxian hope for the eradication of one of its central categories of analysis—class). On the other hand, it is difficult to see how the talent for multiperspectivism, typically attributed to those who occupy the "margins" of society, and frequently celebrated in the literatures of oppression, resistance, and empowerment, would not be retained as one of the desirable capacities of citizens of the ideal society.[14]

Feminism, then, has important affinities with ethical pluralism, although, as I argue later, these affinities are frequently tested within feminism as well as in confrontations between feminist policy agendas and antifeminist resistances to those agendas. There is a key sense in which feminism may be thought of as a constituent part of "the ethos of pluralization," which, according to political theorist William Connolly, is a discernible impulse within "the contemporary condition." Furthermore, feminism also instantiates what Connolly identifies as a "correlation between pluralization and fundamentalization."[15] If pluralism is the occasion of enunciation and opportunity for emergent feminisms, it may also function as an obstacle to the implementation of feminist policies designed to alleviate the conditions of women's disempowerment. When ethical values prescribe—overtly or implicitly—the disempowerment of women, then feminism must oppose them. Stated baldly, *feminism will accommodate ethical pluralism until it confronts ethical values that mandate the disempowerment of women.* But this way of stating things runs the risk of contributing to a misleading impression. For the key terms of this general principle are not transparently meaningful; rather, they are subject to a great deal of interpretation and debate. Feminists do not always agree on whether specific conditions and practices do in fact contribute to the disempowerment of women; and, even if they do, they do not necessarily agree on the appropriate means of opposing them.

SOCIAL REGULATION

As examples from nineteenth-century U.S. women's history illustrate, American women have not been shy about invoking the power of the state to protect, ban, and regulate ethically based differences, which have been implicated in a myriad of issues ranging from suffrage to matters of public policy involving reproduction, education, family, employment, sexuality, and economic status. One of the most notorious examples of U.S. women's influence on public policy—with major repercussions for the social management of pluralism—is the temperance movement. Whether the Women's Christian Temperance Union (WCTU) was a bona fide feminist organization is the subject of continuing debate among historians. (By the end of the nineteenth century, the WCTU boasted the largest membership of all women's organizations in the United States.) One the one hand, the WCTU was clearly committed to the empowerment of women. On the other hand, this empowerment was conceived in instrumental terms. In the name of "Home Protection" and "For God and Home and Native Land," members of the WCTU during the late nineteenth century agitated for "woman suffrage . . ., dress reform, guardianship rights for mothers, greater authority for women in the churches, improved treatment of female prison inmates, better wages and conditions for women workers, and a host of measures to combat prostitution, including tougher statutory rape laws and the establishment of a single (lofty) standard of sexual morality for women and men."[16] What they are most remembered for is their promotion of state-level prohibition, which resulted, in 1919, in the Eighteenth Amendment to the Constitution banning the manufacture, sale, and transportation of liquor in the United States. This coercive and unenforceable amendment was finally repealed in 1933.

From our "sophisticated" and "liberated" vantage, it is easy to dismiss the WCTU leadership and membership as a bunch of prudish women who didn't want men to have any fun; but as many historians have pointed out, during the nineteenth century "liquor" was a powerful point of condensation for many of the problems facing women, including domestic abuse and abandonment.[17] Male alcoholism—in conjunction with patriarchal power—had devastating effects on women and families. Although the WCTU never confronted patriarchal power explicitly, its targetting of male alcoholism was a strategic intervention designed to protect women and families from some of the worst abuses of male power.

The WCTU gives us an instructive example of a protofeminist movement and organization that waged a militant campaign in order to involve the state in *banning* behavior judged to be morally objectionable. But feminists have frequently had to argue for the *toleration* of ethically based differences in order to advance agendas for the empowerment of women. Obstacles to women's empowerment are often lodged within ethical systems, especially religiously based ethical systems, including Christianity, Judaism, and Islam, whose prescriptions for sex- and gender-appropriate conduct constitute oppressive restrictions and requirements for girls and women. When these ethical systems enjoy hegemonic status as state-sanctioned policies, feminists have had to argue on behalf of ethical pluralism. The history of the controversy over contraceptives and morality in the United States is an instructive example. In 1873 the Comstock Act—which defined contraceptives and written information about them as "articles of immoral use" and prohibited their distribution—was passed by the U.S. Congress with no opposition and fifteen minutes of debate. Attempts to repeal the Comstock Act as a violation of free speech rights all failed. During subsequent decades and as a result of powerful religious influence over elected legislators, the Comstock Act was only gradually eroded by means of some court decisions that allowed doctors to prescribe contraceptives for the treatment and prevention of disease. The interest of eugenics groups in contraceptives as a means of slowing down the birth rate among undesirable (i.e., non-Anglo) populations also contributed to the thaw. But it was not until 1965 (*Griswold v. Connecticut*) that the Supreme Court established a new definition of contraception as involving the right of privacy of married couples that would begin the process of invalidating the legacy of the Comstock Act. That process was not completed until 1977 (*Carey v. Population Services International*). In the interim (*Eisenstadt v. Baird*, 1972), the Supreme Court extended the right of privacy to unmarried individuals.

Even though Margaret Sanger had agitated publicly for the legalization of contraceptives and contraceptive information as a women's rights issue, beginning in 1912, U.S. feminist organizations did not actively participate in the national debate about contraceptives until 1970. Nevertheless, the legacy of Comstock, which includes the potent memory of antipluralist religious influence, is an important "negative" (as in, "never again!") feature of contemporary U.S. feminist sensibilities about contraception. For feminists who think of abortion as a method of contraception, and who regard contraception as a key component of what is now termed "reproductive freedom," religiously inspired efforts to abolish legal abortion inspire real terror. The bumper sticker proclaiming "Don't like abortion? Then don't have one!" only barely masks this terror with some humor. The plea for toleration of ethical differences is an unmistakable component of contemporary feminist support for the legalization of contraceptive products, services, and information as well as for the subsidization of their costs for women who cannot otherwise afford them. Furthermore, the contemporary standoff between opponents and supporters of legal abortion is a prime example of the vanishing point of ethical pluralism. When an act that qualifies as "murder" by one group is viewed as a "right" in the service of "freedom" by the other, mutual toleration of ethically based differences is nearly impossible to achieve.

Ethical pluralism is not necessarily composed of antagonistic elements, however. U.S. feminists have also called on the state to protect complementary sex-based differences that were presumed to compose a beneficient (and decidedly heterosexual) whole. The historical example of feminist support for protective labor legislation for women workers during the late nineteenth century, and the continuation of protective legislation policies overseen by the Women's Bureau of the Labor Department into the 1960s, attest to the ideological staying power of the doctrine of separate spheres, which emerged in the aftermath of the Civil War. Women and men were thought to occupy different spheres structured by correspondingly different ethical orientations. Women's domestic sphere required a caring orientation, whereas the public sphere of men, which included the hurly-burly worlds of industrial capitalism, the military, government, and leadership of religious institutions required the "manly" virtues of courage and tough decision making. In an interesting twist of fate and unintended consequences, American women used the doctrine of separate spheres to justify their increasing involvement in civic affairs during the latter half of the nineteenth century and into the Progressive Era. The concept of "social housekeeping" enabled many women to become political and social reformers decades before they managed to secure the vote.[18]

During the 1880s U.S. feminists and other social reformers mobilized to help women workers. Using the separate spheres doctrine of different roles for women (mothers) and men (breadwinners) , these reformers argued that woman's primary role was motherhood and that her failure to live up to the expectations and requirements of that role would jeopardize the health and well-being of her offspring. Social reformers called on the state to institute protective labor legislation so that women's work would not conflict with their primary role. Protective labor legislation was the result: women were barred from some occupations and their work conditions, including hours, were regulated. We need to keep in mind that most U.S. women in the 1920s worked in domestic service and agriculture. Black American women, along with many immigrant women, were predominant in both of these, and protective legislation had absolutely no impact on these jobs. Although protective labor legislation saved some women from the worst abuses of industrial capitalism, it also adversely impacted their competitiveness in the labor market. Not all feminists at the time agreed with protective legislation. In contrast to the social feminists, egalitarian feminists opposed "special treatment" for women. The egalitarian feminists would have to wait until the 1960s for opportunities to influence the political process.[19]

These three examples drawn from the U.S. experience suggest that feminists have not been disinclined to invoke the power of the state to regulate ethically based differences in society; and that they have called on the state to ban differences as well as to protect them. The guiding inspiration and motivation for these diverse attitudes toward ethical pluralism had to do with specific and strategic assessments of the obstacles to and requirements for women's empowerment. As the example of protective legislation also suggests, we need to bear in mind that the empowerment of some women by no means entails the empowerment of all women.

A brief consideration of some contemporary critical characterizations of feminism suggests the residual (and, as always, selective) impact of historical memory. Snide references to "feminazis" (the term was coined by Rush Limbaugh, I believe) evoke the image of the militant ax-wielding, saloon-smashing temperance activist, and imply that feminists are intolerant of differences, have no sense of humor, and seek to impose their prudish morality on everyone else, especially fun-loving men. Public debates about women and the death penalty, which surface periodically in response to the imminent execution of a female, reveal complex anxiety about the combined persistence and demise of a sexual double standard:

are women, unlike men, getting away with murder?[20] And fundamentalist Christian religious opposition to abortion casts feminists as ultratolerant to the point of immorality. In another version of opposition to feminist-identified policies such as liberalized divorce and abortion laws, communitarian critics charge feminists with having capitulated to the egalitarian ethos of liberal individualism, thus abandoning the ethical insights of the nonmarket domestic sphere.[21] In these examples, caricatures and criticisms of feminism cast it, respectively, as a form of repressive antipluralism seeking to impose a single morality on everyone else; as encouraging women's strategic and selective manipulation of a separate spheres-based sexual double standard; and as the handmaiden of liberal schemes designed to dismantle the pluralism of separate spheres in the name of individual rights. Familiar elements of this historical legacy also survive in discussions and disagreements between "equality feminists" and "difference feminists" concerning appropriate paths to empowerment for working women.[22]

Feminist attitudes toward the social regulation of ethically based differences are vigorously debated among feminists themselves, particularly with respect to issues involving the regulation of pornography, which I discuss later. But no general discussion of contemporary feminist attitudes to the social regulation of ethically based differences would be complete without mention of a major issue that has mobilized, divided, and even immobilized some feminists over the past decade. With this issue, we enter the global, international arena of feminist theory and activism, and we encounter the relatively new concept of "women's rights" as a dimension of internationally recognized "human rights." The issue is so controversial that it even has a number of different names, ranging from the relatively bland "female circumcision" to the clinical "female genital surgery" (FGS) to the emphatically disapproving "female genital mutilation" (FGM). This list of categories reveals telling information about some of the interpretive aspects of the controversy. Are we talking about a practice that is parallel to male circumcision, including its initiatory and religious dimensions? Or is this a medical procedure with risks and benefits that need to be weighed against each other? Or, is this practice akin to torture, something horrible and despicable from the outset? FGM has stimulated a passionate and often acrimonious debate among feminists that is centrally preoccupied with the issue of how to respond to ethically based differences worldwide.[23] Although this debate is sometimes figured as a fight between ethical universalists and cultural relativists, these designations do not fully capture the complexity of many of the positions and arguments.

FGS comprises a number of operations on the genitalia of girls (and sometimes of women), including clitoridectomy (removal of the tip of the clitoris); excision (removal of the entire clitoris and possibly the labia minora); infibulation (excision of the clitoris and labia minora, sometimes parts of the labia majora, together with the stitching together of the sides of labia majora); and reinfibulation (the restitching of the vulva after childbirth, divorce, or death of a husband). Because these practices are often part of secret rituals, or practiced in countries that have officially outlawed the practice, or in regions that are not propitious venues for state-of-the-art statistical data gathering, we do not know exactly how many girls and women continue to undergo one or more of these procedures. One figure cites approximately 2 million girls per year, 6,000 per day. Most of these girls reside in sub-Saharan Africa; some of them are members of immigrant families who have settled in other parts of the world, including Australia, Canada, France, the United States, and the United Kingdom.

There has been a flurry of attention to FGS during the past decade. Why? Martha Nussbaum argues that FGM offers a relatively tractable problem in search of a solution.[24] This is what makes it an appealing, high-salience issue. Yael Tamir, on the other hand, suggests that FGM has attracted a lot of notice because it deflects attention from less tractable problems contributing to women's subordination: it is easier to say no to FGM than it is to commit resources to combat illiteracy.[25] Some of the credit for the issue salience of FGM must also go to the social and political dynamics of internationalization and globalization, including UN sponsored conferences on the status of women worldwide—which have put feminists from the industrialized and postindustrialized sectors into contact and communication with women and feminists in other parts of the world—and the transcontinental immigration of Africans. In several cases, for example, immigrant African women have requested political asylum for themselves and their daughters on the grounds of persecution in their home countries; there have been publicized cases of FGM being done to girls of immigrant families residing in countries such as France and Australia where the procedures have been declared illegal; and there has been some controversial discussion of "medicalizing" the procedure and "minimizing" the health risks for daughters of immigrant families who do not want to abandon the cultural heritage altogether and so attempt to come up with a compromise version of the surgical procedure that will be acceptable to the host country.

Feminist debate about these practices is enmeshed in interpretive disagreements about how to define, describe, and label them as well as what to do about them. According to some feminists, FGM has to do with universal ethical issues that transcend national boundaries and cultural beliefs. FGM should be condemned as medically harmful, as a human rights violation, as a violation of women's rights, as an example of child abuse, and as another version of the (all-too familiar and pervasive) patriarchal attempt to control female sexuality and reproduction. According to this view, these practices should be actively discouraged, condemned, and prohibited through criminal as well as civil legislation. International pressure and sanctions should be leveled against countries that do not take pro-active measures to eliminate the practice. Immigrants should not be allowed to reproduce these practices in host countries, even under sanitized and medical supervision.

For other feminists, including African feminists and some African American feminists, these practices are embedded in complex traditions that Western feminists rarely take the time to try to understand. These feminists are aware of some complications in the preceding analysis that are rarely addressed, including the active involvement of women in the procedures, the support of many women for the practice, and the ways that the rhetoric of "univeralism" in human rights discourse obscures existing power differentials in the international arena. Feminists in this camp also emphasize the religious and cultural aspects of the practice, and the fact that in certain regions of the world, it is key to the social acceptance of women who have limited social roles available to them. In the absence of real alternatives to marriage, the life chances of the uncircumcised and therefore unmarriageable woman are by no means an improvement over those of her circumcised sister. Furthermore, as these observers point out, there are many other severe health problems that African women face, none of which have attracted as much sensationalist attention as FGM. These feminists are also disturbed by the systematic disregard on the part of many U.S. and Western feminists for the diversity and incommensurability of cultural meanings.

Given all of these concerns, these culturally sensitive feminists also worry that the very kinds of proposals endorsed by feminists in the first camp will not even work—that they will drive the practice underground and therefore expose women to even more health risks than they currently face. For these feminists, change will only come from the bottom-up and through transitional stages of transformation. Express legislation is not the preferred method for these feminists; more attractive approaches include educational campaigns run by members of the affected communities; structured opportunities for more dialogue between women and feminists in the affected regions and feminists from other regions; closer attention to the ambivalence and tension in feminist discourse on this issue; and a willingness to "complexify" rather than "simplify" the issues.

In a further gloss on the theme of complexity, some critical feminist observers of the discourse and debate have argued a version of "bringing it all back home," by urging attention to the (all too often repressed) constitutive links between criticism of the other and self-criticism. As Yael Tamir puts it: "Candid dedication to the needs of others may blind us to the flaws of our own society, partly as a way of magnifying the evil we are determined to fight."[26] According to Tamir, another (and frequently unrecognized) value of multicultural exchanges is that they confront us with our own deficiencies. The problem with clitoridectomy, according to Tamir, is familiar rather than exotic: "yet another way of oppressing women and locking them at home, of seeing them as the producers of children and as a source of pleasure to others."[27] If we object on these grounds, rather than on the sensationalist and abjected grounds of "barbaric" practice, then the arguments have clear implications for "us" as well as for "them."

CITIZENSHIP

Given women's historic exclusion from many of the rights of citizenship enjoyed by (some) men, feminism has been centrally preoccupied with the civil status of women, particularly in self-proclaimed democratic political systems and in democratizing political cultures. A major stimulant to this preoccupation in the United States was provided by slavery. Abolitionist women like the Grimke sisters soon realized that their efforts to abolish slavery as an immoral practice were hampered by social and legal restrictions on their freedom to assume the full rights and duties of citizenship. In spite of the fact that women were barred from leadership positions in their religious congregations, from public speaking, and from voting and running for public office, Angelina Grimke urged her white sisters in the South to take full responsibility for the immoral practice of slavery; to assume, in effect, the full duties of the citizen who is responsible for what her government is doing, with or without her consent. She called on women to oppose slavery in a variety of ways, ranging from discussing the issue with the men in their families and persuading them to give up the practice and publicly oppose it, to commiting acts of civil disobedience by freeing their slaves, paying them wages for their labor, and teaching them how to read and write. For Grimke, the ethical pluralism involved in the controversy over slavery could admit no accommodation. Slavery was an unmitigated evil and had to be opposed by every ethical means available. Like her counterparts in the temperance movement, Grimke adopted a commitment to feminism in the service of her commitment to another cause.[28]

A great deal of modern feminist activity in the United States and Great Britain during the second half of the nineteenth century and into the early twentieth century went into securing the vote for women. This "First Wave" of feminism encountered a great deal of resistance and is still remembered for the militancy of the British suffragettes, who endured imprisonment and forced feedings in order to publicize their cause and embarrass their opponents. In the United States, theories of natural rights and popular sovereignty, in conjunction with universal white-male suffrage and democratization in the early 1800s, set the stage for the first formal demands for women's suffrage.[29] The Seneca Falls Declaration of Sentiments and Resolutions in 1848 proposed a number of remedies for women's subordination to the rule of "mankind," including women's equal right to the franchise. This was the only resolution not passed unanimously by the convention. As Dorothy Stetson explains, many of those who were commited to improving the situation of women feared that this demand was just too radical and would discredit the "Woman Movement": "Ideas of equality, liberty, and inalienable rights were competing in American culture with common-law and religious traditions of the unity of husband and wife. The husband acted for and ruled the wife. The stability of the family and society depended on it. To separate men and women, which a doctrine of individual rights required, would threaten social peace."[30]

The fact that it took seventy years for passage of the Nineteenth Amendment underscores the deep controversy that was engendered by the prospect of equal voting rights for women. This stalemate might very well have lasted even longer had it not been for the doctrine of separate spheres, which helped to soften the potentially radical implications of women voting as self-interested individuals. The idea that women might bring a special voice to politics because of their experience and expertise as wives and mothers served to accommodate female suffrage with the sex- and gender-differentiated family. With this new definition of the franchise in place, "social peace" (a euphemism for the question of gender roles) would be safe until new questions about the meaning of "equality" and rights for women emerged in the early 1970s.

With the benefit of hindsight, the Equal Rights Amendment (ERA) has assumed a great deal more significance for feminists as a result of its defeat than it had when it passed Congress in 1972 and awaited ratification by thirty-eight states.[31] Particularly for younger feminists, many of whom had been politically socialized in the movements of the New Left and who had a skeptical view of the political utility of liberal political rhetorics of "law" and "rights," the ERA was a merely symbolic effort. Many of these younger and left-leaning feminists assumed that the ERA would pass. Some of them eventually became involved in efforts to mobilize state-level public support for the amendment after the extension of the time limit for ratification, when it became obvious that there was a great deal more resistance to the concept of equal rights for women than had been expected. But by 1982 the ERA had become "too controversial." Opponents of the ERA raised concerns about the security of homemakers; they predicted that women would be drafted into the military and forced into combat positions. Unisex bathrooms, homosexuality, and abortion were invoked to discredit the ERA. And states' rights arguments fueled opposition in the southern states. Like the "radical" proposal for women's voting rights from the previous century, the ERA summoned the specter of social chaos and immorality. Given the difficulty of amending the U.S. Constitution, anything short of near social consensus would not suffice for ratification. In this case, we could say that a version of ethical pluralism—the separate spheres arguments—trumped feminism. The ERA became a condensation point for unresolved anxieties in the political culture: anxieties having to do with sexual roles, gender identities, family life, and quality-of-life issues that do not admit of easy translation into rubrics of "equality" and "rights." The involvement of high-profile women in the opposition to ERA also discredited the claims of feminists that this would be good for all women.

Although most feminists would agree that the ERA should have passed on the merits of its straightforward message—"Equality of rights under the law shall not be denied or abridged by the United States or by any State on account of sex"—the question of how civil society should deal with ethically based disagreements on the rights and duties of citizenship is not thereby answered. As the history and politics of race in the United States confirm, morality cannot be legislated from the top down, in the absence of change-making efforts down on the ground. Changes in women's civil status have had and will have powerful ramifications at the level of everyday life. In this respect, certain opponents of the ERA were absolutely right in fearing the consequences of constitutionally protected equal rights for women. On the other hand, to the extent that "equal rights" is a powerful and popular constitutive feature of political culture in the United States, it is doubtful that the defeat of the ERA will succeed in turning the tide altogether. For feminists, the question of how to handle dissenting positions on the civil status of women is, in the end, a strategic question of long-term persuasion and incremental reforms that will occasionally take dramatic and contestatory forms. The important thing is to keep the public "conversation" about women's civil status alive and to ensure that women are active participants in that conversation. For many feminists, the defeat of the ERA also confirmed the continuing need for feminism, for work and agitation on behalf of the empowerment of women.

To the extent that the rights and duties of citizenships are mutually entailing (as Angelina Grimke understood so well), the issue of women in the military, which includes the controversial issue of women in combat, is an important component of the contemporary public discussion in the United States about women's civil status. This issue is controversial among feminists as well as within society at large. With the issue of women in the military, questions concerning the rights and duties of citizenship in the context of a basic presumptive political equality between men and women come to the fore.

Historically, the rights of citizenship have been linked to the duties of soldiering, of defending the nation. Today, this linkage is discernible in statistics that reveal that candidates for electoral office in the United States who have served in combat are more likely to win office than those who have not.[32] Even though women have been far more involved in military activities than the gendered mythology of war admits,[33] their official exclusion from combat preserves a gendered narrative of masculine protectors and feminine protected that disadvantage women.[34] This analysis prompts some feminists to argue that women will not achieve equal citizenship until they are full participants in the military. Other feminists argue that the real challenge and task is to develop alternative models of citizenship that do not rely on the trope of the citizen-warrior. They propose to draw on the historical tradition of pacifism and peacemaking by women.[35]

As increasing numbers of women enter the various branches of our volunteer military forces, questions about equal rights in the military jostle with opportunity structures that typically require training for combat positions from which women are excluded. Furthermore, as wars become increasingly "high tech," the distinction between combat and noncombat positions becomes fuzzier and more arbitrary. It may just be that dissenting positions on the civil status of women, which derailed passage of the ERA, may in due time be overridden by the policies and practices of the military. That would indeed be an ironic turn of events, and in more than one respect. In self-proclaimed democracies like the United States, the military is not accorded an official role in social policy making. Furthermore, there is a well-established political tradition of pacifist feminist opposition to militarization and war making.

LIFE-AND-DEATH DECISIONS

With the language of "reproductive rights" and "reproductive freedom," which gained currency in the 1970s, U.S. feminists have called on the state to protect women's access to procreative and contraceptive information, services, and products; and to help ensure that these services and products are safe, available to all women, and administered properly.[36] The salience of these issues within feminism cannot be overestimated. For feminists, women's ability to make informed decisions about reproduction and to use safe and reliable methods and technologies for the purposes of preventing, postponing, or inducing conception are key quality-of-life issues. Women of lesser economic means in the United States and throughout the world have stressed that reproductive freedom entails the right to bring children into the world along with the right to choose not to do so. They have alerted us to the injustices of sterilization abuse, the distribution ("dumping") by unscrupulous companies of untested and unsafe contraceptives in the Third World that damage the health and future reproductive prospects of women; and the everyday hazards of poverty, nutritional deficiencies, unsafe working environments, and environmental pollutants for women's reproductive lives. Recent advances in fertility technologies have also underscored the procreative dimensions of reproductive rights.[37]

Some of the new technologies and practices, including surrogacy and the ability to create "designer embryos," have also created dilemmas for feminists. Feminists have been notably divided on the issue of surrogacy (an age-old practice with some new spins) when contracts and financial payments to the surrogate mother are involved. They worry about the commercialization of motherhood and the exploitation of women of lesser economic means by wealthier men and women. These feminists are not so sure that the state should be called on to enforce surrogacy contracts. Other feminists are pleased by the desentimentalization of biological motherhood, which puts female reproduction on a par with that of men, and encourages people to think about "reproduction" and "parenting" as distinct activities and commitments. New fertilization technologies raise a number of issues, including medical-ethical and availability concerns. These technologies are notoriously expensive: does the state have the obligation to subsidize the costs of these treatments for infertile individuals and couples who cannot afford them? And, when we can design an embryo not only absent the gene for sickle cell anemia, but with specified and desired attributes of sex, intelligence, and athletic abilities, should this be allowed, regulated, or banned outright by the state? Feminists will surely be grappling with these issues in the years to come.

To the best of my knowledge, feminism does not yet have much to offer on the question of decision making concerning death, unless we are willing to include abortion within this rubric. For the most part, feminists have been unwilling to render ordinary abortions (by which I mean elective abortions that do not involve the inmediate life of the mother) into the vocabulary of "life and death." This, of course, is exactly the vocabulary that opponents of abortion use, in order to promote the claim that every abortion involves a murdered fetus. Most feminists who support legalized abortion have consistently refused to pit "the life of the (prospective) mother" against "the life of the fetus." Rather, they have treated the fetus as a "potential life." This use of different vocabularies to describe abortion, coupled with the powerful rhetoric of "rights" that is deployed by both groups (rights of the fetus versus rights of the mother), accounts for the discursive stalemate on abortion that is the subject of much analysis and commentary.[38]

Issues of reproductive freedom and decision making are high-salience issues for feminists for a number of reasons. Women's bodies endure many more of the physical consequences of reproductive decisions (and nondecisions) than men's bodies do. Although mortality figures associated with pregnancy and parturition have declined, women's lives are still at risk. Furthermore, the typical conflation of biological and social maternity (which is only upset under "extraordinary" circumstances such as adoption and surrogate motherhood), and analyzed by feminists under the rubric of "motherhood as institution," means that reproductive outcomes typically translate into parenting outcomes, the responsibilities of which are disproportionately carried by mothers. Finally, women's capacity to bring life into the world and to nurture it are viewed as important quality-of-life components. For these and other reasons, freedom in reproductive decision making is viewed by feminists as a women's issue with major implications for women's overall quality of life and state of empowerment. In view of ethically based conflict on reproductive issues, much of which is religiously based, feminists have appealed to ethical pluralism in their efforts to maintain a wide range of meaningful choices for women in the sphere of reproductive decision making.

But, as Carole Pateman has pointed out, ethical pluralism has also been invoked by those who oppose freedom in reproductive decision making for women. One sense of ethical pluralism, harkening back to the "separate spheres" claim that morality is sexually differentiated, is clearly discernible in the "pro-life" arguments of those who oppose women's exercise of reproductive choice. While these critics of reproductive choice oppose the toleration of ethical differences in society at large, they subscribe to the view that there is something special about women in their capacities as mothers. As Pateman points out, it is interesting to think about forced motherhood as an exception to the general agreement that forced labor has no place in a modern democracy.[39] What enables this exception to flourish in the minds of those who support "the right to life" against "the right to choose" is the underlying sense that women-as-mothers occupy a distinct social sphere. The relative silence of antichoice activists on a number of related matters, including the ethics of capital punishment and the obligations of men and society at large to support the burdens of mothering, which are disproportionately borne by women, provide additional evidence for the claim that a separate spheres argument is indeed at work here.

While a great deal of public attention has pitted the "right to life" of the fetus against women's "right to choose" whether, when, and under what circumstances to become mothers, women's basic "right to life" has received far less attention. Several years ago the economist Amartya Sen calculated that, worldwide, more than 100 million women who ought to be alive according to standard demographic expectations are "missing."[40] As a result of female infanticide, nutritional and medical deprivations, and other forms of abuse and neglect, girls and women in many parts of the world are not surviving, much less thriving. To the extent that these disturbing statistics reflect ethical diversity in the basic assessment by different societies of the value of girls and women, ethical pluralism poses major hazards for the basic life chances of females.

In the matter of death, we should expect many, although not necessarily all, feminists to favor policies supporting death with dignity. This would include adequate provisions for pain relief (even when such relief may hasten death) and an emphasis on palliative care over heroic and costly measures to prolong life. The "ethics of care" endorsed by some feminists would certainly support such a stance. Furthermore, to the extent that women shoulder the burden of care for the sick and dying—as professional health care workers and as family members—we would expect that they have good reasons to support death with dignity. On the other hand, we should not discount the appeal of religiously based claims to the sanctity of life. Many feminists are religious believers and are especially persuaded by arguments based on respect for human life. Finally, we should bear in mind that some feminists are alert and sensitive to the fact that sick and elderly women may be especially prone to the dynamics of female undervaluation and neglect. Under circumstances in which elderly females who have outlived their social usefulness and their family relations are viewed as expendable, "death with dignity" runs the potential risk of justifying neglectful medical and social practices.

HUMAN SEXUALITY

Along with reproduction (which is impossible to disentangle from human sexuality, even though it was discussed under the previous heading), issues of sexuality have also been central feminist concerns, although it is important to specify that this is not because feminists regard women as being any more (or less) "sexual" than men. Rather, women's sexuality, along with their reproductive capacities, has been subject to a great deal of regulation and social control. Furthermore, what should or should not be labeled as an issue of "sexuality" is also explicitly thematized and problematized by feminists. When Susan Brownmiller, in her pathbreaking analysis of rape, *Against Our Will*, proposed in 1975 that rape was not about sex, but rather about power, she was attempting to shift the discursive field from an understanding of rape as the excess sexual impulsivity of individual males to an alternative thematization of rape as a structure of power with pervasive effects on all women. In an apparently (but only apparently) opposite move, when Catharine MacKinnon asserts that a particular paradigm of (hetero)sexuality is the model for power relations between men and women—he is the "fucker" and she is the "fucked" one—she is attempting to create a new theoretical paradigm for the understanding of women's situation of disempowerment.[41] Each of these analyses has been the object of controversy and debate within feminism as well as without. Each also exemplifies a sensibility that is central to contemporary Western feminism: sexuality and politics are thoroughly intermingled, to the point that it is difficult, if not impossible, to disentangle them. The consequences of this fundamental insight, however, do not translate into a single feminist position on ethical pluralism and human sexuality.

Feminist interest in human sexuality is manifested in a number of issues, including prostitution and other forms of sex work, pornography, rape, sexual harassment, sexual abuse of children, and illict forms and practices of sexuality, including homosexuality, lesbianism, bisexuality, sadism and masochism (S&M), pedophilia, and incest. (It is important to recall that the concept of "sexual harassment" did not even exist until 1975, when feminists finally gave a name to an age-old practice.) Because of the close relationship between the social regulation of sexual behavior and reproduction, and the institution of marriage, feminists have critically scrutinized various family forms, including the modern nuclear family; they have also explored and proposed alternative family forms deserving of social acceptance and legal recognition.[42] As a result of the modern medicalization of sexuality, feminists also monitor the practices and theories of the medical establishment, particularly as these involve definitions and treatments for sexual dysfunctions. The issue of female sexual pleasure—how to define it and how to enable women to pursue it—has been a key concern for "second wave" feminists. Feminists have also subjected heterosexuality—reconfigured as an institution—to a great deal of critical scrutiny.[43] Moderate feminist organizations such as the National Organization for Women (NOW) were not originally eager to ally themselves with lesbians and lesbian issues, for fear of appearing too "radical" or "marginal." Nevertheless, lesbians constitute a visible and active presence in feminist organizations, activities, and culture; and feminists tend to support rather than oppose legislation designed to eliminate discrimination against lesbians, although the impetus for such legislation tends to come from gay and lesbian rights organizations.

As Dorothy Stetson points out, "two great ideologies of sexuality" have structured the discursive field of sexuality in the United States from colonial times to the present: "Moralists, inspired by religious convictions and rules, want to use public policy to contain sexual expression in heterosexual marriage and procreation and to punish deviations from the norm.

Libertarians discourage coercive moral standards and ask government to leave people alone to live their sexual lives in private."[44] To a very great extent, "the moralist-libertarian axis" sets the terms for disagreement and debate. As Stetson and others have observed, it is very difficult for feminists seeking to participate in and influence public debate on issues of sexuality to avoid placement on this axis, although there have been a number of theoretical efforts to do so.[45] No issue illustrates this claim more vividly than the feminist debate regarding pornography.

Feminist concern and activism on the pornography issue emerged during the 1970s in the form of a number of activist organizations such as Women against Pornography (WAP) and Women against Violence against Women (WAVAW). The aim of these groups was to reduce or eliminate pornography, which was linked to various modes of violence against women and to a broader cultural pattern of male domination and female devaluation and oppression.[46] In 1985 the feminist strategy against pornography took a distinctive turn with a new legal argument proposed by Andrea Dworkin and Catharine MacKinnon. The Dworkin-MacKinnon strategy defined pornography as an infringement on the civil rights of women and proposed that women could sue the producers and distributors of pornography for civil damages based on harm. Ordinances to this effect were proposed for a number of cities, including Indianapolis, where it was eventually struck down as unconstitutional. The Indianapolis ordinance mobilized concerned feminists to oppose publicly the work of antipornography feminists. Feminists against Censorship Taskforce (FACT) challenged the link between pornographic images and violent behavior against women; in particular, they opposed what they saw as censorship, and they worried that the antipornography campaign would, in the end, undermine women's freedom, particularly women's rights to sexual exploration and expression.[47] Alliances between feminist antipornography groups and religious conservative groups seeking to introduce antipornograpy ordinances in a number of cities fueled the allegations of the anticensorship feminists that antipornographic legislation was simply too "dangerous" for feminists to mix with. These strange alliances, in turn, confirmed the difficulty of charting a separate feminist path for considerations of pornography outside of the ideological axis of moralists versus libertarians: one is either against pornography and for censorship, or for First Amendment rights of free expression and against any limitations on those rights. As Alida Brill points out, "If in the ideal WAP vision *Playboy* must be removed from the newsstands, then the FACTs must argue that nothing can be eliminated, and if the WAPs hear that nothing can be eliminated, they in turn must cling to the position that each and every piece of pornography must be eliminated."[48]

The feminist debate concerning pornography has by no means been resolved. What this debate reveals is that specifically feminist attitudes toward ethical pluralism are, in the end, subordinated to the attitude that constitutes feminism itself: a commitment to the empowerment of women. We see that some feminists are prepared to strenuously oppose ethical pluralism in the domain of sexual expression and practice on the grounds of harm to women. By contrast, other feminists discern the threat of harm and impediments to women's empowerment in efforts to legislate sexual morality.

Historically as well as today, prostitution is thematized as a key feature of the sexual exploitation of girls and women. Feminists have argued that it is not only the prostitute who is exploited, although her exploitation alone would constitute good enough reason to oppose the practice. The prostitute's objectification and commodification is thought to degrade and dehumanize all women, who are treated like actual or potential "sluts" by their male sexual "partners" (sic). Prostitution, then, disempowers women and therefore ought to be discouraged actively through policies designed to punish or embarrass the men whose "demand" keeps the industry flourishing even where it is illegal. Prostitution should be illegal without exception and vigorous efforts should be made to stamp out the practice. Feminist arguments against prostitution do not assign blame or responsibility for the practice to prostitutes themselves, and they tend to advocate that state-sanctioned disciplinary measures be levied against the johns and pimps and not against the prostitutes.[49]

This critical assessment of prostitution has been vigorously and eloquently contested by none other than some of the prostitutes themselves, and in the very name of women's empowerment. The organization COYOTE (Call Off Your Old Tired Ethics) was founded by Margo St. James in San Francisco in 1973 and supported by a number of prostitutes and their allies who argued for the decriminalization of prostitution on the grounds that this would do more to improve the situation of prostitutes than either criminalization or regulation. Invoking the free-market vocabulary of free trade and entrepreneurship, St. James and her supporters claimed the right to choose their profession and insisted that they were not victims, except insofar as the illegality and stigma of their profession made them vulnerable to control by criminal elements. Prostitutes have also argued persuasively that they are far more empowered than their legitimate counterparts in the nuclear family: housewives who must provide an array of unpaid services to their husbands, including sexual services. In 1986 the International Committee for Prostitutes' Rights (ICPR) issued a draft statement on prostitution and human rights based on the European Convention on Human Rights of 1953: "The World Charter of Prostitutes' Rights . . . demands that prostitution be redefined as legitimate work and that prostitutes be redefined as legitimate citizens. Any other stance functions to deny human status to a class of women (and to men who sexually service other men)."[50]

As a result of recent events and trends in the world at large, prostitution continues to attract a great deal of feminist attention and concern. Economic dislocations brought about by the fall of the Soviet Union have had especially severe consequences for young women in Eastern Europe, many of whom have become involved in prostitution as they migrate (often illegally) to the more prosperous areas of Western Europe. Immigration restrictions offer opportunities and incentives for unscrupulous businessmen to lure women into prostitution under false pretenses. The existence of extensive black markets in the sex trade in Europe is now well documented.[51] Uneven patterns of economic development in Asia have contributed to the notorious phenomenon of sex tourism in countries such as Thailand and the Phillipines. Eager to attract capital in whatever form they can get it, governments are complicitous with the development of a sex tourism industry designed to attract Japanese, European, and American businessmen, many of whom have a penchant for young virginal girls. The sex tourism industry is replenished by a steady supply of girls and young women from the impoverished countryside, most of whom have no idea what kind of work awaits them in the cities to which they have been sent. Those who do not succumb to premature death as a result of sexually transmitted infections have virtually no prospect of marriage or economic security in the future. Recent reports from India paint a ghastly picture of child prostitution in Bombay.[52]

These examples of nonconsensual prostitution need to be distinguished from consensual forms of sex work. Although consent is not a sufficient indicator of the legitimacy of prostitution for many feminists in this matter as well as others (e.g., surrogate motherhood), most feminists would agree that there is a meaningful difference between the situation of a child who is forced into prostitution, who works in hazardous, unhygienic conditions, whose future life prospects, including expected life-span and basic quality-of-life expectations will be severely compromised; and the situation of an adult woman with some choices, who elects to sell her sexual services and exercises some influence over her working conditions. The feminist who acknowledges the significance of these distinctions (as, I believe, nearly all feminists would) is not necessarily prepared to endorse prostitution under "proper" and "appropriate" circumstances. But all feminists would, I believe, have serious concerns about prostitution whenever the case can be made that girls and women are coerced into prostitution, and that their working conditions adversely affect their life chances.

CONCLUSIONS

Historically, as we have seen, feminist attitudes toward ethical pluralism have been forged in the context of specific assessments of the status of and requirements for women's empowerment. Ethical pluralism has on occasion been invoked to justify the differential and unequal treatment of girls and women. As the history of separate spheres in the United States suggests, feminists have sometimes opposed this version of ethical pluralism in the name of "equality"; but under other circumstances, they have succeeded in advancing demands for women's empowerment within the rubric of separate spheres. The claim that morality is sexually differentiated, which suggests that "the conduct and social place of men and women should be regulated by different moral principles," is, in key respects, an increasingly untenable claim, as Carole Pateman has suggested.[53] As a result of feminism's finally winning equal civil and political standing for women in Western countries, and economic changes that have thrust increasing numbers of women into the official economy, the conditions and conceptions for the woman-mother/male-breadwinner distinction have eroded to a significant extent. Nevertheless, this development is vigorously opposed by contemporary antifeminist movements. In response to antifeminist arguments, feminists have invoked an alternative conception of ethical pluralism in order to make the case for women's empowerment. In this alternative conception, the "separate spheres" formulation is treated as one among a number of plural conceptions of women's proper role in society, and is thereby demoted from its previously hegemonic status.

A third sense of ethical pluralism having relevance for feminism has emerged from time to time within domestic contexts, but with increasing frequency as a result of globalization. This sense of ethical pluralism is concerned with modes of assessing culturally specific practices affecting women. In domestic contexts, this version of ethical pluralism concerns the rights of cultural self-determination for minority communities and national minorities. In international and global contexts, it concerns the rights of immigrants to carry their cultural practices with them, and the rights of various regions, nations, and cultures to set the terms of acceptable and expected practices and behaviors for their populations, including women.

Western feminists are awkwardly positioned with respect to global and international dimensions of ethical pluralism. Efforts by Western feminists to intervene on behalf of women in "other" cultures are susceptible to the charge (not at all unfounded) of Western imperialism. On the other hand, failure to draw attention to the plight of women around the world implicates Western feminists in the accusation that they are only concerned with the empowerment of (a select number of) their own women. Recently, the question of global, multicultural pluralism was called by political theorist Susan Okin, in an essay provocatively entitled, "Is Multiculturalism Bad for Women?"[54] Her answer is a resounding yes, although a number of critical and offended responses to her essay have suggested that posing the question in these terms is perhaps unproductive. (After all, multiculturalism is in the eye of the beholder. Members of minority groups and disempowered regions of the world have been acutely aware of multiculturalism well in advance of majority groups and empowered regions.) As the example of FGM demonstrates, indigenous feminist critics and dissenters are actively involved in efforts to reform and abolish specific practices and attitudes that impede the empowerment of women. And many women and women's groups from around the world (not merely those from the northern West) have been active in efforts to promote an international women's rights agenda. It is interesting and relevant to note that the U.S. government continues to hold out against signing the Convention on the Elimination of All Forms of Discrimination against Women (CEDAW), although 153 other countries in the world have seen fit to do so.

Feminism has entered a new phase of reflection and activism in an increasingly complex, interrelated, and conflict-ridden global environment characterized by travel and immigration (legal and illegal, forced and voluntary); economic dislocation and imbalance, opportunity and exploitation; new communications technologies; traveling cultures and their attendant forms of creative hybridization; extreme stratification in power and wealth; and capital's hungry pursuit of resources, markets, and profits. Ethical pluralism is an abiding feature of the global environment with which feminists must reckon. Whether feminists will celebrate the ethical pluralism in their midst, or tolerate it, or seek to eliminate it in the name of universal ethical values is as yet an open question. A great deal will depend on feminist interpretations and assessments of the state of women's empowerment.

NOTES

I am indebted to a number of colleagues for their very thoughtful responses to the initial draft of this essay. Angela Ginorio, Susan Glenn, Richard Madsen, Carole Pateman, Tracy Strong, Priscilla Wald, and Shirley Yee gave me much to think about, for which I am grateful, even though I was not able to address all of their concerns and criticisms in this essay.

1. Consult the following texts for descriptions, discussions, and analyses of some of these varieties of feminism: M. Jacqui Alexander and Chandra Talpade Mohanty, eds., *Feminist Genealogies, Colonial Legacies, Democratic Futures*

(New York: Routledge, 1997); Judith Butler and Joan Scott, *Feminists Theorize the Political* (New York: Routledge, 1992); Irene Diamond and Gloria Ferman Orenstein, eds., *Reweaving the World: The Emergence of Ecofeminism* (San Francisco: Sierra Club Books, 1990); Rosemary Hennessy and Chrys Ingraham, eds., *Materialist Feminism: A Reader in Class, Difference and Women's Lives* (New York: Routledge, 1997); Gloria T. Hull, Patricia Bell Scott, and Barbara Smith, eds., *All the Women Are White, All the Blacks Are Men, but Some of Us Are Brave: Black Women's Studies* (Old Westbury, N.Y.: Feminist Press, 1982); Alison M. Jaggar, *Feminist Politics and Human Nature* (Totowa, N.J.: Rowman and Allanheld, 1983); Stanlie M. James and Abena P. A. Busia, eds., *Theorizing Black Feminism: The Visionary Pragmatism of Black Women* (London: Routledge, 1993); Chandra Talpade Mohanty, Ann Russo, and Lourdes Torres, eds., *Third World Women and the Politics of Feminism* (Bloomington: Indiana University Press, 1991); Vandana Shiva, *Staying Alive: Women, Ecology, and Development* (London: Zed Books, 1988); Rosemarie Tong, *Feminist Thought: A Comprehensive Introduction* (Boulder: Westview, 1989); Imelda Whelehan, *Modern Feminist Thought: From the Second Wave to "Post-Feminism"* (New York: New York University Press, 1995).

2. For recent data on the worldwide condition of women, see Naomi Neft and Ann D. Levine, *Where Women Stand: An International Report on the Status of Women in 140 Countries, 1997–1998* (New York: Random House, 1997). Women currently account for more than 70 percent of the world's population living in poverty.

3. Carole Pateman, "Comments on Christine Di Stefano, 'Feminist Attitudes toward Ethical Pluralism,' " Ethikon Institute Conference on Attitudes toward Ethical Pluralism, La Jolla, Calif., June 1999.

4. On African American feminism, see Patricia Hill Collins, *Black Feminist Thought* (Boston: Unwin Hyman, 1990) and bell hooks, *Feminist Theory: From Margin to Center* (Boston: South End Press, 1984); on Marxist feminism, see *Selected Writings of Alexandra Kollontai*, trans. and introd. Alix Holt (London: Allison & Busby, 1977).

5. Uma Narayan, e-mail correspondence with the Futures of Feminist Theory discussion group, October 1997.

6. See Claudia Card, ed., *Feminist Ethics* (Lawrence: University of Kansas, 1991); Eve Browning Cole and Susan Coultrap-McQuin, eds., *Explorations in Feminist Ethics: Theory and Practice* (Bloomington: Indiana University Press, 1992); Marsha Hanen and Kai Nielson, eds., *Science, Morality and Feminist Theory* (Calgary, Alberta: University of Calgary Press, 1987); Virginia Held, ed., *Justice and Care: Essential Readings in Feminist Ethics* (Boulder: Westview, 1995); Alison M. Jaggar, ed., *Living with Contradictions: Controversies in Feminist Social Ethics* (Boulder: Westview, 1994); and Rosemarie Tong, *Feminine and Feminist Ethics* (Belmont, California: Wadsworth, 1993).

7. Gregor McLennan, *Pluralism* (Minneapolis: University of Minnesota Press, 1995), 21.

8. For essential historical and documentary information regarding modern Western First Wave and Second Wave feminisms, consult the following works:

Rachel Blau Du Plessis and Ann Snitow, eds., *The Feminist Memoir Project: Voices from Women's Liberation* (New York: Three Rivers Press, 1998); Alice Echols, *Daring to Be Bad: Radical Feminism in America, 1967–1975* (Minneapolis: University of Minnesota Press, 1989); Sara Evans, *Personal Politics: The Roots of Women's Liberation in the Civil Rights Movement and the New Left* (New York: Random House, 1980); Eleanor Flexner, *Century of Struggle: The Women's Rights Movement in the U.S.* (New York: Atheneum, 1973); Dawn Keetley and John Pettegrew, *Public Women, Public Words: A Documentary History of American Feminism*, vol. 1: *Beginnings to 1900* (Madison, Wis.: Madison House, 1997); George Klosko and Margaret G. Klosko, *The Struggle for Women's Rights: Theoretical and Historical Sources* (Upper Saddle River, N.J.: Prentice-Hall, 1999); Miriam Schneir, ed., *Feminism: The Essential Historical Writings* (New York: Random House, [1972] 1992); Miriam Schneir, ed., *Feminism in Our Time: The Essential Writings, World War II to the Present* (New York: Random House, 1994).

9. For a discussion and comparison of "equality feminism" and "difference feminism," but which is weighted on the side of "equality feminism," see Judith Evans, *Feminist Theory Today: An Introduction to Second-Wave Feminism* (London: Sage, 1995).

10. See Grace Clement, *Care, Autonomy, and Justice: Feminism and the Ethic of Care* (Boulder: Westview, 1996).

11. For a classic exposition of this view, see John Stuart Mill, *On the Subjection of Women*, ed. Susan M. Okin (Indianapolis, Ind.: Hackett, 1988).

12. An important proponent of this view is the French theorist Luce Irigaray. See *je, tous, nous: Toward a Culture of Difference*, trans. Alison Martin (New York: Routledge, 1993).

13. See bell hooks, *Ain't I a Woman: Black Women and Feminism* (Boston: South End Press, 1981); Shane Phelan, *Getting Specific: Postmodern Lesbian Politics* (Minneapolis: University of Minnesota Press, 1994); and Elizabeth V. Spelman, *Inessential Woman: Problems of Exclusion in Feminist Thought* (Boston: Beacon Press, 1988).

14. For a classic exposition of multiperspectivism, see the discussion of "double consciousness" in W.E.B. DuBois, *The Souls of Black Folk* (New York: Penguin, 1989). For a more recent version, see Patricia Hill Collins, *Black Feminist Thought* (New York: Unwin Hyman, 1990).

15. William E. Connolly, *The Ethos of Pluralization* (Minneapolis: University of Minnesota Press, 1995), p. xii.

16. Suzanne Lebsock, "Women and American Politics, 1880–1920," in Louise A. Tilly and Patricia Gurin, eds., *Women, Politics and Change* (New York: Russell Sage Foundation, 1990), pp. 35–62, esp. p. 40.

17. See Linda Gordon, *Heroes of Their Own Lives: The Politics and History of Family Violence: Boston, 1880–1960* (New York: Viking, 1988).

18. See Paula Baker, "The Domestication of Politics: Women and American Political Society, 1780–1920," *American Historical Review* 89 (1984): 620–47; Paula Giddings, *When and Where I Enter: The Impact of Black Women on Race and Sex in America* (New York: Bantam, 1984), and Lebsock, "Women and American Politics, 1880–1920."

19. See Jo Freeman, "From Protection to Equal Opportunity: The Revolution in Women's Legal Status," in Tilly and Gurin, *Women, Politics, and Change*, pp. 457–81.

20. See Timothy Kaufman-Osborn, Renee Heberle, and Barbara Cruickshank, "Symposium: Gender and the Death Penalty," *Signs: Journal of Women in Culture and Society* 24, 4 (Summer 1999): 1097–1129.

21. See Jean Bethke Elshtain, *Power Trips and Other Journeys: Essays in Feminism as Civic Discourse* (Madison: University of Wisconsin, 1990) ; and Mary Ann Glendon, *Abortion and Divorce in Western Law* (Cambridge, Mass.: Harvard University Press, 1987).

22. See Joan Scott, "Deconstructing Equality versus Difference: Or, the Uses of Poststructuralist Theory for Feminism," in Marianne Hirsh and Evelyn Fox Keller, eds., *Conflicts in Feminism* (New York: Routledge, 1990).

23. For a sampling of the literature on this complicated and compelling issue, see the following: Catherine L. Annas, "Irreversible Error: The Power and Prejudice of Female Mutilation," *Journal of Contemporary Health Law and Policy* 12 (1996) 325–53; Layli Miller Bashir, "Female Genital Mutilation in the United States: An Examination of Criminal and Asylum Law," *Journal of Gender & the Law* 4 (Spring 1996): 415–54; David Fraser, "The First Cut Is (Not) the Deepest: Deconstructing 'Female Genital Mutilation' and the Criminalization of the Other," *Dalhousie Law Journal* 18 (Fall 1995): 310–79; Mary-Jane Ierodiaconou, " 'Listen To Us!' Female Genital Mutilation, Feminism and the Law in Australia," *Melbourne University Law Review* 20 (1995): 562–87, esp. p. 563; Stanlie M. James, "Shades of Othering: Reflections on Female Circumcision/Genital Mutilation," *Signs: Journal of Women in Culture and Society* 23, 4 (Summer 1998): 1031–48; Nancy Irene Kellner, "Under the Knife: Female Genital Mutilation as Child Abuse," *Journal of Juvenile Law* 14 (1993): 118–32, esp. pp. 118–19; Hope Lewis, "Between *Irua* and 'Female Genital Mutilation': Feminist Human Rights Discourse and the Cultural Divide," *Harvard Human Rights Journal* 8 (1995): 1–55; L. Amede Obiora, "Bridges and Barricades: Rethinking Polemics and Intransigence in the Campaign against Female Circumcision," *Case Western Reserve Law Review* 47 (1997): 275–378; Judith S. Seddon, "Possible or Impossible?: A Tale of Two Worlds in One Country," *Yale Journal of Law and Feminism* 5 (1993): 265–87; Sylvia Wynter, " 'Genital Mutilation' or 'Symbolic Birth?' Female Circumcision, Lost Origins, and the Aculturalism of Feminist/Western Thought," *Case Western Reserve Law Review* 47 (1997): 501–52.

24. Martha Nussbaum, "Double Moral Standards?" *Boston Review* 21, 5 (October–November 1996).

25. Yael Tamir, "Hands Off Clitoridectomy," *Boston Review* 21, 3 (Summer 1996); and "Yael Tamir Replies," *Boston Review* 21, 5, October–November 1996).

26. "Yael Tamir Replies," p. 32.

27. Tamir "Hands Off Clitoridectomy," p. 22.

28. See Angelina Grimke, "Appeal to the Christian Women of the South," and "Letters to Catherine Beecher," in Sue Davis, ed., *American Political Thought* (Englewood Cliffs, N.J.: Prentice-Hall, 1996), pp. 228–34, and 234–36, respectively.

29. See Ellen Carol DuBois, *Feminism and Suffrage: The Emergence of an Independent Women's Movement in America, 1848–1869* (Ithaca: Cornell University Press, 1978); and Flexner, *Century of Struggle.*

30. Dorothy McBride Stetson, *Women's Rights in the U.S.A.: Policy Debates and Gender Roles* (Pacific Grove, Calif.: Brooks/Cole, 1991), p. 46.

32. For analyses of the defeat of the ERA, see Mary Frances Berry, *Why ERA Failed* (Bloomington: Indiana University Press, 1986); Joan Hoff-Wilson, ed., *Rights of Passage: The Past and Future of ERA* (Bloomington: Indiana University Press, 1986); Jane Mansbridge, *Why We Lost the ERA* (Chicago: Chicago University Press, 1986).

32. See Sheila Tobias, "Shifting Heroisms: The Uses of Military Service in Politics," in Jean Bethke Elshtain and Sheila Tobias, eds., *Women, Militarism and War* (Totowa, N.J.: Rowman and Littlefield, 1990).

33. See Cynthia Enloe, *Does Khaki Become You? The Militarization of Women's Lives* (Hammersmith: Pandora Press, 1988).

34. See Judith Hicks Stiehm, "The Protected, the Protector, the Defender," *Women's Studies International Forum* 5, 3–4 (1982): 367–76.

35. See Sara Ruddick, *Maternal Thinking: Toward a Politics of Peace* (Boston: Beacon Press, 1989); and Amy Swerdlow, *Women Strike for Peace: Traditional Motherhood and Radical Politics in the 1960s* (Chicago: University of Chicago Press, 1993).

36. See Linda Gordon, *Woman's Body, Woman's Right* (New York: Penguin, 1977); and Rosalind R. Petchesky, *Abortion and Woman's Choice: The State, Sexuality, and Reproductive Freedom* (New York: Longman, 1984).

37. For an excellent collection of work on reproduction in the context of globalization, see Faye D. Ginsburg and Rayna Rapp, eds., *Conceiving the New World Order: The Global Politics of Reproduction* (Berkeley: University of California Press, 1995).

38. See Ruth Colker, *Abortion and Dialogue: Pro-Choice, Pro-Life, and American Law* (Bloomington: Indiana University Press, 1992); Faye D. Ginsburg, *Contestations: The Abortion Debate in an American Community* (Berkeley: University of California Press, 1989); and Kristin Luker, *Abortion and the Politics of Motherhood* (Berkeley: University of California Press, 1984).

39. Pateman, "Comments."

40. Amartya Sen, "More Than One Hundred Million Women Are Missing," *New York Review of Books* 20 (December 1990). I would like to thank Carole Pateman for reminding me about Sen's important research and its relevance for the issues under consideration in this volume.

41. Catharine A. MacKinnon, *Toward a Feminist Theory of the State* (Cambridge, Mass.: Harvard University Press, 1989).

42. See Iris Marion Young, "Reflections on Families in the Age of Murphy Brown: On Gender, Justice, and Sexuality," in Nancy J. Hirschmann and Christine Di Stefano, eds., *Revisioning the Political: Feminist Reconstructions of Traditional Concepts in Western Political Thought* (Boulder: Westview, 1996), pp. 251–70.

43. Adrienne Rich, "Compulsory Heterosexuality and Lesbian Existence," *Blood, Bread, and Poetry: Selected Prose, 1979–1985* (New York: W. W. Norton, 1986).

44. Stetson, *Women's Rights in the U.S.A.*, p. 204.

45. See Drucilla Cornell, *The Imaginary Domain: Abortion, Pornography and Sexual Harassment* (New York: Routledge, 1995); Ann Ferguson, Ilene Philipson, Irene Diamond, Lee Quinby, Carol S. Vance, and Ann Barr Snitow, "Forum: The Feminist Sexuality Debates," *Signs: Journal of Women in Culture and Society* 10 (Autumn 1984): 106–35; and Ann Snitow, Christine Stansell, and Sharon Thompson, eds., *Powers of Desire: The Politics of Sexuality* (New York: Monthly Review Press, 1983).

46. See Andrea Dworkin, *Pornography: Men Possessing Women* (New York: Perigee Books, 1981).

47. See Ellen Willis, "Feminism, Moralism, and Pornography," and Lisa Duggan, Nan D. Hunter, and Carole S. Vance, "False Promises: Feminist Antipornography Legislation," in Alison M. Jaggar, ed., *Living with Contradictions: Controversies in Feminist Social Ethics* (Boulder: Westview, 1994), pp. 161–64 and 165–70, respectively.

48. Alida Brill, "Freedom, Fantasy, Foes, and Feminism: The Debate Around Pornography," in Tilly and Gurin, *Women, Politics, and Change*, pp. 503–28, esp. p. 525.

49. See the following selections from Jagger, *Living with Contradictions*: Evelina Giobbe, "Confronting the Liberal Lies about Prostitution," pp. 120–26; and Carole Pateman, "What's Wrong with Prostitution?" pp. 127–32.

50. International Committee for Prostitutes' Rights World Charter and World Whores' Congress Statements," in Jagger *Living with Contradictions*, pp. 133–43, esp. 139.

51. See Jacqueline Berman, " '(Un)Popular Strangers': The European Political Community, Discourses of Sex-Trafficking, and the Panicked State of the Modern Nation" (unpublished manuscript, 1999).

52. Robert I. Friedman, "India's Shame," *Nation*, 8 April 1996.

53. Pateman, "Comments."

54. Susan Moller Okin, with respondents, *Is Multiculturalism Bad for Women?* (Princeton: Princeton University Press, 1999).

Feminism and the Varieties of Ethical Pluralism

Carole Pateman

Feminism, as Christine Di Stefano demonstrates, stands in a complex relationship to ethical pluralism. To complicate matters further, feminism also has its own conflicts, which include questions about ethical pluralism, with the other traditions represented here. But how should feminism be characterized? Di Stefano begins with this question and offers a "minimalist" definition in terms of "a basic commitment to the empowerment of women."

Empowerment is certainly a feminist goal, a necessary part of a feminist agenda, but it is not obvious that it is sufficient to establish what is *distinctive* about feminism as a tradition of political and ethical argument. For instance, someone who is not a feminist might nevertheless claim to share the goal of empowerment when advocating some degree of separation of the sexes and different spheres of activity for men and women. This arrangement, it might be argued, empowers women because they can develop their specific capacities and talents in their own sphere free from competition with and unwanted attention from men.

As Di Stefano notes, few individuals are born into feminism, unlike major religions or some political ideologies, but a feminist tradition of argument has a much longer history than is often supposed. Reflecting on that history, and on the neglect of, or hostility toward, feminist argument, has led me to suggest that the distinguishing feature of feminism is concern with a specific problem—namely, the problem of the power exercised by men over women, and the claim by men to have right of government over women in all areas of social and political life. Other forms of power—such as that of kings, lords, slave masters, the bourgeoisie, elites, and vanguard parties—have been called into political and ethical question. With few exceptions, however, those who have challenged the legitimacy of these forms of power have excluded women's subordination from criticism by treating it as ordained by nature, or God, or as necessary for a well-ordered polity, or for the preservation of tradition and culture. Men's power, therefore, has been widely assumed to pose no pressing ethical or political questions.

It is precisely the question of the legitimacy and justification of men's government of women that has been raised by the feminist tradition of argument since at least the late seventeenth century. To press this point is not meant, as Di Stefano charges, to "tell the whole story." Rather it has three purposes: first, to distinguish feminism from other traditions; second, to indicate that men's power over women has to be confronted before empowerment can take place; and third, to help elucidate how feminism is both critical of and interconnected with other traditions of thought. The women (and sometimes men) who have contributed to the development of feminist argument have always drawn from other traditions and been concerned with other problems, such as racism, capitalism, temperance, or welfare. Yet because they are conscious of a distinctively feminist problem, their perspective on other issues differs, to varying degrees, from more familiar approaches.

The early feminists attacked men's domination in two areas in particular: their power as husbands and their monopoly of education. Not until the 1790s did women's standing in the "public" world, and their political self-government, their natural (in today's terminology, human) rights, and citizenship, become prominent questions. One of the achievements of the early feminists was to draw attention to both the denial of natural rights to women and to (what I have called) men's special rights,[1] that is, the rights that are part of men's government of women. In this insight they anticipated some of the contemporary feminist arguments about ethical pluralism.

Two different senses of "ethical pluralism" appear in Di Stefano's discussion. In order to highlight and expand upon some of the complexities to which she draws attention I shall call the first ethical pluralism I (EPI) and the second ethical pluralism II (EPII). Di Stefano also refers to a third sense, "plural conceptions of women's proper role in society." However, this seems to me part of, and a consequence of the success of, feminist argument and political campaigns rather than a third sense of ethical pluralism. Feminists have always been concerned to open up ethical space so that women, like men, can be and do many things, in many different ways.

I was invoking EPI, which involves the view that morality is sexually differentiated, in my remarks on empowerment. The conduct and social place of men and women, it is argued, should be regulated by different ethical principles, and so the two sexes should each have their own—complementary—spheres. Much of Di Stefano's discussion focuses on EPI. The second sense of ethical pluralism, EPII, is involved in current controversies over multiculturalism, and over women's human rights. EPII is concerned with the justification of cultural rights and practices, with claims about the value and preservation of religion, custom and tradition, and with cultural self-determination for minority communities and national minorities. EPI and EPII are interrelated.

Feminists, as Di Stefano's examples show, do not by any means speak with one voice, and there is more than one feminist response to issues surrounding ethical pluralism. For example, some feminists, like conservatives and many of their left-wing opponents, are very suspicious of rights. Thus, not surprisingly, the feminist response to EPI has never been straightforward.

Much feminist argument has criticized institutions and practices based on the notion of separate ethical spheres, differential rights for the two sexes, and the identification of men with the public world and women with the private realm. Feminists have criticized EPI because the ostensibly separate spheres are connected through the power that men exercise in both the household and public life, and because this view of ethical pluralism has been bound up with the denial of women's access to education, employment, and the rights of citizens. But women have had to live in the world of EPI, and they have also valued womanly activities and their associated virtues (a line of argument that has resurfaced in the contemporary debates about an "ethics of care"). From the 1790s onward, feminists have argued that the societal contribution that women have made from within their own sphere, especially as mothers, has been insufficiently valued, and that it deserves public assistance and recognition. Some feminists went further and argued not only that women's "private" contribution, service, and sacrifice of life[2] were a qualification for citizenship, in the same way that men's service as soldiers has been a qualification, but that women's contributions were part of citizenship.

The major controversy in the United States in the interwar period over "protective" legislation for mothers and their children and women workers is a good example of the complexities of feminist argument about policies directed to women but not to men. Many former suffragists, who were, therefore, in favor of rights and equality, and who supported protective legislation, nevertheless opposed the Equal Rights Amendment (first introduced into Congress in 1923). They believed that the proposed amendment would lead to the dismantling of existing protective legislation, and that if women were forced to compete with men in the labor market their already disadvantaged position would be exacerbated. But not all former suffragists supported protective legislation or opposed the ERA. Leading proponents of the ERA believed that protective policies aimed only at women reinforced the view that women were unable to be self-governing or to enjoy equal rights and were, at best, lesser citizens. Such legislation, they argued, worked to the detriment of women.

This earlier controversy was between feminists, that is, between advocates of political equality and legal reform to improve women's position. In contrast, the controversy over ratification of the ERA in the 1970s was a battle between feminists and antifeminists. A major part of the antifeminist campaign revolved around the catastrophic effects that were held to be sure to follow ratification of the amendment. They declared that EPI would finally be eliminated, and that the protection that was provided to women by separate spheres of activity for the sexes would come to an end. Such arguments are still heard from antifeminist movements in the 1990s in the conflicts over "family values."

Antifeminists are usually willing for the state to step in to uphold EPI, and, looking back over the past century or more, the question for feminists, as Di Stefano comments, has not been state regulation as such. Rather, feminists have grappled with the problem of what kind of reform or regulation would best undermine men's legal privileges, their monopoly of political authority, and access to economic and other resources. They had to decide which measures would aid women's self-government and citizenship, while improving their standing in the sphere allocated to them within a sexually differentiated ethical and political system.

But EPI has crumbled in Western countries, and although a vigorous rearguard action is being fought by antifeminists of various stripes, it is now increasingly difficult to justify. The changes of the past quarter-century have meant that the economic conditions that buttressed EPI, and the ideology of the male "breadwinner" with his economically dependent wife, are no longer there, nor are the legal props. Thanks to the campaigns of the feminist movement, women have finally won equal, formal civil and political rights and standing. Moreover, conceptions of masculinity and femininity and norms of sexual behavior have also undergone considerable transformation.

In these new circumstances it is not surprising that feminists now disagree about state intervention. The controversies have been particularly heated around matters of sexuality. For example, feminists who have criticized pornography or prostitution and advocated legal intervention have been presented as being "antisex" by other feminists. In the case of prostitution, however, it does not necessarily follow that feminist critics support legal prohibition. In my own attempt to show what is ethically wrong with prostitution I do not, as is sometimes erroneously suggested, advocate that it be made illegal.[3]

Di Stefano discusses in some detail the major controversy that has raged around female genital mutilation, and in this case accusations of cultural imperialism have been a prominent feature. Female genital mutilation has received enormous publicity (no doubt some interest is merely prurient) but, as Di Stefano indicates, the debate has not always been productive. A more useful way to discuss the problem might be to address the practice as a (public) health question, both for the women concerned and for the burden it imposes on public resources. It is, to be sure, by no means the only medical issue that women face in the relevant regions, but, especially in the most extreme forms, excision makes a significant contribution to the toll of preventable health problems. There is a good case for prohibiting female genital mutilation in Western countries,[4] and some governments of the countries where the practice is widespread have banned it. Legislation can be a very important ethical symbol, but in many matters associated with sexuality and "private" life, it is not always a very effective instrument on its own. Information and education are crucial, and the problem of genital mutilation is best dealt with through the many local activist movements now working on the issue, or by following the example of certain villages in Senegal where the elders have taken the lead.

The interrelationship between EPI and EPII, and the critical question of where feminist lines are to be drawn in debates about ethical pluralism, are both raised in the case of female genital mutilation. Di Stefano emphasizes that where ethical values disempower women, feminism ceases to accommodate ethical pluralism. Similarly, where women suffer physical harm or death, or their self-government is denied, ethical pluralism and feminism come into conflict. The friction is evident in recent debates about multiculturalism in Western countries, and in the problem of women's human rights around the world.

In most academic discussions of multiculturalism in the 1990s questions about women's position and men's power were seldom raised as a serious problem—which prompted Susan Okin's intervention.[5] She points out that women are seen as central figures in the preservation and transmission of culture, and that religious and cultural groups are usually concerned with family law and the regulation of women's conduct and activities, yet this aspect of multiculturalism hardly appears in the best-known discussions. In short, claims for cultural rights and the preservation of customary ways of life (EPII) usually entail that EPI is upheld to a greater or lesser degree. For example, governments sometimes leave jurisdiction over marriage and the family to minority religious or cultural groups, and their regulations can differ from wider state law or principles of citizenship. For some feminists this evokes uncomfortable echoes of past treatment of relations between spouses as a "private" matter from which the law stood aloof, even when criminal assault took place. More generally, the question is raised of why citizenship rights, or human rights, should stop at the door to the household.

As Di Stefano illustrates, feminists who have asked such questions about the intersection of EPI and EPII, have been accused by other feminists of cultural imperialism and imposing alien ethical values, of showing lack of understanding of other ways of life, or of unjustifiably presuming to speak for other women. In these feminist controversies three important points are sometimes neglected. First, that traditional ways of life are now carried on within modern states. Many of these states have been constructed quite recently by (almost exclusively male) political actors who use political ideas—not least national self-determination and the modern "state" itself—that are Western in origin. Accusations of cultural imperialism imply that what is sauce for the nationalist gander is improper for the feminist goose. Moreover, the impact of bureaucratic and military apparatuses, predatory elites, the globalization of capitalist markets, and the emergence of vicious ethnic conflict are doing far more to undermine traditional cultures than any feminist ideas, writings, protests, or efforts at legal reform.

Second, cultures are not monolithic or static, and the invention of tradition is a very flourishing enterprise. Who has the power to interpret what "traditional culture" encompasses, or a particular religious text prescribes, is a key question and central to many power struggles. Women around the globe are now demanding to participate in the task of interpretation. Few cultures today are without their own internal critics and dissenters—just as ideas such as "rights of citizens" have been bitterly contested in Western countries.

Third, underlying the interrelationship between EPI and EPII is the problem of whether girls and women, and the lives of girls and women, are valued, or valued to the same extent, as boys and men and their lives. This question is highlighted most graphically by the demographic data on the "missing women," but it is also brought to the fore by the distressing level of violence against girls and women in all countries.[6] I hope that feminist scholars will make a much larger contribution than is the case at present to the debates over the ethics of euthanasia, care of the chronically sick and terminally ill, patenting of life-forms, and the very rapid developments in genetics. However, one of the most basic global issues of life and death of concern to feminists is nutrition and health care for women, and their bodily integrity and security.

If there are feminists who want to "eliminate" ethical pluralism "in the name of universal ethical values," they are harboring a strange ambition. Ethical values are necessarily couched in general terms, which is why major religious and cultural traditions can subscribe to some of the same fundamental principles. The difficulties arise over their interpretation and implementation. Ethical pluralism is hardly likely to vanish given the wide latitude available for plausible interpretation of general principles within and between ethical traditions. Recent intellectual trends that are very suspicious of, or have rejected, universalism have been very influential within feminism and have fueled the controversies within feminism over EPII. But, as often happens, intellectual fashion has been overtaken by political developments. Particularly since the U.N. conferences on human rights in Vienna in 1993 and on women in Beijing in 1995, women's human rights, and hence universalist language, have become central to the campaigns of a multitude of women's organizations around the globe. This does not mean, however, that these organizations will all agree on the interpretation of particular rights or how they should best be implemented within different ethical and cultural contexts.

There are hard questions to be resolved about the character of the changes that are required, and how regulatory principles and everyday practices are to be assessed if women's human rights are to be upheld within EPII. For instance, what of dress codes? Under the Taliban government a (harshly enforced) dress code for women was part of an extremist regime that denied girls and women access to education or employment. In London or Paris, in contrast, a young woman might decide to wear the *hejab* as a mark of her religious beliefs while participating in a variety of ways in the "majority" culture. In France a major controversy erupted recently when a few schoolgirls began to cover their heads. Some feminists insisted that their action demonstrated that the young women were mere subordinates within their familial culture, and that the *hejab* was an affront to republican, secular education. Other feminists take the view that (uncoerced) dress is a matter of ethical indifference. The important issue is not how women dress, but to what extent they are self-governing, and whether they can take a full part in all aspects of the social and political life of their societies.

The more general problem for feminists is that the conjunction of EPI and EPII so often rests on special rights for men and the denial of the basic right of self-government to women. Self-government is an ethical and political principle that lies at the heart of democratic theory and practice. Now that almost all governments around the world at least pay lip-service to democracy, the questions raised by feminists about ethical pluralism can no longer be ignored.

NOTES

1. Carole Pateman, "Democracy, Freedom and Special Rights," in David Boucher and Paul Kelly, eds., *Social Justice: From Hume to Walzer,* (London: Routledge, 1998), pp. 219–22.

2. Feminists drew attention to the high maternal death rate in the early twentieth century and emphasized that casualties exceeded the sacrifice that men made on the battlefield.

3. Carole Pateman, *The Sexual Contract* (Stanford: Stanford University Press, 1988), pp. 189–209. The global sex industry and the traffic in girls and women has grown enormously since I wrote my book, fueled by the collapse of many economies, the growth of "mafias," and increasing inequality.

4. In the past, the practice was used by medical practitioners in the West to "cure" women who exhibited "abnormal" behavior.

5. Susan Okin, *Is Multiculturalism Bad for Women?* (Princeton: Princeton University Press, 1999). See also, e.g., Ayelet Shachar "Group Identity and Women's Rights in Family Law: The Perils of Multicultural Accommodation," *Journal of*

Political Philosophy 6 (1998): 285–305; and "On Citizenship and Multicultural Vulnerability," *Political Theory* 28, 1 (2000): 64–89.

6. Publicity is being given to the extent of what is now called domestic violence, and to "everyday" rape around the world. But the violence includes honor killings; dowry deaths; the systematic use of rape as a weapon, and one of spoils, of war; and the taking of girls and women into slavery in some conflicts.

PART IX

Critical Theory and the Challenge of Ethical Pluralism

William E. Scheuerman

It would be a mistake to claim that early critical theory was insensitive to the significance of ethical pluralism for human freedom. Originally conceived during the darkest days of a Europe haunted by the specter of National Socialism, the Frankfurt School's eclectic brand of Hegelian-Marxism powerfully described the many ways in which contemporary social and economic forms delimit the possibilities for authentic ethical and moral choices in contemporary society. From the perspective of the emigré left-wing intellectuals who made up the core of the Frankfurt School (Theodor Adorno, Walter Benjamin, Erich Fromm, Herbert Marcuse, Max Horkheimer, Otto Kirchheimer, Leo Loewenthal, and Franz Neumann), the readiness with which so many men and women subjected themselves to totalitarian trends in our century provided indisputable evidence for the fundamental bankruptcy of contemporary capitalism.[1] Capitalist society ultimately generates, in Marcuse's telling phrase, a "one-dimensional man" exhibiting only a truncated and unsatisfying form of human existence; totalitarian regimes simply represented the most egregious manifestation of this one-dimensionality. For the Frankfurt School theorists, the basic institutional structure of modern society necessarily results in authoritarian political trends, a constriction of intellectual debate, cultural mediocrity, and a profound hostility to novel forms of intimacy and sexual life. Experimentation with alternative forms of life is only possible within a narrow set of parameters determined by the oppressive logic of advanced capitalism. Potential attacks on the status quo too often merely function to reinforce it, and seemingly subversive challenges are subverted by the structural dynamics of a society in which capitalist accumulation and a truncated form of "instrumental rationality" reign supreme: young people begin wearing jeans in order to revolt against rigid forms of bourgeois self-presentation, but within a short time their revolt simply generates another way for large corporations to profit by marketing a limited conception of selfhood to young people.[2] Contemporary society systematically excludes some forms of life, while simultaneously privileging those meshing neatly with the structural imperatives of its flawed institutional core.

Moreover, the Frankfurt School's critique of contemporary society was driven by a vision of emancipation inspired by what one commentator has aptly described as "those traces and moments of otherness . . . cracks in the crust of the totality of the administered world."[3] Marcuse looked to social groups (students, the ghetto poor, the women's movement) locked out of the "one-dimensional" logic of contemporary society and whose sensibilities purportedly pointed the way to a superior mode of human existence, whereas Adorno hinted that aesthetic experience might harbor a chance for "the subject to let itself go, to deliver itself over to which is not itself, to remain 'by itself in otherness.'"[4] Because capitalist society suppressed the emancipatory potential of its "wholly other," its claim to constitute a truly pluralistic society was fraudulent. Pluralism could never be genuine in a society whose institutional core privileged forms of existence based on civic privatism, consumerism, and the cult of violence, while suppressing alternative ways of life as expressions of unacceptable modes of alien "otherness."

Nonetheless, early critical theory clearly failed to tackle some of the more striking normative and institutional implications of what John Rawls has famously described as "the fact of pluralism." Even if writers like Marcuse and Adorno were right to underline the *incomplete* and *distorted* character of pluralism in contemporary capitalist society, modern societies rest on fundamental ethical and religious divides: contemporary political life must start from the "fact" of "a diversity of opposing and irreconcilable religious, philosophical, and moral doctrines," even if contemporary institutional structures unduly restrain opportunities to express certain forms of "otherness" as viable alternatives to society's mainstream.[5] Unfortunately, the most obvious *normative* and *political* dimensions of this problem—how, for example, a democratic society should decide how to regulate conflicts stemming from ethical pluralism—were neglected by early critical theory. This failure is part of a more general theoretical weakness, namely early critical theory's "distrust towards questions of legitimacy and the normative dimensions of political institutions."[6] To the extent that critical theory remained committed to the possibility of a postcapitalist society, it occasionally seemed to assume, in the spirit of Marx, that socialism would render such questions either irrelevant *or* easily resolvable. In this way, the Hegelian-Marxism that haunts even the most innovative versions of early critical theory arguably made it ill-equipped to tackle questions of normative political theory.[7] Similarly, the Frankfurt School always remained imprisoned in a model of action according to which *work* or *production* represented the primary activity in the making of self and society. Unfortunately, this model was poorly suited to the task of making sense of human intersubjectivity or the dynamics of public life. Early critical theory never was able to develop a defensible political theory—and thus an account of how political institutions should grapple with ethical pluralism—because its basic conceptual framework prevented it from doing so.[8]

Even those Frankfurt School writers, namely Franz Neumann and Otto Kirchheimer, who went furthest in developing a coherent political theory, never succeeded in providing an adequate analysis of the problem of ethical pluralism. Although Neumann and Kirchheimer made valuable contributions toward the formulation of a critical theory of democratic institutions and the rule of law, they too ultimately were plagued by a brand of Hegelian-Marxism that prevented them from acknowledging the full significance of the "fact of pluralism." The centerpiece of Franz Neumann's political theory, his idiosyncratic social democratic defense of modern *formal* law, is telling in this respect. Whereas modern liberals have often defended the ideal of clear, general, and *formal* legal rules as a way of undergirding the liberal state's need to guarantee neutrality in the face of ethical and moral pluralism, Neumann instead defended modern formal law chiefly because he saw it as a protection for subordinate social groups. In his account, the threat to formal law comes from privileged sectors of the capitalist economy that manipulate vague, amorphous, and moralistic legal standards (e.g., "unconscionable," "in good faith") as a social weapon against the working classes. To his credit, Neumann acknowledged that the abrogation of formal law could constitute a potentially disastrous attack on modern political and ethical pluralism; he criticized National Socialism in part for precisely this reason. Yet his primary concern always remained the way in which antiformal trends in the law tend to undermine the social achievements of the less-well-off.[9]

Fortunately, more recent critical theorists have proved adept at tackling both the challenge of ethical pluralism and its implications for political theory. Although in many ways intellectual offspring of the early Frankfurt School, second- and even third-generation critical theorists have been busily reconstructing a critical theory of society that does justice to "the fact of pluralism," while outlining a model of a democratic civil society able to take advantage of the normative and political fruits of modern pluralism. In particular, Jean Cohen and Andrew Arato have formulated an ambitious democratic theory whose very raison d'être is the quest to provide a starting point for the democratization of "societies which are pluralistic and composed of individuals with distinct and differing conceptions of the good life."[10] Because Cohen and Arato consider civil society the primary site in which we "learn to value difference," they have taken valuable steps in formulating a model of civil society attuned to the "fact of pluralism."[11] In my view, they have successfully overcome crucial weaknesses of early Critical Theory, which lacked both a sufficient understanding of the significance of modern pluralism *and* a model of civil society appropriate to it. First, I examine the details of their complex model of civil society while responding to a number of criticisms recently directed against it. Then I underline the merits of their model as a conceptual starting point for grappling with difficult conflicts concerning the coordination of ethical pluralism. In my view, we can build on Cohen and Arato to begin addressing a series of difficult policy questions. In a concluding section, I try to underline some of the weaknesses of contemporary critical theory discourse about civil society. Although contemporary critical theorists are right to break with the conceptual foundations of early critical theory, they have downplayed their predecessors' concerns about capitalism's built-in hostility to difference. No account of the relationship between ethical pluralism and civil society remains complete, however, unless it acknowledges the manner in which present-day globalizing capitalism prevents the full realization of the potentialities of modern ethical pluralism.

GENERAL CONSIDERATIONS: CIVIL SOCIETY AND ETHICAL PLURALISM

Nowadays it is commonplace to begin any discussion of contemporary critical theory with an analysis of the intellectual achievements of its most impressive contemporary representative, Jürgen Habermas.[12] As far as critical theory's account of civil society goes, however, that would probably be inappropriate. Although they clearly have been inspired by Habermas's attempt to formulate a neo-Kantian *discourse ethics* as a foundation for moral and political decisions, Habermas himself has borrowed substantially from two North American critical theorists, Jean Cohen and Andrew Arato, who have developed the most sophisticated normative and institutional concept of civil society within the critical theory tradition. In fact Habermas is merely summarizing the results of Cohen's and Arato's impressive theoretical work, when he writes in *Between Facts and Norms* that the institutional core of civil society

> comprises those non-governmental and non-economic connections and voluntary associations that anchor the communication structures of the public sphere. . . . Civil society is composed of those more or less spontaneously emergent associations, organizations, and movements that, attuned to how societal problems resonate in the private life spheres, distill and transmit such reactions in amplified form to the public sphere.[13]

Given the centrality of their model of civil society to contemporary critical theory, it is imperative that we sketch out its main features. In particular, I hope to underline ways in which the problem of ethical pluralism has been central to the conceptualization proffered by Cohen and Arato.

In their model, civil society consists of those activities composing the intimate sphere (including different forms of family life), associations (especially voluntary associations), social movements, and forms of public communication *distinct from* the activities of the state and economy. Characterized by "relations of conscious association, of self-organization and organized communication," civil society nonetheless presupposes legal protections (most important, basic rights) for its institutionalization because "in the long run both independent action and institutionalization are necessary for the reproduction of civil society."[14] Put somewhat more blandly: enforceable rights (e.g., the right to assembly) help make autonomous modes of self-organization within civil society possible.

In addition, civil society requires a minimum of economic efficiency and material well-being, only achievable within the context of a modern market economy, as well as forms of state administrative coordination; in this account, markets and the state administration represent potential *threats to* but also *presuppositions of* a democratic polity resting on a vibrant civil society. Yet administrative and market processes simultaneously depend on a lively civil society in which freewheeling debate and independent activity are commonplace, at least to the extent that their operations are to be rendered compatible with a political order committed to the principles of democratic legitimacy. Markets and bureaucracies cannot generate democratic legitimacy. Market and administrative processes necessarily exhibit structural features that make them poor sites for uninhibited communication or self-mobilization. But "the political legitimacy of modern constitutional democracies rests on the principle that action-orienting norms, practices, policies, and claims to authority can be contested by citizens, open to their input and revision, and must be discursively redeemed."[15] In Habermas's original terminology, markets and bureaucracies partake of a "systems-logic" that necessarily conflicts with a model of normative integration based on an ideal of freewheeling, open debate and political exchange. Yet the core intuition of this claim hardly depends on recourse to systems theory: modern bureaucracies and markets perform indispensable functions, and we cannot realistically hope to supplant or replace them altogether with mechanisms characterized by the boisterous, freewheeling debate and political exchange constitutive of a robust civil society. As Cohen and Arato note, actors engaged directly in administrative and market processes simply "cannot afford to subordinate strategic and instrumental criteria to the patterns of normative integration and open-ended communication characteristic of civil society," in part because they face rigid time restraints and considerations of efficiency.[16] Civil society thereby becomes the *main* site for the generation of democratic legitimacy. Cohen and Arato acknowledge the difficulty of institutionalizing discourse ethics' ambitious claim that a norm

of action is only valid if all those possibly affected by it could, as participants in a practical discourse, reach agreement that the norm deserves to
possess validity. In their account, a freewheeling, pluralistic civil society,
based on a commitment to open debate and exchange, is the most likely
candidate for producing this legitimacy, in part because civil society is
free of the pressing restraints on deliberation evident within administrative and market processes.

Is this model of democracy thereby rendered excessively "defensive,"
in light of the fact that it occasionally seems to envision civil society primarily as a counterweight to the operation of (nondemocratic) markets
and bureaucracies?[17] Such a reading obscures central features of Cohen's
and Arato's model. They also argue that we should recognize the existence
of distinct political and economic "societies" as constituting mediating
spheres between civil society and administration and markets. Parties,
political organizations, and publics directly involved in government decision making, for example, mediate between civil society and the imperatives (e.g., the time constraints and formalities) of the state administration, whereas labor unions and other mechanisms guaranteeing labor
representation play a similar role in the present-day political economy.
In some contrast to Habermas, whose recent political theory arguably
contains a number of overly defensive features,[18] Cohen and Arato unam-
biguously acknowledge the pressing need today to experiment with new
modes of interaction between civil society and political and economic
society, as well as novel forms of organization within the economy and
state. Their point is merely that such experiments will have to respect
some limits imposed by the constraints of modern markets and bureaucracies. Because some forms of political and economic organization are undoubtedly inconsistent with a flourishing civil society, a "defensive strategy of democratizing only civil society must fail and . . . complementary
strategies of democratizing state, economy, and civil society, albeit to different degrees, are possible."[19] Cohen and Arato explicitly comment that
"democratization [within the economy] is not per se incompatible with
efficient functioning."[20] In my reading, their model leaves substantial
room for institutional experimentation, while rightly acknowledging that
democratization within the state and economy will need to take approaches different from those appropriate to civil society.

So how then does this model of civil society confront the challenge of
ethical pluralism? First, Cohen and Arato take the "fact of pluralism"
seriously by breaking with early critical theory's tendency to dismiss the
pluralistic self-portrait of contemporary society as little more than a
"veil" masking its one-dimensional character. Following Max Weber, they
acknowledge that ours is a "disenchanted" (*entzaubert*) world in which
no overarching comprehensive moral doctrine can claim universal valid-

ity. *Contra* Weber, who believed that modern pluralism necessarily renders political authority more or less arbitrary, Cohen and Arato follow Habermas in trying to outline a procedural and formal model of democratic legitimacy faithful to the core achievements of modern rationalism. At times reminiscent of influenial currents within contemporary liberal theory, discourse ethics for them is a *political ethic* that need not commit its defenders to any specific moral philosophy.[21] A universally acceptable system of democratic legitimacy is possible alongside substantial ethical pluralism: for Kantians and utilitarians, as well as socialists and free-marketeers, the only reasonable way to resolve conflicts about enforceable societal norms is by engaging in freewheeling debate and deliberation, resting on mutual and reciprocal recognition, in which everyone affected by a norm under consideration is given an equal chance to participate.[22] Although presupposing demanding procedural standards (symmetry, reciprocity, and reflexivity), this model of legitimacy is seen as embodying minimal preconditions of normative coordination and commonality already implicit in deliberative practices at work within contemporary society.

From this perspective, attempts to achieve ethical uniformity necessarily represent an attack on the core preconditions of modernity itself, and civil society inevitably becomes the main forum for the debate and contestation about the societal coordination of ethically based differences. It also becomes a site for *experimenting* with forms of life and identities that may conflict with those of society's mainstream. One of the most important achievements of Cohen and Arato's model for critical theory is that they devote substantial energy to the task of *valorizing* ethical difference for civil society *without* succumbing to a romanticized view of difference that would necessarily undermine the shared preconditions of democratic legitimacy. Here as well, they go well beyond Habermas, whose own views on occasion have suffered from a certain insensitivity to the virtues of difference.[23] Because every democratic consensus is, of course, always empirical, fallible, and thus subject to change, "individual judgement, differing ways of life, and experiments with new ways must be granted autonomy from the current consensus on what is just" because the need to correct or revise previous political decisions requires respect for ongoing experiments with alternative "ways of life."[24] In this model, pluralism is not only a "fact" to be accommodated, as the issue has been formulated within certain strands of liberal theory; it represents one of the strengths of modern society, because it heightens our collective capacity to resolve conflicts successfully concerning societal norms. Civil society needs to leave the widest possible room for experimentation based on ethically based differences concerning any of a host of controversial issues.[25] Only by doing so can we hope to formulate enforceable legal norms that can make a real claim to do justice to the richness and diversity of modern ethical experience. Indeed, the deliberative processes essential to a thriving civil society necessarily presuppose the autonomy of the individual moral conscience—namely, individuals able to distance themselves potentially from their own moral positions and criticize those of others in a principled manner as well. A freewheeling civil society is only possible if the political system provides protection for the cultivation of an independent moral standpoint and distinct ways of life potentially in conflict with those of a majority of society's members.[26] But an independent standpoint of this type is only likely to be achieved in a civil society that places a premium on ethical diversity and acknowledges that fundamental ethical and existential questions ultimately belong to the sphere of individual moral conscience.[27]

SOCIAL REGULATION

The formal and procedural character of the concept of civil society described here precludes an unambiguous determination of any particular political community's posture toward many ethically controversial topics concerning gender roles, intimacy, sexuality, and life-and-death issues. From the perspective of discourse ethics, the specific way in which any democratic polity deals with ethical debates of this type ultimately can only be determined in a process of freewheeling debate and political give-and-take. Nonetheless, the approach described here does clearly suggest that a political community is only likely to succeed in resolving such conflicts reasonably if it provides adequate protections for a heterogeneous civil society capable of serving as a terrain for experimentation with a vast range of different answers to difficult ethical questions. Formalism need not be "empty" or "content-less": the critical theory model of civil society contains real normative "muscle" or substance, albeit of a rather abstract type, and thus there are plausible reasons for suggesting that critical theorists are likely to be committed, at the very least, to a particular *range* of policy options concerning the societal regulation of ethical differences. To be sure, policy preferences cannot be mechanically deduced from the model of civil society defended here. Yet some policy options surely cohere with that model better than others.

Cohen and Arato appropriately emphasize that a variety of relatively distinct institutional versions of democracy are consistent with this picture of civil society. At the same time, they underscore why civil society should not be conceived as a sphere in which the politicization of personal matters is necessarily desirable. For sure, discourse ethics suggests that the only legitimate way to draw the boundary between the sphere of individual moral judgment and those matters deserving of general societal regulation is by means of a discussion including everyone potentially affected. Only in open debate can we determine what rightly constitutes a "private" matter; we might describe this as the radical democratic normative core of discourse ethics.[28] But an institutional concretization of this view, in which the public-private divide is effectively tossed out the window as a consequence of (an oftentimes justified) skepticism toward the way in which the public-private boundary has historically been drawn, simultaneously risks destroying civil society to the extent that it would subvert the emergence of the independent moral standpoint on which civil society rests in the first place: a radical democratic *normative* model is hardly inconsistent with legal protections for individuals along the lines that liberal theorists, traditionally have viewed as essential to a worthwhile polity. Cohen and Arato agree with liberal theorists like J. Donald Moon, who have pointed out that "[t]here must be a limit on the extent to which they [i.e., individual citizens] can be required to reveal themselves to others and on the necessity to defend their basic values and commitments if their participation in political activity is not itself to be coercive."[29] But they refuse to accept Moon's view that securing privacy rights is inconsistent with the idea of discourse ethics.[30]

Cohen develops this line of inquiry by outlining a robust defense of privacy rights that both acknowledges the socially and historically contingent character of the boundary between public and private *and* insists that "the boundary line must be drawn somewhere."[31] By necessity, substantial debate and exchange within civil society should be concerned with scrutinizing the division between those activities requiring societal coordination and those essentially private in character. Yet this debate is only likely to take a fruitful form—for both the individual and broader system of democratic legitimacy—if undertaken under the auspices of a legal system guaranteeing a set of privacy rights capable of providing protection to a zone of privacy in which the sanctity of individual moral autonomy is taken seriously. In modern pluralistic societies we inevitably find ourselves disputing the scope of this zone; the ongoing debate about abortion is an obvious illustration. But the fact that the precise scope of privacy inevitably remains controversial hardly means that no zone of privacy therefore can be effectively protected. In this account, privacy guarantees provide an effective counterweight to the moral paternalism often characteristic of majoritarian pressures: privacy means "the right not to have an identity imposed upon one by the state or third parties that one cannot freely affirm and embrace."[32]

Now one might counter that privacy rights risk removing too many controversial issues from the scope of democratic politics: privacy rights risk ejecting an excessive dose of liberalism—which has always emphasized individual legal protections—into the radical democratic core of discourse ethics.[33] To be sure, this worry needs to be taken seriously. None-theless, it would be wrong to see privacy rights as entailing a quest to *remove* certain controversial moral matters from the political process *altogether*; they simply entail providing *enhanced legal protection* to some forms of activity, which hardly entails withdrawing them from the political sphere, any more than the Bill of Rights enjoins American citizens to cease disputing the practical significance of freedom of the press or habeas corpus. At least since John Stuart Mill, we should know that there is more to democratic politics than majority rule-making, and thus we would do well to acknowledge that antimajoritarian legal devices some-times can play a healthy role in buttressing political debate and exchange, and thereby helping to secure the more fundamental principle of popular sovereignty.

In Cohen's view, recent constitutional jurisprudence in the United States has taken important initial steps in grounding just such a protected sphere of privacy; the Supreme Court has been right to acknowledge both "the right to be left alone" (freedom from official intrusion and surveil-lance) and "decisional privacy" (freedom from undue regulation) in the intimate details of personal life. Privacy rights entitle "one to choose with whom one will attempt to justify one's existential decisions, [and] with whom one will communicatively rethink conceptions of the good," and they are constitutive of moral agency.[34] Arguing against communitarians who consider the Court's privacy jurisprudence pernicious, Cohen insists that privacy rights mesh well with an intersubjective model of personal identity, as well as an awareness of the historical and contextual origins of ethical and moral value. Communitarians are simply wrong to assert that recent decisions on abortion, contraceptives, marriage, sexual rela-tions, and child rearing necessarily rest on a crude form of contractual thinking or embody an indefensible atomistic conception of the self. Whatever the specific flaws of the Court's reasoning in individual rulings, privacy rights function as a puissant protection for individuals to grapple autonomously with fundamental existential questions, and there is no reason to assume that their normative justification necessarily rests on untenable variants of moral and political theory.

From this perspective, there is no simple answer to the question of how much ethical pluralism would be acceptable in a particular polity, or when the state should suppress such differences. Of course, "[r]adical pluralism . . . cannot be so radical as to exclude meaningful normative coordination and commonality."[35] Some forms of life—most obviously, those predi-cated on violence—would surely be inconsistent with this model of civil society. Others raise difficult questions for a critical theory perspective, just as they do for anyone who takes the disenchanted character of our moral universe and the "fact of pluralism" seriously: what is the appropriate status of religious communities (for example, the Amish) whose practices hardly seem especially "deliberative" in character? At the same time, there are pressing prima facie reasons for maximizing possibilities for experimenting with alternative forms of intimacy, sexuality, and gender organization, and for guaranteeing a protective shield for the unique identities and intimate choices of concrete persons. Privacy rights potentially provide one instrument for doing so.

For some critics, calls for privacy rights merely divert attention from the basically antipluralistic character of the model of civil society described here. If the boundary between the sphere of individual moral judgment and the sphere of general societal regulation is to be resolved by debate and deliberation, will that not mean that those unsuited to the highly "rationalistic" modes of discourse allegedly privileged by Habermasians like Cohen and Arato not be excluded from this determination?[36] Who, in fact, is the likely subject of deliberative processes based on demanding normative standards of symmetry, reciprocity, and reflexivity? Might not this model provide a flawed picture of civil society by secretly harboring an exclusionary logic favoring some social groups (whites, Europeans, men) over others (peoples of color, women). Moreover, does this model not posit an unrealistic view of politics, in which the obviously nondeliberative character of so much political life is obscured?[37] Might it not obfuscate the contestable and agonistic character of political life, in which participants are more likely to "talk past one another" than engage in politically efficacious debate capable of generating meaningful results?

In my view, part of the answer to these anxieties is to acknowledge the dangers of an overly narrow model of real-life political deliberation. It would be silly to deny the difficult questions raised by the need to contextualize the normative standards of discourse ethics; in some settings— think of a policemen who swings his club menacingly at those protesting police brutality—even a guttural shout of defiance ("No!") can constitute an important public statement and "argument." Iris Young is right to suggest that political discourse can legitimately consist of forms of greeting, rhetoric, and narrative that mesh poorly with some of Habermas's own descriptions of the deliberative processes constitutive of civil society.[38] At the same time, a normative theory of democratic legitimacy will need to maintain some minimal standards of impartiality and fairness, *even* as it acknowledges the contestable character of every application of those standards to particular forms of political exchange in particular situations.[39] Here, as well, difficult questions are sure to arise. By the same token, it is difficult to see how even those bent on challenging the very existence of such minimal standards cannot simultaneously avoid appealing to them: left- and right-wing Nietzscheans who delight in defending an agonistic conception of politics while belittling "rationalistic" Habermasian discourse inevitably rely on some minimal common standards of human understanding and scientific validity, at least to the extent that they hope to be taken seriously by their interlocutors.

As far as the accusation of political naiveté is concerned, this model is *not* committed to the obviously implausible claim that all ethically based political conflicts can be neatly resolved by deliberation and debate. There is no built-in guarantee that a civil society relying on freewheeling debate will necessarily generate agreement—or even an agreement to disagree—in reference to any of a host of difficult normative and policy questions. By the same token, "[w]e must resist the temptation to take all our disputes and disagreements as given" by wrongly assuming "that all the problems we face are tragic, unbridgeable, or irreconcilable."[40] Of course, we often do simply "talk past each other"; this is one of the reasons we need to figure out how to institutionalize the best possible nexus between civil society and the economy, on the one hand, and state institutions, on the other, so as to allow the political community to make the most fruitful use of freewheeling debate and exchange. Clearly, this task raises a host of difficult contextual issues as well, and the theoretical approach to civil society described here hardly intends to obscure the significance of such questions. But it does remind us of something too often downplayed by competing intellectual perspectives: only a rambunctious civil society, in which we both experiment with difference as we argue about it, will allow us to identify which conflicts are tragic or irreconcilable in the first place.

CITIZENSHIP: THE CASE OF GENDER

Critical theorists today can be fairly described as striving to avoid the widely documented dangers of two influential competing notions of citizenship. On the one hand, the model of what we might describe as the "supercitizen," found in much republican and participatory democratic theory and according to which political participation represents the highest of human goods, is untenable given the pluralistic character of modern society. Because we live in polities composed of individuals with differing conceptions of the good life, it is unreasonable and probably dangerous to privilege "the life of the *polis*" too much. The functional requirements of modern markets and bureaucracies conflict with this ambitious model of citizenship as well; there are good reasons for doubting the possibility of making either markets or bureaucracies sites for ambitious expressions of participatory citizenship oriented to the "common good." On the other hand, critical theorists simultaneously hope to avoid the denigration of political life implicit in the idea of the "citizen-taxpayer" found in some strands of classical liberalism as well as its most influential contemporary offshoot, libertarianism. In that model, citizenship is reduced to yet another form of bourgeois economic activity; the citizen becomes a mere taxpayer or consumer acting in correspondence with a narrow model of economic rationality.[41] To the extent that this model sacrifices pluralism by making *economic man* the paragon of human virtue, it reproduces the antipluralist thrust of participatory democratic theory. Whereas participatory democratic theory overstates the possibilities for democracy within markets and bureaucracies, the libertarian view fails to provide room for even the most minimal forms of freewheeling, open-ended political debate and deliberation. From a critical theory perspective, this truncated, economistic notion of the "citizen-taxpayer" represents a vivid illustration of the manner in which contemporary capitalism inappropriately "colonizes" facets of contemporary human life in which economic standards and procedures are utterly inappropriate.

The model of civil society described here suggests a model of citizenship in some ways less demanding than participatory democracy but more demanding than libertarianism. Critical theorists aspire for a political community in which citizens will be able to engage in relatively ambitious forms of deliberation and political exchange, and where independent political action is far more commonplace than in contemporary liberal democracy. Citizenship of this type is seen as indispensable if we are going to assure both a reasonable and legitimate model of political decision making, in which the voices and interests of *all* those affected by governmental action have a real chance of gaining meaningful acknowledgment. Civil society needs to be as inclusionary and egalitarian as possible. Otherwise, it not only will lack sufficient legitimacy, but it is likely to fail, in practical terms, to deal effectively with the daunting political tasks of our time.

From this perspective, it should come as no surprise that contemporary critical theorists have been outspoken defenders of a whole series of attempts to break with traditional gender structures that "force" particular identities onto women and men in a manner that discourages a reflexive relationship toward cultural traditions and mores. Paternalistic attempts to preserve legal privileges for the traditional patriarchal family, for example, are inconsistent with the underlying normative principles of a modern democratic civil society (symmetry, reciprocity, and reflexivity). Communitarians are, of course, right to remind us that people do not willy-nilly invent forms of child rearing and parenting into which they then are socialized. Nonetheless, in modern pluralistic societies, individuals reinterpret and reinvent pregiven norms, traditions, and customs; legal regulations that expressly hinder this process of reinterpretation and reinvention by perpetuating an illusory "naturalization" of gender relations represent an assault on the self-organization and free association constitutive of civil society. *Contra* some strands within communitarianism, envisioning gender and sexual relations in this light is *not* the same thing as claiming that identity is based on "a set of preferences which we can pick and choose like clothes."[42] Moreover, it is wrong to assume that traditional family structures alone can provide a solid foundation for democratic civil society. Communitarians who lament the decline of "the" family miss that the ongoing pluralization of forms of intimacy is a far more ambivalent normative and sociological process than communitarian rhetoric of moral decline typically captures. Nor does experimentation with new forms of family life and gender relations stem from the philosophical ills of the much maligned "unencumbered self" or an irresponsible "permissive" culture of the 1960s. Instead, experimentation in this sphere represents a legitimate quest to develop new forms of self-organization and free association in the face of a series of profound social transformations that have undermined traditional family structures.

> What is yearned for [in much communitarian discourse] are the cultural certainties and clear boundaries between roles and spheres of life typical of industrial society . . . in particular, its gendered division of labor, its neat separation between family and paid work, complemented by the care ethic for women and work ethic for men, and its overall strategy of distinguishing between public and private in order to handle contentious issues.[43]

Particularly in light of contemporary social and economic conditions, the communitarian insistence on refurbishing traditional gender roles represents a rearguard agenda only likely to succeed by means of repressive and potentially authoritarian measures. At times eerily rehashing classical republican political theory's patriarchal strands, some forms of communitarianism risk succumbing to an antipluralistic conception of the family that bodes poorly for a model of civil society allegedly committed to buttressing trust and solidarity.[44]

SEXUALITY

From the critical theory perspective defended here, we need to achieve a civil society that allows all of its members to "test" traditional practices by comparing them, on an even plain, to (oftentimes unpopular) alternatives. Sexual relations have changed dramatically over the course of the past half-century; civil society should serve both as a forum for an open discussion about those changes, as well as a site where possible answers to the ambivalent situation we face today in the arena of sexual relations are experimented with and thereby scrutinized. How can we even begin to have a reasonable debate about same-sex marriage unless encouraging cautious experimentation with it? Recall that the critical theory model expressly *includes* the "realm of intimacy" within its scope; critical theorists do *not* see sexual relations as somehow external or prior to civil society. For sure, sexual identity is probably not something that we either shed or embrace in the same way that "we can pick and choose clothes." Yet it remains a legitimate site for reformulating tradition and pregiven forms of practice in accord with the ideals of free association and self-organization. By implication, critical theorists should be skeptical of any legal privileges enjoyed by traditional forms of sexuality in relation to a whole host of alternative modes of "family" and sexual life (including cooperative child rearing, various types of extended families, and a vast range of unorthodox gay and straight relationships, including same-sex marriages between consenting adults). To the extent that legal discrimination against same-sex couples, for example, rests on a moral paternalism inconsistent with the experimental character of civil society, it must be considered suspect: such discrimination hinders the reinterpretation and reinvention of tradition constitutive of a modern democratic civil society. Moreover, since legal (and, for that matter, social) privileges for traditional forms of sexuality arguably perpetrate power inequalities between gays and straights and help squelch the voices of those outside the sexual mainstream of society, they have to be considered problematic as well. The inclusionary and egalitarian model of civil society defended here requires us to be skeptical of any inequalities deriving from the traditional tendency to privilege heterosexuality, just as it calls for skepticism in the face of privileges traditionally enjoyed by men in relation to women.

In this spirit, critical theorists would have to be supportive of trends, now evident in a number of foreign countries, pointing toward a significant improvement in the legal status of same-sex couples. Whereas twenty-nine U.S. states and even the federal government have passed laws expressly forbidding same-sex marriage, courts and legislatures in Canada, Holland, and Scandinavia have sought to provide heightened protections to same-sex couples, even if thus far most of these legal innovations still leave them with rights inferior to those enjoyed by heterosexual couples. Nonetheless, the second-tier spousal rights enjoyed, for example, by Canadian gays and lesbians (who recently gained the right to have their "conjugal" partnerships acknowledged as common-law marriages) represent a substantial advance over the reactionary state of affairs in the United States, where even "liberal" politicians are hesitant to push for the legalization of same-sex marriage, and major universities still deny the extension of employee benefits enjoyed by straight couples to their gay and lesbian peers.[45] Needless to say, a presupposition of legalizing same-sex marriage is the decriminalization of sodomy, which remains a crime in many parts of the United States. When the Supreme Court appeals to "community standards" (e.g., in *Bowers v. Harwick*) in order to uphold such laws, critical theorists will need to add their voices to the chorus of commentators who rightly remind us that a genuinely *democratic* community is one in which discriminatory and potentially arbitrary laws have no rightful place.

Although often neglecting the details of contemporary policy disputes like those concerning same-sex marriage, critical theorists have described many ways in which civil society might serve as a site for "learn[ing] to value difference." Many of their comments on this matter are suggestive for those grappling with the place of ethical conflicts about sexuality in civil society.

Nancy Fraser has plausibly argued that a civil society in which social groups advance unpopular identities and ethical standpoints will have to consist of a "multiplicity of publics" where distinct groups can develop culturally specific modes of action and deliberation. Particularly in socially stratified societies where mainstream political and cultural patterns often exclude alternative identities, it will be important for marginal groups to develop "subaltern publics" as a challenge to the dominant—and oftentimes biased—forms of cultural and political identity. As Fraser points out, American feminists have created a "subaltern counterpublic, with its variegated array of journals, bookstores, publishing companies, film and video distribution networks, lecture series, research centers, academic programs, conferences, conventions, festivals, and local meeting places" in order to develop and defend dissenting positions on women's role within society.[46] Of course, gay and lesbians have long pursued a similar strategy, as they have made civil society both a site for their alternative conceptions of intimacy *and* a forum for an ongoing debate about sexual and gender issues. Is this a recipe for a civil society in which separatism would be allowed to run amok? Separatism is always a danger, but it can be counteracted if those operating within civil society continue to grasp the *publicist* orientation of their activities: if only because desirable legal changes require appeals to a broader constituency within society at large, subaltern publics would do well to continue communicating with those located outside of them.

For their part, Cohen and Arato see civil disobedience as the most appropriate device for negotiating the complex intersection between the spheres of legality and morality. "[I]n the case of a conflict between conceptions of the good life and legality, it should not be deemed unethical for the individual to follow his or her moral conscience or judgment and to act accordingly," even if this requires an abrogation of legality.[47] But such illegal action must strive symbolically to acknowledge the legitimacy of the basic principles of democratic legitimacy; in practice, this means that civil disobedience should take a self-limiting—but hardly uncontroversial—form. By the same token, a legal system respectful of civil society as a site for learning to deal with difference will necessarily respond to such actions so as to distinguish it from common criminality. In this way, gays and lesbians might challenge practices—homophobic AIDS-related policies, for example, or marriage laws—that degrade or discriminate against them. Needless to say, civil disobedience promises no easy resolution to oftentimes explosive conflicts between legality and morality; it is just as likely to be employed by those who seek to defend traditional views of gender and sexuality. It does offer an important way to force civil society as a whole to reconsider the validity of some set of legal practices—while respecting the basic ethos of reciprocity and equality on which civil society should rest.

Others working in the critical theory tradition have suggested that the guarantee of special group rights (e.g., a veto for gays and lesbians over legislation having special significance to them) should contribute to the protection of forms of ethical life threatened by society at large.[48] Given the relatively formal character of the model of democratic civil society described here, it seems to me that there can be no a priori reason for dismissing the idea of group rights out of hand. In some political and historical settings, group rights *may* make sense as a device for guaranteeing a rich and lively civil society. At the same time, some conceptions of group rights are suspect to the extent that they potentially hypostatize forms of collective identity and thereby generate new forms of moral paternalism. In any event, the appropriateness of group rights as a device for contributing to ethical pluralism can only be determined with reference to a complex mix of contextual factors.

LIFE-AND-DEATH QUESTIONS

In contrast to controversial disputes concerning gender and sexuality, critical theorists have had little to say about ongoing policy disputes concerning the state's role in the regulation of controversial life-and-death questions such as physician-assisted suicide.[49] Nonetheless, their emphasis on the virtues of a heterogeneous civil society might lead them to support the liberalization of legal regulations concerning physician-assisted suicide. From the perspective defended here, legally enforced discrimination against unpopular answers to fundamental ethical questions risks depleting the moral resources that alone make a thriving civil society possible: not only would a "disenchanted" and pluralistic society do well to accept the fact that individuals are likely to harbor legitimate ethical differences about physician-assisted suicide, but the legalization of physician-assisted suicide also arguably represents one way of acknowledging the supremacy of individual autonomy in those matters of greatest existential significance to us. Hostility to suicide runs deep within Western political and moral thought. But a *critical* appropriation of tradition is consistent with the legalization of physician-assisted suicide as a way of allowing those who hope to experiment with alternative answers to fundamental life-and-death questions a fair and equal chance to do so. It also requires a careful examination of the ways in which entrenched power and societal inequality (e.g., the capitalist allocation of health services in the United States, or state funding for churches in many European countries) potentially undermines an open debate about physician-assisted suicide. Not only is it the task of critical theorists to bring attention to how inequality subverts the procedures constitutive of democratic politics, but critical theorists would probably do well to fight (e.g., in the recent Oregon referendum on physician-assisted suicide) to protect the rights of those who seek to end their own lives as they see fit.

CONCLUSION:
GLOBALIZATION AND ETHICAL PLURALISM

I have tried to suggest that recent critical theory has rightly acknowledged the depth of the problems posed by the "fact of pluralism" and thus has been able to overcome one of the key failings of the early Frankfurt School. If I am not mistaken, this shift also leaves critical theory well positioned conceptually to begin dealing with the implications of the ongoing process of globalization, in which the necessity "to mediate among the very different cultures and ways of life of different people" is destined to take on heightened significance.[50] J. Donald Moon nicely points to the tasks at hand when he notes that in recent history "[t]he migration of peoples has thrown formerly separate cultural and ethnic groups together, and a variety of economic and social changes has undermined both the integrative values and the structures of hierarchical encapsulation that formerly limited or contained moral pluralism."[51] All evidence suggests that the trends described by Moon are now rapidly gaining in magnitude, as global economic integration spawns unprecedented movements of people across borders along with fundamental challenges to settled forms of life everywhere. The intensity of recent conflicts concerning "identity" is an intrinsic component of globalization. Whereas past civilizations often were able to keep "the other" at a relatively safe distance, the simultaneity and instantaneousness constitutive of contemporary human existence means that no one today can escape a sense of the unmediated presence of competing ways of life. To an ever greater extent, ours is a global village whose members immediately face neighbors whose ethical and religious choices often seem both alien and profoundly threatening. As we enter the twenty-first century, we need a model of how a transnational civil society, resting on the solid conceptual fundaments provided by Cohen and Arato, can grapple with the imperatives of an ethical pluralism that makes most of its former historical manifestations, which operated primarily within the confines of nation-state borders that today prove ever more irrelevant, seem like child's play.

I also tried to defend the institutional model of civil society formulated by Cohen and Arato from critics who consider it excessively defensive and inadequately anticapitalist in character. The model of civil society defended here *does* allow substantial room for political and social democratization; in this way, Cohen and Arato remain in the shadows of the Frankfurt School's oftentimes impressive critique of contemporary society. Where they arguably break with the Frankfurt School is in their tendency to underplay the ways in which contemporary social institutions—especially capitalism—place real limits on ethical pluralism in present-day society. Busily integrating the most important insights of contemporary liberal political theory into a critical model of civil society, Cohen and Arato at times "seem to be [primarily] concerned with . . . the proper form of a theoretical justification of political liberalism, as if capitalism no longer existed."[52] The ways in which capitalism constrains the flourishing of a "right to be different" has *not* played a central role in their thinking about civil society and ethical pluralism.

Globalization suggests that contemporary critical theory would do well to take this "traditional" theoretical concern seriously, even if doing so calls for the reformulation of critical theory of contemporary society that breaks with the widely documented errors of the early Frankfurt School. For example, globalization entails the worldwide embrace of neoliberal economic policies: conscious political decisions and state policy drive the liberalization of global markets, but global economic integration then subsequently functions to create a series of "economic facts" that generate strong incentives for political actors to opt for a narrow range of neoliberal policies. The most familiar result of this tendency is a dramatic heightening of market pressures on many forms of social activity (e.g., the educational system) that arguably possessed a greater degree of independence from the immediate imperatives of economic rationality during the heyday of the welfare state. Exaggerated rhetoric about the alleged requirements of globalization indeed should be challenged and discredited.[53] By the same token, the political employment of that discourse is working to create an altered economic environment in which political actors necessarily find themselves driven by structural factors to contribute further toward a very real process of globalization.

Globalization should again remind us that the modern "fact of pluralism" is structured and prefigured by capitalism. As the German critical theorist Hartmut Rosa points out in an important recent essay, contemporary capitalism of course privileges the pursuit of some conceptions of the good life while discriminating against others. Some forms of moral pluralism are *not* easily cultivated in capitalism. Those of us who are asked every semester to provide sound "practical" advice to college undergraduates concerned about the job market are unlikely to recommend forms of existence devoted to asceticism, meditation, artistic creativity—or even academic scholarship—for the obvious reason that such varieties of pluralism mesh poorly with the economic imperatives of contemporary capitalism. In light of the fact that the "capitalist system necessitates that all or most people develop identities in which production, in particular the professional career, and consumption are given priority," it is "obviously wrong to think that a capitalist economy simply provides the safe and neutral basis upon which we can pursue *all kinds* of lives."[54]

Such reflections may seem to take us far from the main concerns of this essay. Obviously, the fact that globalizing capitalism constrains ethical pluralism hardly provides easy answers to difficult normative and policy questions concerning sexuality, life-and-death decisions, or other intimate matters. Yet it does suggest that any attempt to grapple with such normative and policy questions will need to devote more attention to the ways in which contemporary capitalism privileges some answers to them over others. Only by acknowledging the ways in which hitherto unquestioned institutional choices—for example, in favor of a particular form of economic life—lead us to exclude the serious consideration of some ethical answers while instinctively embracing others can we tackle the challenge of ethical pluralism head-on. Anything less risks culminating in yet another attempt to deny the modern "fact of pluralism," by preventing the rational consideration of forms of ethical pluralism suppressed by historically contingent forms of social practice.

In this way, one of the "oldest" concerns of critical theory also remains the most contemporary.

❖   ❖   ❖

The author would like to thank Simone Chambers, Richard Madsen, Tracy Strong, and Iris Young, for their detailed written criticisms of earlier versions of this paper. Joseph Chan, William Galston, Donald Moon, Carole Pateman, and James Tully also clearly took some time out of their busy schedules to think through some of the issues raised by it, as did the other participants at the Ethikon Institute Meeting in San Diego where it was presented.

NOTES

1. Herbert Marcuse, *One-Dimensional Man* (Boston: Beacon Press, 1964).

2. In light of their original affiliation with the Institute for Social Research in Frankfurt, Germany, this first generation of critical theory is commonly described

as the Frankfurt School. Most of its members, however, ultimately found their way to New York City during the late 1930s, where they established the Institute for Social Research at Columbia University. Although rooted in the Marxist tradition, their analyses typically displayed a real appreciation for those elements of social life (including culture, psychology, and law) typically downplayed by orthodox Marxism. For surveys of their ideas, see Martin Jay, *The Dialectical Imagination: A History of the Frankfurt School* (Boston: Little, Brown, 1973), and Rolf Wiggershaus, *The Frankfurt School: Its History, Theories, and Political Significance* (Cambridge, Mass.: MIT Press, 1994). The most important contemporary representative of critical theory, Jürgen Habermas, was a student of Horkheimer and Adorno (both of whom returned to Germany after World War II), and has dedicated his enormous intellectual energy to reformulating the original project of the early Frankfurt School.

3. Seyla Benhabib, *Critique, Norm, and Utopia: A Study of the Foundations of Critical Theory* (New York: Columbia University Press, 1986), p. 222.

4. Ibid., p. 210.

5. John Rawls, *Political Liberalism* (New York: Columbia University Press, 1993), p. 4. From the standpoint of my essay, "otherness" need not be antithetical to pluralism. As we will see, one of the tasks of critical theory is to provide as broad a terrain as possible for forms of existence unfairly suppressed by certain structural trends at work in contemporary society.

6. Benhabib, *Critique, Norm, and Utopia*, p. 348.

7. From a Rawlsian standpoint, the early Frankfurt School could be seen as endorsing just another ill-fated attempt to privilege "the good" over the "the right," and therefore ultimately incapable of grappling with the full implications of modern pluralism.

8. This is a central argument of Benhabib's *Critique, Norm, and Utopia*.

9. On Neumann and Kirchheimer, see William E. Scheuerman, *Between the Norm and the Exception: The Frankfurt School and the Rule of Law* (Cambridge, Mass.: MIT Press, 1994).

10. Jean L. Cohen, "Discourse Ethics and Civil Society," *Philosophy and Social Criticism* 14, 3 (1988): 322.

11. Jean Cohen and Andrew Arato, *Civil Society and Political Theory* (Cambridge, Mass.: MIT Press, 1992), p. 23.

12. Breaking with the Hegelian-Marxism of his predecessors within the Frankfurt School, Habermas relies on a rich diversity of theoretical sources, while striving to salvage emancipatory elements of Enlightenment liberal-democratic thinking for the purposes of formulating a critique of contemporary capitalist society. On many points, Habermas appropriates liberal philosophical and political positions, to the consternation of critics on the left who worry that Habermas has abandoned too many of the radical impulses motivating early critical theory.

13. Jürgen Habermas, *Between Facts and Norms: Contributions to a Discourse Theory of Law and Democracy*, trans. by William Rehg (Cambridge, Mass.: MIT Press, 1996), p. 367. Habermas takes over many core features of Cohen's and Arato's model. Within the critical theory tradition, the concept of civil society also plays a role in the work of Ulrich Rödel, Helmut Dubiel, and

Günter Frankenberg (*Die demokratische Frage. Ein Essay* [Frankfurt: Suhrkamp, 1989) and Ulrich Press (*Revolution, Fortschritt, und Verfassung. Zu einem neuen Verfassungsverständnis* [Berlin: Wagenbach, 1990]). In my view, Cohen and Arato have gone furthest in developing Habermas's model of discourse ethics as an institutionally nuanced political theory. Within the critical theory tradition, critical remarks on the notion of civil society can also be found in Axel Honneth, *Desintegration. Bruchstücke einer soziologischen Zeitdiagnose* (Frankfurt: Fischer Verlag, 1995), pp. 80–89; in a more ambitious manner, Ingeborg Maus, *Zur Aufklärung der Demokratietheorie* (Frankfurt: Suhrkamp, 1992).

14. Cohen and Arato, *Civil Society and Political Theory*, pp. ix–x. This model does raise some difficult questions in reference, for example, to organizations like the Catholic Church, which occasionally have played an important role in movements for democracy without easily fitting the model of free associations suggested by Cohen and Arato. I am grateful to both Simone Chambers and Tracy Strong for bringing this point to my attention.

15. Jean Cohen, "Does Voluntary Association Make Democracy Work? The Contemporary American Discourse on Civil Society and Its Dilemmas," in Mark Warren, ed., *Democracy and Trust* (Cambridge: Cambridge University Press, 1999).

16. Cohen and Arato, *Civil Society and Political Theory*, p. ix.

17. For this criticism, see Iris Marion Young, "State, Civil Society, and Social Justice," in Ian Shapiro and Casiano Hacker-Cordon, eds., *Democracy's Value* (Cambridge: Cambridge University Press, 1999), pp. 141–62.

18. William E. Scheuerman, "Between Radicalism and Resignation: Habermas' *Between Facts and Norms*," in Peter Dews, ed., *Habermas: A Critical Reader* (Oxford: Blackwells, 1999), pp. 153–76.

19. Cohen and Arato, *Civil Society and Political Theory*, p. 611, n. 50. In a more recent paper, Cohen writes "that wherever important decisions, investments, or developments are occurring (be it in the scientific, corporate, media or educational establishments) public spaces involving criticism and self-criticism, articulation of alternatives and counterpowers must be provided for and protected." Cohen, "Does Voluntary Association Make Democracy Work? The Contemporary American Discourse of Civil Society and Its Dilemmas."

20. Cohen and Arato, *Civil Society and Political Theory*, p. 416.

21. For a fine discussion of the ongoing debate about the utility of discourse ethics for both moral and political theory, see Simone Chambers, *Reasonable Democracy: Jürgen Habermas and the Politics of Discourse* (Ithaca: Cornell University Press, 1996), pp. 140–52. Cohen and Arato use discourse ethics as a basis for conceptualizing democratic legitimacy and for determining where we should distinguish between legality and morality; Chambers suggests that a more ambitious employment of it, as a device for covering moral issues, is justified as well. Contemporary critical theorists are divided on this point, as they are about the specific implications of their model for the reform of both the state and economy.

22. Habermas sees these standards as *built-in*, in what he has described as a "quasi-transcendental" manner, to human communication itself. Needless to say, this remains a controversial point, both within critical theory and outside it.

23. Benhabib, *Critique, Norm, and Utopia*, pp. 309–16.

24. Cohen and Arato, *Civil Society and Political Theory*, p. 357.

25. There is surely an echo here of Mill's defense of social experimentation, but one should note that the normative grounding and basic institutional model provided by Cohen and Arato are obviously distinct in many important ways from Mill's.

26. Cohen and Arato, *Civil Society and Political Theory*, pp. 355–58; Jean Cohen, "Democracy, Difference, and the Right to Privacy," in Seyla Benhabib, ed., *Democracy and Difference: Contesting the Boundaries of the Political* (Princeton: Princeton University Press, 1996), p. 198. On this matter, critical theory may even go beyond Rawls in its appreciation of the potential strengths of pluralism, at least to the extent that Rawls occasionally seems to see pluralism as little more than an empirical "fact" to be accommodated, but hardly something whose cultivation should be encouraged given that it is basic to some of the most worthwhile features of modern political experience.

27. Cohen and Arato, *Civil Society and Political Theory*, p. 356.

28. In a similar vein, see Nancy Fraser, "Rethinking the Public Sphere: A Contribution to the Critique of Actually Existing Democracy," p. 129; Seyla Benhabib, "Models of Public Space: Hannah Arendt, the Liberal Tradition, and Jürgen Habermas," pp. 89–93, both in Craig Calhoun, ed., *Habermas and the Public Sphere* (Cambridge, Mass.: MIT Press, 1992).

29. J. Donald Moon, *Constructing Community: Moral Pluralism and Tragic Conflicts* (Princeton: Princeton University Press, 1993), pp. 198–99.

30. For Moon's criticisms of Benhabib on this point, see ibid., pp. 87–97. Cohen's work on privacy rights should be read as an attempt from within critical theory to respond to criticisms of this sort.

31. Cohen, "Democracy, Difference, and the Right to Privacy," p. 202.

32. Ibid., p. 201.

33. I am indebted to Simone Chambers for encouraging me to take this problem seriously. See her critical comments on my essay in this volume.

34. Cohen, "Democracy, Difference, and the Right to Privacy," p. 203. Cohen is responding to writers like Michael Sandel, who criticizes the Supreme Court's jurisprudence on privacy matters in *Democracy's Discontent: America in Search of a Public Philosophy* (Cambridge, Mass.: Harvard University Press, 1996), pp. 91–119.

35. Cohen and Arato, *Civil Society and Political Theory*, p. 373.

36. In this vein, James Tully, *Strange Multiplicity: Constitutionalism in an Age of Diversity* (New York: Cambridge University Press, 1995), p. 131.

37. Michael Walzer, Max Horkheimer Lectures, University of Frankfurt, May 1998.

38. For the most sophisticated version of this view, see Iris Young, "Communication and the Other: Beyond Deliberative Democracy," in Benhabib, *Democracy and Difference: Contesting the Boundaries of the Political*, pp. 120–36. Young's relationship to Habermasian critical theory is complicated. Although inspired in some ways by Habermas, Young has also eagerly integrated modes of "postmodernist" theory into her account in a way that tends to worry more rigorous Ha-

334 ❖ Critical Theory

bermasians. For these reason, I treat her here both as a practitioner *and* critic of contemporary critical theory.

39. Seyla Benhabib, "Toward a Deliberative Model of Democratic Legitimacy," in Benhabib, *Democracy and Difference: Contesting the Boundaries of the Political*, pp. 81–84.

40. Chambers, *Reasonable Democracy: Jürgen Habermas and the Politics of Discourse*, pp. 158, 160.

41. For this reason, "rational choice" models of citizenship, inspired by neoclassical economic theory, typically exhibit strong libertarian biases. For a discussion of this conceptual nexus in the work of a leading libertarian legal theorist, see my "Free Market Ant-Formalism: The Case of Richard Posner," *Ratio Juris* 12, 1 (March 1999): 80–95.

42. Cohen, "Democracy, Difference, and the Right to Privacy," p. 200.

43. Cohen, "Does Voluntary Association Make Democracy Work? The Contemporary American Discourse of Civil Society and Its Dilemmas."

44. On classical republicanism, see Joan Landes, *Women in the Public Sphere in the Age of the French Revolution* (Ithaca: Cornell University Press, 1988).

45. On the situation in Canada and a number of other countries, see E. J. Graff, "Same-Sex Spouses in Canada," *Nation*, 12 July 1999, pp. 23–24. On the extreme caution widespread among the present Democratic Party contenders for the presidency, see "Bradley Favors Expanding Homosexual Rights," *New York Times*, 17 September 1999, p. A17. My own former employer, the University of Pittsburgh, is an example of one institution that continues to oppose granting health benefits to same-sex couples.

46. Fraser, "Rethinking the Public Sphere: A Contribution to the Critique of Actually Existing Democracy," p. 123. It may be the case that subaltern groups often seem to rely on some more or less shared "culture," and thus hardly in themselves constitute sites of a pluralistic, deliberative civil society. But they surely can play a major role as part of a broader network of associations and organizations making up such a civil society.

47. Cohen and Arato, *Civil Society and Political Theory*, p. 356.

48. Iris Young, *Justice and the Politics of Difference* (Princeton: Princeton University Press, 1990), pp. 183–91.

49. At the same time, some of the issues alluded to earlier in the essay (including abortion and AIDS policy) arguably fall under the rubric of life-and-death questions. As we saw, critical theorists have had quite a bit to say about those issues.

50. Moon, *Constructing Community*, p. 35. Given the manner in which globalization has become ingrained in fashionable political jargon as of late, we need to be careful about how we are using the term. A careful discussion of this problem transcends the boundaries of this essay, but let me point to a useful attempt to come to terms with the concept of "globalization": Jan Aart Scholte, "Beyond the Buzzword: Towards a Critical Theory of Globalization," in Eleonore Kofman and Gillian Youngs, eds., *Globalization: Theory and Practice* (New York: Pinter, 1996), pp. 43–57.

51. Moon, *Constructing Community*, p. 35.

52. Hartmut Rosa, "Does Capitalism Threaten Pluralism?" *Constellations* 5, 2 (June 1998): 205.

53. Pierre Bourdieu, *Acts of Resistance: Against the Tyranny of the Market* (New York: New Press, 1999).

54. Rosa, "Does Capitalism Threaten Pluralism?" 203. Iris Young has also underlined the ways in which capitalism encourages a "client-consumer orientation toward citizenship." Young, *Justice and the Politics of Difference*, p. 72. In my reading of Young's work, however, this theme often takes a rear seat to a more pressing concern for the manner in which traditional modes of liberal universalism contribute to the suppression of cultural diversity.

Substantive and Procedural Dimensions of Critical Theory

Simone Chambers

Much of contemporary critical theory has been influenced by Jürgen Habermas, especially Habermas's theory of discursive ethics. Jean Cohen and Andrew Arato, the two theorists Bill Scheuerman discusses, are no exception. While going significantly beyond Habermas in their theory of civil society, they nevertheless understand the democratization of civil society (the normative goal within their theory) in essentially Habermasian or discursive terms. Now one of the early criticisms of Habermas was that discourse ethics—and the political philosophy to emerge from that theory—was antithetical to pluralism.[1] The crude version of this accusation went something like this: because discourse ethics places consensus at the heart of legitimacy this must mean that discourse ethics contains a presumption in favor of agreement (agreement is good) and against disagreement (disagreement is bad). This misreading led some liberal theorists to conclude that for critical theory the fact of pluralism was a regrettable fact to be overcome through authentic and legitimate consensus.

Bill Scheuerman unequivocally lays this criticism to rest. He finds no antipathy between critical theory and ethical pluralism; in fact, critical theory welcomes ethical pluralism. Ethical pluralism is a necessary condition of healthy democratic discourse: "a freewheeling, pluralist civil society, based on a commitment to open debate and exchange, is the most likely candidate for producing (discursive) legitimacy." The agreements that we do reach (even the agreement to disagree) have legitimating force only if produced within a context that safeguards and promotes autonomous identity formation and difference. This represents an essentially procedural approach to ethical pluralism. In what follows, I want to pursue some implications of this approach and draw a few distinctions in a slightly sharper way than Scheuerman does.

For Cohen and Arato, civil society is the most important site of democratic self-determination because within civil society citizens can free themselves from "the pressing restraints on deliberation evident within administrative and market processes." Within civil society and the public sphere (the political voice of civil society), citizens can engage in authentic deliberation in search of solutions to their most pressing shared problems of coordination. This view of civil society offers the critical theorist two

avenues of argument and research: questions are either procedural or substantive. A procedural approach involves investigating the conditions
under which we deliberate about and resolve ethical disputes. A substantive approach concerns the arguments we champion within such disputes.
Substantive arguments may appeal to procedural grounds, when, for example, we defend government-subsidized day care on the grounds that
such support is required if women are to enjoy equal citizenship. Although the procedural-substantive distinction is sometimes blurry, it is
useful for distinguishing the sorts of questions that might animate a critical theory of ethical pluralism.

Let me try to illustrate this using the case of physician-assisted suicide.
Scheuerman speculates that on this issue a critical theorist would probably emphasize "the virtues of a heterogeneous civil society" and so would
support the liberalization of legal regulation. This liberalization acknowledges "the supremacy of individual autonomy in those matters of the
greatest existential significance to us" and further would allow for experimentation with alternative answers to fundamental life and death questions. I would not disagree that many (but I would venture to say not
all) critical theorists would support the legalization of physician-assisted
suicide. It is important, however, to ask whether they do so on procedural
grounds that a right to die is essential to democracy or on other nonproce-
dural grounds. Scheuerman seems to favor the former. We can in a sense
"deduce" the legalization of physician-assisted suicide because such a
freedom would be considered part of the autonomy that must be guaranteed for authentic identity formation. And authentic identity formation is
a necessary condition of a democratized civil society. But what if this
dispute, although existentially fundamental, is not really fundamental to
questions of democracy? Then a critical theorist would investigate the
"pure" procedural question: how would it be resolved by those affected
in a fair discourse.[2] Although Scheuerman acknowledges that there are
many issues that must be left up to the democratic will of each community,
he never explores this approach to ethical pluralism. At some point the
critical theorist is wedded to the unpredictable outcome of deliberative
procedures. Critical theory is obligated to investigate where that point
lies. Furthermore, deference to the opinion of those affected reinforces
the centrality of that branch of critical theory concerned with the institutions of opinion and will-formation.

The "pure" procedural approach can investigate the conditions of deliberation and consent at both the individual as well as collective level.
At the individual level critical theory is interested in the ways in which
we promote informed, free, and authentic deliberation in any given case.
Further questions animate this type of investigation. Can the chronically
ill, for example deliberate in a way that is safeguarded from distortion and

manipulation? How much power do physicians have in this conversation? What about individuals who cannot speak for themselves but must rely on advocates? Does the educational or economic level of the individuals involved affect their perspective on life-and-death decisions? A critical theorist might also investigate how discursive role playing shapes the issues under investigation.[3] There are a number of interesting venues for investigation in this area, all of which would concentrate on the intersubjective conditions, indeed the very possibility, of autonomous judgment and consent with regard to a decision to die.[4]

At another level of analysis critical theory is interested in how society as a whole must make the decision to allow or not allow physician-assisted suicide. This is clearly a different type of question than how we ourselves might deliberate about our own death or that of a partner or of a patient. Again, a critical theorist would be concerned with conditions and procedures. For example, in the 1998 Oregon referendum on physician-assisted suicide, while a critical theorist may have articulated many arguments in favor of legalization (perhaps along the lines that Scheuerman spelled out), also central to such a perspective would be the conditions under which this debate took place. Various questions animate this approach. What type of opportunities do citizens have to explore this issue in a meaningful way? Is the debate overly dominated by power or money perhaps in the form of the American Medical Association, the insurance industry, or organized religion? Are there groups that have been systematically excluded or silenced in this debate? Are there groups like the poor or mentally impaired who might have a special interest but have not been given a voice? Whatever the outcome (and to some extent a critical theorist must accept the outcome if the procedure was healthy and discursive), what is important to the critical theorist is that conditions are met for authentic opinion and will-formation.

The pure procedural perspective is not appropriate for all issues. There are some ethical disputes that we do not want to leave entirely to the democratic process particularly when our democratic process often falls very short of discursive ideals. There are some issues that deal with the conditions of democracy itself. For example, while I think that it was appropriate for the citizens of Oregon to determine the legal status of physician-assisted suicide, I do not think one can make the same argument with regard to, say, *Bowers v. Harwick* where the courts deferred to the community standards set by Georgia with regard to the criminalization of sodomy. While the issues in both cases are procedural, the sodomy case touches on the rules of the game so to speak in a way that physician-assisted suicide does not. Sodomy laws (or constitutional amendments like Amendment 2 in Colorado) affect the ability of gays fully and equally to participate in civil society, for even if those laws are never enforced, knowledge that the community supports their continuation creates a chilling effect on self-expression and free identity formation.[5] This in turn can be seen as violating conditions of symmetry and reciprocity needed for authentic democracy. As I have noted before, I am not convinced that the same can be said with regard to physician-assisted suicide. Although questions of euthanasia are in some ways more fundamental to each of us than nonenforced sodomy laws, they do affect our status as equal citizens in the same way.

I do not have the space to defend fully the claim that physician-assisted suicide is a question that must be left up to the democratic community to work through together while sodomy laws jeopardize the very idea of a democratic community. Instead, I simply assert that wherever one does draw the line, some such line is built into the critical theory perspective. How and where we draw the line is a question that critical theory cannot avoid and it is a central question in any adjudication of disputes over ethical pluralism.

I wish to raise a second distinction important in the relationship between ethical pluralism and the conditions of democracy. Generally speaking most critical theorists adhere to the view that some form of ethical pluralism is a prerequisite for healthy democracy. They sometimes disagree, however, about what form that ethical pluralism ought to take. We can recognize two types of ethical pluralism; let's call them type A and B. Ethical pluralism A is wedded to notions of autonomy, critical self-reflection, and independent identity formation. This pluralism contains experimentation in life-styles, resistance to conformity, unpopular stands vis-à-vis the majority, and the privacy of conscience. It is a pluralism that focuses on the individual, although the individual is understood as achieving autonomy through communicative interaction. Kant and Mill are the fathers of this type of pluralism. Ethical pluralism B is associated with multiculturalism. This type of pluralism refers to a freedom for different communal and cultural ways of life to flourish. Here it is not the Millian eccentric who needs protection so much as the Amish or Navajo way of life. These two types of ethical pluralism can clash in various ways.[6] Take, for example, the practice of veiling. On the one hand, we might want to promote pluralism and autonomy by encouraging a reflexive and critical attitude toward cultural traditions and mores like veiling. This appears to be the type of pluralism that Scheuerman and Cohen endorse as a precondition of democracy. This might, however, be seen as an attack on ethical pluralism B as it attempts to limit the role and influence of traditional interpretations of ethical and family relations. Ethical pluralism B could also be seen as a necessary condition of democracy as it might promote safe havens of communal and group identity formation from which citizens gain a voice or supply the conditions of autonomy.[7] Again, I do not have an answer to this dilemma, I only pose it and suggest that critical theory is somewhat ambiguous about how individualist is its interpretation of ethical pluralism.

Individualist—indeed, quite Millian—leanings are clearly present in Scheuerman's final and well-aimed criticism of contemporary critical theory. He points out that theorists like Habermas and even Cohen and Arato tend to "underplay the ways in which contemporary social institutions—especially capitalism—place real limits on ethical pluralism in present day society." But when he comes to identifying the sort of diversity and difference that capitalism might stifle, he is concerned that college students are unlikely to choose forms of existence devoted to asceticism or artistic creativity. Less pressing for Scheuerman is the loss of collective solidarities to the homogenizing pressures of global capitalism.

NOTES

1. For an interpretation of Habermas along these lines, see, for example, Stephen Lukes, "Of Gods and Demons: Habermas and Practical Reason," in John B. Thomson and David Held eds., *Habermas: Critical Debates* (Cambridge, Mass.: MIT Press, 1982), p. 144. Also Wolfgang Schluchter, *Religion und Lebensführung* (Frankfurt: Suhrkamp, 1988), 1: 322–33. Quentin Skinner, "Habermas's Reformation," *New York Review of Books*, 7 October 1982, pp. 35–38.

2. The term "pure" proceduralism is taken from Rawls and refers to a procedure where there "is no independent criterion for the right result: instead there is a correct or fair procedure such that the outcome is likewise correct or fair, whatever it is, provided that the procedure was properly followed." John Rawls, *A Theory of Justice* (Cambridge, Mass.: Harvard University Press, 1971), p. 86.

3. An example of this approach can be seen in Alfons Matheis, "Ethik und Euthanasie. Diskurethische Kritik von Peter Singers Konzept Praktischer Ethik," in Karl-Otto Apel and Matthias ettner, eds., *Zur Anwendung der Diskursethik in Politik, Recht und Wissenschaft* (Frankfurt: Suhrkamp-Verlag, 1992), pp. 232–60.

4. One argument against physician-assisted suicide from this pure procedural view is that, even if there are persuasive arguments to the effect that this should be an individual choice, there is no way to safely guarantee that individuals are not being manipulated while under deep psychological stress. On this reading, the risk is too great to legalize it.

5. Frank Michelman argues along these lines. See "Law's Republic," *Yale Law Journal*, 97, 8 (July 1988): 1493–1537.

6. For a good discussion of the problem, see Susan Moller Okin, *Is Multiculturalism Bad for Women?* (Princeton: Princeton University Press, 1999).

7. See Will Kymlicka, *Multicultural Citizenship: A Liberal Theory of Minority Rights* (Oxford: Oxford University Press, 1995).

PART X

Pluralisms Compared

J. Donald Moon

The writers of the main essays collected in this volume were asked to respond to five broad questions within the framework of a particular tradition or perspective. The purpose of this chapter is to identify some of the broad similarities and differences among the ethical perspectives, as described in this collection, and to identify the possibilities for dialogue across these lines of difference. The first question is the most general—whether the perspective in question aims at ethical uniformity or accommodating ethical pluralism. One difficulty in comparing responses to this question is rooted in the different ways in which the term "ethical pluralism" is used. In one obvious sense, all of these traditions acknowledge the existence of a plurality of human values, and even the existence of conflicts among them. Every society, as Walzer has argued, is marked by different "spheres," different areas of social life organized according to different principles and values: the religious life is oriented to the achievement of goods that are different from those of family and domestic life; the virtues of the soldier are distinct from those of the artist or scholar.[1] In that sense, all of the perspectives seek to accommodate "ethical pluralism" as what I shall call "structural" or "social structural" pluralism. A related use of the term "ethical pluralism" refers to the plurality of cultures in the world and, increasingly, within different countries, reflecting the fact that different cultures are characterized by different patterns of structural pluralism.

"Ethical pluralism" is used in a second, and quite different sense, to refer to a specific theory of value or axiology. According to this theory, value is inherently plural in that different values cannot be reduced to a single, underlying measure or form of value (such as pleasure or utility), nor can they be rendered commensurable so that they can be arranged in a rationally ordered hierarchy specifying the correct or appropriate "trade-offs" among them. This position is often attributed to Isaiah Berlin, who argued that "the belief that some single formula can in principle be found whereby all the diverse ends of men can be harmoniously realized is demonstrably false," concluding that "the possibility of conflict—and of tragedy—can never wholly be eliminated from the human condition."[2]

The idea that value is inherently plural is sometimes used to explain the forms of social pluralism discussed here. Thus, the plurality of value is expressed in the incommensurate values or goods characterizing different social spheres, such as the values of domestic, religious, or economic life. In a similar vein, different cultures can be seen as instantiations of different and incommensurate systems of value, each giving expression to some aspect of human possibility. Value pluralism does not rule out all moral judgment about different forms of social life, or about different "spheres" within a society: one can be a value pluralist but still affirm some minimal standards of decency, proscribing certain types of society (e.g., Nazism) or spheres within a particular society (e.g., a criminal underworld).[3] But the value pluralist denies the possibility of ranking different forms of life that meet these minimal standards of decency.

For Berlin, value pluralism is the ultimate basis for a liberal political order, but none of the perspectives presented here, including liberalism, advocates or is based on ethical pluralism in this sense. It appears that, in some of their variants, liberalism (both classical and egalitarian), critical theory, and feminism are compatible with the view that values are inherently plural, but they do not require that controversial view. The other traditions represented in this collection reject value pluralism as a theory of value and envision the moral world as inherently ordered. That does not mean that these older traditions do not recognize the possibility of conflicts among values or other moral considerations; indeed, such conflicts are obvious and lie behind some of the different schools of thought within each tradition. Nonetheless, the traditions provide the frameworks—the concepts, values, principles, norms, and perhaps most important, modes of reasoning—to which adherents can appeal to sort out conflicting moral considerations and to establish reasoned priorities among them.

The recognition of complexity and the possibility of disagreement within all perspectives brings us to a third sense in which the term "ethical pluralism" is used, what we might call pluralism as reasonable disagreement, or what I sometimes refer to as "perspectival pluralism."[4] In contrast to the type of disagreement that arises within a particular tradition, ethical pluralism as reasonable disagreement acknowledges that the very frameworks within which ethical issues are framed may themselves be the object of reasonable disagreement. One who accepts the possibility of ethical pluralism as reasonable disagreement explicitly acknowledges that one's own perspective does not provide an authoritative framework within which disputes must be argued, unlike the disagreement that arises *within* a particular perspective. Because its most basic presuppositions may be challenged, one who acknowledges pluralism as reasonable disagreement, *and* who seeks to live with others on the basis of norms (in a broad sense) they also have reason to accept (or, at least, do not have sufficient reason to reject), may find it necessary to abandon important, even fundamental aspects of one's own framework in order to reach a reasonable accommodation with others.

The distinction between reasonable disagreement that arises within a particular perspective and that arising between perspectives is not hard and fast. As the essays in this volume show, there are many differences within each perspective, so much so that the boundaries marking any particular perspective are themselves subject to dispute. In some cases one perspective may shade off into another, as in the case of classical and egalitarian liberalism.[5] Nonetheless, this is an important distinction, marking real differences among the traditions represented in this volume.

Perhaps the most important difference is that some perspectives, most obviously the two forms of liberalism and critical theory, take the accommodation of ethical pluralism as reasonable disagreement to be (one of) their principal objectives, and even to define the problems to which the perspective seeks to provide an answer.[6] Based on the recognition of perspectival pluralism, these perspectives become self-limiting. Seeking to provide a framework that can accommodate competing perspectives, they limit the range of questions to which they offer answers. Thus, Kukathas stresses that classical liberalism "is a *political* philosophy rather than an ethical doctrine," which "does not purport to answer a range of important questions." Galston emphasizes that extensive "zone of moral indeterminancy" in egalitarian liberalism that "can be filled by varied individual and group decisions." And Scheuerman points out the important parallel between modern liberalism and critical theory, because the latter incorporates a "*political* ethic that need not commit its defenders to any specific moral philosophy."[7]

These three perspectives, then, are "partial" or limited, as opposed to the comprehensive perspectives represented by Confucianism, Judaism, natural law, Christianity, and Islam. Unlike the partial perspectives, the latter are comprehensive in the sense that they seek to provide answers to a wide range of questions about the nature of human life and the human good, our place in the cosmos, the ideal forms of character, and the principles that should govern a wide variety of relationships among people.

The self-limiting character of liberalism and critical theory also shows itself in their presupposing that (at least some)[8] people will accept another perspective, one that addresses a broader range of issues and that may be, in some respects, incompatible with the overarching framework itself. These perspectives, then, presuppose that people are capable of entertaining a high level of cognitive complexity. Not only do they recognize the possibility of reasonable disagreement among competing perspectives, but they also suppose that people in their own thinking and sensibility will simultaneously occupy different and in some respects incompatible perspectives. In the case of the two forms of liberalism, one obvious source of cognitive pluralism is the different religious perspectives surveyed in this volume. One of the historical sources of liberalism is the plurality of religious traditions and the conflicts to which that plurality gave rise. By seeking to overcome conflicts by creating a limited state based on nonreligious principles and a commitment to toleration, liberalism assumes that people have the capacity to manage a significant degree of cognitive complexity, in that they (or at least some) will accept both liberalism and a particular religious perspective. But because liberalism imposes limitations upon the claims of any particular comprehensive or religious perspective, this feat requires one to be able to distance oneself from one's own comprehensive beliefs, at least to the extent of being able to see those beliefs as one possible perspective among others, a possible object of sincere and even reasonable disagreement. One's comprehensive perspective, then, cannot be taken to be "natural" or "self-evident," or in some other way beyond dispute. In short, the cognitive complexity that liberalism (and critical theory) demands requires that each comprehensive ethical perspective be able to acknowledge the possibility of affirming perspectival pluralism within its own conceptual resources.

As the essays in this book make clear, all of the comprehensive perspectives have the resources to acknowledge perspectival pluralism at least to some degree. In the first place, all perspectives are internally complex, marked by more or less well defined traditions of interpretation and/or different sects, and the arguments among these traditions and sects in large part define the perspective itself. No one can avoid the experience of having to confront opposing arguments and ideas and, as a result, developing the capacity to view one's own ideas with a certain distance. Further, all perspectives place value on behavior that is sincere, that is motivated by the individual's ethical convictions rather than being coerced. Valuing persuasion, one must learn to engage the other, and so to develop the capacity to see the world through the other's eyes. As the range of possible interlocutors is extended, more and more of one's fundamental beliefs can be contested, culminating in the acknowledgment of ethical pluralism as reasonable disagreement, or perspectival pluralism.

The possibility of comprehensive perspectives acknowledging perspectival pluralism is a major theme in many of the chapters of this collection. In some cases, there are significant resources within a tradition that lead directly to the acceptance of reasonable disagreement. Little describes the important role that "conscience" plays in some strains of Christianity, an emphasis rooted in the "earliest and most formative expression" of the Christian movement, namely, that it 'called out' new adherents by means of individual persuasion, rather than by civil coercion or by appealing to ethnic or other forms of group identity." In particular, the development of "the doctrine of erroneous conscience" led to the view "that an individual's conscientious beliefs, though in error, ought, under some conditions, nonetheless be tolerated."

In other cases, the confrontation of ethical pluralism as reasonable disagreement involved a tradition's encounter with modernity. Fisch, for example, describes the dilemma facing Orthodox Jews who have come to participate actively in the governance of Israel, a modern state that is based in important respects on liberal principles. In Fisch's account, Orthodox Judaism outside of Israel had successfully been able to avoid confronting ethical pluralism by focusing inwardly on the Orthodox community itself, and not engaging the larger society around it except to seek the liberty to maintain its own practices. But in Israel that option has become problematic, as Orthodox parties have increasingly contested political power and taken part in ruling the country. When democratic decision making has led to policies opposed to Orthodox prescriptions, adherents have been placed in the deeply problematic position of implementing policies that violate their fundamental beliefs. Unless the Orthodox are prepared to abandon political life altogether, they thus face the dilemma of either opposing the liberal-democratic form of the modern state or making room "for a religiously meaningful approval of ethical pluralism by rethinking halakha [the code of Jewish law]." In Fisch's analysis, the latter option is possible by drawing on traditions of halakhic argumentation that acknowledge "humankind's profound fallibilism" and acknowledging the need to revise halakhic interpretations in response to criticism. Coming to accept "epistemic humility," one can endorse ethical pluralism as reasonable disagreement because the challenge represented by opposed systems of belief enables one to discover and correct errors in one's own, thereby enriching one's life and one's community.

Fisch's proposal represents one possible way in which Orthodox Judaism could come to accept perspectival pluralism but, as Seligman reminds us, this development is by no means inevitable.[9] In particular, as long as the acceptance of pluralism is based only on epistemic grounds, toleration (let alone celebration) of differences is limited by the need to balance the value of criticism and correction of one's beliefs against other considerations. In Fisch's example, the person who is required to implement a law that violates his fundamental beliefs could see some value in doing so, in that epistemic modesty leads him to accept perspectival pluralism. But that argument only goes—and should only go—so far. There may well be policies that are so wrong, from the point of view of one's comprehensive perspective, that even acknowledging the value of pluralism one cannot rightfully carry them out. But it should be noted that this problem is not unique to Orthodox Judaism. Even those who affirm perspectival pluralism not only on grounds of epistemic modesty but also out of respect for individual autonomy or the claims of individual conscience may face that dilemma. Acknowledging the possibility of reasonable disagreement does not mean that tolerance let alone celebration of difference is an overriding value. The possibility of continuing conflict is an aspect of the cognitive complexity discussed earlier.

So far I have distinguished four senses in which the term "ethical pluralism" has been employed: as structural pluralism (the idea that different values and principles govern different spheres of society), as cultural pluralism (the idea that different societies are structured in accordance with different systems of value), as value pluralism (the idea that value as such is inherently plural, in the sense of being incommensurate), and as perspectival pluralism (the idea that there can be a basis for reasonable disagreement among adherents to different ethical perspectives). I have also stressed the difference between comprehensive ethical perspectives, which seek to provide a general account of all or most aspects of human life, and partial perspectives, which seek to accommodate different comprehensive perspectives by providing a political order that can manage their differences. In his chapter on "Pluralism as a Matter of Principle," Skillen points out that the coexistence of different ethical perspectives in society will necessarily involve some pattern of structural pluralism. In the case at hand, if a society is to be religiously pluralistic, then there must be a separation between the political and the religiously sphere, and the political sphere will necessarily be "monistic," at least in the sense that everyone must observe certain norms (such as toleration).

Each of the ethical perspectives represented in this collection has significant implications for the patterns of structural pluralism that are morally acceptable and, by implication, for the acceptable range of cultural diversity across societies (or among subcultures within any particular society). Egalitarian liberalism, for example, precludes social hierarchies that involve the assignment of different rights and duties to ascriptive groups, such as ethnic, religious, or caste groups. Structural pluralism is a particularly important issue for feminism. Like liberalism and critical theory, it is a partial perspective, but unlike the former, it does not take as a primary task the management of perspectival pluralism. Although there is controversy about how to describe what is distinctive to feminism, feminists agree that women's "life chances are unjustly and adversely impacted as a result of practices and values that prescribe norms of conduct and treatment" for them, and all seek to correct that situation.

As Di Stefano points out, "one is never simply a feminist"; rather, feminism is always combined with other ethical perspectives, which help to specify the conditions that contribute to the "empowerment" or enhance the "life chances" of women. As a result, feminists can be found on opposite sides of many political issues. "Equality" feminists, for example, argue that women should be treated as persons by being "brought under the purview of an impartial justice from which they have been too long excluded," while "difference" feminists claim that "discursive space and political opportunity . . . should be allocated to women as women rather than persons."

In addition to wrestling with this internal plurality, feminism must also confront structural pluralism, because, in virtually all societies, "the conduct of men and women" has been "regulated by different ethical principles" (Pateman), and women's principal roles have been confined to particular spheres, in ways that have inhibited their agency. Feminism, like the other ethical perspectives considered in this volume, refuses to take any existing system of structural pluralism as normative, and insists upon judging it, and calling for its reform, according to its own normative commitments. This stance leads to a conundrum, shared to some extent by liberalism and critical theory, when considering the problems posed by cultural diversity. Committed to enhancing the agency of women, many Western feminists have been reluctant to criticize social practices out of respect for the women who participate in those practices, and the desire not to undercut their agency by imposing alien standards upon them. At the same time, to the extent that these practices disempower women, feminism is committed to opposing them. Indeed, feminist political movements in the West have had great success in attacking analogous forms of structural pluralism in their own societies; this dilemma sometimes threatens to place them in the awkward position of being radicals in their own cultures but tories about others.[10]

Because feminism encounters plurality at so many levels and in so many ways, feminists have made significant efforts not so much to transcend these differences (in the manner, say, of liberalism), as to extend the range of understanding of alternative positions, to be able to grasp the different ways in which women's life chances and capacities for agency can be enhanced, and how they can vary with differences in culture and social situation. An example of this is the thoughtful and nuanced discussion of female genital surgery-mutilation in the chapters by Di Stefano and Pateman. Feminism thus contributes a distinctive sensibility to the task of learning how to engage in dialogue across difference, one that cultivates both an openness to others and the identification of new possibilities.

SOCIAL REGULATION

Should the power of the state ever be invoked to protect, ban, or otherwise regulate ethically based differences? If so, where and how should the state be involved?

All of the perspectives examined in this volume would use the state to regulate behavior, even when that behavior is motivated by ethical differences. And it could hardly be otherwise. A social order by definition is constituted by a set of social norms, and the maintenance of those norms requires their enforcement. More significant, these traditions have more substantive points in common: all permit some scope for toleration of differences rooted in perspectival (not to mention other forms of) pluralism, and all share at least some modes of reasoning about the regulation of ethically based differences.

Not surprisingly, the most capacious perspectives are those that take the accommodation of difference as their point of departure—liberalism and critical theory. While all perspectives have some capacity to acknowledge perspectival pluralism, and so to tolerate differences that challenge their own presuppositions in fundamental ways, liberalism and critical theory are committed not only to tolerating but also to protecting differences. At the heart of liberalism is a commitment to individual rights and liberties, including especially freedom of expression and conscience, designed to protect individuals' ability to develop and communicate their beliefs. And critical theory goes beyond the concern for individual rights to critique social and economic institutions, particularly market capitalism, that impose an unnecessary and stultifying uniformity on modern society. Although there is scope for toleration in all of the perspectives, only liberalism and critical theory make toleration a foundational principle.

In general, comprehensive perspectives, precisely because of their commitment to ethical uniformity, contain the conceptual resources to legitimize a substantial degree of social regulation, limiting the ways in which people may express and act on ethical ideals contrary to those embodied in the perspective in question. The problem is posed forcefully by Joseph Chan's discussion of Confucianism, whose ethical ideals can be invoked to justify regulations that require individuals to conform to the norms that Confucianism regards as ethically sound. Unlike some other perspectives, as Chan points out, this proclivity is not counterbalanced by a commitment to individual autonomy, or even a developed theory of individual conscience, nor does it endorse a separation of private and public morality. Nonetheless, Confucian support for social regulation is limited by its commitment to *ren*, to action based on individual virtue, and virtue must reflect conviction, not coercion. Too much regulation, then, would be counterproductive, preventing the realization of the highest moral ideal.

Some other comprehensive perspectives are even more receptive to limits on social regulation. In the case of Christianity, the significance of individual conscience, as described by Little, provides a powerful justification for toleration and individual liberty in matters of belief and, to a lesser extent, ways of life. Indeed, respect for conscience provides a (defeasible) justification for not only tolerating but also for protecting differences by permitting exemptions from various laws and policies, ranging from allowing for conscientious objection to military service to permitting Sikhs to ride motorcycles without wearing helmets. Similarly, as Boyle points out in his discussion of the natural law perspective, there are important human goods that can only be realized through conscientious individual action, and so cannot be achieved through legal enforcement of norms.

As Chan observes, limits on social regulation based on the desirability of allowing individuals to act on their own moral (and religious) judgments can be overridden in cases where the "damage" that might be done by allowing a greater liberty would be worse than enforcing restrictions on opportunities to express virtue. On the other hand, Confucianism, like the other comprehensive perspectives, also supports pragmatic limits on the tendency toward social regulation. Implicit in Chan's discussion is a recognition that, at least in some cases, the effort to require proper behavior may cause more evil than it avoids. This kind of reasoning figures explicitly in the natural law perspective, as described by Haldane. Even in what might seem to be a paradigmatic case of justified regulation, such as encouraging norms of good parenting, Haldane points out, "prevention or cure may be more harmful than the disease," so "prudence may need to temper idealism."

Third, all of the perspectives at least implicitly acknowledge that there are times when the correct answer to a moral question is indeterminate, thereby undercutting justifications for social regulation and enlarging the area within which individuals should be free to act on their own judgments. The natural law perspective, for example, holds that "moral questions admit of objective answers, though not necessarily of exclusive ones" (Haldane), and in a similar vein Chan talks of the importance of moral discretion and the need to revise or selectively use rites when one confronts new or unanticipated circumstances.

The wide range of grounds on which impulses to social regulation can be checked suggests the possibility that the scope for practical agreement among different ethical perspectives is much greater than might be thought, considering the ways in which their fundamental principles may be opposed. While a perspective might unequivocally condemn a particular practice, that condemnation does not by any means translate into a justification for suppressing it. Still, the differences between liberalism and critical theory, on the one hand, and the comprehensive perspectives on the other, are important. Many of the pragmatic tests involved in determining whether to tolerate an activity, for example, are dependent on the relative balance of power of contending groups, as the costs of suppression will vary directly with the size and resources available to the groups involved. Small and marginal groups, then, are much less likely to receive protection in a society organized by one of the comprehensive perspectives than they would in a society based on the principles of liberalism or critical theory.

CITIZENSHIP

How should ethically based disagreements on the rights and duties of citizenship be dealt with? For example, how should dissenting positions on the civil status of women be handled in civil society?

Citizenship is not a concept that is shared across all of the perspectives presented in this volume. As Chan points out in the case of Confucianism, "there are no citizens, only subjects and rulers." In contrast, egalitarian liberalism and critical theory are premised upon the idea of citizenship. In many cases, then, addressing this question involves extending a tradition, developing its ethical ideals, and applying them to contemporary circumstances. Needless to say, different adherents to the same tradition can reach quite different conclusions. Fisch describes how rabbinical authorities reached diametrically opposed positions in the case of citizenship rights for women in what would become the state of Israel, and Chan outlines a range of possibilities that exist within Confucianism, some of which point to the clear subordination of women and their exclusion from citizenship altogether, while others support a reinterpretation of Confucian ideals that would legitimate equal rights between men and women. In those strains of Christianity in which the ideal of conscientious individualism is prominent, a strong, perhaps even compelling case can be made for equal citizenship for men and women, but as Little's discussion of this issue implicitly suggests, the same cannot be said for other variants of Christianity.

If there is considerable indeterminacy within various traditions about the rights and duties of citizens, particularly the civil status of women, their responses to ethically based disagreement about citizenship are even less clear. In his account of Christianity, Little describes how such disagreement might be resolved regarding the duties of citizens, particularly in the case of conscientious objection to military service. While he is clear that there can be no general exemption from such duties because of ethical disagreements with the state's laws, he points out that a strong case can be made for conscientious objection to military service, on the grounds that "mixing conscience and force is highly problematic."

Fisch also addresses this question explicitly, arguing that the question of citizenship poses the same problem as other areas of ethical disagreement. So far as the practice of orthodox Jews is concerned, the halakhically correct answer to the question of citizenship binds their adherents, but the orthodox are essentially indifferent to the practices of others. If, for example, the rabbis had decided that Orthodox women could not participate in political life on equal terms with men, then in Fisch's view the women would have observed that restriction "while grudgingly accepting the fact that other women" would not. A problem would only arise for those Orthodox Jews who assumed leadership positions in the society and came to have responsibilities for facilitating women's participation, thereby finding their political obligations in conflict with their religious duties. And that, as Fisch observes, is a special case of the general type of conflict that can occur between the demands of Orthodox Judaism and the modern democratic state.

Interestingly, in spite of their commitment to perspectival pluralism, the "modern" perspectives, notably liberalism and critical theory, have little tolerance for dissenting positions regarding the rights of women. Both insist upon equal citizenship. To the extent that citizenship involves the exercise of various rights, such as voting and running for elective office, liberalism and critical theory can accommodate ethical perspectives that reject equal rights for women, or reject the idea that women should play a significant role in public life. Female members of such groups are free simply not to exercise these rights. But to the extent that citizenship involves duties, as Galston observes, liberalism and critical theory cannot be so accommodating. While most democratic regimes do not require voting on the part of all citizens (let alone more active forms of participation), they do require preparation for citizenship, notably in the form of compulsory (secular) education, so this exclusionary or nonaccommodating aspect of liberalism and critical theory is of real significance.

LIFE-AND-DEATH DECISIONS

To what extent, if any, should the power of the state be utilized to regulate decision making on life-and-death issues? For example, how should ethically based conflict on physician-assisted suicide be handled?

Life-and-death issues, such as abortion and euthanasia, are among the most difficult issues confronting any ethical perspective. Indeed, with the partial exception of the natural law perspective, none of the perspectives represented in this volume has a clear, unequivocal position on these issues, and few appear to have a specific response to how ethical disagreement on these matters should be resolved. Among the comprehensive perspectives, there appear to be significant debates within Judaism and Confucianism on these issues. This is hardly surprising, because they have become salient in part at least because of recent advances in medical technology. The natural law perspective has always placed a high value on human life, and has been adamantly opposed to any deliberate taking of human life,[11] including suicide, and it appears to come closer to offering a definite position on these issues than the other traditions. Not only is it opposed to abortion and physician-assisted suicide, it tends to support their legal prohibition, but even here there is debate on a number of specific points. In all of these cases, the arguments about these issues move within the basic concepts and principles that define the perspective in question, and none of the perspectives appears to address the question of how ethically based disagreement, disagreement rooted in alternative perspectives, might be handled.

These issues are of central concern to feminism, though it too does not speak with one voice on these matters. Historically, women have borne much of the responsibility of caring for the young and the dying, and the regulation of life-and-death issues has significantly affected their capacities to exercise agency and to resist the power that men exercise over them. Many feminists support the right to abortion as necessary to the ability of women to make their own reproductive decisions; many also support measures to permit "death with dignity," a stance broadly consonant with the "ethics of care" that many feminists endorse. But because feminism is always combined with other ethical perspectives, other feminists, particularly those who hold strong religious views, oppose such measures.

Liberalism and critical theory, as might be expected, offer accounts of how ethically based disagreement about these issues might be handled, accounts that are essentially applications of their general approaches to these particular issues. Classical liberalism insists that the state should not take sides on these morally contested questions insofar as possible and, to the extent that it must do so, calls for compromises, including allowing different subunits or jurisdictions within the state to regulate them in different ways. Egalitarian liberalism leans heavily toward a permissive posture, permitting such practices, though like critical theory it cautions against the ways in which differential power and advantage might lead to abuses in the case of physician-assisted suicide.

Human Sexuality

To what extent, if any, should conflicting ethical positions on sexual relationships be accommodated? For example, should society agree or decline to recognize same-sex unions as a form of marriage?

In general, the comprehensive ethical perspectives examined in this collection endorse some form of heterosexual marriage. The natural law perspective appears to take the strongest position, holding that the proper function of sexual relationships is reproduction, and concluding that sex should be confined to heterosexual marriage. Even so, that does not mean that there is an absolute bar to same-sex unions; as we have seen in other cases, natural law reasoning is open to a variety of considerations, and "where there is strong demand for alternatives [to exclusively heterosexual forms of marriage] it will consider the cost of opposing this, . . . and may elect to tolerate what it cannot endorse" (Haldane). Confucianism also strongly endorses heterosexual marriage, but offers no principled objection to nonmarital homosexual relationships. Nonetheless, given the centrality of the family and male-female relationships to the Confucian tradition, it is far from clear that any room could be made within Confucianism for same-sex unions as a form of marriage. The Christian tradition of conscientious individualism, at the other extreme, offers the materials from which a strong case can be made for equal legal rights regardless of sexual orientation, which could be employed to support some form of same-sex marriage.

With the exception of the natural law position, whose response to ethical pluralism is largely based on pragmatic considerations, none of the comprehensive perspectives offers a specific account of how to manage ethically based differences regarding same-sex marriage. The same is true of feminism, which once again tends to reproduce the differences among ethical perspectives within itself, as a result of the fact that feminism is necessarily tied to other ethical frameworks. Thus, we find feminists on both sides of such issues as whether pornography and prostitution should be legalized. While all feminists are opposed to practices that contribute to the subordination of women, and while they can agree in rejecting practices in which women are coerced into positions of inferiority, they disagree among themselves what practices necessarily involve subordination and whether they should be legally proscribed.

Liberalism and critical theory, as one might expect, do not take a direct position on what constitutes valuable or worthwhile forms of human sexuality; rather, their central concern is to determine how issues regarding sexuality should be politically regulated, given the existence of ethical pluralism. Their positions on this issue are, as in the case of life-and-death decisions, applications of their general account, and not specific to questions of sexuality. Both egalitarian liberalism and critical theory tend to take a more definitive position on sexuality than on life-and-death decisions. Both have a strong tendency to reject discriminatory treatment based on sexual orientation, and to support some kind of legal recognition of same-sex unions. For both accounts, justifications for state support of a particular type of marriage or family relationship are too closely tied to ethical perspectives that are objects of reasonable disagreement and, absent more compelling arguments for such policies, must be rejected as bases of state action.

Classical liberalism (as it is described here) differs in an important respect from egalitarian liberalism and critical theory on the issue of sexuality, a difference that also bears on life-and-death decisions. While egalitarian liberalism and critical theory differ in important ways, it is not too much of an oversimplification to say that both seek to accommodate ethical pluralism by regulating behavior according to norms that transcend the differences between the perspectives, norms that adherents to all perspectives can accept. In practice, as the discussion of sexuality in Galston's essay shows, that means that authoritative norms must be justified by reference to empirical claims and to goods (and moral considerations generally) that are shared by different perspectives or, at least, that none has good reason to reject. Thus, absent a justification that can be shared, egalitarian liberalism and critical theory reject public policies that involve unequally burdening different groups of citizens, based on their different conceptions of the good, at least when the burdens are severe for some groups. Given the enormous importance of the benefits conferred by the legal institution of marriage, such as the right to participate in medical decisions if one's partner becomes unable to make such decisions, the case for same-sex marriage or marriage-like arrangements is hard to answer.

Classical liberalism, although committed to the state's not "presuming the correctness of one ethical stance as against another on matters of marriage and sexuality," nonetheless does not endorse the case for same-sex unions in societies where the scope of public policy requires the state to determine what counts as a family or what children should be taught about sexuality in the schools. As Kukathas argues, the stance of ethical neutrality cannot plausibly be regarded as anything but a substantive position by those whose ethical perspectives differ. Taxpayers whose idea of the family envisages only husband and wife, and their children, may not condone public definitions that include same-sex, polygamous, or incestuous relationships. Thus, the classical liberal response is to allow people "to distance themselves from the ethical position of the state—to disengage from 'mainstream' society." In the case at hand, for those "who wish to live in same-sex unions, there would be the opportunity not so much to have such unions recognized as a form of marriage as to reject the salience or necessity of such recognition altogether."

Without spelling out what this proposal would require, it's hard to tell whether it would be acceptable to egalitarian liberalism or critical theory, but adherents of the latter positions would undoubtedly dispute the premise from which the argument proceeds. While it may be true that believers in the traditional family (such as those who hold a natural law perspective) might regard state allowance for same-sex unions as a non-neutral, substantive position, that would not be decisive. Critical theory and egalitarian liberalism do not attempt to handle ethical disagreements by finding a "neutral" position among the different perspectives represented in a morally pluralist society. Rather, in their view public policy should be neutral only in the sense that it is not designed to advance a particular conception of the good, a particular (comprehensive) ethical perspective; to the extent that it seeks to realize particular values, they must be values that all have reason to accept (or, at least, not reject). Such policies will often not be neutral, in the sense that they may make it easier for some groups to reproduce themselves over time than it is for others. Education policies, for example, might make it more difficult for groups that reject a way of life that valorizes career success to sustain themselves by recruiting new members over time. But so long as the purpose of the policy is not to promote a particular ethical perspective at the expense of another, such differential advantage does not constitute an adequate reason to reject the policy in question, from the point of view of egalitarian liberalism or critical theory.

Even if this line of reasoning is successful in handling ethically based disagreements about same-sex unions, it cannot readily be extended to many life-and-death decisions. Opponents of abortion, for example, justify their position by reference to a universally shared value, life, and not (or at least not only) to a particular, disputed ethical perspective. Similarly, as Galston's discussion makes clear, the case of physician-assisted suicide does not admit of an easy answer. From the point of view of egalitarian liberalism and critical theory, the problem in these cases is not that there is no "neutral" policy but that one can find reasonable, widely shared grounds on which any particular policy might be rejected. That does not mean that ethical pluralism in the case of life-and-death decisions cannot be accommodated, because the resources for doing so are richer than those available even within those perspectives specifically designed for that purpose.

DIALOGUE ACROSS DIFFERENCE

As several of the essays in this volume emphasize, contemporary societies are marked by significant degrees of ethical pluralism, in the sense that they contain adherents of opposed ethical perspectives, and so the accommodation of difference has come to be a central concern of contemporary political theory. For many commentators, this condition has been a cause of alarm. MacIntyre famously describes our condition as one of "civil war carried on by other means."[12] But this bleak view is not supported by this survey of the actual pattern of differences revealed by the essays in this volume. While the ethical perspectives surveyed here differ from each other in fundamental ways, there are important areas of overlap, and important ways in which they are mutually compatible. In the first place, not all perspectives aim to be comprehensive, to provide accounts of the values and principles that should properly guide all or most areas of human life. The two versions of liberalism and critical theory define themselves as limited perspectives, designed in part to provide a method to accommodate what I have called "perspectival pluralism." Second, each of the comprehensive perspectives represented here contains the conceptual resources to acknowledge reasonable disagreement with other perspectives, and to accommodate, at least to some degree, those differences. Third, we have seen that feminism, a perspective that is perhaps uniquely internally plural and which arises in large part in response to the experience of structural pluralism, contributes a sensibility that encourages dialogue across difference—a dialogue aimed not so much at resolving or transcending differences as in enlarging our understanding and opening up new possibilities. Finally, we have found that the variety of resources available to negotiate difference makes possible practical agreement or accommodation on many issues, even where fundamental disagreement on principle remains. This is not to say, I hasten to add, that our differences can or should be dissolved in some happy harmony—only that we have reason to persist in our arguments with each other, that we can opt for politics rather than war.

Notes

1. Michael Walzer, *Spheres of Justice* (New York: Basic Books, 1983). Structural pluralism is also central to the essays by Skillen, Di Stefano, and Pateman in this volume.

2. Isaiah Berlin, "Two Concepts of Liberty," in his *Four Essays on Liberty* (New York: Oxford University Press, 1969), p. 169.

3. This seems to be Berlin's position. See, for example, his reference to "rules so long and widely accepted that their observance has entered into the very conception of what it is to be a normal human being, and, therefore, also of what it is to act inhumanly or insanely" (p. 165).

4. See Charles Larmore, "Pluralism and Reasonable Disagreement," in his *The Morals of Modernity* (Cambridge: Cambridge University Press, 1996), pp. 152–74, for a helpful discussion of the distinction between pluralism as a theory of value and pluralism as reasonable disagreement.

5. Indeed, throughout this essay I use the term "liberalism" to encompass both classical and egalitarian variants, because in many contexts their positions do not differ significantly.

6. This characterization of critical theory follows Scheuerman's account and reflects recent developments in this tradition of thought. As Kukathas points out, other variants of critical theory rest on a "vision or promise of human liberation," which would make them an example of a "comprehensive" ethical perspective.

7. The emphasis on "political," as opposed to the more general "ethical" or "moral," in these quotations is in the original.

8. Some people, perhaps most people, do not hold well-articulated systems of belief, and so it would be misleading to say that they hold two distinct perspectives simultaneously.

9. Although the main thrust of his comments is to review the obstacles to the acceptance of ethical pluralism within Judaism, Seligman also suggests additional avenues within Orthodoxy that could lead in that direction.

10. This phrase, I believe, is Gellner's.

11. A possible exception is capital punishment for major crimes, which finds some support within this tradition.

12. Alasdair MacIntyre, *After Virtue*, 2nd ed. (Notre Dame, Ind.: University of Notre Dame Press, 1984), p. 253.

Contributors

BRIAN BARRY is the Arnold A. Saltzman Professor of Comparative Constitutionalism at Columbia University, a former editor of *Ethics* and the *British Journal of Political Science*, and a member of the editorial board of *The Ethikon Series in Comparative Ethics*. He is a fellow of the British Academy and of the American Academy of Arts and Sciences. His publications include *Political Argument*; *The Liberal Theory of Justice*; and *Power, Democracy, and Justice*, his collected essays.

JOSEPH BOYLE is professor of philosophy and principal of St. Michael's College at the University of Toronto. He has published extensively on applied ethics and moral theory and is coauthor with John Finnis and Germain Grisez of *Nuclear Deterrence, Morality, and Realism*. A past president of the American Catholic Philosophical Association, much of his work is part of the contemporary effort to understand and develop Catholic natural law theory.

SIMONE CHAMBERS is associate professor of political science at the University of Colorado at Boulder. She is the author of *Reasonable Democracy: Jürgen Habermas and the Politics of Discourse*, for which she received the American Political Science Association's award for the Best First Book in Political Theory. She has also published a number of articles on deliberative democracy and is currently working on democratic models of constitutional reform.

JOSEPH CHAN is associate professor of political theory at the University of Hong Kong. He has published articles in major journals, including *Ethics*, *History of Political Thought*, *Journal of Democracy*, and the *Oxford Journal of Legal Studies*. His current research focuses on Confucian political philosophy, human rights in Asia, liberalism, and Aristotle's political philosophy.

CHRISTINE DI STEFANO is associate professor of political science at the University of Washington, Seattle, an associate editor of *Signs: Journal of Women in Culture and Society*, and past president of the American Political Science Association's Section for Women and Politics Research. She is the author of *Configurations of Masculinity: A Feminist Perspective on Modern Political Theory* and coeditor (with Nancy Hirschmann) of *Revisioning the Political: Feminist Reconstructions of Traditional Concepts in Western Political Theory*.

DALE F. EICKELMAN is Lazarus Professor of Anthropology and Human Relations at Dartmouth College and a former president of the Middle East Studies Association of North America. His books include *Moroccan Islam*; *The Middle East and Central Asia: An Anthropological Approach*; *Knowledge and Power in Morocco*; and *Muslim Politics* (with James Piscatori). He has also edited and coedited a number of books and published numerous articles and contributions to edited books. He has been a Guggenheim Fellow, a fellow at the Woodrow Wilson International Center for Scholars, a member of the Institute for Advanced Study,

Princeton, and Muhammad Bin-Ladin Visiting Fellow at the Oxford Centre for Islamic Studies.

MENACHEM FISCH is professor of history of the philosophy of science at Tel Aviv University and senior fellow at the Shalom Hartman Institute for Advanced Judaic Studies, Jerusalem. He is the author of *William Whewell, Philosopher of Science* and *Rational Rabbis: Science and Talmudic Culture* as well as many journal articles on the philosophy of science. He is also an active participant in interfaith dialogue projects focused on toleration and the management of diversity.

WILLIAM A. GALSTON is professor in the School of Public Affairs and director of the Institute for Philosophy and Public Policy at the University of Maryland, College Park. Formerly deputy assistant to President Clinton for domestic policy, he is now executive director of the National Commission on Civic Renewal, co-chaired by Sam Nunn and William Bennett. He also serves as a senior advisor to the Democratic Leadership Council and the Progressive Policy Institute. He is the author of six books and numerous articles on political philosophy, public policy, and American politics.

JOHN H. HALDANE is professor of philosophy at the University of St. Andrews in Scotland and director of its Centre for Philosophy and Public Affairs. He has published widely on aesthetics, the history of philosophy, metaphysics, philosophy of mind, and political and social philosophy. He is the author of *Faithful Reason: Essays Catholic and Philosophical* and coauthor (with J.J.C. Smart) of *Atheism and Theism* in the Great Debates in Philosophy Series. He is coeditor (with Crispin Wright) of *Reality, Representation, and Projection* and also writes the column Credo for the *Times* (London).

CHANDRAN KUKATHAS is senior lecturer in politics at the University of New South Wales (Australian Defence Force Academy), and coeditor of the *Journal of Political Philosophy*. He is the author of *Hayek and Modern Liberalism*; *The Theory of Politics: An Australian Perspective* (with David Lovell and William Maley); and *Rawls: A Theory of Justice and Its Critics* (with Philip Pettit). He is also the editor of *Multicultural Citizens: The Philosophy and Politics of Identity*.

DAVID LITTLE is Dunphy Professor of the Practice in Religion, Ethnicity, and International Conflict at the Harvard Divinity School. He has also been a senior scholar in religion, ethics, and human rights at the United States Institute of Peace and a member of the U.S. State Department Advisory Committee on Religious Freedom Abroad. His books include *Human Rights and the Conflict of Cultures: Freedom of Religion and Conscience in the West and Islam* (with John Kelsay and Abdulaziz Sachedina), *Religion, Order, and Law: A Study in Pre-Revolutionary England*, and *Comparative Religious Ethics* (with S. W. Twiss).

RICHARD MADSEN is professor of sociology at the University of California, San Diego, and a coauthor (with Robert Bellah et al.) of *The Good Society* and *Habits of the Heart*, which received the Los Angeles Times Book Award and was jury-nominated for the Pulitzer Prize. A former Maryknoll missionary, he has authored or coauthored four books on China, including *Morality and Power in a Chinese*

Village, for which he received the C. Wright Mills Award; *China's Catholics: Tragedy and Hope in an Emerging Civil Society*; and *China and the American Dream*.

MUHAMMAD KHALID MASUD is Academic Director of ISIM (International Institute for the Study of Islam in the Modern World), Leiden. His Ph.D. is from McGill University, and he has a special interest in Islamic law and jurisprudence, especially law and social change

J. DONALD MOON is professor of political theory at Wesleyan University and a former chair of the Conference for the Study of Political Thought. He is the author of *Constructing Community: Moral Pluralism and Tragic Conflicts*; "Logic of Political Inquiry," in the *Handbook of Political Science*; and a number of articles on the political theory of the welfare state, the philosophy of social inquiry, and other topics. He is also the coeditor of *Dissent and Affirmation* and editor of *Responsibility, Rights, and Welfare*.

CAROLE PATEMAN is professor of political theory at the University of California, Los Angeles, past president of the International Political Science Association, and series editor of *The Ethikon Series in Comparative Ethics*. A fellow of the American Academy of Arts and Sciences, she is the author of *Participation in Democratic Theory* and *The Sexual Contract* as well as many journal articles. She is also vice chair of the Ethikon board of directors.

WILLIAM E. SCHEUERMAN is associate professor of political science at the University of Minnesota (Twin Cities), where he teaches political and legal theory with a special interest in recent continental European thought. He is author of *Between the Norm and the Exception: The Frankfurt School and the Rule of Law* and *Carl Schmitt: The End of Law*. He is also the editor of *The Rule of Law under Siege: Selected Essays of Franz L. Neumann and Otto Kirchheimer* and coeditor of *From Liberal Democracy to Fascism: Political and Legal Thought in the Weimar Republic*.

ADAM B. SELIGMAN is professor of religion and research associate at the Institute for Economic Culture at Boston University. He has taught in the United States, Israel, and Hungary, where he was a Fulbright Scholar from 1990 to 1992. His books include *The Idea of Civil Society, Innerworldly Individualism: Charismatic Community and Its Institutionalization*, and *The Idea of Trust*. He is currently working on issues of authority and toleration.

JAMES W. SKILLEN is president of the Center for Public Justice, located in Washington, D.C. and Annapolis, Maryland. He has directed the center since 1982 and edits its quarterly *Public Justice Report*. He holds a Ph.D. from Duke University in political science. The author or editor of a dozen books, he regularly writes essays, book reviews, and commentaries for popular magazines and academic journals.

TRACY B. STRONG is professor of political science at the University of California, San Diego and former editor of *Political Theory: An International Journal of Political Philosophy*. He is the author of *Friedrich Nietzsche and the Politics of Transformation*; *Right in Her Soul, the Life of Anna Louise Strong*; *The Idea of*

Political Theory: Reflections on the Self in Political Time and Space; and *Rousseau and the Politics of the Ordinary*.

JAMES TULLY is professor of political science at the University of Toronto, fellow commoner, Christ's College, Cambridge University, and adjunct professor of philosophy at McGill University. He is the author of seven books and numerous articles on contemporary political philosophy, European political thought, liberalism and democracy, contemporary issues of rights and pluralism, and the demands of indigenous peoples. His most recent book is *Strange Multiplicity: Constitutionalism in an Age of Diversity*, based on the inaugural Sir John Robert Seeley Lectures, which he gave at Cambridge University in 1994.

LEE H. YEARLEY is the Walter Y. Evans-Wentz Professor of Oriental Philosophies, Religions, and Ethics at Stanford University, and a past Henry Luce Professor of Comparative Religious Ethics at Amherst and the Five Colleges. A specialist in comparative ethics, he is the author of *Mencius and Aquinas: Theories of Virtue and Conceptions of Courage* and *The Ideas of Newman: Christianity and Human Religiosity*. He has contributed chapters to eleven books and published numerous journal articles. His special interests include the comparative study of Thomism and Confucianism, and the theology of Cardinal Newman.

Index